Letters and Papers

of

CHARLES, LORD BARHAM

Admiral of the Red Squadron

1758-1813

Volume I

Elibron Classics
www.elibron.com

Elibron Classics series.

ISBN 1-4021-3917-9 (paperback)
ISBN 1-4212-9230-0 (hardcover)

This Elibron Classics Replica Edition is an unabridged facsimile of the edition published in 1907 by the Navy Records Society, London.

PUBLICATIONS

OF THE

NAVY RECORDS SOCIETY

Vol. XXXII.

The Barham Papers

VOL. I.

This volume—LETTERS AND PAPERS OF CHARLES, LORD BARHAM (Vol. I.)—announced for last year, has been unavoidably delayed, but is now issued on the 1906 *subscription.*

October 1907.

LETTERS AND PAPERS
OF
Charles, Lord Barham

ADMIRAL OF THE RED SQUADRON

1758-1813

EDITED BY

SIR JOHN KNOX LAUGHTON, M.A., D.Litt.

HON. FELLOW OF CAIUS COLLEGE, CAMBRIDGE
FELLOW OF KING'S COLLEGE, LONDON

VOL. I

PRINTED FOR THE NAVY RECORDS SOCIETY
MDCCCCVII

THE COUNCIL

OF THE

NAVY RECORDS SOCIETY

1907–1908

INTRODUCTION

CHARLES MIDDLETON, a captain of 1758, rear-admiral in 1787, and created Lord Barham in 1805, was, throughout a long life, in the closest possible touch with the opinion and the administration of the navy. Captain of cruizing and harbour ships, comptroller, senior sea lord, and ultimately first lord of the admiralty, it is difficult to conceive conditions under which a man could be better informed of the state of affairs. Active-minded, fond of noting down his ideas, not afraid of expressing them, and eager to get hold of those of others, he accumulated a large mass of documents of various sorts, which —quite independent of official papers, now in the Record Office—comprise—

1. 'In letters:' letters addressed to him; some private; many semi-official, but partaking largely of the freedom of a private character.

2. 'Out letters:' letter books and drafts of letters written by him, including many to William Pitt,

the finished copies of which are now in the collection of 'Chatham Papers' belonging to Rear-Admiral John Eliot Pringle, who has most kindly permitted the present Editor, in the interests of the Society, to have free access to them.

3. Drafts of representations on points of service.

4. Miscellaneous memoranda.

These, by the broad-minded liberality of their owner, the Earl of Gainsborough, on the suggestion of his cousin Admiral Sir Gerard Noel—both of them Barham's direct descendants in the fourth generation—have been put at the disposal of our Society, to be printed in this and succeeding volumes.

Charles Middleton—son of Robert Middleton, a collector of customs, and of Helen, daughter of Charles Dundas, said to have been a captain in the navy, but more probably in the mercantile marine—was born at Leith on the 14th October, 1726. On the father's side, his great-grandfather, Alexander[1] (d. 1684)—a younger brother of John Middleton,[1] who, after an adventurous career as soldier of fortune, was created Earl of Middleton, and died, governor of Tangier, in 1673; uncle of Charles,[1] 2nd Earl of Middleton and titular Earl of Monmouth, secretary of state to the titular James III.—was a doctor of divinity and principal of King's College, Aberdeen; as also, in succession, was his grandfather, George Middleton[1] (d. 1726). On the mother's side his great-grandfather was Robert Dundas, Lord Arniston[1] (d. 1726), a lord of session, as his father had

[1] See *Dictionary of National Biography*.

been before him; his grand-uncle, also Robert[1] (1685–1753), was a judge of the court of session, whose son, Henry Dundas,[1] first cousin of Barham's mother, was created Viscount Melville in 1802. The family history, thus briefly outlined, is interesting as showing how distinctly action, law and organization,[2] business and religion were represented in Barham's pedigree, and as thus explaining much that is complex in Barham's character.

Young Middleton entered the navy as 'captain's servant' on board the Sandwich, in April 1741; and his service at sea, with the intervals of half-pay, as made out from the respective pay-books, was as shown by the table on the following page.

His earlier service is more exactly given by his passing certificate, dated October 4th, 1745:—

Ships	Rating	Time			
		yrs.	m.	w.	d.
Sandwich . . .	Captain's Servant	0	1	2	6
Duke	Do.	0	4	0	0
Do.	Do.	0	1	2	3
Flamborough . .	Do.	0	5	2	2
Do. . .	Able	0	1	0	4
Do. . .	Mid.	3	0	0	5
Do. . .	Mr's. Mate	0	2	0	3
Loyal Jane, merchant ship	—	3	1	0	2
		7	4	1	4

[1] See *Dictionary of National Biography.*

[2] 'The great family, or rather the great dynasty, of Dundas did for a long time govern Scotland and filled many of the principal positions in that country. In a comparatively short time two presidents of the court of session sprang from the family of Arniston, and innumerable judges, lord advocates, and what not. In fact, the whole system of jurisprudence in Scotland would

Ship	Guns	Rank	Date of Entr	Date of Discharge	Captain	Stations
Sandwich .	90	Captain's Servant	25 April 1741	11 June 1741	Sam. Mead	Portsmouth & Channel
Duke . .	90	,,	12 June 1741	20 Nov. 1741	Mead to 2 Oct.; then Alex. Geddes	,,
Flamborough .	20	CS, Mid., Mr's Mte.	21 Nov. 1741	4 Nov. 1745	Jos. Hamar	Coast of Carolina & Georgia
Chesterfield .	40	Lieut.	5 Nov. 1745	15 July 1749	Wm. Gordon to Nov. '47; then O'Brien Dudley	Channel to Jan. '48; then Atlantic, W. Coast of Africa, West Indies
Half-pay .	—	,,	16 July 1749	2 June 1752	—	—
Culloden .	74	,,	3 June 1752	15 Nov. 1752	Matt. Buckle	Guardship in the Medway
Half-pay .	—	,,	16 Nov. 1752	10 Jan. 1753	—	—
Anson . .	60	,,	11 Jan. 1753	21 Mar. 1754	Charles Holmes	Portsmouth to Gibraltar; Portsmouth
Monarch .	74	,,	22 Mar. 1754	26 July 1754	Roger Martin	Portsmouth to Gibraltar and back
Anson . .	60	,,	27 July 1754	25 Feb. 1757	Holmes, to Feb. '55; then Rob. Man	Portsmouth; to Gulf of St. Lawrence in '55; then Leeward Islands
Speaker . .	12	Commander	26 Feb. 1757	13 July 1758	Seniority, 26 Feb. '57	Leeward Islands
Barbados .	12	,,	14 July 1758	28 Feb. 1759	—	,,
Arundel . .	24	Captain	1 Mar. 1759	14 July 1760	Seniority, 22 May '58	,,
Emerald . .	28	,,	15 July 1760	26 Oct. 1761	—	,,
Half-pay .	—	,,	27 Oct. 1761	10 Mar. 1762	—	—
Adventure .	32	,,	11 Mar. 1762	2 April 1763	—	Coast of Normandy
Half-pay .	—	,,	3 April 1763	22 Mar. 1775	—	—
Ardent . .	64	,,	23 May 1775	6 Nov. 1776	—	Nore
Prince George	90	,,	7 Nov. 1776	2 Feb. 1778	—	Nore & Portsmouth
Jupiter . .	50	,,	3 Feb. 1778	21 July 1778	—	Building & fitting
Half-pay .	—	,,	22 July 1778	Appointed Comptroller of the Navy	—	—

The differences are trifling, and the only point worth noting now—then it was only a matter of course—is the three years allowed for time at sea in the Loyal Jane. As the service in the navy, from April 1741 to October 1745, is continuous, these three years were prior to the earlier date, beginning, at the latest possible, in March 1738, when the boy was a few months over eleven. We have no record of how he really passed these years, but presumably at school, while the skipper of the Loyal Jane, not unwilling to do a friendly turn for the collector of customs, bore the name of the boy as an apprentice on his ship's books.

Whether Middleton's service in the Sandwich and Duke had any more reality than that in the Loyal Jane cannot now be told; we do not get on sure ground till we note his joining the Flamborough, a small 20-gun frigate, fitting out for the Carolina station, and the protection of the colonial trade from the Spanish privateers. With her head-quarters at Charleston and its neighbourhood, she cruized to the southward, at times stretching down as far as the coast of Cuba. It was a service that must have been peculiarly trying in many respects; so that, after three years of it, Middleton—notwithstanding the bogus time in the Loyal Jane—was able to pass his examination, then entirely practical, satisfactorily. A month later, 5th November, 1745, he was promoted to be lieutenant of the Chesterfield, a 40-gun ship, fitting for Channel

hardly, apparently, have been able to go on, had there not been always a Dundas to help it.'—Lord Rosebery, in the *Times*, 15 July, 1907.

service, and employed during the next two years in convoying the coasting trade from Plymouth to Bristol, with occasional short spells on the coast of Ireland or in the Soundings.

The third year of the commission was more lively. The Chesterfield sailed from Sheerness on the 1st January, 1748, and in a leisurely navigation —stopping three weeks at Spithead, two in Cork harbour, a month at Gibraltar, and a fortnight at Madeira—came by the beginning of May to Teneriffe, in the neighbourhood of which she cruized for nearly a month. On the 13th June she anchored in Porto Praya Road, where she had two men killed and several wounded in an affray with the 'negors.' Thence she went over to the mainland, lay for a fortnight at Sierra Leone; and, after proceeding leisurely along the coast, anchored off Cape Coast Castle on 7th October.

On the 15th the master wrote in the log [1]:—

> At noon I came on shore to Cape Corse Castle to refresh myself, being very much afflicted with the rheumatism. The ship being carried out of the Road the same night by the people on board, I was left behind with the captain, 2nd [Wm. Forster] and 3rd [C. Middleton] lieutenants, purser, surgeon, master's mate, five midshipmen and five men.

The story is given by Beatson [2] correctly enough, except in the matter of date—10th October instead of 15th. The ship was retaken by the efforts of the boatswain, who brought the men back to their duty,

[1] Official Number, 370.
[2] *Naval and Military Memoirs*, iii. 89.

and made prisoners of Samuel Couchman, the first lieutenant, and the other chiefs of the mutiny—one of whom, John Place, carpenter's mate, pronounced by the court-martial 'to have been a principal in this whole affair,' was afterwards said to have been 'one of Roberts'[1] men.' As Roberts was killed twenty-six years before, the story seems improbable. Couchman, who certainly acted as a madman, pleaded that he was mad drunk, which was very likely true; but, as an extenuation of his crime, the plea was not accepted, and he was duly shot, as Beatson has recorded. Captain Dudley was tried for being out of the ship with so many of his officers; but he had no difficulty in proving that he and the whole party were employed in making a survey of the station; that they remained for the night 'at the earnest request of the president and factory to let as many officers be on shore as could possibly be spared, to give them countenance;' and that there was absolutely no suspicion of any felonious design. And indeed, as far as Couchman was concerned, there does not appear to have been any such design; though we must believe that the attempt had been already planned by Place and some of the others.

Before the boatswain recovered the ship, she had got too far out to be able to regain the anchorage, so she was taken across to the West Indies, where, in English Harbour, on 7th March, 1749, Dudley, with the other officers, resumed the com-

[1] *Sc.* Bartholomew Roberts, pirate, slain in fight with Sir Chaloner Ogle in 1722. See *D.N.B.*

mand, but was superseded on the 9th April by Captain James Campbell, who had been sent out from England. On 23rd April she came out of the harbour, sailed for England on the 30th, and anchored at Spithead on the 14th June.

Middleton's service in the Culloden, his first service in the Anson, and his time in the Monarch call for no comment; even when he joined the Anson for the second time, in July 1754, Europe was still at peace; but a few months later the political outlook was more threatening, and, in the spring of 1755, the Anson, now commanded by Captain Robert Man, was one of the fleet under Boscawen sent out to North America, with the avowed intention of preventing the French reinforcing their positions on the St. Lawrence.[1] Though war was not yet declared the expedition was the nearest approach to war service, on the grand scale, that fell to Middleton's lot to see; a circumstance that gives an especial interest to the following extract from Man's Journal :—[2]

1755. *8th June.*—Cape Race, N 27° E, 25 lgs. Moderate and fair. Saw several strange sail: two hoisted their colours: in the evening, saw 3 large ships to the westward. In the morning saw the same 3 sail: made the signal to the admiral: the whole fleet gave chase. At 11 a.m. the Dunkirk coming up fast with the chase, the admiral made the general signal for engaging the enemy. The French ship hoisted her colours and fired a gun to windward. At ½ past 11 the Dunkirk engaged,

[1] Cf. Beatson, i. 425 *seq.*
[2] Official Number, 4115.

and in less than ½ an hour the French man-of-war submitted, by striking his colours. We and most part of the fleet continued the chase after the other two ships. Sounded, 50 fms.

9th June.—Do. Cape, N 31° E, 18 lgs. Do. weather. At 1 p.m. the admiral made the signal to call in most of the fleet, which soon joined the admiral. The Defiance and Fougueux continued the chase. At 2 we had orders to send our boat with an officer and 34 men on board the prize, which proved to be the Alcide, a 64-gun ship, commanded by Monsieur Hocquart.[1] At 5 one of the other ships struck to the Defiance and Fougueux, which was the Lys, a 64-gun ship, but had but 24 on board and 600 troops. We received 35 prisoners from the Alcide. The fleet bore down to the Defiance and Fougueux. We found, by the prisoners, that the third ship was the Dauphin Royal, of 64 guns. The latter part of this 24 hours was foggy, and sometimes blowed fresh: repeated the fog signals.

After this the fleet went off Louisbourg, and then to Halifax, where it remained till towards the end of October, when it returned to England. By the end of November the Anson was in Hamoaze, and there she continued during the winter. In March she went round to Portsmouth, and on 27th April sailed, in charge of the trade, for the West Indies. On the 7th June she was off Carlisle Bay, Barbados; and on the 12th moored in St. John's Road, Antigua, which for the next six months was her head-quarters, though she was pretty actively employed, cruizing

[1] Beatson points out that this was the third time that Hocquart had fallen into Boscawen's hands. Cf. Lacour-Gayet, *La Marine Militaire sous Louis XV*, p. 532.

round about the Leeward Islands in the protection of commerce. Turning over the leaves of her log,[1] the names that continually meet the eye are Deseada, Barbados, St. Kitts, S. end of Guadeloupe, St. Eustatius, Anguilla, Dominica, Marie Galante, St. Lucia, and so forth.

She remained on this service till June 1757; but meantime, on the 24th February, a court-martial[2] had made a vacancy in the command of the Blandford, and Middleton was promoted to the rank of commander. At first he was sent to the Blandford as acting captain; a month later he was moved to the Saltash sloop, and finally to the Speaker sloop, to which he had apparently been commissioned from the first; but the curious point is that, from the 26th February to the 28th March, he was borne, as commander, on the books of both Blandford and Speaker; and that—which, in the middle of the eighteenth century, is almost more curious—he was only paid for the Speaker.

On the 22nd May, 1758, Middleton was advanced to post rank, although the Barbados, which he joined in July—possibly before his promotion came out—was certainly not a post ship. He continued in her, however, till March 1759, when he moved into the Arundel, from which, in July 1760, he was transferred to the Emerald, always on the same station

[1] Reference Number, 47.

[2] On Captain Richard Watkins, for having 'treated Rear-Admiral Frankland in a highly contemptuous and disrespectful manner, and likewise been disobedient to his orders . . . in neglecting to put them in execution with that diligence so expressly required of him.'—'In Letters,' 5296.

and on the same service—the protection of commerce, his views of which are explained, in full detail, in his letters to Mr. Pringle (pp. 1–20) and to Sir James Douglas (pp. 27–38), embodying a clear exposition of the method he proposed for keeping down the force of the enemy's privateers. That, as worked by him, it answered very well would seem to be proved by the thanks of the assembly and the gold-hilted sword voted to him in 1761 by that highly critical and far from uninterested body, the merchants of Barbados.

On paying off the Emerald in the end of October 1761, Middleton—not without considerable objection on the part of the admiralty—took a few months' holiday and married; but the war was still going on; it was no time for an active-minded officer to remain on half-pay; and in March 1762 he joined the Adventure, of thirty-two guns, for service in the Channel, and actually employed during the next twelve months in a close blockade of the north coast of Normandy, more especially from Cape d'Antifer to Cape de la Hague, though the names of Alderney, Guernsey, and the Caskets appear in the log—occasionally Beachy Head or Bolt Head, and sometimes Spithead and the Sound, to clean the ship or refresh the men. It was, no doubt, a strenuous time; and though the blockade was carried on in an easy-going fashion that now seems curious, very good work was done. Several small but troublesome privateers were captured; three or four West Indiamen, prizes of the privateers, were recovered; one Dutch vessel, of 300 tons, carrying timber for ship-building from Havre to Brest, was brought to

Spithead for adjudication—a measure which seems to have put an end to that nefarious traffic.

The number of petty prizes, too, was considerbale; small coasting vessels, laden, for the most part, with country produce; butter for Rouen; glass and millstones from Rouen for Granville; a small sloop laden with pitch and tar; and, on one occasion, a large lugger laden with oysters, which were 'distributed to the ship's company.' As often as not the Adventure was at anchor, very frequently off the mouth of the Seine or off Cape Havre (la Hève), where, once at least, at a distance of four miles from the shore, they quietly 'heeled the ship, scrubbed the starboard side, and boot-topped with tallow.' The active cruizing seems to have been commonly done by the boats, and by the small prizes used as tenders.[1]

At the end of the war the Adventure was paid off, and Middleton, begging to be excused taking up a commission to the Pearl, went on half-pay for the next twelve years. During this time his life, so far as we are concerned, is a blank. In the summer of 1763 he visited Holland 'on private business;' but, with the exception of the two or three formal letters (dated from Teston) asking for leave and reporting his return, we have no information as to his doings, though we may be sure that they did not involve anything of general interest.

When war again broke out, he obtained employment as captain of the Ardent, guardship at the Nore;

[1] Log of the Adventure (No. 1122); Official Letters ('In Letters,' 2114–5).

his order book in which (pp. 39–45)—and especially if compared with that of Prince William Henry in the Andromeda, thirteen years later[1]—bears witness to an enlightened mind, singularly in advance of his day. It will, in fact, be noticed that several of the measures tending to health, comfort, and efficiency, suggested by Kempenfelt in 1780–81, had been actually ordered by Middleton in 1775.

In November 1776 Middleton was appointed to the Prince George, a ninety-gun ship, kept—according to a then prevailing custom, long extinct, but recently revived—nominally in commission for home defence, with a greatly reduced or, in the language of to-day, nucleus crew—a deception to parliament and the nation, and a real danger in time of need. He held this command for upwards of a year, quitting it on 2nd February, 1778, to take charge of the fifty-gun ship Jupiter, still on the stocks. It was certainly an *interim* appointment, pending some other of which we know nothing; for on the 14th July Maurice Suckling, the comptroller of the navy, died. Middleton was appointed to succeed him, and on the 21st July his active service came to an end.

For nearly twelve years he held the post of comptroller, his work during the War of American Independence being rewarded with a baronetcy on 23rd October, 1781. In 1784 he was elected M.P. for Rochester. In 1787 he successfully asserted his right to his flag, and—against the decision of Lord Howe, then first lord of the admiralty—was made a rear-admiral on 24th September. His further pro-

[1] *N.R.S.* xxiv. App. A.

motions, in course of seniority, were: vice-admiral, 1st February, 1793; admiral, 1st June, 1795. On 9th November, 1805, he was one of the newly made admirals of the red, and so he remained. In March 1790, finding it impossible to carry out certain reforms in the navy board, on which he had insisted, he resigned his office, though without ceasing to take a lively interest in the course of naval administration.

In May 1794 he joined the admiralty, of which the Earl of Chatham was then the head, and remained a member of the board, under Earl Spencer, till November 1795. Ten years later, on the resignation of Lord Melville (30th April, 1805), he was appointed first lord of the admiralty, and, at the same time (1st May) was raised to the peerage as Baron Barham of Barham Court and Teston, in the county of Kent, with succession, in default of male issue, to his daughter and to her heirs male. The extent of his share in the great events of that year will be described and discussed in a future volume; it is enough here to record that he was the responsible minister of the navy antecedent to and at the date of Trafalgar.

On the death of Pitt (23rd January, 1806), and the consequent reconstruction of the ministry, Barham, being then in his eightieth year, retired from public life; and though he lived for another seven years, taking an intelligent interest in public affairs, and especially in all that related to the navy, he had no longer any share in their conduct. He died at Barham Court, in his eighty-seventh year, on 17th June, 1813.

Some twenty or more years after Lord Barham's death, his former secretary, Sir J. Deas Thomson, undertook to write his life; but, after a good deal of preliminary work, the project does not seem to have got any further than the printing of a prospectus, of which the following is a copy, though it seems unnecessary to display it, as in the original.

Preparing for publication in the ensuing Autumn,

A BRIEF MEMOIR OF THE LIFE AND PUBLIC SERVICES OF THE RT. HON. CHARLES MIDDLETON, LORD BARHAM, OF BARHAM COURT AND TESTON, IN KENT,

Admiral of the Red, one of His Majesty's Most Honourable Privy Council, Comptroller of the Navy from 1778 to 1790, one of the Elder Brethren of the Trinity House, a Member of the Board of Inquiry into the state of the Woods, Forests, and Land Revenue in 1787, Senior Sea Lord of the Admiralty in 1794–5, Chairman of the Board for Revising the Civil Affairs of the Navy in 1804, 5, and 6, and First Lord of the Admiralty during the latter part of Mr. Pitt's Administration in 1805–6.

TOGETHER WITH AN APPENDIX CONTAINING

Extracts from his Correspondence with the Earl of Shelburne, and Mr. Pitt, when Prime Ministers; with Lord George Germaine, when Secretary of State for the War Department; with the Earl of Sandwich, Viscount Keppel, Earl Howe, and the Earl of Chatham, when respectively at the head of the Admiralty; with Admirals Sir George Bridges Rodney, Sir Samuel, afterwards Lord Hood, Barrington, Graves, Digby, Kempenfeldt, &c. when in command during the American war; and with Admirals Lord Keith, Lord Nelson, Cornwallis, Collingwood, Sir John Duckworth, &c. during the period when he (Lord Barham) presided at the Admiralty in 1805–6. The whole selected with the permission of his grandson, the present Lord Barham, from the originals in the Repositories at Barham Court in Kent, by

SIR J. DEAS THOMSON, K.C.H., F.R.S., F.L.S.,

His Lordship's Private Secretary when at the Head of the Admiralty in 1805-6, and from that period Commissioner and Accountant-General of the Navy till the extinction of the Navy Board in June 1832.

From Thomson's close personal as well as family connection with Barham, it must, in some respects, be regretted that the proposal was never carried out. He would, beyond all doubt, have been able to give a portrait of the old admiral, such as the present editor cannot even attempt. On the other hand, his course of life seems to have unfitted him for historical research. The inaccuracies in the list of Barham's correspondents, here printed, and numerous faulty memoranda, as, for instance—

List of the ships in which Lieut. Charles Middleton served :—

1745—Shark.
1752—Culloden.
1758—Aldborough.
1760—Barbados.
1765—Ardent, Captain—

show that, notwithstanding his long-continued relations to the admiralty and the navy board, he was curiously ignorant of the navy as a fighting service. From the historical point of view, the memoir he would have written could not have been satisfactory.

On 22nd December, 1761, during a short period on half-pay, Middleton, then a post captain, and having, it would seem, made a good deal of prize money in the West Indies, married Margaret, younger daughter of James Gambier, Warden of the Fleet, and of his wife Mary, daughter of —— Mead, probably also a sister of that Captain Mead who, twenty years before, had introduced Middleton into the navy. The Gambiers were very numerous; and, as many of them and their connections are mentioned in the following pages, an extract[1] from the family tree will not be out of place.

Nicolas Gambier, Huguenot, escaped from France on the revocation of the Edict of Nantes.

- James = Mary Mead.
  - John, Lieutenant-Governor of the Bahamas.
    - Samuel, a commissioner of the navy.
      - Many sons and daughters.
    - James, Lord Gambier, admiral of the fleet; *d.s.p.* 1833.
    - Other sons.
    - Mary = Samuel Pitchford, nephew of Sir S. Cornish, whose name he took on inheriting his large fortune. Captain of the Arrogant on 12 April, 1782; *d.*, admiral, 1816.
    - Margaret = W. Morton Pitt, Wm. Pitt's second cousin and family friend.
    - Other daughters.
  - James, admiral; *d.s.p.* 1789.
  - Other sons.
  - Susan = Sir Samuel Cornish, bart., vice-admiral; *d.s.p.* 1770.
  - Margaret = Charles Middleton, Lord Barham.
  - Other daughters.

As Margaret Gambier,[2] Mrs. Middleton had contracted a school-girl intimacy, which ripened into a lasting friendship, with Miss—or, as she was

[1] For fuller details, consult Collins's *Peerage*, ed. by Brydges, ix. 387.

[2] Lady G. Chatterton, *Life of Lord Gambier*, i. 139.

usually called in later years, Mrs.—Bouverie,[1] a cousin of the Radnor family, a woman of very considerable property and of large-hearted charity, the friend of Wilberforce, Hannah More, and others of the religious philanthropic society of the day. Into this set Margaret Gambier was naturally drawn, and, after her marriage, her husband with her; they spent much of their time at Teston,[2] with Mrs. Bouverie, who, at her death in 1798, left Barham Court and the Teston estate, in Kent, to Middleton, who was also appointed sole executor and residuary legatee. This clause in her will,[3] dated 12th October, 1786, runs:—

To Sir Charles Middleton, of Hertford Street, in the parish of St. George, Hanover Square, in the county of Middlesex, Bart., and his heirs and assigns for ever, all that my mansion house situate and being at Teston, wherein I now dwell, and all houses, outhouses, buildings, gardens, lands, meadow pasture, and wood grounds thereto belonging or therewith used, and all the rest and residue of my manors, lands, tenements, hereditaments, and real estate whatsoever and wheresoever, not herein before otherwise devised or disposed of, and also all the rest, residue, and remainder of my personal estate and effects of what nature or kind soever and not herein before disposed of.

[1] Elizabeth Bouverie was daughter and eventually sole heiress of Christopher, younger son of Edward Bouverie (1621–94), 'an eminent Turkey merchant;' brother of William Bouverie (baronet 1714), whose grandson, William, was 1st Earl of Radnor, and of Anne, who married Sir Philip Boteler, of Barham Court.—Collins, v. 32–4; G.E.C[okayne], *Complete Baronetage*, vol. ii.

[2] Middleton's letters to the admiralty when on leave, 1762–3, 1775–8, are mostly dated from Teston.

[3] Now in Somerset House (Walpole, 635).

The value of this bequest it is impossible even to guess at, and indeed it is no business of ours. We may, however, believe that it was very handsome, though, apparently, all the estates which Miss Bouverie had inherited, directly or indirectly, from her father were left to her Radnor cousins, and the legacies to relations, friends, and charities were both large and numerous. The Teston estate she had inherited from her cousin, Sir Philip Boteler, who died without surviving issue in 1772, and probably considered it more especially her own. But it is a little curious that, though the will is dated six years before Lady Middleton's death, her name is not in any way mentioned in it; there is to her neither legacy nor expressed remembrance; though there are legacies of 100*l.* to her one daughter, Diana, and to Diana's husband, Gerard Noel Edwards. Mr. Edwards, who married Diana on 20th December, 1780, was nephew, on the mother's side, of the Earl of Gainsborough, on whose death (1798), without direct heirs male, the title became extinct; and Edwards, succeeding to the estates, assumed the name of Noel. On the death of Lord Barham in 1813, Noel, by the terms of the patent, succeeded to the baronetcy, and Mrs. Noel to the barony, as Lady Barham. She had a large family; and in her eldest son the title of Earl of Gainsborough was revived.

When Middleton was appointed comptroller the navy was labouring in a period of unexampled depression. One of the doubtful advantages of that system of party government, which its admirers acclaim as the palladium of our political liberties, is that—whichever party may be in office—the treasury is unwilling to spend money on our armaments, knowing that, at the next election, it will be denounced as a flock of vultures who have been battening on the very vitals of the poor. It follows that, when need arises, when an enemy, seeing our unprepared state, proposes to take advantage of it, we have to arm in a hurry, imperfectly, and at a lavish cost; spending in a few months many times the amount which, if invested year by year, on business principles, might have obviated all need for war, by making it too clearly dangerous; and if not that, would at least have placed the country in a state to meet the enemy's assault without apprehension, and above all without panic.

During the autumn of 1777 the ministry had been warned, not only by neutral members but by the opposition, that the House of Bourbon was only waiting for an opportunity to take the part of the revolted colonists. But timely preparation would have cost money, and might have seemed to invite a war. *Laisser aller* policy and fear of the opposition were as lively and as costly in 1777 as they were in 1898; more so; for the resources of the kingdom were infinitely less, and—under a dishonest administration—the navy as well as the army was at the lowest ebb.

When, in March 1778, it was known that France had recognized the independence of the American Colonies, and had made a treaty of alliance with them, then, indeed, the government deemed it necessary to act. But, unarmed as they were, they could not at once accept the challenge. Some time before, and at the particular request of the king, Keppel had accepted the command of the Channel fleet, on the assurance that there were forty-two ships of the line in commission, thirty-five of which were completely manned and ready to put to sea at a moment's warning. But when he went to Portsmouth on 22nd March, he found only six, to use his own words, 'fit to meet a seaman's eye.' The others, although indeed in commission, were not manned and were in need of more or less extensive repairs, while the store-houses at Portsmouth, as also at Plymouth, were empty.

Now, indeed, every effort was made; and, at once to hasten the equipment and encourage the country, the king visited the several dockyards—Chatham, Sheerness, and Portsmouth—where he reviewed what was called the fleet, held a levée on board the Prince George, Keppel's flagship, and conferred baronetcies, knighthoods, and promotions. Against very great difficulties the work was pushed forward, and by the beginning of May a considerable fleet had been got together.

Then the admiralty received belated news that the French were equipping a squadron at Toulon, under the command of the Comte d'Estaing, either to join the fleet at Brest or to go to America. Whatever was its destination, the obvious course was to intercept it at Gibraltar; and a squadron of twelve ships of the line, selected from Keppel's fleet, was ordered to hurry on their equipment and get to sea with all possible despatch, under the command of Vice-Admiral Byron. To do this, heavy toll was laid on the rest of Keppel's ships; they were cleared of men, of stores, of provisions, and stripped, in many cases, of their running rigging, to satisfy the needs of those ordered to Gibraltar. With all the haste that could be made, it was not till 9th June that Byron got to sea and sailed for America, as it was already known that D'Estaing had passed the Straits on 18th May. Hurriedly fitted out, with raw crews, and rigged largely with twice-laid rope, the ships suffered severely from the heavy weather they experienced, and finally reached New York more fit for the friendly assistance of the hospital or the dockyard than for active hostilities against the enemy.

And in the meantime Keppel, having gone out with, in the first instance, a fleet of twenty ships, returned to Portsmouth on ascertaining that the French fleet at Brest numbered thirty-two. When, reinforced, and with practically equal numbers, he again appeared off Brest, the roadstead was empty. The French fleet was at sea; and though he got sight of it on the 23rd July, it was not till the 27th that he was able to bring it to action, and then only partially. The celebrated battle was, in truth, little more than a passing skirmish; and though it looms large in our naval history, it is only by reason of the quarrel which broke out between Keppel and Palliser, the third in command. Keppel was tried by court-martial on a charge of misconduct, and was honourably acquitted; Palliser, too, was tried and acquitted, though not without a certain suggestion of blame, in what Sir Charles Douglas happily described as a 'censoriously acquitting sentence' (p. 267).

This quarrel, however, deplorable as were its

effects, which rent the navy into tatters, was itself political rather than naval, and can now only serve to accentuate the noble maxim traditionally ascribed to Blake—'It is not for us to meddle with State affairs, but to keep foreigners from fooling us.' Where politics come in, considerations of strategy and the art of war are laid on one side.

But with one accord, those Englishmen who have written about the battle from the naval point of view have represented it as an English success, which only the cowardly flight of the French prevented becoming a crushing victory. Of course it was no such thing; the French fleet was probably in better order than the English; its gunnery was probably better; its commander was probably a better tactician; and Kempenfelt, writing whilst the details of the battle were fresh before him, expressed a decided opinion that the advantage was with the French. 'Why they did not profit from it, I can't conceive' (p. 291).[1]

The grounds on which he based this opinion are no doubt disputable; and it is certain that throughout the long Revolutionary and Napoleonic wars we continued—as we had done since the time of Elizabeth and our great victory over the Spanish Armada—to fire into the hull of our enemy's ships rather than at their masts and spars, a rule which

[1] As soon as the lines drew clear of each other D'Orvilliers made the signal for the van to wear in succession; but the signal was not obeyed. It has been and is still disputed where the fault lay; but at the time, the Queen, the Court, and public opinion loudly denounced the misconduct, or, as they called it, the *lâcheté*, of the Duc de Chartres, then in command of the van. It seems, however, certain that the blunder cannot be attributed to D'Orvilliers.—Chevalier, i. 89–96; Lacour-Gayet, ii. 130, 135.

the French admiral Jurien de la Gravière earnestly recommended to his countrymen as the sounder in principle. It may, however, be doubted whether the French purposely aimed at the rigging; whether it was not merely that, to avoid losing their shot in the sea, they were trained to fire on the upward roll of their ship.

But what confirmed our forefathers in their adhesion to the old rule of firing into the hull was rather that throughout the eighteenth century, as in the great war, the French tactics were governed by the false strategy of 'ulterior aims.' Their fleets, as their single ships, were sent out with instructions to keep themselves, before everything, fit for some further service, which they could not do if they fought a stubborn enemy to a decisive issue. Consequently they rarely engaged, if engaging could be avoided; and when it could not be they quitted the action at the first convenient opportunity. This was certainly not 'running away,' as our officers pretended to believe; it was strategy, often a very cunning strategy; and though, as Colomb, Mahan, and others have shown, wrong in principle and incapable of leading to decisive results, it cannot be denied that it not unfrequently led the French to the end at which they were aiming.

Thus on the 11th February, 1744, they wished to break the blockade of the coast of Italy and to open the communication with the Spanish ports. They succeeded in doing so; not indeed permanently, but sufficiently for their immediate purpose. Thus on the 20th May, 1756, they succeeded in preventing the English fleet relieving Minorca; and, again, sufficiently for their purpose. On the 5th September, 1781, in the action off the Chesapeake, which fills so much of our vol. III (*Hood's Letters*), and is so frequently referred to in the present volume, it is clear that the purely defensive tactics adopted by the French accomplished all they then wanted, and left their fleet intact for further service—the capture of St. Kitts, for instance. Of course they also left the English fleet, which they ought to have destroyed, to form the nucleus of that which met them on the 12th April, *dies cretâ notanda*, when they would fain have avoided action, or rendered it abortive; have dismantled the English ships and gone away to attempt the capture of Jamaica, had not the accident of the wind and the genius of Rodney combined to bring their plan to nought. When in 1804–5 Napoleon gave stringent and reiterated orders to Ganteaume at Brest to avoid an action—'parce qu'une victoire même n'aurait fait que s'opposer, par des avaries inévitables, à l'exécution des désirs de sa Majesté'[1] —he was merely following the strategical principle which had become traditional in the French navy, though he had utterly discarded it from the practice of the French army.

But, after all, the effective result of the battle of the 27th July is always overlooked. We know the course of the war which it ushered in; have we ever considered how that might have been changed if the battle had ended in an overwhelming victory for one side or the other? For the French, for instance? There would have been no essential

[1] Desbrière, *Projets et Tentatives de Débarquement aux Iles Britanniques*, iv. 514.

difference, though the pace might have been quickened. England would have been left with less power of resistance than she already had, Gibraltar must have fallen, and there could have been no countervailing 12th April. Or for the English? If the 12th April, pushed to its issue in the sense imagined by Hood (p. 161), had been anticipated off Ushant on the 27th July? With the French navy crushed, the assistance of France to America could not have been given; D'Estaing must have been at once recalled; Spain would have remained neutral, and the colonies would, for the time at least, have returned to their allegiance. Nothing of this happened, because we could not defeat the French fleet on the 27th July; because Keppel's notions of tactics were crude; because his fleet was a mere congeries of ships, and their crews a mob of newly raised, untrained men. The price we then paid for the neglect of the government, as approved by the country, was the loss of our prestige in Europe, the loss of our colonies in America, and an increase of more than one hundred millions to the national debt.

Thus begun, the war continued. There had been no foresight, no preparation; and the political animosity, brought by the admiralty into the service afloat, destroyed any chance which the previous maladministration might have left. Keppel resigned the command of the Channel fleet; no officer on the active list was willing to undertake it; and Sir Charles Hardy, the governor of Greenwich Hospital, was drawn from his retirement to fill the vacant post. Under Hawke, Hardy had been an adequate second in the battle of Quiberon Bay and afterwards; but he had never held an independent command; had not been at sea for nearly twenty years;[1] and though only sixty-four, was, in body and mind, an old man. Kempenfelt was appointed his first captain, a fortunate event to which we owe the interesting series of letters now printed.

It will be noticed that these are not news letters. They make no pretence of relating the current history. They tell us nothing of the invasion of the Channel by the combined fleets of France and Spain; nor of our forbearing to oppose the sailing of De Grasse for the West Indies, and thanking God we were rid of him, so that Gibraltar might be safely relieved; nor, indeed, of the whole course of events during these critical years. But the bare story of all this was published in the Gazettes of the day, and may now be read in Beatson's *Memoirs*, or, more concisely related, in the admirable chapter by Captain Mahan in the voluminous work of the late Sir W. Laird Clowes. Beatson, however, had only an imperfect knowledge of, and it was not in Mahan's plan to dwell on, the political situation which controlled the action of the English fleet; and the difficulties in its way have remained things which might sometimes be guessed at, but were never clearly set forth till now.

When Hardy died in the spring of 1780, the command was offered to Barrington (p. 366), who absolutely refused it, though he consented to act as

[1] Such jobbery was not all on one side. The other party sinned in very much the same way, and without the same excuse, in sending Pigot out to the West Indies. See *post*, p. 209.

second with Geary, then an old and frail man, quite unequal to the fatigues of the post which, after the summer cruize, he resigned (pp. 329, 370), to be succeeded by Vice-Admiral Darby.

With both Geary and Darby, Kempenfelt continued as first captain, even after his promotion to flag rank, till 18th November, 1781, when he hoisted his flag in the Victory, and, in command of a detached squadron, performed one of the most brilliant actions recorded in our naval history. Kempenfelt's letters and the Victory's log (pp. 350–60) give or correct many of the details of this remarkable story, of which a complete sketch cannot fail to be interesting.

About the middle of November the admiralty had intelligence that a large convoy, carrying supplies and reinforcements for the West and East Indies, was on the point of sailing from Brest, and Kempenfelt was appointed to the command of a small squadron, with instructions to intercept it. His letters (pp. 351–3) show some of the indignation which he naturally felt at the conduct of the admiralty in trying to make him go to sea, as if voluntarily, with an inferior force. It appears that the squadron, as first detailed, consisted of fourteen ships of the line and one of fifty guns; and though this was inferior in force to the fourteen larger and heavier ships reported as forming the French escort, it does not appear that he would have complained, although it would have been quite easy to give him an overwhelming superiority, from the ships on the point of sailing for the East and West Indies. But when the Namur, of ninety guns, and the Hercules, of seventy-four, were withdrawn, he could not help letting Middleton, and, through Middleton, Lord Sandwich, know of his discontent at being finally ordered to sea with only twelve ships and very few frigates, to intercept a convoy guarded by fourteen ships individually more powerful. As a matter of fact, the French squadron consisted of nineteen sail of the line, under the command of Guichen, who had with him the Marquis de Vaudreuil, La Motte-Picquet, D'Entrecasteaux, and two other flag officers. The aggregate of guns carried by the French squadron was 1,582, as against 996 by the English.

What happened on 12th December, when the two squadrons came in sight of each other, Kempenfelt has well and modestly told (pp. 356–7), and how, having effectually spoiled Guichen's voyage, he returned to Portsmouth.[1] Brilliant as the affair was, and honourable to Kempenfelt, it was felt by the country at large to be most discreditable to the admiralty that he should have been ordered to sail with a force so markedly inferior. If he had done so much with so little, what might he not have done had he been properly supported? If the government did not know that the French were sending out nineteen ships of the line, their ignorance was culpable; if they did know, their neglect was treasonable.

But an administration which had survived the surrender of Saratoga and Yorktown was not to be overthrown by an outcry such as this; nor, although badly shaken, was it overthrown till the news came of the surrender of Minorca on 4th February, 1782.

[1] Cf. Beatson, v. 415 *seq.*, vi. 317–21; Chevalier, i. 278–80; Lacour-Gayet, ii. 377–8.

Amid greater disasters and anxieties, the loss of this important fortress and harbour was little noticed by the public, nor was it, perhaps, fully appreciated till some ten or fifteen years later. But in parliament it served as a fresh proof of incapacity; and after several stormy debates and close divisions, the government, including Lord Sandwich, resigned on 20th March. Keppel, raised to the peerage, became first lord of the admiralty, having Harland and Pigot as two of his colleagues. Darby, the junior lord under Sandwich, gave up his seat at the admiralty and his command of the Channel fleet, to which Lord Howe succeeded. With him was Barrington, as second in command; and, among other junior flag officers, Kempenfelt, with his flag in the Royal George, till she foundered at Spithead on 29th August, 1782.

That in her

> Kempenfelt went down,
> With twice four hundred men,

is perhaps all that a large proportion of readers have previously known about him, though many know also that it was largely due to him that an improved system of signalling was, shortly after this date, adopted in the service. And in his letters we have the workings of his mind on the solution of that problem. He made no secret of his indebtedness to the French; and if, as he believed, the real author of the numerical code was La Bourdonnais, the genius of that remarkable man must be placed on a still higher level than that which it has already held. But it is not only the detail of his system of signalling that will captivate the attention; almost more interesting are his discussions on the discipline of the navy, his proposals for reforms, and perhaps most of all his insistence on the necessity of tactical study. This, in an age when the whole mystery of naval tactics was supposed to be embodied in the Fighting Instructions, is sufficiently remarkable; but as we read his letters it is impossible to avoid being struck by the breadth of his suggestions, which are so frequently described as having been first made by Clerk of Eldin.

Clerk embodied them in book form, and a claim —quite untenable—of having been Rodney's teacher has been made on his behalf. It will scarcely be maintained that he was also the instructor of Kempenfelt, whom we here find enunciating the principle of Clerk's system in July 1779, several months before Clerk's book was written—the principle of concentration of effort. It is requisite, he wrote (p. 292), 'to watch and seize the favourable opportunity for action, and to catch the advantage of making the effort at some or other feeble part of the enemy's line.' The particular manner in which this was to be done he did not explain; but we are warranted in assuming that he had no cut and dried rule; the principle was what he insisted on; the way in which it was to be carried out might properly be left to be decided according to circumstances. One way he illustrated on the 12th December, 1781.

But again, in September 1779, we have him insisting on the use that ought to be made of fire ships—which, in point of fact, were not used as fire ships during the whole course of the war—and writing (p. 296), 'In the line, the fire ship has as much chance to succeed when the masts are standing as when they are gone, without the ship she point for bears away; and then the line is broke, and an opening made for their defeat.' For, indeed, breaking the line was no new idea; and though the Instructions did not provide for it, we may be quite sure that it appealed to many capable officers as the problem of the day; otherwise such a remark as Douglas's—'Drake stood firmly on, in close impenetrable order' (p. 278)—would have little or no significance.

But the largest share of the interest of this present volume belongs to the war in American and West Indian waters, on which the letters of Young, Rodney's flag captain, and Hood, second in command under Rodney and under Pigot, throw much new light. After D'Estaing's failure to surprise Howe in Delaware Bay, his refusal to attempt 'the passage perilous' of Sandy Hook, and his somewhat inglorious meeting with the little English squadron outside, he went to the West Indies, where—on 15th December, 1778, at the Cul-de-Sac of St. Lucia—he sustained a still more shameful repulse from Barrington. For this he consoled himself by the easy seizure of Grenada, which he permitted his troops to pillage, and by a 'strategic' victory—such as those already referred to—over Byron (6th July), which he declined to push to any decisive issue, either then or a few days later (22nd July) at the Basse Terre of St. Kitts. From St. Kitts he took the fleet to Cape Français in St. Domingo, and thence to the coast of North America, where he co-operated with a land force in the siege of Savannah. When that proved hopeless he re-embarked his men and returned to France.

The career and character of D'Estaing have not to be considered here, and it is sufficient to say that, while Guérin and other writers of the sort have indulged in excessive laudation of his 'bravoure bouillante,' French naval officers did not think highly of him, even in this respect. According to Chevalier (i. 154), 'la plupart des officiers ne croyaient pas à la capacité maritime du comte d'Estaing;' and Lacour-Gayet (ii. 229) quotes La Clocheterie—a man whom we know—as saying, 'C'était un poltron et un homme sans talents.'[1]

After an interval of some months, D'Estaing was succeeded by the Comte de Guichen, a very different style of man; a Breton by birth, trained in the navy from his early youth, and now a lieutenant-general in his 68th year. He had served with credit through all the wars of the century, and was distinguished among his compeers for his skill, as a captain, in manœuvring his ship, as an admiral, in manœuvring his fleet. On the 23rd March, 1780, he arrived at Fort Royal of Martinique, bringing with him sixteen ships of the line, which, joined by the six already on the station under the command of the Comte de Grasse, raised his force to twenty-two; and though, after the disastrous Channel campaign of 1779, when pestilence had carried off the seamen by thousands, there had been some difficulty in manning the ships, they were now in such excellent

[1] Cf. Mahon, *Hist. of England* (cabinet edit.), vi. 272.

order that the English, on seeing them manœuvre, came to the conclusion that they had entered large numbers of American sailors.[1] They do not, in fact, seem to have had any; and the credit of this excellence must be awarded to Guichen and his officers, though we have Kempenfelt's assurance (p. 311) that it was not unusual in the French navy of that time.

The man destined by the fortune of war to be his opponent was Sir George Brydges Rodney, admiral of the white squadron, and at this time just sixty-one, but effectively perhaps the older of the two. He suffered horribly from gout, gravel, and their kindred complications; so that, at times, for days together, he was quite incapable. In his youth he had been a fine, dashing officer; and even now, when but the wreck of his old self, gave forth marks of genius and energy which have raised his name to a lofty pinnacle of glory; but these seem to have been intermittent, and there were long periods when he had neither the power to decide himself nor the temper to permit others to decide for him. Well or ill, he was determined to be commander-in-chief; and his juniors, who sometimes thought that they were better qualified to do the work, did not always like it.

This was particularly the case with Rear-Admiral Sir Samuel Hood, who came out as second in command, and was often indignant because Rodney—who possibly always thought of him as one of his old midshipmen—would not let

[1] Beatson, v. 65.

him be first. In editing his letters, Mr. Hannay formulated the opinion that 'Hood detested his commander-in-chief,'[1] but it would perhaps be more correct to say that he detested the want of energy, decision, and self-restraint which his commander-in-chief too often exhibited, the vanity and the greed which seemed to dictate his plans, and above all the *hauteur* intended to keep a subordinate in his proper place. To what we already knew of this, the further letters from Hood, now printed, add nothing; but they are curiously corroborated by those from Walter Young, who, as flag captain, was more intimately associated with Rodney than Hood ever was; who probably owed his promotion and certainly owed his position to Rodney, and was thus, in a measure, bound to maintain Rodney's opinions; and yet his judgment of Rodney is very similar to Hood's.

Of Young, personally, nothing is known beyond what we have in these letters. It may be assumed that he was a Scot (p. 71), and it is clear that he had —in Scots phrase—'an unco gude conceit o' himsell.' Whatever the employment he had had under the navy board, it had made him personally acquainted with Middleton; and the flag captain on a station so important as the West Indies then was, was a person worth cultivating, even by the comptroller. It will be seen that he virtually claims the credit of much that was done—of the battle off Cape St. Vincent, for instance. 'Had Sir George,' he says, 'followed my advice in making the land, probably the whole

[1] *N.R.S.* iii. x.

[of the Spanish fleet] would have been secured by four in the afternoon' (p. 65). Or again—

> When the Bedford made the signal for the number she discovered, I wished to have had the signal for a general chase made, as night was coming on. This the admiral opposed, and ordered the signal for a line of battle ahead at two cables' distance. This I opposed in turn, conscious that a great deal of time and distance would be lost, and proposed the signal for a line of battle abreast at a cable's distance. At the same time—as he was confined to his bed—I kept out a stiff sail on the Sandwich, that no time might be lost; and as soon as I discovered the enemy making sail to get off, the signal for a general chase was made. When our ships got up, the signal to engage to leeward and in succession, and the signal for close action at the same time. The admiral's ill state of health, and his natural irresolution, occasioned our shortening sail frequently, which prevented me bringing the Sandwich so early into battle as I could have wished; and it was with difficulty that I succeeded at last, as he attempted several times to have the ships called off from chase.

This may be taken as a crucial instance; and as no amount of vanity could make Young think the admiral was 'confined to his bed' if he was on the poop or quarter-deck, we must believe that the orders were really given by Young in the way he describes, though whether he did so on his own initiative may be doubtful. The unhesitating dash at the enemy has been often referred to as an illustration of Rodney's character, the engaging to leeward as a stroke of Rodney's genius. Young implies that these were all his own; that Rodney had nothing to do with them. Confined to his bed, Rodney could evidently only see with Young's eyes, and must have been, to a great extent, guided by Young's opinion; but the exact measure of the dependence must be left to the judgment of the reader, who will bear in mind that Young, though a middle-aged man,[1] was a very junior captain—of less than four months' seniority.

Rodney sailed from Spithead on 27th December, 1779, in command of a large fleet, having under its escort a vast number of store-ships for the relief of Gibraltar, then in pressing need. Off Cape St. Vincent, on 16th January, he fell in with and demolished the Spanish squadron under Langara; passed on and relieved the fortress; and then, while the bulk of the fleet returned to England, he, in the Sandwich and with three other ships of the line, went to the West Indies, and in Gros Islet Bay of St. Lucia, on 27th March, joined Rear-Admiral Hyde Parker, who had been in temporary command since Byron and Barrington had gone home. A more aggressive officer than Guichen might have overwhelmed Parker in the first place and Rodney afterwards; but while he was trying to reconcile an attack on sixteen ships by twenty-two bigger ones with the principles of French strategy, Rodney's arrival, by increasing the number of the English to twenty, settled the question, and Guichen withdrew to Fort Royal Bay.

Thither Rodney followed him on 2nd April, and,

[1] He can scarcely have been less than 25 and was more likely over 30 in 1763, when he accepted a master's warrant. This would make him about 45 or 50.

by way of offering battle, remained in the bay for two days, approaching at times within random shot of the fortress. Mere fighting, however, was not Guichen's idea of the use of his fleet; and Rodney, finding that his challenge was not accepted, returned to Gros Islet Bay, connecting his anchorage with the enemy's position by a chain of fast sailing, coppered frigates.

On 13th April Guichen came out, partly to cover the approach of a large convoy on its way to Cape Français, and principally intending an attack on Barbados, for which purpose 3,000 soldiers had been embarked, under the command of the Marquis de Bouillé. The uncertainty of the wind under the lee of the island delayed him for a couple of days, and he was still struggling to get to windward of Dominica when, on the 16th, the English fleet came in sight in the south-east quarter. Before nightfall it was sufficiently near to permit the enemies to count each other's force. The two fleets, as eventually ranged in line of battle, on the starboard tack, were as shown on pp. xlv, xlvi.

By the morning of the 17th the two fleets were, roughly speaking, abreast of each other to the west of Martinique; the French, formed in a very extended line ahead, towards the south, on the port tack; the English, in a much closer order, in line towards the north, on the starboard tack, some ten or twelve miles to windward of the French. At a quarter to seven Rodney signalled his intention to attack the enemy's rear, in accordance with a special instruction he had given out some little time before, but which, apparently, nobody understood. A few

ENGLISH.[1]

—	Ships	Guns	Captains	—
1	Stirling Castle .	64	Rob. Carkett . .	Hyde Parker, Rear-Admiral
2	Ajax . .	74	Sam. Uvedale . .	
3	Elizabeth . .	74	Hon. Fred. Maitland	
4	Princess Royal .	90	Harry Harmood .	
5	Albion . .	74	Geo. Bowyer . .	
6	Terrible . .	74	John Douglas . .	
7	Trident . .	64	A. J. P. Molloy .	
8	Grafton . .	74	Thos. Newnham .	Thos. Collingwood, Commodore
9	Yarmouth .	64	Nath. Bateman .	
10	Cornwall . .	74	Tim. Edwards . .	
11	Sandwich . .	90	Walter Young . .	Sir G. B. Rodney, Admiral
12	Suffolk . .	74	Abr. Crespin . .	
13	Boyne . .	70	Chas. Cotton . .	
14	Vigilant . .	64	Sir Geo. Home .	
15	Vengeance .	74	John Holloway .	Wm. Hotham, Commodore
16	Medway . .	60	Wm. Affleck . .	
17	Montagu . .	74	John Houlton . .	
18	Conqueror .	74	Thos. Watson . .	Joshua Rowley, Rear-Admiral
19	Intrepid . .	64	Henry St. John .	
20	Magnificent .	74	John Elphinston .	

Greyhound, 28, W. Dickson; Venus, 36, J. Ferguson; Pegasus, 28, John Bazely; Deal Castle, 24, Wm. Fooks; Andromeda, 28, H. Bryne; Centurion, 50, Rd. Braithwaite, to assist the rear in case of need.

[1] Official list, attached to Rodney's despatch, with Christian names added, checked by the Pay-books.

FRENCH.[1]

—	Ships	Guns	Captains	—
1	Hercule	74	Cte. d'Amblimont	
2	Artésien	74	Chev. de Peynier	
3	Sphinx	74	Cte. de Soulanges	
4	Robuste	74	Chev. de Longueville	Cte. de Grasse, chef d'escadre
5	Magnifique	74	Chev. de Brach	
6	Triton	64	Brun de Boades	
7	Intrépide	74	Duplessis-Parscau	
8	Actionnaire	64	De Larchantel	
9	Indien	64	Chev. de Balleroy	
10	Palmier	74	Chev. de Keroulas de Cohars	Chev. de Monteil, chef d'escadre
11	Couronne	80	Chev. de Buor de la Chenalière	Cte. de Guichen, lieut. général
12	Fendant	74	Cte. du Chaffault de Chaon	Mqs. de Vaudreuil, chef d'escadre
13	Victoire	74	Chev. d'Albert Saint-Hippolyte	
14	Caton	64	Cte. de Framond	
15	Citoyen	74	Mqs. de Nieuil	
16	Solitaire	64	Cte. de Cicé-Champion	
17	Souverain	74	Chev. de Glandevez	
18	Triomphant	80	De Gras-Preville	Cte. de Sade, chef d'escadre
19	Pluton	74	Chev. de la Martonie	
20	Saint-Michel	60	Chev. d'Aymar	
21	Vengeur	64	Chev. de Retz	
22	Destin	74	Cte. Dumaitz de Goimpy	

Résolue, 32; Iphigénie, 32; Courageuse, 32; Médée, 32; Gentille, 32; Cérès, 18.

[1] From the lists given by Chevalier and Troude, compared with Lacour-Gayet. As French writers dwell on the advantage the English had in their three-deckers, it is well to point out that, in every material respect, the French 80 was a more powerful ship than the English 90; she was bigger, more roomy, carried her guns better, threw a heavier broadside, and had a larger complement.

minutes later, signal to close the line to one cable, and at half-past eight to form line abreast.

At this time, then, the English fleet was concentrated abreast of the French rear, and was leading down towards it. Guichen was quick to see his adversary's intention, and wore his line, all together. This would have brought the English attack, if persevered in, on his van, instead of his rear; to prevent which, Rodney wore also, and came to the wind on the port tack. After standing to the southward for rather more than an hour, he again wore (10h. 10m. a.m.), thus coming on the same tack as the enemy—heading towards the north. At 11, signal to alter course to port; and at 11.50 'for every ship to bear down and steer for her opposite in the enemy's line, agreeable to the 21st article of the Additional Fighting Instructions.' This article ran—

> If the squadron should be sailing in a line of battle ahead to windward of the enemy, and the commander-in-chief would have the course altered, in order to lead down to them, he will hoist an union flag at the main top-gallant mast-head and fire a gun; whereupon every ship in the squadron is to steer for the ship of the enemy which, from the disposition of the two squadrons, it may be her lot to engage, notwithstanding the signal for the line ahead is kept flying; making or shortening sail in such proportion as to preserve the distance assigned by the signal for the line, in order that the whole squadron may, as near as possible, come to action at the same time.

It was on these two signals, the one made at

7 o'clock in the morning, the other at noon, with at least two important evolutions between, and in a reversed position of the fleets, that Rodney's plan of the action depended. He wished his line, in close order, to go straight down on the enemy's rear—twenty ships against a much smaller number, and crush them. In his mind, the ship of the enemy which it was the lot of any ship to engage was that ship which was abreast her when the signal was made; and he conceived the former signal—to attack the enemy's rear—as strengthening and explaining the order. But in fact neither captains, nor commodores, nor junior admirals, so understood it. To each of them, the ship which, by the disposition of the two squadrons, it was his lot to engage was the corresponding number in the enemy's line. Carkett, a gallant old officer,[1] so understood it, and made sail to engage the leading ship of the French line; Parker so understood it, and though some of the captains in his division began to see there was something wrong, he took all the van away; Collingwood so understood it, and went ahead; Bateman—a fine old fellow, who had been an able seaman of the Marlborough, and put on the quarter-deck for his gallant conduct in the action off Toulon (11th February, 1744)—so understood it, and counted the ninth ship as the one it was his 'lot' to engage (p. 393); but as the distances increased and the line got into disorder he lost

[1] He was first lieutenant, left—by the death of the captain—in command of the Monmouth when she captured the Foudroyant in 1758. He was promoted the next day to be captain of the big prize.

confidence, did not know what to do, and being, apparently, a puzzle-headed sort of man, did nothing. What is, perhaps, still more damnatory, Clerk of Eldin—who was certainly not a puzzle-headed man—so understood it; understood Rodney's signal to mean 'that his headmost ship should attack the headmost of the enemy, and so on, in succession, throughout his fleet.'[1]

And, indeed, the question must arise, if it did not mean that, what could it mean? The wording of the 'instruction' is, in fact, a valuable object lesson to those critics of the admiralty who have decried the use of teaching English to our young officers. It is not going too far to assert that nine-tenths of the miscarriages and blunders made in the eighteenth century arose out of the inability of the commanding officers to give an intelligible order, or of the commanded to understand one if given. Howe[2] was, of course, an extreme instance of this, and it might be argued that Molloy was victim to it; this 21st article of the Additional Fighting Instructions is certainly another, and Bateman was the sacrifice; but of far more consequence than the ruin of poor Bateman was the loss of the great opportunity that Rodney held.

For what did the order mean? According to Rodney's estimate, the French line was extended over four leagues (twelve miles). This enormous length—probably a gross exaggeration—may have had several gaps, though none are mentioned; but if we are to suppose that the enemy's ships were

[1] *Naval Chronicle*, xxv. 403.
[2] Cf. Laughton, *From Howard to Nelson*, p. 335.

pretty evenly distributed along it, the average distance between them was rather more than 1,000 yards. As, then, the English ships were at 400 yards, it follows that the whole English line, going down in the way understood by Rodney, would have closed on nine ships, a theoretical victory that might have become an overwhelming reality. But there was no instruction as to its being the 'lot' of two or three ships to engage one; the Fighting Instructions made no provision for any such thing. Twenty-nine years afterwards, Sir Gilbert Blane, the physician to the fleet, wrote—

> Lord Rodney himself at various times informed me that, two days before the action, he did, either by oral or written communication, acquaint each captain in his fleet that it was his intention to attack that of the enemy; not their entire fleet of 23 sail with his inferior one of 20, but a part of theirs—as, for example, 15 or 16—with his whole fleet.'[1]

If Blane's memory was not playing him false, if Rodney really did this, we can only say that power of exposition was altogether wanting to him; for it is quite certain that not one man to whom he thus explained his intention had the faintest notion of what Rodney wanted him to do, or how he wanted him to do it. It has often been said that the failure on this occasion must be attributed to the very inefficient system of signalling then in use. The facts before us scarcely seem to bear this out; and when we remember how—with a very much improved system of signalling at his service—Nelson

[1] *Naval Chronicle*, XXV. 402.

spent several weeks before the battle of the Nile, and quite three before the battle of Trafalgar, in explaining his ideas to—in discussing them with—those who were to give effect to them, so that at the critical time the only signal necessary was 'Engage the enemy more closely'—a signal which could be made as well in 1780 as in 1805—it is not difficult to see where the cause of the failure really lay.

It is unnecessary to say more. The letters of Young and Maitland (pp. 53–5, 101–7) and the evidence at the Montagu and Yarmouth courts-martial (App. A) give the details of the fighting with a fulness and precision never before attempted. The case of the Montagu may perhaps explain the rather curious fact that, with one exception, every account of the battle hitherto printed[1] describes the lines as standing to the south on the port tack; and that, though the signals given in Mundy's *Life of Rodney* (ii. 402), essentially the same as those on pp. 390–1, distinctly show that they were on the starboard tack.

It may, however, be pointed out that Blane's contention[2] that 'Rodney did break the French line in order to cut off a part of their fleet' is not in agreement with the evidence before us. It is, on the contrary, quite clear that he had no idea of doing so, but simply intended—which would have been equally effective—to overwhelm a part with vastly superior numbers. As to his 'breaking the line,'

[1] Including Beatson, Mahan (*Influence of Sea Power*), Chevalier, Lacour-Gayet. The one exception is Mahan's chapter in Clowes's *Royal Navy*, in writing which the author had before him abstracts of the courts-martial.

[2] *N.C.* xxv. 402.

which Blane substantiates by quoting from the *Gazette*[1] that 'before the Sandwich engaged the Couronne she had beaten three ships out of their line of battle, had entirely broke it, and was to leeward of the wake of the French admiral' (*ib.* 403)—a statement with which Young's account is in exact agreement—it is evident that no attempt was made to improve or take advantage of the position, to segregate the French rear, or to engage the Couronne to leeward. Quite the contrary, indeed. The Sandwich, having got through the enemy's line, waited, astonished at her own success, until, as Young says in so many words, 'the French admiral, seeing us unsupported . . . with his two seconds wore out of the line and came abreast of the Sandwich, and brought to the wind on the same tack, at their own distance, and continued battering of her for an hour and a half' (p. 55). That the English fleet, in close order, might have cut through the enemy's line and engaged to leeward, that it might have enveloped and overwhelmed the enemy's rear, may be admitted; but the one certain fact is that it did not; that the first was never ordered nor contemplated; and that the second, though ordered, was not understood. We can see that Rodney's design was excellent. We can quite accept Blane's statement that

'the mortification which the gallant commander felt on this occasion no words can express. Of his victory on 12th April, 1782, I know that he thought little. He had a contemptuous opinion of the naval

[1] An imperfect and verbally inaccurate version of Rodney's despatch (26 April) is in Mundy's *Life of Rodney*, i. 283 *seq.*

character of De Grasse, but always spoke in the highest terms of that of Guichen, whom he considered as the best officer in the French service; and he looked on this opportunity of beating such an officer with an inferior fleet as one by which, but for the disobedience of his captains, he might have gained immortal renown.'

But the expression 'disobedience of his captains' shows that he never recognized the true reason of his failure.

If, however, as the French had laid down, and as seems logically correct, a battle which leads to the accomplishment of the ulterior aim, or prevents the enemy accomplishing his, is to be considered a victory, then the 17th April, unsatisfactory as it was from the tactical point of view, was strategically a victory for the English. Guichen had intended an attack on Barbados; and though, after refitting at Guadeloupe, by means of stores supplied from St. Eustatius by our treacherous allies, he got to windward of Martinique, the two rencounters of 15th and 19th May (pp. 56–60) finally put it out of his power to do any mischief—if, indeed, he was then trying to do anything more than return to Fort Royal. This he eventually did, and later on went to Cape Français, whence in August he sailed for Europe with the greater part of his fleet, leaving the few remaining ships under the command of M. de Monteil.

Rodney could only learn that he had sailed; he believed that he had gone to North America, that the allies were meditating some heavy blow, that—in his own words—'his Majesty's territories, fleet, and army in America were in imminent danger of being overpowered.' So he followed, 'without,' he wrote to the admiralty, 'any person whatever in the West Indies, General Vaughan and Mr. Hotham excepted, having the least surmise that I had left that part of the world.' And thus, sweeping the whole coast line northwards, he anchored unexpectedly off Sandy Hook on 14th September.[1]

The insolent and mutinous reception which Arbuthnot gave to Rodney is familiarly known; and it has at least been conjectured that the cause of it was not so much the being superseded by a senior as the loss of a large share of prize money, which it entailed; for when there was only one admiral on the station he got the whole flag share —one-eighth—of all prizes; when there were two, the junior—who in this case was Arbuthnot—got only one-third of that one-eighth. Young, it will be seen, had no doubt that this was the true reason of Arbuthnot's behaviour.

No one with any competent knowledge of the history of naval war can possibly accept the proposal to neutralize private property;[2] but none the less, it is quite certain that the old system of prize money was the frequent cause of serious injury to the public service. Without going further afield than this present volume, and independent of this extreme case of Arbuthnot's, it may be pointed out that ships sent to Jamaica on special duty were detained by Sir Peter Parker (p. 129); that the

[1] Mundy, i. 376.

[2] Cf. Mahan on 'The Question of Immunity for Belligerent Merchant Shipping' (*National Review*, June 1907).

service was delayed by Rowley taking Hood under his orders (p. 261); and that this latter constantly felt himself cramped by the apprehension that measures which he thought necessary would be attributed to selfishness or greed (pp. 126, 230–1).[1]

In Arbuthnot's case, the situation seems to have been aggravated by the rascally character of his secretary. This has been somewhat plainly hinted at before now; but Young does not hint; his charges are categorical, though he does not say that he had legal proof of them. Whether he had or not, the bringing them prominently forward would certainly have involved Arbuthnot, who had good interest, and might probably have involved officials in much higher places than Arbuthnot's. In clearly explaining the swindle to Middleton, Young was, in all likelihood, doing the best that was in his power.

When the fleet returned to the West Indies, it was almost at once occupied with punishing the Dutch treachery by the capture of St. Eustatius. It is a confused story, for the amount of property seized was very large, and perjury could be liberally paid. Here we have little to do with it, beyond pointing out that Young's estimate of the value seems to corroborate Rodney's, unless, indeed, it is the same, which is not improbable. That given (p. 98) by Middleton's anonymous correspondent differs exceedingly. At St. Eustatius Young died, without having heard of the encounter which Hood, who had just come on the station, had

[1] *N.R.S.* iii. 154.

with the Comte de Grasse, who came out in succession to Guichen.

Hood's letters which follow are, to a large extent, complementary to those already published by the Society in vol. III; and many which he wrote to Middleton are virtually the same as those which he wrote to Jackson. Most naval officers have experienced the difficulty of writing accounts of the same events to two or three different people, and are probably quite familiar with Hood's method of solving it; but an interesting feature of it is that, busy man as Hood was, he found time to write out the two editions of these long letters with his own hand. They are nearly all holographs. Still, it has not appeared necessary to reprint letters so nearly identical; but all differences of any significance have been noted.

By far the most important of these letters are those relating to the fatal skirmish off the Chesapeake on 5th September, 1781, though the cream of them has already been given in vol. III. Those that are now new do little more than confirm our previous knowledge of our commanders' utter ignorance of De Grasse's plans. On this point much has been written, blame has been wildly scattered, and explanations which are no explanations have been insisted on. The real explanation is that the enemy's plans were not fixed till the very last; and that if Clinton and Graves believed that the combined effort by sea and land—if made at all—would be against New York, it was that Washington believed so too. The question is one of very great interest both from the historical and naval point of view; and the only reason why it has not been fully answered long ago is that, in respect of it, historians have neglected the familiar maxim 'fas est ab hoste doceri.' The answer is to be found in the correspondence of the enemy's commanders.

When, in the beginning of July, Rear-Admiral Thomas Graves took over the command from Arbuthnot, he found himself in a most difficult position. His squadron was a very small one—not more than equal to that which the French had at Rhode Island, now under the command of M. de Barras—and he was given vaguely to understand that De Grasse might at any moment appear with a part or the whole of the West Indian fleet. The general, Sir Henry Clinton, was convinced that the allies intended to attack New York; and, in fact, that was what had been agreed on by Washington and the French general, the Comte de Rochambeau, not only with a view to winning a position so important, but still more in the hope of taking the strain off the southern States, then hard pressed by Cornwallis.[1]

They had written jointly to De Grasse to this effect; and Washington had urged that, in any case, it would be better that his first appearance on the coast should be off Sandy Hook, 'because, by coming suddenly there, he would certainly block up any fleet which might be within, and he would even have a very good chance of forcing the entrance before dispositions could be made to oppose him.

[1] Washington to Greene, 1 June 1781 (*Washington's Writings*, edit. by Sparks, viii. 62).

Should the British fleet not be there he could follow them to the Chesapeake, which is always accessible to a superior force.[1] Rochambeau, however, was rather inclined to operations in Virginia, and wrote privately to De Grasse to the effect that he must know very well the difficulty of forcing the passage into the harbour of New York, since he was in the fleet under D'Estaing, who had vainly offered an enormous sum to the pilots to take his ships across the bar; that an enterprise in Chesapeake Bay, against Cornwallis, would be more practicable, and the least expected by the enemy, who counted on the distance of the allied army. Finally, he begged him to despatch a frigate with his answer as soon as possible, so that arrangements might be made for them to join him at the point assigned in the Chesapeake.[2]

De Grasse complied with Rochambeau's representations, and wrote, on 8th July, that he hoped to sail from Cape Français on 3rd August. It was the middle of August before this letter was received at Newport, a fact which fixes the date at which Washington changed his plans. On 17th August he wrote to De Grasse—

In consequence of the despatches received from your Excellency by the frigate Concorde, it has been judged expedient to give up, for the present, the enterprise against New York, and turn our attention towards the south, with a view, if we should not be able to attempt Charleston itself, to recover and secure the States of Virginia, North Carolina, and

[1] Washington to Rochambeau, 13 June (*ibid.* p. 77).
[2] *Ibid.* p. 77, *note; Mémoires de Rochambeau,* ii. 277.

the country of South Carolina and Georgia. For this purpose we have determined to remove the whole of the French army, and as large a detachment of the American as can be spared, to the Chesapeake, to meet your Excellency there.[1]

He was naturally careful to conceal his change of plan from Clinton, who did not learn, till the beginning of September, that Washington was decidedly marching southward, and then—having no knowledge of De Grasse's movements—without understanding the meaning of it.

When, on 28th August, Hood came off Sandy Hook, Graves, still thinking that De Grasse was coming there, ordered him to cross the bar, and only yielded to Hood's remonstrance. When, on the news that Barras had gone south, Graves determined to follow, it was in hopes of smashing him before he could join with De Grasse; and when, on 5th September, he saw a crowd of French ships lying in the mouth of the Chesapeake, he took for granted that it was Barras's squadron with a number of storeships. It was only as the crowd of ships resolved itself into a French line of battle that he understood what he had before him.

The way in which the action that followed was fought has been often told from Graves's despatch.[2] He attempted to obey the 19th Article of the Fighting Instructions,[3] and failed, as everybody else failed. Hood, who was a man of genius and dis-

[1] Sparks, viii. 130. The letter was signed by both Washington and Rochambeau.

[2] *N.R.S.* iii. 40; Beatson, v. 273–4.

[3] *N.R.S.* xxix. 198.

dained pettifogging routine, saw how very differently it could and should have been fought, saw what a great opportunity had been lost, and could not help writing bitterly about it.[1] Of the angry controversy which afterwards arose as to whether Graves, in ordering and enforcing the signal for the line of battle, meant something else, or whether Hood gave the signal a too literal interpretation, it is useless to speak. The old evidence is most contradictory,[2] and we have no new, except Graves's remarkable memorandum of 6th November (p. 127), which seems—as Hood's endorsement suggests—to propound some such conundrum as : When is a line of battle not a line of battle ?

Whatever the truth of all this was, the mischief was done. De Grasse had gained as much of a victory as served his purpose and wanted no more. He went back into Lynnhaven Bay ; the fate of Cornwallis was sealed, and with it the independence of the American Colonies. When Creasy wrote his *Fifteen Decisive Battles*, his attention was too closely fixed on land war, or he would surely have recognized that not Saratoga, but this petty rencounter off the Chesapeake was the 'decisive battle' of this war, the battle which gave birth to the United States.

The details here given of the loss of St. Kitts are merely supplementary to the story, as told in vol. III ; and Hood's account of the battles of 9th and 12th April, of his discontent at the imperfect conclusion, and of his conversation with Sir

[1] *N.R.S.* iii. 28–31. [2] Cf. Clowes, iii. 500, *note*.

Charles Douglas, is essentially the same, though the interest of the narrative, and its occasional variations, seemed to warrant the repetition. The sequel is more important, giving, in fuller detail than ever before, the story of the war during the next twelve months.

We are very much in the habit of thinking that the war ended on the 12th April; that the French naval power in the West Indies was broken, and that peace was virtually, if not formally, concluded. Hood's later letters show how entirely false such a notion is, and emphasize his remarks (p. 177), written—it will be noticed—exactly one month after the battle.

Had Sir George done what he might and ought, we should all most probably have been peaceably at home by our firesides in the course of another year! How he can stand the reproaches of his own mind, if he is not perfectly callous, for doing so little, when a vast deal of honour and glory might so easily have been gathered for his poor country, almost a bankrupt in both, I cannot reconcile. The French could never have rose again this war; America would have shaken off her unnatural connection with them; Spain, in all human probability, would have seen her error, and have been glad of the first opening to have withdrawn herself; and England would have been the admiration and envy of every Court in Europe. Now, the whole business will be to come over again; for further than the glory of his Majesty's arms having appeared with lustre, and the danger probably removed for the present from Jamaica, I can see no great benefit can arise from so perfectly complete and unrivalled a victory. The very important and favourable opportunity that has been lost for raising Great Britain's glory is melancholy in the extreme to think of, and there is no dwelling upon the subject with any degree of temper.

It is evident that, as the months passed on, Hood considered the state of affairs far from secure. In November he certainly thought that the danger said to be threatening Jamaica was very real (pp. 220 *seq.*); that Vaudreuil at Boston was a force to be reckoned with (p. 229); and that when he had come south he stood 'a chance to be abominably thrashed' (p. 232). We can see now that his anxious care somewhat exaggerated all this; for, as he knew later on (App. C), Vaudreuil's squadron, though respectable in point of numbers, had no disposition to fight; but the news did not reach him till too late to be of any use; peace had already been signed.

The relations of Hood to his commander-in-chief call for a short notice, the more so as they seem to throw some light on his bitter criticisms of Rodney. When Pigot first came out, his second in command formed a very poor opinion of his abilities, and wrote, on 30th August, 'Do you think a certain noble Viscount has acted upon true patriotic principles, as a real friend to his poor distracted country, in placing an officer at the head of so great a fleet so very unequal to the very important duty, having never had the command of a squadron before, or scarce seen salt water since the year '63?'[1] The detailed criticism which follows seems fair; or rather, knowing Hood's ability, is fair, though perhaps un-

[1] *Post*, p. 209; *N.R.S.* iii. 148.

necessarily bitter. Gradually the bitterness dies out; his notices of his commander-in-chief become friendly, and by the end of October we have him writing (p. 210)—

> Admiral Pigot and I have lived upon the best terms possible; my sentiments have ever been expressed most clearly and without reserve, having no private view to gratify; and I believe the admiral to be very perfectly satisfied with me; for however I may have differed in opinion with him in some material points, I never lost sight of keeping up a most cordial unanimity in the fleet, and I may venture to say greater harmony never existed in any fleet than in the one under Admiral Pigot's command.

The difference in tone, both from the former letter and from his several mentions of Rodney, is very marked, and asks for an enquiry as to its cause, which may possibly be that Rodney, when in health, was a most capable man, and at all times a strong-willed one, who would not relinquish one jot of his authority; Pigot, at once ignorant and weak, was rather glad that Hood should take the burden off his shoulders and tell him what to do. If this is the true explanation it must be put to Hood's credit that he did not unduly push his advantage, but allowed the admiral all possible credit (p. 247).

As he concludes this introductory notice of the more important contents of the volume, the Editor would express his gratitude to Mr. Julian S. Corbett, who has read the proof slips and offered many valuable suggestions; and also to the officials of the Public Record Office, more especially to Mr. Hubert

Hall, for much friendly assistance in the research which the work has entailed.

Bibliographical Note.

The following list of books referred to in the notes, and of some others relating to the War of American Independence, will probably be found convenient.

Beatson, Robert. *Naval and Military Memoirs.*

Charnock, John. *Biographia Navalis.*

Clowes, Sir W. Laird. *The Royal Navy: a History.* Vol. iii. Chapter by Captain A. T. Mahan.

Dictionary of National Biography.

Keppel, Admiral the Hon. Augustus, Minutes of the Court-Martial on.

Keppel, Rev. Thomas. *Life of Viscount Keppel.*

James, William. *Naval History of Great Britain.*

Matthews, John. *Twenty-one Plans of Engagements in the West Indies.*

Mundy, General Godfrey Basil. *Life of Lord Rodney.*

Palliser, Vice-Adml. Sir Hugh, Minutes of the Court-Martial on.

Schomberg, Captain Isaac. *Naval Chronology.*

White, Captain Thomas. *Naval Researches.*

Bouclon, Adolphe de. *Liberge de Grandchain.*

Chevalier, Cap^ne^ E. *Histoire de la Marine Française*—

i. *Pendant la Guerre de l'Indépendance Américaine.*

ii. *Sous la Première République.*

Duro, C. Fernandez. *Armada Española.* Vol. vii.

Lacour-Gayet, G. *La Marine Militaire de la France*—

i. *Sous le Règne de Louis XV.*

ii. *Sous le Règne de Louis XVI.*

Noailles, Vicomte de. *Marins et Soldats Français en Amérique pendant la Guerre de l'Indépendance des Etats-Unis.* Portraits.

Troude, O. *Batailles Navales de la France.*

CONTENTS

LETTERS AND PAPERS

OF

LORD BARHAM

MIDDLETON TO MR. WALTER PRINGLE[1]

[*Holograph.*] Barbados: at sea. 21st October, 1758.

Dear Sir,—Agreeable to your request, I have considered your queries concerning the number of ships that may be necessary for protecting the Leeward Islands and their trade, and from the little experience I have had, I am of opinion that the following plan, well executed, would in a great measure defend our merchant ships from the enemy, and be a great means of suppressing their privateers.

To effect this I would require—

Two ships of 40 guns,
Two ,, of 20 ,,
Eight brigantines of 16 guns, built on the Bermudan plan, with a little variation; to be allowed 110 men each, and
Two sloops of 10 guns.

[1] A cadet of the family of Pringle of Stitchell, settled at St. Christopher's as a merchant and planter. It does not appear that he had any official post, though he may very well have been

This force I would have distributed in the following manner:—

To victual at Barbados.		*At Antigua.*	
1 ship	40	1 ship	40
1 ship	20	1 ship	20
3 brigs		5 brigantines	
		2 sloops	

The Barbados brigantines to cruize to windward of that island, and at such distances as they find the enemy's cruizers kept at; in my time, they have generally resorted at about seven leagues' distance, and seldom further than twelve. They ought never to stretch beyond the north and south latitude of the island after being to windward, and to endeavour at daylight each morning to be in the mid-latitude; for by that method they will be in the fairest way to fall in with our own trade and the enemy's privateers. I would never have them chase to leeward of the island without the greatest probability of the chase being an enemy, and that they can come up with her; for when to leeward, it takes a long time to beat up again, and much mischief may be done during their absence; whereas the enemy's being drove there is sufficiently guarding the island from his attempts.

I would likewise have one of the cruizers, if two are out, to be always in sight of the island, and another to make it at least every fourth day, and to carry all merchant vessels they meet with so near in as to be out of danger; but not to run beyond the windward part of the island with them, as they are there out of danger, and you have it in your power

chairman of the local chamber of commerce. He, together with his wife, was lost at sea in 1776, leaving a son, Thomas, a captain in the navy, who commanded the Valiant on 1 June, 1794, was commander-in-chief at the Cape of Good Hope in 1797, and died, an admiral, in 1803.

to get to your station; whereas if you go lower down you may be days of beating up again, and of course doing no service.

The Antigua brigantines must cruize to windward of that island at such distances as they find enemies to go to; but one of them constantly to be in sight and pretty near. Their cruizes must be from Guadeloupe as far to the northward as 18° 30′, for to that distance do the enemy stretch; and in their return, I would have them who are to victual at St. John's, cruize a few days under the lee of Barbados and as far to the northward of it as seven leagues. These cruizers I would have restricted, though not so much as the Barbados ones; for to that island there is only one channel, and that the enemy endeavour to keep in. To Antigua, St. Christopher's, Nevis, Montserrat, Jamaica, &c., there are many, and all must be looked after; so that the cruizers there must have a larger latitude given them; only disposed in such a manner as that all will be serviceable, which the commanding officer will best judge of, from his being on the spot and knowing the circumstances of his cruizers.

As some stations will be more profitable than others, and to prevent the cruizers being tempted to leave the bad and stretch into the good, I would have them shifted now and then, and to give great discretionary orders to those who can be trusted with them, as 'tis impossible to lay down any rule or give orders that are effectual, the enemy varying in their stations, either as they are drove or our merchant vessels lead them.

The 40-gun ship at Barbados I would have cruize from the latitude of 14° to the latitude of 16°, and as near in a meridian with Deseada as he can. The 20, I would have cruize from 16° 40′ to 15° 30′, at about three leagues eastward of Deseada, by which means the enemy will be interrupted in carrying their prizes into Martinique, Marie Galante and Guadeloupe by windward; but should the enemy alter their method, ours must likewise alter.

The 40-gun ship from Antigua I would have cruize from Englishman's Head[1] as far south as Basse Terre Bay, and a sloop of 10 guns to accompany her; by which means I think nothing could get in this way. The 20-gun ship and other sloop to be a relief to these two; and when not wanted there, to cruize so as to be there at the proper time of relieving. The Deseada station, when left to one ship, as it often may be, to be looked after from three leagues to windward of that to fifteen degrees of latitude.

I have now, I think, disposed of all the frigates and vessels wanted for the protection of the trade, and I think I have guarded against every principal channel which the enemy at present make use of to secure their prizes when taken, except the Bay of St. Pierre and Grandtier.[2] The first, I have in a great measure made provision for by the Barbados frigates cruizing to windward of Dominica, as most of the French endeavour to make the south part of that island, to avoid our privateers, who cruize more to the southward, and run over in the night from Martinique. I therefore rather choose to put the frigates there than nearer in, and by that means guard not only against that port, Marie Galante and Guadeloupe the south way, but keep these cruizers out of danger from any ships of force which the enemy may now and then have falling into

[1] Tête à l'Anglais, off the NW point of Guadeloupe; thus covering the west side of the island.

[2] Presumably the bay on the east side of Grande Terre of Guadeloupe, but it may perhaps be that on the north—Grand Cul-de-Sac Marin and the harbour of Port Louis.

Martinique. The Bay of Grandtier must be trusted to the Antigua brigs, who will often make that island, and to the 20-gun ship who stretches 20′ to the northward of Deseada, and which island the privateers make with their prizes when bound in that way. The 20-gun ship and sloop, too, when at sea and not off Basse Terre may cruize off Grantier, by which means they are guarding that bay and ready to supply the 40 and sloop's place who are to leeward. St. Pierre's Bay, and the windward part of Martinique is generally the station left to our line of battleships when here, so that I may say we are now guarded in most places against the enemy; our trade in a way of being protected, and enemy and privateers open to our cruizers; and I will venture to affirm that, with such a guard, the enemy would not only soon give up privateering but starve, while our islands are in plenty.

The number of large ships necessary for the protection of these islands depends so entirely upon intelligence of the enemy's intentions in these parts, that it can only be answered by saying that, as many of our islands are weak and open to attacks, we ought to be superior to them in sea force.

And now I have answered those parts of your queries which fall most particularly to my way of life, there only remains my reasons for some things which may be objected to, either from want of knowledge or experience. And it may be asked: Why I must have two fortys, two twentys, eight brigantines and two sloops, in preference to any others, and that they should be so disposed?

First then as to the ships. I choose them as being sufficient to protect our small cruizers in case the French should attempt to interrupt them by a frigate or frigates which may casually be at Martinique; and as they are very sufficient for recaptures, convoys to the northward, and may be easily spared from the great number of them employed, I mention them preferable to others.

My reasons for the Deseada cruizers victualling at Barbados are: Because two such ships are necessary for the protection I before mentioned, for carrying such merchant ships to the northward, as may be ready at different times in Barbados, and because the trade winds in general will admit of their doing all this duty without loss of time; whereas if they victualled at Antigua, a very great part of their time would be lost in beating up to their station, and this inconvenience happen every time they left it. The same reasons of convenience and service are applicable to those stationed at Antigua.

Why I would choose brigs for the protection of the trade before any other kind of vessel is: Because, if they are of the kind I mentioned, they have greater advantages over sloops and schooners (which vessels the enemy generally use against us in this country) than any other kind can have; are much cheaper to the government than ships, and full strong enough for the service they are employed upon; and as they are fittest for this business, so are sloops for the inshore stations if accompanied with a ship, as they are easily worked, can go into shoal water, and be managed with oars in a calm.

These in general are my thoughts concerning the trade of these islands. I have drawn them up unconnected and in a hurry; I wish you may be able to make them out, and that you may find any amusement in them, as I wish for every opportunity of obliging you; and am,

Dear sir,
Yours very affectionately,
C. MIDDLETON.

Since my last I have taken a small privateer, but have no farther hopes, as the Arundel is soon expected, and we see nothing to windward.

You will observe that I have said nothing about convoy. As they are, the Leeward Islands may do with them and reap their benefit; but Barbados cannot; for as a great part of their sugars are clayed,[1] and that not finished till September, a convoy in the middle of July and one in October would suit them better than the present; but if they could get that last to the present two, 'twould be still better for them; and this last convoy is more on account of insurance than any other real benefit that can accrue from it, as no fleet could keep together home at such a season of the year. This is the state of Barbados; the other islands you are better acquainted with than I am, and must judge accordingly. In short I believe if this third convoy was granted, and that a 20-gun ship only, the Barbadians would agree to your time for the sailing of the other two.

I beg my best wishes may be made acceptable to Mrs. Pringle and Beck; and once more, believe me yours,

C. M.

I am in great want of madeira and claret; and I have told Governor Pinfold that I would intercede with you to get him some of the last, as he is much in want.

You must make this out as well as you can, for I am in general so very seasick that writing is a great task upon me. Adieu.

[*What follows is written on the inside of the wrapper.*]

[1] 'Refined with clay'; i.e. by a process in which clay is used. —*N.E.D.*

What is within may be contradicted for contradiction's sake, as Mrs. P. says our sea people are fond of that and their own opinions; but they must be very well acquainted with the situation of these islands in general, the practice of French privateers in cruizing and the securing of their prizes, who find fault with it; and I own to you I should have been a stranger to all, had I not been particularly employed upon each station, conversant amongst most of the islands, and successful in captures, by which last, I get acquainted with many of their methods. But I am surprised that the more easy and effectual means of keeping our trade from danger, by sending home all the prisoners, has not been practised. I have heard all the arguments against, and think them without either reason or foundation.

Middleton to Pringle.

Arundel: St. John's Road. 4th December, 1759.

There are two identical copies of this letter, both in a clerkly hand; but one, written on seven pages of two sheets of foolscap, has been corrected or modified by Middleton, who has added, on the last page of the second sheet, the autograph letter here given on p. 17. It would seem from this that this is the copy actually sent to Mr. Pringle; but, if so, the question naturally arises how comes it among Middleton's papers? The letter to Sir James Douglas (*post*, p. 27) suggests that, when writing it, Middleton asked Pringle to return this, as well as to give Douglas a copy. The corrected copy is the one here followed, but, as the corrections seem sometimes to strengthen, sometimes to weaken, the argument, and as it is especially interesting to note the uncertainty in Middleton's mind as to whether the 'danger zone' was twenty leagues broad or forty; whether the alleged loss of time was two-thirds or one-third of the whole, it has seemed better, and indeed important, to present both versions. The words given in *italics* are those finally approved; words or sentences in [square brackets] are those first written, but afterwards deleted.

Dear Sir,—The injury which our trade has received of late, the clamour it has raised, and the inclination you showed some time ago to be informed how it might be best protected, has induced me *again* [once more] to trouble you upon that subject. Guadeloupe, too, when I last wrote to you, and its neighbouring islands were in possession of the French; so that the plan I then sent, by the late transition [1] is become obsolete and of no use, which you will perceive on comparing it with this.

Our merchant ships in general, bound to the island of Guadeloupe, Antigua, Montserrat, Nevis and St. Christopher's, are obliged and do either make Marie-Galante, Deseada [or] Antigua *or St. Martin*, whose extremes from south to north are [20] *40* leagues, or from 16° to [17°] *18°* latitude; and which the enemy's privateers are so well acquainted with that they confine themselves to the same parallels; and as the uncertainty of their easting [2] makes it necessary that they should fall in from 100 to 150 leagues to windward, you will easily perceive that any distance within that, and between 16° and [17°] *18°* latitude, is as good a station as

[1] Guadeloupe had surrendered on 1st May; the other islands on the succeeding days, to the land and sea forces commanded by Major-General Barrington and Commodore John Moore.

[2] Till long after this date there was no way of determining the longitude at sea except by Dead Reckoning, which was extremely uncertain, by reason of currents then quite uncharted, of the rude way of computing, and most of all, of the inaccurate way of marking the log line, on which the knot was anything the master chose, from 40 to 50 feet with a half-minute glass. In 1755, the Winchester, on her passage out to the West Indies, was 100 leagues out in her reckoning, from Madeira to Barbados, in consequence of having her log line marked to 42 feet with a 30-sec. glass.

being near*er* the islands, for intercepting them; and for many reasons a better one, as they thereby avoid our cruizers who are improperly confined, have an opportunity of carrying in their prizes with less risk, and meet with no interruption in cruizing or chasing. Their privateers, too, being so numerous that we may, within compass, allow forty—which is only one-half of the list I have now by me—to be constantly upon this station; it is impossible that one-half of our trade can escape them, or rather that the greatest part must not fall a prey to their numbers; and that this must be the consequence from the present direction of our squadron, I will endeavour to explain, by painting our own conduct, by showing the accidents which we are liable to and cannot avoid; and afterwards propose what to me appears to be the best, though not an effectual remedy.

To begin then with our cruizers, I must inform you that the present practice of stationing them is between the latitude of 16 and 19, at confined distances from the shore, and to windward of the islands. Their cruizes finished, they return to Antigua for provisions and further orders, and they either water at some leeward island before or after their arrival at Antigua. The consequences of such orders are that, as they cruize from the latitude of 16° to 19°, which is 60 leagues, they are employed in sailing [40] *20* of them without a chance of protecting our own trade or annoying the enemy; and as the captains no doubt adhere strictly to their orders [two days] *one day* out of three or [two-thirds] *one-third* of their cruize *while upon their station* is employed to no purpose; for if you recollect, I observed before that our trade is obliged to keep within a tract of [20] *40* leagues, and to which the enemy confine themselves [likewise]. That third part of their cruize, too, which carries an appearance of doing something, is also rendered useless by their being confined in their easting; for the enemy, finding that they can be safe at a greater distance, do proceed there and continue for the reasons I have already given.

[Their] *The windward cruizers* returning to Antigua and one of the other Leeward Islands causes at least a fortnight loss of time to each cruizer at the end of every cruize, which will appear obvious from what I shall say hereafter. Now allowing that we have two frigates constantly employed on this station confined to the [20] *40* leagues I propose, and that the enemy have only *in that tract* [30] *20* privateers, and supposing that they are daily in chase and take two privateers each in their cruize, will the danger that the merchant ships are to run through be lessened any more than as two to [30] *20*, and that increased to the number that they take only on the days of taking them? and will there not remain every day till the captures are made [28] *18* in security, or at least [24] *16*; and will any man of common sense say that these are not sufficient to destroy our trade and distress the islands? Surely no; nor will it appear a paradox that our frigates take privateers without lessening the number; that they are cruizing for the protection of the trade without doing it; and that the government are sufferers as well as the merchants by their appointment, and would be some thousands of pounds in purse if they were employed anywhere else. For has not the squadron within these two years past taken upwards of fifty privateers, and have they not more at this day than ever was known from the French islands? Has not our losses in trade increased instead of diminished, and does the number of captures even in Europe amount to what they have done here within these six months past? Has not the government paid upon this station upwards of 20,000*l.* for head money, and has the intention of granting that bounty been answered in any *one* respect? The French lose a hull which they easily replace; the government lose the premium which they cannot replace; and the poor merchants receive no other consolation than in having a free country to complain in.

Where the errors are requires little penetration. The commander of the squadron is in fault if his ships are improperly disposed of, but he is not answerable for the ill-consequences of a cartel from which all our evils spring. Had no such agreement been made, half the cruisers that are now here would have protected the trade; a commanding officer could not have erred in the disposal of [them] *his ships*; the enemy's privateers would have remained in port for want of men, and we should not have had the same prisoners eight or ten times in our jails; nay, many of them returned upon their cruizing station before the ship who took them. I have heard all the arguments that are made use of in support of this subject—they are too many to enter on, and too prejudicial to insist upon. However, it has its advocates, and they complain too at the non-exertion of our squadron. [To such I would give the vulgar answer which I remember to have heard a captain of a 20-gun ship give to his men when they complained to him that their provisions were so bad that they could not eat it; which was, 'Jump up, and damn yourselves.' The meaning of which is, captains of those ships were formerly pursers of them, but on complaints of their not doing justice between the government and the seamen, that office was taken from them and given to another.] But I desire that you may not think I mean *from this* to vindicate the error of our sea commanders by laying a stress upon those of the land; far from it. I only would convince that [we have given] a rod *has been given* to scourge [ourselves] *yourselves* with, and [we] *you* are angry that another will not break it for [us; we load] *you*; the sea officer *is loaded* with the [folly of our own] *bad effects of your* proceedings [without seeing that] *when* his own are sufficient to bear him down; but [you will say that our own error is not to be mended, and 'tis too late to repine, and in this I agree with you, and will therefore return to our subject wherein I have already proved that our trade is not protected, nor the number of the enemy's privateers lessened. I will next endeavour to find a remedy, and by obviating where our errors lie show where they may be remedied], *as the error you have committed cannot be recalled, we will return to what may be remedied.*

To begin then: The commanding officer, if he has the sole direction of the squadron, and if its destination here is the protection of the islands and its trade, commits an error in stationing the frigates so far to the northward as 19° latitude; for I have observed before that our trade in general and the enemy's privateers *in general,* go no farther than [17] *18°*; and it is a great oversight to confine them in their easting, as the enemy, by that means, avoids us by going farther to windward, and with the advantages to themselves which I have shown before.

Secondly: The ordering the windward cruizers to return so often to Antigua and to the Leeward Islands seems to me a want of knowledge of their situation, and of the worst consequences; as loss of time is lessening our force and augmenting our danger. For if instead of running 40 leagues to leeward they run 60 upon a meridian, *which the common trade winds will admit of both ways,* they might victual and water at Barbados, and return again to their station without receiving any interruption from winds or lee currents, both of which are their opposites when at Antigua.

Thirdly: The employing the frigates to leeward when the great ships would serve as well, is losing the use of them; and their running so often from island to island, when they might be protecting the trade, is an addition to that error, and an encouragement to the enemy; and

Lastly: The not guarding the passages to Martinique is of all the greatest blunder we have yet committed; for as I have already made it pretty evident that it is impossible for any number of men-of-war to prevent captures where merchant ships are confined to parallels, we therefore ought to be the more careful of retaking them, especially when we know the very ports they are to carry them into, and have strength enough to block it up.

But these are our errors; and to remove them, I would desire two of the best sailing frigates and the Antigua brig to cruize and be employed to windward of Antigua *and Deseada* only, as the fittest to annoy the enemy's privateers; and they ought to be confined in their latitude to [the enemy's] *their* tracts, but left to their own discretion in their easting, as it is difficult to determine what must depend on the motions of another. The two first, as soon as the cruizes are finished, should be ordered to victual and water at Barbados, as a windward island; and never to Antigua, but when they are in want of repairs or in other cases of necessity; and by this means much time that is now lost will be saved, and the strength of our squadron augmented by making a more proper disposition of it. The Antigua brig I would have always ordered back to that island, and when convoys from it or any of the other ones are ready, she may carry them as far to the northward as the latitude of 19°, upon a wind, and there leaving them, stretch back into her cruizing station again ; and to be continued on this service except when it is necessary to employ her upon more material ones.

I would have another frigate stationed from 3 to [10] *15* leagues to windward of the north part of Martinique; and a fourth about the same distance to windward of the south part of it, as it is very well known that the enemy bring most of their captures from to windward, carry all *by choice* into Saint Pierre, and must come round one of these two points. The two frigates stationed here I would have to increase their distances from the shore to windward at the latter end of their cruizes, and when finished proceed to Barbados for water and provisions, from which place they may recover their station in twelve hours, whereas they cannot from Antigua in less than a week; and to prevent what may escape them from getting into port, I would station two line-of-battle ships attended by two sloops to cruize between the Pearl and Diamond rocks, and that when relieved they should be ordered to victual at Antigua, and either water at Montserrat or Dominica in their way to it, or on their return to their station, the trade winds admitting of either without loss of time.

The Barbados brig I would have to remain there for the protection of that island, and the convoy belonging to it to be carried to the northward by the windward Antigua cruizers, who thereby lose no more time than running twenty leagues beyond their station; whereas settled convoys not only take up a great deal, but employ cruizing ships for several days off their stations.

If it was thought convenient by the government, I would add a brig for carrying the merchant ships from St. Christopher's, Montserrat, Nevis, and Guadeloupe to the northward, who should constantly rendezvous at the just mentioned island; and at such times as this service did not require her, she should cruize off St. Eustatius, to intercept the trade between that and Martinique;[1] so that here you see the whole station guarded by two line-of-battle ships, four frigates, three brigs, and two sloops, and I have only to find relief for the ships to windward and leeward of Martinique, the other stations being of little consequence when compared with this. Therefore, if the ships upon the station are at any time too few for such a relief, I would then take one from to windward of Antigua, or place large ships where I want small; for we must not imagine, nor vainly flatter ourselves, that the taking or destroying of privateers only, while the present cartel subsists, will either protect our own trade or lessen the enemy's numbers. It is only striking off a hydra's head; and as it is impossible to prevent captures, we must endeavour to hinder their being carried in, and put up with the loss of salvage to avoid greater evils; for by retaking only is the trade of these islands to be preserved; and he who fancies to himself other ways will find his mistake when it is too late.

That this plan cannot always be strictly followed, and that many circumstances may happen to prevent it, I am very well aware of, and at such times would keep as near it as I could, leaving naked what is of

[1] Earlier in the year, during the reduction of Guadeloupe, Moore had not scrupled to blockade St. Eustatius—a neutral port—from which supplies were being sent to the enemy (Gardiner, *Expedition to the West Indies*, p. 42; Moore to Clevland, 5 March—hoping that their Lordships will approve). It appears now an extreme measure, but—as Boscawen also showed in Lagos Bay—in 1759 neutral rights did not count for very much if they were not upheld by adequate force.

least consequence, and adding to what is of most. If such a conduct is observed, and such a disposition made of our squadron, I will venture to say that our present misfortunes will soon diminish; our enemy's privateers will be reduced for want of supplies, and the inhabitants of Martinique will once more feel the extremities which Mr. Pocock's per severance and vigilance subjected them to.[1]

I have much more to say on this subject, but fear I have already tired you, and if so you must thank yourself. It was you first led me into the subject, and 'tis to please you I pursued it. Adieu.

Memorandum.[2]—When I say the trade is confined to parallels I mean, in general; because some few fall in to leeward. Idle ships may attend convoys and intercept the enemy's trade.

On the blank page of the sheet, in autograph.

Dear Sir,—You can see that though I have not wrote you many letters of late, yet I have been employed for you, so it must make amends for my seeming neglect. I am but just anchored here from a month's cruize to windward of Antigua, where I only retook two merchant vessels, and sent two privateers back to Martinique. I wished for a leeward chase, but could not find one; and if I had not met with near twenty days' calm I should have made a plentiful cruize. 'Tis the only chance I have yet had in the Arundel, and fortune interfered; for of late she has forsaken me, and I will assure you the Arundel is not [in] fault. I am now going on shore, and as my foremast is sprung, I will hope I am to heave down. Wherever I go I will hope that you will believe me to [be], dear Sir,

Yours most affectionately and sincerely,

CHAS. MIDDLETON.

[1] In 1747–8. [2] In Middleton's hand.

I hope my good friend, Mrs. Pringle, and Beck is well; pray remember me to them and the little ones. Would I could see you all; but I water at Dominica, while others ——

Middleton to Pringle.

[*Rough draft. Autograph.*] [1759.]

Sir,—The advantages that brig cruizers has over sloops and schooners has been so obvious in this country that I cannot help expressing my wonder at the alterations already made, nor my fears lest the error should propagate, and by that means render useless the vessels that I hear are to be commissioned. What can be said in favour of such changes I own myself a stranger to, and yet I am not ignorant of the qualities of either. I have considered both, and can assure you that the following are facts which I have proved not only from experience but practice, and which may be easily confirmed or confuted by trying the Antigua [1] with the Barbados,[1] in their present forms.

1st. That brigs of the Bermudian kind have more advantages over sloops and schooners than any other kind of vessel that can be found in this country.

2nd. That they will beat either sloop or schooner considerably in every point of sailing, and can be beat only in one circumstance, which is in blowing weather when close upon a wind.

3rdly. That they can never be in danger from any number of the enemy while they preserve this superiority in sailing in every kind of weather; and that they will be an overmatch for any single privateer, from the advantages of their tops, which the enemy are not ignorant of; and

[1] They were both rated as twelve-gun brigs.

Lastly. That they have singly taken upwards of thirty privateers in these seas.

These are truths within my own knowledge, and it is easy to assign reasons for their being so; but I will only at present trouble you with one, which is, that a brig, in every variation of the wind, can carry a greater proportion of sail than either sloop or schooner, and which no other vessel can do but themselves.

The advocates for schooners have, I fear, little considered the subject. Indeed, such as I have seen have been little acquainted with it, and novelty with them has been substituted for judgment; for to give all the merit to a sloop or schooner which is their due, I shall even then be very much at a loss to find the whole of their good qualities equal one of those I have attributed to a brig; and sailing, my good friend, is the primitive one in a cruizer.

Sloops in blowing weather, it is true, will carry sail when a brig cannot; and in action they are easier worked, require less men, and have but few ropes to be carried away. These are their advantages; but let me ask if the enemy have not them in common with ourselves; and as they purchase the best sloops they can get, and have more skill in trimming and sailing them than those belonging to ships of war, may it not be reasonably supposed that they will outsail ours in general? or if not, that they will sail as fast? and if either, what one advantage can we propose to ourselves from employing sloops against sloops? and how many has not our success proved that we have by continuing brigs?

That the not being subject to alarms from every squall of wind, that the sleeping undisturbed at nights, and being free from much trouble and fatigue, are considerations material to those employed in brigs, and that they wish them otherways, is very reasonable; but it surely is not so to suppose that the public service is to give way to their ease, or that good cruizers are to be made otherways from their whimsical representation.

I could add much upon this subject, but my present time will not permit. When more at leisure I will state fairly the advantages and disadvantages of these different kinds of vessels, and leave you to make a judgment upon them, though I think the Speaker[1] and Antigua have already proved beyond words how right we have already been in our choice, and I wish future experience may not likewise teach us how wrong we are like to be in our alteration. A Guadeloupe is to be purchased, and I think the Nonpareil as good a one as will present soon, which you may inform Sir James of, as well as my opinion of the different kinds of vessels above mentioned. I desire my best wishes may be made acceptable to Mrs. P., and that you will believe me to be, &c.

COUNCIL AND MERCHANTS OF BARBADOS TO JOSEPH PICKERING[2]

[*Copy. Autograph.*] [1759.]

Sir,—We have written you a long letter by this fleet upon a variety of subjects, and we wish we could have there closed our correspondence by the present opportunity; but our duty calls upon us to remonstrate without delay against the gentleman entrusted with the command of his Majesty's great fleet upon this station, whose superiority, by a strange course of conduct, for which we are at loss to find a name, has failed of every hopeful advantage

[1] Is not named in any printed list.
[2] Agent for Barbados in London.

which was to be derived from it; the enemy, with a squadron much inferior to Mr. Moore's, have traversed these seas, unmolested, from one of their settlements to the other, first making a bold attempt to relieve the island of Guadeloupe, and there actually landing a large body of regulars, who, but for the spirited operations of our troops, which had just then[1] compelled the enemy to surrender, had utterly defeated the design of that conquest, if not destroyed our brave little army, upon the point of reaping the glory and reward of all their labours; next, sailing from Martinique a second time (having been suffered to return in safety to that island from Guadeloupe, though absent above a fortnight), in order to protect some store ships lying at the Grenades,[2] which durst not venture to Martinique from thence but under convoy, and performing this service also without any interruption from the English fleet, which was the more painful to reflect upon, as every captain under Mr. Moore's command had gallantly distinguished himself at the attack of Basseterre, and no doubt burnt with impatience to complete the glorious work of conquest appearing by Heaven designed for them in the daring spirit of Bompar.

Yet the disgrace to his Majesty's navy has not been the only melancholy consequence of this unparallelled neglect. The enemy's privateers have preyed upon our poor merchant ships, and filled the stores at Martinique with plenty, whilst ours are drained for the supply of the forces at Guadeloupe, and all our resources from the North American colonies daily cut off; for no less than 175 or 180 sail of vessels have been carried into Martinique

[1] May 1, 1759. The French troops, to the number of 600 regulars and 2,000 buccaneers, were landed on Grande Terre the same day.

[2] Grenadines.

since the arrival of Bompar's squadron, which we once flattered ourselves were come only to add to the spoils of Britain, little imagining it could have so foiled her glory. Could we assign one argument in favour of the commodore's proceedings, our charity, if not our personal regard, had wrought in us to stifle our suspicions of his ill conduct; and gladly we had caught at anything to save us the present irksome task which we are enjoined to. But when every appearance of blame is his, when every circumstance of distress is ours, how can we in justice to our country, in honour to the nation, or in duty to his Majesty, forbear complaining?[1]

We do therefore desire that the contents of this letter may be fully communicated to Mr. Secretary Pitt, whose injury on this occasion we feel as sensibly as our own, that the designs of an upright

[1] This complaint of the merchants really involves the story of the reduction of Guadeloupe, where our troops, covered by the squadron, landed on the 24th January. On the 11th March, Moore had news that Bompar, with eight ships of the line, had arrived at Martinique, where there was already a 74-gun ship; and believing that, from off Basse Terre, he would be unable to prevent a relief force from landing at Grande Terre, he judged it right to take up a position more to windward, in Prince Rupert's Bay, of Dominica. This concentration of the squadron, and calling in the cruizers, permitted exceptional activity among the enemy's privateers, and a great many merchant ships were captured, though the 180 is probably an exaggeration, or made up by counting every petty country vessel. That Moore's conduct was severely criticised is quite certain, and the complaint here printed is only one of many; but the Admiralty, then presided over by Anson, would seem to have approved of it. He was made a baronet in 1766, and died an admiral in 1779. Cf. *D.N.B. s.n.* Moore, John; Beatson, *Naval and Military Memoirs*, ii. 248 *seq.* (virtually an abstract of Moore's despatch); Gardiner, *Expedition to the West Indies*, p. 45 *seq.* (the story of a marine officer who did not love the commodore); and Mante, *Hist. of the Late War in America and the Islands of the West Indies*, p. 180 *seq.* (entirely favourable to Moore).

and spirited administration should be thus defeated by the very hands intrusted with the execution.

And if such behaviour in a chief commander is to pass uncensured or unobserved, it will be in vain that a great minister appears to plan and to design for the good and glory of a nation, when the officer who leads the powers that are raised, cannot catch a spark of that ambition in the field which flames so brightly from the cabinet.

We are, &c., &c.,

FRERE, ROUS, HUSBAND, of the Council.

B. MELLOWS, J. G. ALLEGRE, S. WOOD, J. DENNY, of the Assembly.

JOSEPH PICKERING TO THE BARBADOS COMMITTEE

Great Queen Street, Lincoln's Inn Fields.
21st November, 1759.

Copy.]

Gentlemen,—Since my last to you by this ship I have had the honour to wait on Mr. Pitt, accompanied by Mr. Gibbons, when I delivered him the two addresses to his Majesty forwarded by you to me. The one congratulatory on the taking of Guadeloupe; the other for an engineer and stores, together with the list of stores mentioned to be wanted. I likewise communicated to him your letter of complaint of Mr. Moore, and his letter to Mr. Alleyne, with Mr. Alleyne's answer thereto, and your letter accompanying them to me; to which Mr. Pitt was pleased to say that he was sorry to hear such complaints suggested against Mr. Moore; for that during such time as he was before Martinique and Basseterre he appeared to him to have behaved with great zeal and spirit. That the complaint did not properly lie before him; but that Mr. Moore had his superiors, to whom, if any complaint was formally and properly made, he was very sure it would meet with a proper regard. That Mr. Moore had in charge, when he went upon that command, the protection of the trade and care of our islands, and he was very sorry to hear he had neglected them. That he thanked the gentlemen of the island for the honour they had done him in their letter, and he should take care to do everything in his power for the service of the island in regard to the engineer and stores, and would talk with Lord Ligonier thereon and see how far the request could be complied with. That he thought Mr. Moore was much to blame in writing such a letter to Mr. Alleyne, for that the island had certainly a right to make their complaints here; otherwise it could never be known when a commander had neglected his duty; and that he thought Mr. Alleyne's letter a very sensible, genteel answer, wherein he had properly upheld the several matters stated by the Committee's letter with a becoming spirit.

In regard to the matter mentioned concerning the illicit trade carried on, and Captain Taylor's having been arrested by the owner of the vessel, he said that he was glad to find the island was determined to prosecute such offenders; that it was a laudable resolution, and he wished all the other islands would follow the example of Barbados, and show the same zeal for the honour of their country.

Mr. Gibbes[1] then acquainted Mr. Pitt with the sentiments of the island, whilst he was upon the spot, with regard to Mr. Moore, and that he was

[1] This is, apparently, the same as the Gibbons named above. The writing, in both cases, is quite clear.

of opinion, in case the enemy should escape the vigilance of our fleets at home, though inferior in strength to Mr. Moore's fleet, the island would be in great danger; for that no assistance was to be expected from Mr. Moore; and this, he said, he thought himself warranted to say from the experience he had of his former conduct, by which alone he could be judged. And that if the legislative of the island were to be restrained from making necessary and just complaints by any threats of a commanding officer upon the station, it might be attended with extreme bad consequences.

To which Mr. Pitt replied, that he thought it not only prudent, but highly necessary for the legislative of the island to make their complaints when there was occasion so to do; otherwise his Majesty would be entirely ignorant of any misbehaviour of his officers; and it would not be possible for him, without such complaints, to know that his orders had not been executed. Upon the whole, Mr. Pitt professed a great regard for the islands; said he thought them of vast consequence to their mother country, and that he should always be for defending and supporting them; but declined taking up the complaint for the reasons before mentioned.

Therefore, if you should think fit to pursue this complaint against Mr. Moore, it will be proper to send home an address to his Majesty, or a memorial to the lords of the admiralty, against him; but then it must be remembered that in case any such formal complaint should come home, it must be accompanied with *vivâ voce* evidence to support it; for there is no doubt but, upon such complaint, a hearing would be ordered before the lords of the admiralty, and Mr. Moore would have notice given him to put himself upon his defence; and in that case, if proper evidence is not supplied to warrant the complaint, it will, of course, fall to the ground. I mention *vivâ voce* evidence, because in matters of this sort the law will not condemn or censure any man upon *ex parte* depositions, taken when the party had no opportunity to cross-examine the witness. However, I submit my thoughts to your better judgment, and be assured in whatever manner you shall please to command me you shall find me devoted to, and ready in every instance for the service of our islands. I have waited on the commissioners of the sick and wounded office with your accounts relating to the French prisoners, which they have promised to look into; which when done, I shall solicit for their report thereon, and will use my best endeavours to get this money repaid, and wish I may be so happy to succeed; in which case you may depend on my giving you the earliest advice that offers. In all other matters committed by you to my charge no care shall be wanting in me to obtain them.

I am sorry to acquaint you that Monsieur Bompar arrived safely at Brest with his fleet on the 8th inst., richly laden, the very day that Sir Edward Hawke was blown off his station by tempestuous winds. It is said, too, that Monsieur Conflans is sailed from Brest with eighteen ships of the line besides frigates; but this is a matter of report only, and no certain account come of it as yet.

I am, &c., &c., &c.,

(Signed) JOSEPH PICKERING.

Dear Sir,[1]—Since I wrote you I got sight of the above letter, and have but just time to send copy.

Yours affectionately,

A. STEVENSON.

[1] Presumably Middleton. There are no other letters from Mr. Stevenson.

MIDDLETON TO SIR JAMES DOUGLAS

[*Rough Draft.* Endorsed by Middleton: Letter to Sir James Douglas concerning the Station and protection of the Leeward Islands trade. 1760.]

Sir,—As you have done me the honour to ask my opinion concerning this station in general, and how its trade may be best protected, I have desired Mr. Pringle to trouble you with a copy of a letter which I once wrote him upon that subject. In it you will find I have mentioned the channel of our trade, the beat of the enemy, and the ports they commonly make use of for the security of their prizes; but as that never was intended for the eye of a commanding officer, and only to amuse a friend, I have, in what I now present you, made many alterations, and shall be glad if it is found worthy of your attention.

Barbados and Barbuda are the two extreme islands to windward; and this tract, which reaches from 13° to 18° N, is the channel in which all our European, African, and greatest part of our American trade come down.

Barbados is reckoned the most considerable, not only in extent, but in its great number of inhabitants, and extensive trade; and is so happily situated, at a great distance from the other islands, and so far to windward of the French islands, that they are seldom pestered with privateers, and have suffered but inconsiderably in their inward trade. For the enemy, finding the time in beating up to be very precarious; the station when reached but narrow, the channel of their trade being only twenty-five miles—the breadth of the island; the difficulty of lying concealed; and the length of time they remain in that jail for want of frequent cartels, have contented themselves with only visiting them in beating up to their other station, which reaches from 16° to 18° 10′. As this comprehends all Guadeloupe, Antigua, Montserrat, Nevis, and St. Christopher's, with some part of the Jamaica runners, it is here that the body of the French privateers have always cruized and given the greatest annoyance to our trade.

The nature of the trade winds obliging all ships bound to these islands to confine themselves to the latitude I have mentioned, every part of it, from Deseada to a hundred leagues eastward, is equal good for cruizing in, and comprehends so very great a space that it is impossible for any number of ships to guard against privateers in it, or prevent captures being made. I have mentioned Deseada, because French privateers on that station seldom have come to leeward of it, since the reduction of Guadeloupe, except when chasing or being chased; whereas formerly they were often within sight of Antigua, and, by reason of the proximity of their own harbour, could secure any prizes taken there in a few hours after. But since our possessing these ports, the carrying their prizes to leeward of Deseada is become hazardous, would oblige the privateer to attend them and run a risk in passing through our islands; which they now avoid by keeping the wind till they have reached the latitude of Martinique before they bear away.

The danger, then, that we are most exposed to is to windward, for very few besides the St. Christopher's northward traders fall in to leeward, and these are so inconsiderable in value, that privateers of force seldom cruize for them; and though many are taken, yet it is more by reason of their great numbers, and their own bad conduct in not endeavouring to avoid vessels they see, than to any design of the enemy. I do not remember to have heard of a fixed cruizer of the enemy being employed against them; and they have themselves given me the reason for it—that they find them of little consequence when taken, compared with European vessels. The privateers indeed sometimes appear about Anguilla and St. Martin, when they expect our convoys going that way to the northward; and sometimes beat up to windward from thence, but never make any long stay.

Though a considerable attention must on this account be paid to the windward station, where the privateers generally cruize, yet they are so numerous and the exchange of prisoners, by means of the present cartel, is so easy, from our Leeward Islands, that even had our cruizers every imaginable success against them, their numbers would not be in the least diminished. Our extensive trade has too many allurements for them; the vessels they make use of against us are such as they have taken from us, and would be hauled ashore for want of purchasers if not employed in this way. Their trade to and from Europe is blocked up, and necessaries and stores of all sorts are scarce at Martinique; they have everything to expect from privateering, and scarcely anything to fear.[1] And while things are in this situation, the utmost that can be done against them is, by a proper disposition of ships off their ports, to render as difficult as possible the carrying

[1] For a curious account of the Martinique privateers and the illicit trade from St. Eustatius in the former war (1746–8), see *MSS. of Lady Du Cane* (Hist. MSS. Comm.), p. xxxiv, and the references there given. Lacour-Gayet (*La Marine Militaire sous Louis XV*, p. 367) says that at this time (1758–9) there were actually at sea in that neighbourhood 180 privateers, and that during the war they made 1,400 prizes. M. Lacour-Gayet's statements, however, will not always bear critical examination.

in of such prizes as our cruizers to windward cannot prevent from being taken.

Martinique is the only island they by choice carry their prizes to, and St. Pierre or Fort Royal the places of sale. The first of these towns they fit out at, and take in their supplies; for Trinity Bay, the only considerable one on the east side of Martinique, they only use to secure their prizes when forced in to it, or as a rendezvous, when they do not choose to break up their cruizes. St. Eustatius and Curaçao they only touch at when provisions or stores are very scarce at Martinique. Their usual route on going upon and ending their cruizes, or carrying in their prizes, is round the north or south point of the island. The proper guarding of these channels will, therefore, be the most likely method of intercepting both them and their prizes, while they continue to carry them to the same ports.

The next danger to which the trade lies exposed is when vessels leave our islands. This, though inconsiderable when compared to the risk vessels bound from Europe or America suffer, may in a great measure be prevented, by granting convoys—not at all times when they are demanded, but at such times as more material services will admit of them, and contrived so as to serve as many islands as possible. For when the great extent of the station, and the usual number of ships appointed to guard it, is considered, it will be found that without taking the advantages of the winds and of the situation of the islands, and without using the greatest economy in the disposal of the ships, the squadron will prove far inferior to the services expected from it.

But of convoys I shall be more particular, when I have mentioned what I am of opinion will answer best for the protection of the trade bound to the islands. To answer this end, two of the best sailing frigates may be appointed for cruizing between 16° and 18° 30',[1] and be confined to that latitude, but left to their own discretion in their easting, because the enemy's privateers will move to the eastward when they find themselves disturbed, and may there cruize with equal advantages and less risk if the frigates have not the range of this station, and cannot follow their lead. I have mentioned the best sailing frigates for this place, because the privateers are here most numerous, and the fastest sailers are the only ships proper to take them. These ships when their cruizes are finished should be ordered to victual and water at Barbados, as it lies to windward, and may be reached in twenty-four hours from the south limit of their station and recovered again in the same time, with another advantage, which I shall mention when I come to convoys.

In their return to Barbados, they should be ordered to fall in between twenty or thirty leagues to windward of it, if they can fetch so far, and run down its mid-latitude, which is 13° 07', by which means they cannot avoid seeing any privateers that are there; and this alone, with the Barbados sloop, will be sufficient to keep the trade bound to that island secure against the enemy. But, should it happen that any time a number of the enemy may be collected to windward of that island—as may be the case when they find themselves pushed to the northward—the frigates who are there may be allowed discretionary orders for dispersing them when such intelligence appears founded upon truth.

Yet as many captures will be made notwith-

[1] It will be noticed that he began (p. 9) with the limits 16° and 17°; extended them to 16° and 18°, and now to 18° 30', thus coming very near to the 19°, which he denounced (p. 10) as useless expenditure of force.

standing these frigates are stationed to windward, two other small ships would be necessary to cruize from the south windward point of Martinique to the south point of Dominica, each being allowed to stretch to the middle of the island of Martinique, to comprehend the enemy's present tract in beating to windward, in returning from their cruizes, and sending in their prizes. Their station should be from the land to fifteen leagues to windward, increasing their easting to the greatest at the latter end of their cruize, from whence they may reach Barbados in twelve hours to victual and water, and may return again in less when that is completed, the trade winds in general admitting of either. This station appears to me the most important, and to merit the greatest attention; and if practicable, two ships ought to be kept constantly on it, which, I think, may be done by employing three on this particular service. When frigates are wanting, large ships might supply their places; either being capable of retaking our merchant vessels which, since we cannot hinder from being taken, will by this method be most easily recovered. But allow me again to add, that though this station is soon reached, and the service may be easily executed while the ships water to windward, yet it will be found impracticable if they are ordered to victual and water to leeward, unless when services more material than the protection of the trade require their attendance otherwise.

The chief objection against the frigates stationed to windward watering at Barbados, is the difficulty of getting stores and of giving intelligence of their progress to the commanding officer; but this may in a great measure be prevented if, when they come in from their cruize, they always lodge their journals and demands for supplies at the custom-house, to be sent down by such ships as are going to heave down, or are otherwise obliged to repair to the Leeward Islands; and as on account of cleaning, and many unforeseen circumstances, there will be a continual succession of ships going to leeward, the commanding officer will, from time to time, be acquainted with all their proceeding, and the remaining ships be furnished with such small stores as they may happen to want between their times of cleaning. The stores brought up for the different ships may be left at Mr. Francis Jones, shipbuilder in Carlisle Bay, who has always supplied what has been wanting in that part, and what small stores could not be had at Antigua. If an appendix were made to each journal containing the time, particular latitude, and longitude from the nearest island, in which ships are first seen, it would be a great means to enable the commanding officer to judge of the enemy's motions and make what dispositions or alterations might be proper in consequence of them.

These ships may cruize during the whole hurricane season, as the enemy's do, taking care, on the usual signs of a hurricane, to stretch to the southward and from the shore. The brig at Barbados, when I commanded her, had general orders to heave down there at the end of every three months, unless when particular service prevented it.

Two ships of force, attended by two small sloops of ten or twelve guns, kept constantly employed, except during the hurricane months, to cruize under the lee part of Martinique, and as near the shore as they can with safety, would intercept what escapes the windward cruizers, straiten the enemy's privateers, obstruct the trade carried on between St. Eustatius and Martinique, and prevent their supplies from getting in. These ships should always return to Antigua, and water by the way at Dominica, Guadeloupe or Montserrat, which may be done at either without much loss of time; or even at St. Christopher's, should they happen to chase so far to leeward—though, to render ships of the greatest service on a station in this country, they ought never to chase far to leeward of it; the lee currents, which generally prevail, and the trade winds make the regaining of it difficult and tedious, while during their absence much mischief may be done in it, and opportunities of annoying the enemy lost.

I mention small vessels as proper to cruize with the large ships here, because such are best for working in all alterations of the wind which happen under high lands; are of force sufficient to retake anything the enemy can take, or even attack their largest privateers, while they have such assistance at hand, and can go nearer the shore than the large ships will venture to do.

As these ships will lie in the way of any French squadron coming to Martinique, the frigates to windward may have general orders to carry to them first any intelligence they may get of such, that they may secure themselves against a superior force. By these ships stationed to leeward of Martinique, two to windward of it, and two in the tract of our Leeward Islands trade, with the Barbados brig to windward of that island, our trade would be tolerably secured, or the greatest part of the captures recovered, while every success which arose from this plan would check the enemy's spirit of privateering and lessen our danger from them. Should they alter their procedure, ours may be varied accordingly; and as it is probable the Grenades will be their next port to secure themselves and their prizes, the Barbados trade will of consequence suffer more than it has yet done, and the trade to the Leeward Islands will then be eased; but the same means which was of service in the one will, with only changing our stations, prove useful in the other.

As to the interior trade of the islands, it is impossible to fix any certain plan for its protection. The vessels employed among them are very numerous, and they are running from one to another without interruption. The Antigua is very insufficient for that service alone, though the only one fit to disperse those small privateers which lurk about the shores to interrupt this part of our commerce; but as there is no other, and Guadeloupe, by reason of its extent and number of ports, lying most exposed, she ought to be chiefly employed about it, but not to windward; may be sent at other times about Barbuda, St. Bartholomew, St. Martin, and Anguilla, where the enemy at any time may make their resort, shifting her station as she finds the enemy do theirs.

The trade from Barbados, which is very considerable, may be carried past the islands to the northward by the windward cruisers, without any interruption to their cruising, as the limit of their station reaches to 18° 30′; and a few miles beyond that there is little danger. A frigate on coming in to water and victual may name a day for sailing, and take those ships which are ready along with her; by which means the convoys will be frequent, no unnecessary ships will be employed, and only obstinate people run any risk. Hitherto convoys have been appointed but seldom, and they the ships which cruised to windward off Barbados. The merchant found it ineffectual, and chose to run the hazard rather than delay his voyage in expectation of a doubtful convoy; and the cruizers, on the other hand, lost much of their time.

From Antigua, convoys may be granted to the northward to any number of ships that are ready when a ship is going from thence to windward, that being in general the best way of beating; but if convoys are required when no such ships are ready, they ought to be obliged to make up at least six sail, else they will be too frequent in respect of the ships on the station. They may likewise be informed when any convoy is granted to St. Christopher's, and go down there with the ship appointed on that service.

Convoys between the islands may, without any prejudice to the activity of the squadron, be as frequent as cruizers go and return to their stations; but, if required to the northward by any of the islands, should consist at least of six sail, or, if fewer, they ought to make it appear that they are of considerable value.

The trade of Guadeloupe is so large, that they will need frequent convoys to carry them to the northward of the islands. But as the island is extensive, they should be obliged to rendezvous at the most convenient port—which seems to me to be Basse Terre—except they can collect a sufficient number of vessels to make it necessary to grant them one from any of the other ports. The ships that carry the convoys from thence may be ordered to go under the lee of Montserrat, and to stop one day at St. Christopher's, to collect such ships as may be ready at these islands at the time; and whatever island applies for a convoy—particularly if it is Guadeloupe—they ought to take the first opportunity of acquainting all the islands which lie in the way of that convoy, that it may turn to the most general advantage of the whole.

Fort George, on Grande Terre, is much frequented by ships of value who load there, and may run some risk in getting to Basse Terre, where the whole ought to assemble. The windward cruizers, when ordered to leeward to heave down or on any other service, may run down between Grande Terre and Marie Galante, and call at Fort George to take under her convoy such vessels as may be ready, and then to proceed to Basse Terre, where she may even wait for more vessels while she completes her water, which she ought always to do before she reaches Antigua. If she has collected a sufficient number, she may proceed immediately, by Montserrat and St. Christopher's, to the northward, and afterwards beat up to Antigua.

An intention secondary to the protection of our own trade is obstructing an illicit trade carried on between Martinique, the Grenades, and St. Eustatius; the Dutch receiving their sugars from the other two islands, either to be shipped off for Europe, or in return for provisions and other goods which they supply them. The vessels employed in it come, in general, from the southward directly to St. Eustatius, and return the same way, unless when the winds are much southerly; and then, many of them stretch to the northward and, weathering all the islands, run down for Martinique in its latitude or in the latitude of Dominica, which brings them into the tract of those cruisers proposed to be stationed to windward of Martinique; and they may also be intercepted by those ships stationed to leeward of it. When there are any ships to spare from other services, to the southward of St. Eustatius would be a good cruize for the Grenada trade.

This, sir, is the plan my experience in this country has enabled me to form for the protection of our own trade, and for lessening that incredible number of captures which the enemy every day makes. I am sensible the intricacy of the station requires a great many ships to cover it sufficiently, and that a thousand accidents may fall out to interrupt the best-laid scheme. Your own judgment and circumstances as they happen must, after all, be your chief guide in the disposition of the squadron. I hope it will be attended with every reasonable success.

CAPTAIN'S ORDER BOOK

1st August, 1775.

By Charles Middleton, Esq., Commander of his Majesty's ship Ardent.

Orders to be observed on board and put in execution by the respective commanding officers, the lieutenants and master having each a copy of them; and the master to supply a lieutenant's place till the complement is complete.

1. [The first lieutenant to make out a watch, quarter and chasing bill.] [1]

2. [Mates and midshipmen, petty officers and men, to be classed in four divisions; each division to be under the direction of a lieutenant.]

3. The lieutenants commanding the respective divisions to see that the clothes and beds of the men under them are to be made up to the quantity specified in the following report . . . [to be supplied by the purser, agreeable to the instructions.]

[The report specifies: Jackets, 3; waistcoats, 2; breeches, 2; shirts, 4; frocks, 2; trowsers, 2; shoes, 2; stockings, 4; beds, 1; caps or hats, 2.]

4. [Mates and midshipmen to keep a list of the men belonging to their own classes, and report weekly the state of the clothes; which the lieutenant is to muster at least once in every month, and report o me.]

[1] Articles in brackets are in abstract

Such as are found careless about their clothes or dirty in their persons to be punished through the boatswain's mate by order of the midshipmen commanding them, as far as a few strokes. If habitually so, to be scrubbed in a tub, by order of the lieutenant; but if any are known to sell or traffic in any way with the clothes mentioned in the report, to acquaint me with it.

It is recommended to the mates and midshipmen to cause the men under their care to wear their own hair; and to get so well acquainted with their character and disposition as to be able to answer, at any time, such particulars as may be required concerning them.

5. The Articles of War and rules of discipline, as likewise such of these orders as relate to the men, to be read once in every month [publicly and distinctly; to be hung up in some public part of the ship].

6. To discourage by example and authority every tendency to vice and immorality in those under you, particularly swearing and drunkenness; for which purpose, let a collar be made use of, agreeable to the custom of the navy in such cases.

7. If any seaman or marine gets drunk on board or on shore, he is to be taken care of till sober, and the following morning to be ordered in custody of the master at arms and brought upon the quarter deck, where the purser's steward is to serve him, in presence of the commanding officer and the ship's company, a pint of salt water, which he is to drink. If drunk a second time, to be punished with six lashes; if a third time, with 12 lashes; and if habitually so, to be reported to me.

[Warrant officers are expected to show a good example. Mates and midshipmen never to fail in ordering—'by permission of the commanding officer' —the collar on such as swear, or in reporting such as are in liquor.] Whoever is known to countenance or pass over either of these vices, will be looked upon as unfit for executing the duties of his station and be discharged from walking the quarter deck.

8. [Proper respect to be paid to the chaplain. Every support to be given to him.]

9. The ship to be kept very clean in the inside as well as without; her sides to be washed round every morning, before the ports are hauled up, and particularly about the head and bows; and to preserve, by frequent visitation of the boatswain and master's mates, in the boats, that appearance which a king's ship ought to have.

10. The ventilators to be kept continually worked . . . particularly when the weather will not permit the ports to be open . . . A midshipman frequently to attend to see it performed.

11. The hammocks to be numbered and booked. Such a proportion to be washed daily as will keep the whole clean; and to be stowed in the netting every day when the weather will permit; at other times, under the half deck.[1]

12. To allow of no berths under the decks but such as roll up, whose canvas is to be kept perfectly clean; and at all times, when the ship is ordered to be cleared, the canvas to be laced up. Such as do not comply, in a particular manner, with this in-

[1] This expression, denoting the after part of the main—or, as it then was, the 'upper'—deck, was, in the later days of wooden line-of-battle ships, very commonly corrupted into 'on the half-deck,' which was nonsense, or 'on the aft deck,' which had no meaning. A reference to any of the 17th or 18th century models in the museums at Greenwich or the United Service Institution will at once show that the 'main' was properly called the 'upper' deck, and that its after part was strictly 'under the half-deck.'

struction, to be deprived of the indulgence of an enclosed berth.

13. [Officers' cabins to be reduced to the size allowed by the navy board. Petty officers to inhabit their own berths ;] so that the seamen may not be deprived of the space allowed them, which at best is found full insufficient.

14. When at sea, the men to have canvas bags for their clothes, as fast as the service will admit of it, when only one chest will be allowed to eight men, and which is to be stowed in the hold as soon as the ship is at sea. At such times, they are to keep their wearing clothes in their beds or hammocks.

15. [The commanding lieutenant to keep the keys of the warrant officers' store rooms. A midshipman to attend the delivery of all stores.]

16. [After the master at arms has reported fire and lights, a midshipman to go down at least four times in each watch.]

17. No officer, petty officer or seaman to have leave of absence . . . from the spot, without my permission . . . When on sea service, none to lie out of the ship without my knowledge. [Not more than eight men on shore on leave at any one time, including those who do not return to their time.] Such men as do not return to their time to wear a badge of disgrace, so that the ship's company may know to whom they are indebted for having their leave abridged. Such as attempt to run from the ship to wear this badge at least three months.

18. [Leave only to men who behave well. Men who behave badly on leave will be punished, and have their leave stopped for the future.]

19. Every boat except the guard boat to be hoisted in before the watch is set. . . .

20. [Boats not to be at the calls of men going

or coming on pleasure: but liberty men may take the opportunity of boats going on service.]

21. No mate or midshipman to appear on the quarter deck in any coloured clothes except blue and white, nor go upon duty out of their uniform. [Commissioned officers to show them an example.]

22. [Men not to take up slops or tobacco in excess of their pay, 'without my order.'] Whoever takes up either for the purpose of trafficking or selling will be severely punished.

23. [When the ship is paid, the lieutenants of divisions to see that their men complete their clothes; to encourage no slopsellers who are not reasonable in their prices.] The boats' crews' shirts to be of the same pattern in the check, and all to have caps of the same kind.

24. [Marine sentries 'are to be clean in their uniforms.' In wet or bad weather, they may 'do duty in their sea dress.']

25. [The marines do garrison duty in port; the duty of the ship is to be done by the seamen, who are exempted from night service, except in extraordinary circumstances.]

26. The marine officers are to exercise their men at every convenient opportunity. . . . Men that are not seasoned to be taken out daily until they become expert in their exercise . . .

27. [On Mondays, Wednesdays and Saturdays, the lieutenants of divisions are to exercise their men at the great guns; on the intermediate days, with the small arms. Whenever this duty is omitted, it is to be entered in the log, with the cause of the omission. The most ignorant men are to be exercised daily at the great guns. The midshipmen and the lieutenants to see to this. The gunner and his mates to attend in instructing the men.]

28. [The topmen and boats' crews to be exercised

at every convenient opportunity in the use of small arms.]

29. [The lieutenants of divisions to instruct the officers under them :—

To preserve silence at all times, and give attention to orders.

In firing against an enemy, the guns are to be pointed on the hull, near the mainmast.

Within musket shot, to fire round and grape while the guns are cool; grape only, when they become hot. At point blank distance, double-headed shot singly; out of that distance, round shot only.

A gun is never to be fired when out of distance, nor till well pointed. More than one shot is not to be put in a gun, unless ordered; nor any rubbish, such as crows or marlin spikes.

Sponges are never to be wetted in time of action.

In addition to the boys quartered for supplying the guns with powder, the lieutenants are to appoint active persons to assist. A cartridge is never to be carried out of its box.]

30. The topmen and boats' crews to be exercised at great guns as well as small arms. The topmen to be exercised in the use of hand grenades, for which purpose false ones are to be constructed and made use of. [In time of action, to clear the enemy's tops and quarter deck with grenades, swivels and small arms.]

31. [Stations of officers for working ship when the hands are on deck.]

32. [The men are to be frequently exercised at their stations. The officers to muster them.]

33. ['The commanding officers in general'—sc. the lieutenants of divisions—to punish lesser crimes through their own authority; by the boat-

swain and his mates, or by confinement; so as to prevent the too frequent use of flogging. To punish in cases of drunkenness, according to art. 7 of these instructions.]

34. [When men are sent to do duty on shore or on board any other ship, the midshipmen, in whose classes they are, are to be sent with them.]

35. [The ship is to be kept at all times fit for service.]

36. [No men are to be entered who are not 'complete seamen,' active and good in health.]

37. [Every lieutenant will be supplied with a signed copy of these instructions, and will sign a receipt in my book.]

No woman of any kind to be permitted to continue on board, who are not wives to the officers or men.

38. [The coxswain of a boat is answerable for his crew.]

39. [Any man beating another is to be severely punished by the master-at-arms, 'who is to carry a stick for this as well as the other purposes of his office.' If the man who is beaten attempts to redress himself, he also shall be punished. No fighting nor quarrelling shall be permitted on board.]

40. [Such men as behave well will have the preference in every kind of indulgence, and in leave. Those who behave badly will not have leave till they reform.]

REV. JAMES RAMSAY[1] *TO MIDDLETON*

Prince of Wales: Gros Islet, St. Lucia.
23rd April, 1779.

Dear Sir,—I have just had transmitted to me your kind favour mentioning the receipt of mine by Mr. Armstrong, from which I conclude that your letter by Captain Lockhart has miscarried. You flatter me by wishing to have me near you, and yet I think I might make the tedious part of your business easier to you; I am sure I should have pleasure in the endeavour. I persuade myself you will not be content with just doing things well while you are in office, but that you will lay the foundation of lasting improvements. It would be my ambition to clear away the rubbish and act under you. Could that same living cast up, my wishes for my family would be completed.

We are still lying here inactive. Part of the French squadron, consisting of three ships of the line and seven frigates, have been parading about the Leeward Islands, and actually took up near a fortnight in conducting to and from St. Eustatius a

[1] Chaplain of the Prince of Wales. Twenty years before he had been assistant-surgeon of the Arundel, with Middleton, but had since taken orders, and been doing clerical duty in the West Indies. In 1781 he was appointed by Middleton to the vicarage of Teston, and apparently assisted him as private secretary. Many of Middleton's papers of the 80's are in his handwriting. He died in 1789. Cf. *post*, vol. ii. index, and *D.N.B.*

convoy of upwards seventy sail. On the 12th instant, the very day on which they returned to Martinique, we despatched two ships of the line and two frigates to intercept them, several frigates happening at that time to be to leeward on other errands. On the 21st two ships of the line and two others, supposed to be storeships, passed in sight of our fleet bound from old France to Fort Royal. Five ships under Admiral Parker were detached after them, which saw them safe into port. This is the second reinforcement that has arrived to the enemy since Commodore Rowley joined us, which many think might have been intercepted had we kept, as it is thought we might, a squadron to windward. The fact is, that never was so mighty a force kept doing so little.

Meanwhile, time is passing away without any better hopes. Lee currents appear to be the raw head and bloody bones of our present chief.[1] And yet the necessity of the thing has obliged him, we are told, to form the resolution of cruizing about Martinique, while the convoy is collecting, which is appointed for June 15th. If such a thing can excuse him for encountering lee currents, why should not the keeping out of supplies from an enemy that keeps us all alarmed be also a good reason? Administration must have lost all vigour if it dare not recall such a man. Why might not our commander be advanced to an higher rank and be enabled to send the next[2] to him after the fugitive enemy?

But though everything that looks like censure on present measures be immediately condemned, I will beforehand venture to say that, had he the

[1] Vice-Admiral Byron. As to the lee currents, cf. Beatson, *Naval and Military Memoirs*, iv. 459–60. The expressions are, no doubt, quoted from Byron's despatches.

[2] Sc. Barrington, who had his flag in the Prince of Wales.

command, the enemy would be confined to his ports till a force could be sent out to take post ashore and assist in destroying him. This is the only part in which we can carry on a war to advantage, and we indeed have an enormous force here, but confined inactive to one spot. The French have very few privateers out. The scarcity of provisions, the stoutness of our merchantmen, the supposed employment of their men in their ships of war, are considered as the reasons.

The French squadron has all the appearance of being healthy. Byron and Rowley's squadrons have been very sickly and are supposed to want, in dead and sick men, near 2,000 effective seamen. The Elizabeth has been one of the most sickly; she has lost fifty-one men and has 230 sick. None of the rest are so bad, and great numbers are on the recovery. As far as I can conjecture, the dead may be about 400.

There seems to be a want of skilful surgeons. Our surgeon, Mr. Fidge, is daily sent for to one ship or another, sometimes in very common cases. It is surprizing to me that so little attention should be paid to so necessary an officer. Half-pay should be extended to every surgeon. A single friend can find employment for a lieutenant or master in time of peace; a whole town or village must conspire against their present surgeon or apothecary to find employment for a discarded navy surgeon; for hardly can a settlement be found unoccupied throughout the kingdom. They should also be supplied with medicines at the public expense.[1] It is not to be concealed that many a seaman's life has been sacrificed to bad and improper medicines. Did these

[1] It seems now almost incredible, but it was not till 1796 that medicines were partly supplied, not till 1804 that they were entirely supplied. See Sir Gilbert Blane's *Select Dissertations*, p. 19 *note*.

encouragements take place, the public would have a right to rise in its demands of learning, skill and application; nor should they be so easy in granting superannuation, which to my knowledge has drawn several experienced surgeons from the service that were still capable of serving. But I tire you. My earnest prayers for your success and the prosperity of your family attend you.

I am, dear Sir,
Your much obliged
and affectionate humble servant,
JAMES RAMSAY

CAPTAIN WALTER YOUNG TO MIDDLETON

Deptford. 13th May, 1779.[1]

Sir,—My suggestions respecting the contractor getting at the masters of the navy victuallers I am now convinced of, as some of the masters have applied to my acquaintances to find what my sentiments were on that head; they have offered a part of the freight (as a bribe) provided I would give them permission to receive on board, in the river, a certain number of casks of pease, &c., &c. I likewise find that the masters mean to avail themselves of the use of their great cabins for the purpose of taking on board those provisions, and to evade, from thence, your demanding freight for them. If this practice should be put in execution by them, I would recommend to you to take up those ships as transports, and make no mention in their charter-party of being victuallers; let them be fitted in every respect as such, and confine the masters to a cabin—such as the masters of transports are allowed—to put a stop to this intended fraudulency.

I have farther to observe to you that, admit[ting] your agents at Cork find those provisions on board,

[1] Walter Young, after serving two years (1763–5) as a master, and having nearly fourteen years' seniority as a lieutenant, had been made a commander on 25 February 1779, and was now on half-pay. His letter indicates that he was acting as transport agent at Deptford, cf. also *post*, pp. 82–3; but no record of his holding any such appointment can be found.

the contractor's purpose is answered, and perhaps at a cheaper rate than Messrs. Muir and Atkinson served him. Added to this, in all probability you have no power to demand or stop freight for the provisions; as, of course, the owners of the transports will plead ignorance of this transaction and throw the whole of the blame on their masters. I am therefore, of opinion that when you take up ships for this service, that this circumstance should be made known to them to prevent their pleading ignorance.

I mentioned this matter yesterday to Commissioner Le Cras, but as he is so much employed in business he may have omitted communicating it to you, I therefore thought it my duty to inform you of it by letter. I have likewise received information that few or none of those large ships, taken up for victualling service by Messrs. Muir and Atkinson, ever had any provisions in their between-decks when they left Cork; consequently an immense quantity of tonnage must have been lost to government, added to their over-measurement.

I thought those hints necessary for your information, and I am, sir,

Your most obedient, humble servant,

WAL. YOUNG.

Deptford. 29th June, 1779.

The owner of the Æolus transport has been with me, in consequence of the protest being made against his ship for not proceeding, and has made a very curious discovery of Governor Paterson's [1] intentions respecting that ship. The governor did inform Mr. Taylor, the owner, that Lord George

[1] Walter Paterson, Governor of St. John's, now Prince Edward's Island, in the Gulf of St. Lawrence.

Germain had ordered this ship particularly for his use, and when the clothing was on board, he was to fill up the ship with what goods he thought proper; but, that things might be carried on smoothly, he offered the owner 50*l.*, provided he—the owner and master—would aid and assist him therein.

As I cannot suppose Lord George could grant, or even countenance, an indulgence of this kind, I think it a duty incumbent on me to acquaint you of it, that Lord George may be acquainted with this, to prevent its being made a handle of by people in trade or opposition; likewise to put a stop to so bad a precedent.

The governor's conduct does not stop here. He went down to the ship yesterday, after receiving a copy of the orders you are under respecting him, and carried with him house carpenters to build up cabins between the guns; and gave peremptory and positive orders to the owner at his peril to suffer the ship to go from Gravesend without his order.

I am much at a loss how to act respecting this said governor. He certainly cannot be an officer by his behaviour. If a trader, he is excusable; but so far, I have given orders that the master is not to suffer any buildings to be put up between the guns in the great cabin and steerage; and that those guns, and all he has, are at all times to be kept clear and ready for defence. I hope this part of my directions to the master will meet with your approbation.

Sandwich: Gros Islet Bay, St. Lucia. 28th April, 1780.[1]

Dear Sir,—As we have had an action with the French fleet, I conclude you would have thought

[1] On 1 Oct. 1779 Young was advanced to post rank, as captain of the Sandwich, then fitting as Rodney's flagship in the

me remiss had I not given you a detail of our proceedings and that of the squadron on that day.

The admiral having cruizers constantly to watch the enemy in Fort Royal Bay, on the 14th instant, at night, the Pegasus boat brought intelligence of the French fleet with the merchant ships having sailed from thence; in consequence of which we got under way immediately, stood for Martinique, and run down to St. Pierre. On the 16th we got sight of the French fleet and gave chase to them; at five in the evening, got pretty near them; they consisted of 23 sail of the line, one 50, three frigates, a lugger and a cutter. The Venus and Greyhound frigates were ordered ahead to watch their motions, which was admirably well attended to by Captain Ferguson.[1] I have understood from him that, from their conduct when they discovered him, they did all in their power to get off. At ten at night we got close to them, and attended to their manœuvres all night, which did not appear to me to be steady.

At daylight in the morning of the 17th we saw them beginning to form in a line of battle ahead on the larboard tack, with their heads to the southward.

West Indies. No record has been found of any correspondence relating to this appointment; and the only time before this when Young may have attracted Rodney's notice was in 1771, when the Guadeloupe, of which he was first lieutenant, was sent to Cartagena to demand explanation and apology for the insulting seizure of the Sir Edward Hawke schooner; for submitting to which, the lieut.-commander was tried by court-martial and dismissed the service. The captain of the Guadeloupe was the Hon. William Cornwallis; but it is possible that Young carried the message on shore and that his conduct on a difficult occasion was favourably represented to the admiral. This is only a guess; but that Rodney had, and continued to have, a high opinion of Young's merit is quite certain. Cf. Mundy, i. 113, 124–9, 358.

[1] James; died, lieut.-governor of Greenwich Hospital, 1793.—Charnock, vi. 519.

We made the signal for a line of battle ahead on the opposite tack, but finding our squadron much extended, at nine o'clock we made the signal for the line of battle abreast, and bore down on the enemy's rear. At ten made the signal that the admiral meant to attack the enemy's rear and to leeward. We continued running down in the line of battle abreast, until the enemy discovered our intention, who wore and formed in line of battle ahead, on the starboard tack. We made the signal for a line of battle ahead on the larboard tack, and stretched along their line on opposite tacks. At half-past ten we made the signal to wear and, after being round, the signal for a line of battle ahead on the same tack with the enemy. At eleven made the signal to prepare for battle. At twelve made the signal No. 21 of the Additional Fighting Instructions, and the signal for close action with the signal for engaging.

At ten past one the headmost ships began to engage, but at too great a distance. Repeated the signal for close action, which signal was continued flying until the business was ended, and struck with the falling of the fore topmast, which was shot away. Had the latter signal been attended to, the day would have been a fortunate one; but, on the contrary, never was a signal more grossly disobeyed, and the Union at the main likewise. I have the pleasure to inform you that we have the general approbation of the officers for bringing two fleets of their numbers so fairly into battle, and confident I am, had the captains attended to the signals and the movements of the Sandwich, the day would have been a glorious one indeed.

On our bearing down on the enemy's centre—that is to say, the second ship astern of the French admiral—we only discharged two discharges, when our opponent bore right up out of the line; and we soon after obliged two others astern of her to follow her example. At this time we had bore up so much that the French admiral and his seconds were open on our weather-bow; his sternmost second engaging the Cornwall, who was more to windward than she ought to have been and suffered for it.

The French admiral, seeing us unsupported by our seconds, and the Yarmouth out of the line, laying to with his main and mizen topsails aback, though his particular signal was out for some time to call him into battle, which he did not attend to—in consequence of his conduct, the French admiral, with his two seconds, wore out of the line and came abreast of the Sandwich, and brought to the wind on the same tack, at their own distance, and continued battering of her for an hour and a half without having any ship to support or take their fire from us except the Cornwall, who was too far to windward. We set our mainsail to get down to them, but they edged away, and after cutting our topsails and courses to pieces, they brought-to, and and we continued driving at them until they bore up, and made sail. Captain Bateman is now in confinement for his conduct, and must answer for it at a court martial; many committed errors, but he has appeared to err most palpably. For further particulars I shall refer you to Sir George's letter.

The fleet is in a shattered condition. For God's sake and our country's send out copper-bottomed ships to relieve the foul and crippled ones, with masts and stores of all kinds. With those, everything will be done; if you do not, nothing but misery and distress must ensue. We chased those French fellows, who got to windward of us, for four days, but could not get them to come to battle; at last we have come here to prevent their getting in to Fort Royal, which they are pushing hard for.

With wishing you and yours health, happiness and success, I am, dear sir,

Yours sincerely,

WAL. YOUNG.

Sandwich: Barbados. 3rd June, 1780.

In my last I informed you of the admiral's intentions respecting the enemy, to prevent their getting into Fort Royal. On the 25th of April they passed by St. John's, Antigua, not in a very good condition, and much at the same time we got off Fort Royal, where we continued until the 27th, when we put into Gros Islet Bay, St. Lucia, to water, land the wounded and sick, and refit the squadron; leaving behind us Commodore Collingwood [1] and five sail of line-of-battle ships, to watch the enemy should they attempt to get in: two frigates were stationed between Martinique and Dominica, one to windward of Point Salines, Martinique, and another to run across to Deseada and Antigua, to look out for their fleet. On the 30th an alarm from Commodore Collingwood's squadron (which proved a false one) brought us all to sea. On the 2nd of May we anchored in Choak Bay,[2] St. Lucia, to complete our water and secure our masts; the Princess Royal's mainmast and the Conqueror's lower masts being in great danger of going by the board, this step was highly necessary.

On the 6th of May the Convert, who was stationed at Point Salines, came into the bay with the signal for the enemy's fleet. The signal for weighing was instantly made, and the squadron got under sail. On the 9th we got sight of them, and on the 12th they bore down with an appearance to give us

[1] Thomas Collingwood, at this time in the Grafton. He died this same month, June 1780.—Charnock, vi. 160.

[2] Anse du Choc.

battle, and to attack us van to van, and each ship opposite to her opponent; but they would have brought to at a distance to windward, and cannonaded us. The admiral, when they were bearing down, moved from the Sandwich to the Venus, to manœuvre our fleet to more advantage; but before he left me I proposed making the signal for our fleet to wear together, and to make Mr. Parker [1] with his division our van, as well for his strength, as to prevent the lame ships of the enemy getting into the channel between Martinique and St. Lucia (as we were far to the southward at this time).

We wore and Mr. Parker led with the starboard tack. This so disconcerted the enemy that they immediately wore and hauled their wind on the same tack, about four leagues to windward, which distance they took great care to preserve until the 16th, when, joined by a line-of-battle ship and four frigates, they again came down in the same manner about noon (when their men had got their wine), and intended the same manœuvre as before. They endeavoured all they could to get their van well pushed on towards ours, but after letting them come pretty near us, the signal was made for our van to make sail; we in the centre made all the sail we could to press up our van, and then we made the signal for the rear to make sail. As we had a fresh breeze this obliged the French to put out all the sail they could; consequently they could not make use of their lee guns until they were near us. The van ship of their fleet, by this means, could get no farther on than the Sandwich, which was the ship he must have brought to action. We waited with patience to get him close to us, as I had the signal ready for our van to tack and gain the wind of the

[1] Rear-Admiral Hyde Parker, the elder (Vinegar).

enemy, which would have been made on seeing what execution the enemy's shot would do, for by that I could have judged of the distance.[1] However, the French admiral, seeing that we had jockeyed him, he made the signal for his fleet to wear, and at the same instant of time I made the signal for our van to tack, and gain the wind of the enemy, which was immediately obeyed by Admiral Rowley's division. We then thought the game was our own, the point was gained. But how uncertain are things in general! Providence brought up a black cloud in the NNW (when they had rigged out the fore topmast studding-sail booms to scout[2] for it), which brought forth a wind from that point, on which they hauled their wind, tacked and weathered the van of our fleet.

The Albion, being the leading ship and so far advanced, there was no judging how to call her off; on she went, and sustained the fire of fifteen of the enemy's ships; the Magnificent was astern of her and received little or no damage, and retorted on the enemy what they gave the Albion, for so it happened, that when the enemy's ships had discharged their cannon at the Albion, the Magnificent was loaded and gave it to them when they opened with the Albion. Some other ships had some men killed and wounded—the Conqueror and some others. This was a mortifying circumstance; however I am certain the sufferings of the enemy was equal to ours.

[1] Although Hadley's sextant was by this time in general use, no one seems to have thought of it as an instrument for telling the distance of a ship, and the estimates were commonly very wild.

[2] Perhaps a variant for 'to scud;' but if we give the 'ou' the French pronunciation, the word becomes marvellously like a bit of modern slang.

Still in sight of each other, the French fleet playing with us, on the 19th our van had a shift of wind which brought them up pretty close to the enemy's centre on different tacks. Mr. Hotham[1] led, and Admiral Rowley's division was the van. The attack was warm on both sides, and the enemy finding their centre attacked, the van bore away and cannonaded us at their own distance; not that they gained much by this, as we find we can cannonade as well as they, and to as good a purpose. On this occasion they were remarkably civil to the Sandwich; their fire was more directed at other ships, though she was farther to windward than any ship in our line; indeed I drew her out to windward as much as I could to get at the fellows, and I flatter myself that our shot did them injury. We had not above ten shot in the hull and sails, and not a man hurt. The Vengeance, Albion, and Conqueror were much shattered and lost a few men. With this I send you a list of the killed and wounded.[2]

At six in the evening we tacked, with an expectation to cut off the rear, particularly one ship who was disabled; but after being round for half an hour, the wind headed us two points, and we saw the enemy had tacked, and that their centre was abreast of our van. We then put about, and stood on the same tack with the enemy, who went on with all the sail they could venture to put out. I was afraid of the consequences of this cursed fighting on opposite tacks, and of some accidents happening to our ships from their powder; as those took place in the day, what must be the consequences at night?

In the morning of the 20th the enemy were at

[1] Commodore William Hotham, created Lord Hotham in 1795, when commander-in-chief in the Mediterranean.

[2] Beatson, vi. Note 188. The Albion lost more than 'a few'—12 killed, 61 wounded.

least six leagues to windward of us, with all the sail they could set, and we brought to, to repair sails and rigging, and collect the state and condition of the ships; and at noon, the weather being hazy, we lost sight of the enemy, who continued standing to the northward.

On the 21st, the Cornwall, Boyne, and Conqueror bore away for Gros Islet Bay, St. Lucia; the two former being leaky, occasioned principally by the effect of their guns in battle on the frame; the latter on account of her lower masts.

If you had sent Mr. Walsingham in time, and he had been here only a week ago, I assure you, sir, Britain would have been mistress of those seas and most of the French fleet in her ports; and if exertion is not made use of with you, and ships sent out, eight or nine sail of fine ships will be ruined, and must leave their bones here, exclusive of what may befall us from the enemy.

I beg you will not make use of Mr. Cole's cast chains for the pumps; they are not to be depended upon, for when our ships have made water by shot, they cannot bear the weight of water, but snap short, and render the chain-pumps useless for some time. I am likewise to advise you that the copper nails are too short; they have not sufficient hold of the wood; for by the shock that the frame of the Sandwich has received in battle they are started from the copper at least the eighth of an inch, and I am apprehensive, if she should sustain such shocks as she already has, the greatest part of it, for seven or eight streaks below the wale, will drop off.

There is no occasion for my describing to you the bad consequences of those irregular attacks: cordage, sails, masts, and men must suffer; I therefore hope you will provide accordingly. Stores of most kinds are wanted: cordage, sails, small stores, pitch, tar, turpentine, and colours; your wise storekeepers at Deptford sent out the latter, but they were all Dutch. Our private signals are made by colours, and many of the ships for want of them are much at a loss.

I have a pipe of madeira for you, which I shall take care of, until I have your directions how to dispose of it. I hope you, Mrs. Middleton, and your family enjoy your healths, to whom I beg you will be pleased to present my best respects, and the offer of my services to procure them anything this country affords; and with wishing you and them all the happiness this world can admit of, permit me, dear sir, to subscribe myself,

Your most obedient and most humble servant,

WAL. YOUNG.

[*Private.*]

I have said in my letter I made signals. This was settled with the admiral after he left me, to make such signals as I saw necessary for the good of the service; which signals I was to show him by hanging them out at where they were to be made; and continued so doing until I saw him blunder, and then I wrote him that I would not be responsible for errors, as I had his flag to defend, as well as to make signals, but that I would repeat any signals he made and give him any information I could.

When the French fleet came down on us the first time, he left me in a confused state, and in short I did not know he was out of the ship. I did by no means approve of his going into the Venus; and he at that time proposed my going with him; but, as the enemy was so near at hand, appearances would have been against me, and I was afraid of the censure of the world to have quitted the Sandwich at that time. However, he shall not leave her again without my being with him, if I continue his captain. I have discharged my duty to him and my country, and will continue to do so, as far as my abilities extend, though my situation requires great patience with so unsteady and irresolute a man. His being in the frigate was of no service, as he always kept to leeward of our line. The enemy being to windward, he could never be a judge of it; but, at last, I got him persuaded to keep between us, which he attended to the last rencounter. I have more to say to you, but shall finish now in hopes of seeing you, with good news.

Sandwich, Gros Islet Bay, St. Lucia. 24th June, 1780.

I have the pleasure to acquaint you that all our possessions in this part of the world are still our own; a proof that the enemy, though superior, are afraid to attempt the capture of any of our islands, though they have had a long and a favourable opportunity to do so. Our squadron is in a distressed situation; the Cornwall sunk in the Carénage, the Fame ordered to share the same fate, from their leaks; and not the smallest probability of disposing of them otherwise. The Boyne may be saved; but this I can with certainty assure you of, if you do not get home the Princess Royal, Albion, Suffolk, Magnificent, Vigilant, Trident, Stirling Castle, Elizabeth, and Grafton—they will in four months share the fate of the two former, who are now totally lost. What Admiral Parker did respecting those ships last hurricane months, by keeping them in this country, he is to answer for; but we have found it a nominal squadron only. And in forming the line of battle large, we have found it impracticable to do it in twelve hours when sailing large, although the Sandwich had no more sail out than to make her answer her helm—that is to say, the topsails lowered down on the caps, and the yards braced contrary ways. From this situation what can be expected from us, the enemy's ships all clean?

The Spanish squadron got into Dominica, where we suppose they have wooded and watered; the French fleet went out from Martinique and cruized off that island to cover them, and we do suppose they left it, and are gone to the westward. Two of our frigates joined us last night, who brought us intelligence that during the stay of the Spaniards an embargo has been fixed, and that they saw the French squadron go into Prince Rupert's Bay, where they anchored. The Russell joined us on the 18th; would to heaven the admiralty despatches had been entrusted to a better officer than he who they sent with them; had this been the case they would have struck the greatest stroke the enemies of our country in any age ever felt.

I beg you will excuse my not being more explicit; but as this vessel is ordered off in a hurry, and we hurried in shifting, I must end here, and assure you that . . .

Princess Royal: Gros Islet Bay. 28th June, 1780.

In my last I gave you an account of the state of the squadron. It is now diminished by the loss of the Cornwall and Fame, who are both ordered to be hauled on shore; the latter is so, and full of water. The fleets of France and Spain are united and safe at anchor in Fort Royal Bay, Martinique; they amount to thirty-four sail of the line. Our line of battle, the Russell and Shrewsbury included, amounts to twenty-two, the Preston included in that number.

To-day we have had a council of war, and I am informed that they have determined to move the squadron here for the defence of this island. I tremble for St. Kitts and Antigua; they must fall without Providence gives assistance. We have been informed that the enemy only intends a feint on our northern islands, on purpose to draw us from this, where they mean to throw in their greatest force, being determined to repossess it at all events. We have lately discovered a part of their scheme, and have several of the planters now under an arrest.

I have pressed the admiral, as much as my situation will admit of, to send all the leaky and crazy ships to England as soon as the enemy quits this country. I wish my Lord Sandwich would send out some more three-decked ships, as they, if well managed, are dreadful to the enemy. Our wants become numerous in the naval line: sails, cordage, masts, yards, and anchors—many of the latter have been lost by negligence and inattention; there is not a seventy-four-gun ship here who has not lost two; consequently they have but two to depend on. I would recommend your sending all the masts and yards ready made, as it is impossible for us to make them as soon here as they are wanted, exclusive of the enormous expense. You will save by freight, and run no risk of disappointment by sending out rotten sticks, which has frequently taken place, and a great deal of labour lost. Our frigates have taken a few of the Spanish transports and some of their trade. We are in want of slops and shoes; thin ones are the most wanted.

I have nothing more to add at present, but to wish you health and happiness. . . .

Princess Royal: Basseterre, St. Kitts. 24th July, 1780.

I am exceedingly sorry that I was not so descriptive respecting the Spanish business[1] as you

[1] To the southward of Cape St. Vincent, 16 Jan. 1780.

wished, and although much time has elapsed, I will give it you as near as I can recollect, and as an assistant the log for the two days.

When the signal was made for seeing them, we could only count eleven in all, nine of whom of the line. I am firmly of opinion there were no more, as two of the line had separated from them two days before in foggy weather. Had Sir George followed my advice in making the land, probably the whole would have been secured by four in the afternoon; but I could not get him persuaded to run into the latitude of the Cape before we bore up to make it, by which blunder we were very near being embayed to the northward of it, and I may with great propriety say very near missing them altogether.

When the Bedford made the signal for the number she discovered, I wished to have had the signal for a general chase, as night was coming on. This the admiral opposed, and ordered the signal for a line of battle ahead at two cables' distance. This I opposed in turn, conscious that a great deal of time and distance would be lost, and proposed the signal for a line of battle abreast at a cable's distance. At the same time (as he was confined to his bed) I kept out a stiff sail on the Sandwich that no time might be lost; and, as soon as I discovered the enemy making sail to get off, the signal for a general chase was made. When our ships got up the signal to engage to leeward and in succession, and the signal for close action at the same time.

The admiral's ill state of health and his natural irresolution occasioned our shortening sail frequently, which prevented me from bringing the Sandwich so early into battle as I could have wished; and it was with difficulty that I succeeded at last, as he attempted several times to have the ships called off from chase; but on representing to him that they were too far ahead to either see or hear our signals, and that it was our business to be at the head or near to them, that we went on and stopped one of the enemy who had prepared to evade us.

I am perfectly of your opinion that it is a dangerous practice to make the signal for a general chase after an enemy equal or superior to you, particularly if they are formed in line of battle, or are near each other; though I own I am an advocate for a close line abreast when there is an intention to attack the enemy, and having the weather-gage; for by this means you get your ships well drawn up; and by so doing the officers are better judges of their distance than in forming in a line ahead, and from the line abreast any evolution is instantly put in practice. From what I have lately seen I am determined never to give a greater distance than one cable; finding that men in general, from high bodies, do not make a proper allowance: if at one cable, it will be two; at two cables, a quarter of a mile.

I have pushed very strenuously, previous to the receipt of yours, to save the Boyne and Fame. The former will come home with the August convoy; the latter will be got to Antigua, where she must be hove down, and may be ready to leave it when the hurricane months are over. I am in hopes we shall be able to send you ten sail of the line to refit and copper.

Your attention to the coppering reflects the greatest merit on you. It is impossible for me to describe the advantages attending it, and indeed exceeds the expectation of everyone. The advantages from the helm alone is immense, as they feel them instantly, and wear in one-third of the distance they ever did; it keeps them tight, and covers the neglects in your dockyards from bad caulking; increases their speed in every situation, more particularly in light winds tending to a calm, which is no small advantage in this and every fair weather country. Its greatest effect is in sailing large; we have frequently made the signal for a line of battle ahead (the squadron all pretty close to us) when going with the wind near aft, our topsails on the caps, the yards braced contrary ways, and the uncoppered ships with every sail they could set, and have not been able to form, though six hours at it, but obliged to give it up.

If you should send old ships to this country, let me advise you to give them their proper lower masts, with reduced topmasts and yards; the mainsails are great sails in beating to windward, and our ships feel it more than any sail in them. I must again repeat the abolishing of Mr. Cole's pumps and chains. Neither are to be depended on; the chains snap and will not bear a heavy load of water or much friction, consequently they are dangerous. The carronades I can say nothing of, the Montagu being the only ship who has them in this country, and, from what I have heard, they were not much used in the action. I own I should not wish to have them near hammocks; indeed I would not make use of them. I think they may be made very useful in small ships as their proper ordnance; for instance, in sloops or the small twenty-gun ships. Those who were only scantlined to carry six-pounders might very well bear twelve-pound carronades and run no risk from fire; added to this as they are narrow, it would give room on the gun-deck.

I am infinitely obliged to you for the share you have been pleased to take in my successes; the obligations I am under to you are such as fall very short of any description I can give of them, but my sensations are such that every time I reflect on what you have done for me, I feel a gratitude glow in my breast, which never can be extinguished but by the termination of my existence; and while I remain on this side of time I hope my conduct will never bring disgrace upon you.

The combined fleets left Fort Royal on the 5th instant at night, and were seen by our frigates on the 7th collecting their trade from Guadeloupe; we have sent six frigates to watch their motions, and expect intelligence every moment. The Andromeda captured a French vessel from Martinique for Rochelle, in which were found a vast many letters from officers of rank to their relations at home, wherein they mention that a part of Monsieur Guichen's squadron is to convoy the trade to France; twelve sail of the line to go to North America, four to Cape Français, and two of the line to continue at Fort Royal. The Russell, Shrewsbury, Culloden, Centaur, and Egmont have joined, as did Mr. Walsingham and the Berwick, with the whole of their convoy, on the 10th instant. Your friend Savage[1] is a captain, I hope at no distance from post; young Pearson, a purser into the Antigua sloop, with a friend of mine who will take care of him.

I shall conclude by begging you to present my respects to Mrs. and Miss Middleton. . . .

Postscript.—As the admiral has detained the packet, I can now inform you that Admiral Parker took three of the frigates with him, who were ordered to follow the combined fleets, by which

[1] Henry; was posted 31 Jan. 1781; died, an admiral, 1823.—Marshall, i. 124.

means, and a blunder of Sir George's orders to two of the frigates, the enemy have escaped, and we are left in the dark. This was what I had constantly represented to guard against. He blames the captains, and they in turn blame him. I unfortunately was not on board when he despatched the frigates, or probably this would not have happened.

From intelligence that the admiral has received he has arranged the squadron as follows :—

Commodore Hotham to command at St. Lucia with the Vengeance, Ajax, Vigilant, Fame, with frigates and sloops to the number of twenty. The Alcide, Torbay and Ramillies, if they come here, are to be under his command likewise.

The Boyne and Preston bring home the August convoy.

Admiral Rowley and Commodore Walsingham sailed this morning for Jamaica with the trade and troops, and the king's ships are the Princess Royal, Thunderer, Berwick, Grafton, Elizabeth, Magnificent, Conqueror, Albion, Stirling Castle, Trident and Barbados brig. Those ships, if not wanted at Jamaica, are to take the trade from thence and proceed to England.

I have delivered the signal books to Sir George for his perusal, though I am apprehensive those are books he will pay little attention to ; but I think the colour of the flags are well adapted, all but the chequered ones, which I would recommend not to be introduced.[1] It would be attended with many good circumstances if you were to allow a complete set of signal colours to each captain, reducing the size of them, and let every ship repeat the signals made by the admiral ; there would then be no excuse for any officer saying he did not see or under-

[1] Cf. *post*, pp. 313, 337–8.

stand the signal, and it would effectually put an end to that of captains stopping of signal colours to make a set for themselves; if they begin to put this in practice the warrant officer has a fine field for embezzling them, which few of them fail to do.

Sandwich: St. Kitts. 31st July, 1780.

Dear Sir,—I was yesterday morning favoured with yours by Captain Douglas.[1] You may be well convinced, sir, that it is my duty, as well as inclination, to serve every person you protect or patronise, and shall use all my influence with the admiral on that head.

I found Captain Brisbane,[2] immediately on his anchoring, had in some measure fixed upon a change with Captain Truscott,[3] of the Preston. When I had an opportunity of seeing Captain Brisbane I represented the impropriety of his scheme, particularly as his nephew and son[4] were both with him; that by his quitting in a month or two for his health he probably might serve both; one was a certainty. This advice he has followed, and I hope will put what I have proposed to him in practice. I have likewise spoke to Sir George on this subject, and have pointed out this vacancy for Captain Douglas, which I suppose we shall bring about; and Brisbane's son may be led on afterwards; but should all those schemes fail, if you are interested in the promotion of Sir James's son, I will at a convenient opportunity quit, on purpose to make an opening for him.

I most sincerely feel with you for your friend

[1] James, son of Sir James Douglas; died, an admiral, 1839.—Marshall, i. 123.

[2] John; died, an admiral, 1807.—Charnock, vi. 447.

[3] William; captain, 1778; rear-admiral, 1795; died 1798.

[4] Charles; died, rear-admiral and K.C.B., in 1829.—*D.N.B.*

Captain Maitland,[1] whose conduct last war was great and spirited; and although I was an utter stranger to him, I felt for his family and character. The censures that were thrown out on him, I spoke publicly of to the captains who were acquainted with him, and said that it was the duty of any friend to acquaint him of what was said, that he might have an opportunity of vindicating himself if innocent. However, I am sorry to say no one put this in practice; consequently the aspersions have still continued. It was a point of too delicate a nature for me to interfere in, being the admiral's captain, and an utter stranger to him; not but my inclination led me to it for many reasons—his family, the country he came from, and his former general good character at large; and, had your letter come in time, nothing on earth should have deterred me from pushing him to do himself justice, if innocent, and punish those who had reviled him, and would have given every other advice and assistance in my power. Admiral Parker becomes the principal accuser; for when he came on board of the Sandwich the day after the action of the 17th of April, on finding that Captain Bateman was confined, he said that one of his captains had behaved in the same manner, and that he was obliged to order Captain Bowyer, of the Albion, to take his station in the line, as he could not get him to obey the signal, but kept to windward and would not bear down on the enemy. I am very apprehensive (from what I have heard) that the admiral was full, if not more guilty than the captain, and for want of example in him other people erred; and he called off those who were in the act of doing their duty, and probably

[1] The Hon. Frederick Maitland. See *post*, pp. 100 *seq.*, and Charnock, vi. 374.

would have effectually finished the day in favour of Britain had he suffered them to go on.

I probably may have omitted acquainting you that I received the signal books and delivered them to Sir George, with whom they may continue for a length of time, and never be looked at or studied. I approve much of the colour of the flags, all but the chequered ones, who ought to be abolished from all signals. Quartered, half, three striped, striped corner ways, half up and down, and pierced, are the only ones that are to be properly distinguished at a distance. Indeed, I wish to see every captain in the navy who commands a line-of-battle ship to have a complete set of flags, and to repeat the signals through the line, as the French do; and I wish most sincerely that an established code of signals were adopted for the use of his Majesty's fleet. I am certain it would be attended with great advantage to our country and the service at large.

The Torbay joined us with the Alcide; we shall continue here until Captain Bateman is tried; when that is over, I suppose we shall go to Barbados, where the admiral intends staying six weeks; we of course shall go to sea, out of the line of the hurricanes. I hope you and your family enjoys good health. Be assured, sir, that no one wishes more a continuance of health, happiness, and success than . . .

Sandwich: New York. 22nd September, 1780.

I have been favoured with yours of the 4th of July, which gave me infinite pleasure to find you enjoyed your health, and uneasiness to find that a report of my leaving the admiral should add to the anxiety you have for the public welfare. Rest assured, sir, that a step of this kind could not be taken without your concurrence. When things were not conducting properly, I might have said so when uneasy; but recollection again taking its turn, I foresaw what would be the consequences. I make no doubt but ample justice have been done me, and probably more than I am entitled to; but, in return, I have discharged the duty of a son to the admiral, as well as that of his captain, and shall continue to do so, both for his advantage and that of my king and country.

I have had no opportunity of answering yours until now, and I am to inform you that I have persevered in putting in practice everything respecting the squadron that you have mentioned. The Fame and another of the bad ships will come home with the October convoy; the Yarmouth will be sent from hence. The expenditure of stores I have paid all the attention to in my power, and have curtailed the demands as much as possible.

Monsieur de Ternay is at Rhode Island with eight sail of the line; and, with the troops he brought has so fortified the island and its environs as to make it too strong for us to attack it. The favourable opportunity has been lost; the cause you will probably hear of by Sir Henry Clinton's letter. I am heartily sorry we were not on the coast a fortnight sooner; probably something might have been done; and I am persuaded had Mr. Graves not taken the East India ship and towed her to this place, he might have been here long before the French, and have defeated them in all their schemes.

I have repeatedly applied to the admiral to give information relative to convoys, and other intelligence both to you at home and to the officers commanding on other stations, which I have been told by him was done. The Spanish convoy is not yet sailed from the Havana, but must soon. France will have no more this year. I am exceedingly sorry to find such disagreements here between our land and sea officers. The army will be much distressed for provisions by some ridiculous conduct; your victuallers lay here empty for near six months, and the admiral would give no convoy because he had no admiralty orders on that head. I would advise your applying for certain ships to attend this service, otherwise there will be no knowing what will be the consequences.

The Sandwich begins to complain. I am apprehensive that she must come home next fall; the clamps of the beams and spirkiting being cut by shot, has weakened her much, but I hope the caulking and repair we are giving her here will keep her up for the time I mention at least. The Triumph fails likewise; the heavy metal tears her to pieces. I wonder much at its being put in her; surely if she could[1] bear it when new, what could be expected after the wear she has had, and the injustice done her at Chatham when intended to relieve the Conquistador.

The field to save the public money in this country is great, both in the naval and victualling departments. I am amazed at their not having store-houses to put the provisions in. They would not only save the enormous expense of shipping, but the provisions also; for the bread is full of vermin, and the other provisions destroyed by the heat of the hold. There are at present here, in

[1] The sense seems to be 'could *not* bear;' and, as 'could' is the last word on one sheet, 'bear' the first word on the next, the 'not' might easily be omitted. It is within every one's experience that no mistake in writing is more common than the omission of a 'not.' The Triumph, built in 1764, was the largest 74 in the navy, by nearly 200 tons. The armament of her class was twenty-eight 32-pdrs., thirty 24-pdrs., sixteen 9-pdrs.; but no instruction to give her a heavier armament has been found. The Conquistador, 60, one of the Spanish ships taken at the Havana in 1762, was at this time guardship at the Nore. Cf. *N.R.S.* xxxi. 214.

vessels, provisions which have been on board eighteen months, without being looked at. I am likewise to acquaint you that the large quantities of butter and oatmeal sent to the West Indies is so much money lost; the butter is not wanted, and the oatmeal hardly made any use of; a large quantity of both was sent home by the last victuallers from St. Lucia. Indeed, I wish a substitute of provisions was made in lieu of the oatmeal; the people and public would reap an amazing advantage by it. I cannot conceive why in the West Indies the men cannot be allowed sugar, coffee, and chocolate, in lieu of the oatmeal; they are a better breakfast for the men, and a much greater anti-scorbutic. I have given encouragement to this mode; but I find the pursers are too rapacious and rob the men, which has obliged me to stop it. They truck with the men at the following rate—viz., for six pounds of bread, one pound of sugar; for three pints of oil, two pounds of sugar, coffee, or chocolate; and in the Sandwich we never expend, on the days that the men are allowed their oatmeal, more than eight gallons, and no allowance made the men on those days for that article. Surely some mode should be adopted by the victualling board on this head. If something is not done the men will be destroyed by the scurvy, which is more predominate in this squadron and in this country, West Indies, than ever was known. Molasses, sugar, coffee, and chocolate to be served them in lieu of their oatmeal will be of infinite use, if rice cannot be had for them on the banyan days.

The signals adopted by Captain Kempenfelt I approve of much, except some particulars: the main topmast shrouds I imagine an omission; I suppose he meant topgallant shrouds: we can at all times make them plain by descending. The chequered flags ought to be avoided; but in the whole of his code I do not see a temporary line of battle, which is absolutely necessary, as detachments may be sent from the main body, and ships separated by chasing. Enclosed with this I have sent one that I have established, for your approbation. I had, on our coming upon the West India station, fixed chasing signals for every point of the compass, and night signals for the same purpose; but I found the captains were averse to them, therefore gave them up, though with much reluctance.

The wine I never meant on any other terms than those you have proposed, as I well knew who I was sending it to; you will be pleased to pay Mrs. Young 29*l.* 10*s.* sterling. It shall be attended to as you have directed.

Enclosure.

Signals for a temporary line of battle.

Whereas from the separation of the ships under my command, it may be necessary from time to time to form a temporary line of battle with the ships who may be in company with the ship my flag is in: that the captains may know the station they are to take in such a line, I will, at the time of making the signal for the line of battle ahead, abreast, or on any bearings as I shall see occasion, hoist the established preparatory flag, which being answered by all the ships, their answering flags are to be hauled down. I will then throw out the captain's signal who is to head on the tack I am on, who is to answer as soon as he can. Immediately after his answering another captain's signal will be made, who is to answer and form next to the ship whose signal was first made; and so on, in succession, until the line of battle ahead is formed; and the last ship's signal that is made is to bring up the rear, and to be the leading ship on the other tack, should the signal for that purpose be made.

Or if sailing large or before the wind, and I should see it necessary to form the line of battle abreast, the signal for the line and the preparatory flag shall be hoisted as before mentioned, and the first captain's signal who is made is to be the wing ship on the starboard side, the second ship's signal who is made next to him, and so on in succession until the line is formed, and the last captain's signal that is made is to be the wing ship on the larboard side. And this order is to be considered and noted as the dispositions of the lines of battle, and the ships are to take their stations accordingly until such dispositions are altered by any other signal.

Each ship to be prepared with a blank form to put down each ship's station in those temporary lines of battle as it shall be signified by the above mode, and when the signal for the line is taken in the captains are to fall into their stations with the commanders of the divisions, as established by the regular line of battle delivered to them. And likewise to observe that when forming the line, as before mentioned, to distinguish the last ship of each division to the officers commanding them and to the captains reciprocally, that they may know the ships of their division and the division they are in, a pennant, striped blue and white, will be hoisted at the fore topgallant masthead at the time the captain's signal is out as a stop pennant, to point out to the officers commanding divisions and the captains that that ship is the last of that division.

In action all the ships are to wear red ensigns.[1]

[1] This, if ever an order, was cancelled by Young's death. On the 12th April the several squadrons wore the colours of their admirals.

A list of the ships in the squadron under the command of Sir George B. Rodney, Bart., admiral of the white and commander-in-chief, &c., &c., &c.

Sandwich Triumph Torbay Alcide Terrible Yarmouth Russell Culloden Centaur Shrewsbury Fortunée	Squadron at New York from the West Indies.	Fame Vigilant	At Antigua, preparing to bring home the convoy.
Boreas Greyhound	Barbados, to join us. Arrived the 25th Sept.	Vengeance Suffolk Ajax Montagu Egmont Albemarle Amazon Venus Blanche Andromeda Bruno Alcmene Deal Castle Cameleon Ætna Vesuvius Carcass	Under the command of Commodore Hotham.
Intrepid Cyclops	At Antigua, to join us. Arrived the 25th Sept.		
Convert Surprise Rover Drake Hornet	At St. Kitts and St. Eustatius.		

The Russell, Culloden, Centaur, and Shrewsbury have joined Admiral Arbuthnot. The Triumph, Terrible, and Alcide are going on a private expedition, and I am ordered to command the latter on this service.

The Greyhound and Boreas on their passage hither have taken three merchant vessels with provisions and lumber, and an American privateer of 24 guns. The Intrepid and Cyclops arrived this morning and have brought in with them two American privateers, one of 24 guns, the other of 41, and two merchant vessels; for further particulars I must refer you to Captain Brisbane, who brings home the admiral's despatches.

Sandwich : New York. 30th October, 1780.

I have the pleasure to acquaint you that I expect we shall sail for our proper station by the latter end of next week. Captain Bateman's trial,[1] has detained us longer than I would have wished; however, I hope Commodore Hotham has been able to keep the enemy in order; at least, our intelligence is that all is quiet.

Our coming to this country has been productive of great consequence to his Majesty's troops and possessions. Had we not made our appearance, this place and the troops must inevitably have fallen a sacrifice to the rebels and French. Our cruizers have been very successful in destroying their privateers; thirteen, of different sizes, having been taken, exclusive of trading vessels, since our arrival.

I informed you in my last of my being ordered out on a cruize in the Alcide under the command of Captain Affleck of the Triumph; we were to have gone into the Chesapeake and to have cut out a French sixty-four *en flûte*, laden with tobacco and a convoy for Bordeaux. The Alcide was intended, with a frigate, to perform this service, but on making Cape Henry I spoke the Triton, who informed us that the ship and convoy had sailed five days before for France. During our cruize we had a heavy gale of wind, wherein the Terrible and Cyclops lost their mizenmasts, the head of the Boreas' rudder broke, and the Triumph complained much but lost

[1] See Appendix A.

no masts. The Alcide met with no damage, having brought her to under a mizen staysail and balanced mizen. The other ships strained much by laying to under their mainsails.

I have endeavoured as much as possible to avoid taking stores from hence, and have curtailed the demands; but there has been a great quantity of cordage and other stores purchased which could not be avoided. Other stores have been ordered to be purchased to carry with us to the West Indies, such as lumber and oars. The admiral has likewise ordered two vessels to be purchased, one a Congress vessel of twenty guns, the other an armed vessel of sixteen; what has been given for them I know not, as this transaction took place when I was absent; they are both good and new vessels, but their fitting must be attended with additional expense, which our foreign yards cannot well bear without going to market. The Sandwich has had a good repair and thoroughly caulked, so that she will be of no expense to the public for some time to come, and ready for service. The other ships of our squadron have gone through the same operation, except the Russell, Culloden, and Centaur, who are with Admiral Arbuthnot.

[*Private.*]

I am exceedingly sorry to inform you that Mr. Arbuthnot does not draw well with either his superior or any other officer. The loaves and fish, in both departments, have occasioned much disappointment; and I am afraid this said prize money is, and will be, the bane of all public service. You will be astonished to hear of the conduct of some of our supposed great men—and of a secretary; in short, sir, Mr. Arbuthnot is so led by Mr. Green, that he is either directly or indirectly in possession of every place under the navy—victualling, sick and hurt, and every other branch where the public money can be got at. Indeed, there is no method that has not been put in practice—such as forgery in pilots' bills, serving the condemned provisions to the French and American prisoners, and charging the government with serviceable, and every other species of villainy. I would therefore recommend it to the public offices in general to pay none of his accounts until they have applied to those gentlemen whose names may be affixed to his bills, to know of them whether they did attest them or not; and proof likewise in every other circumstance where the said Mr. Green or Admiral Arbuthnot have been concerned respecting the market prices. The abuses of the hospital are beyond description; this Mr. Green has had the physician discharged (turned out) and every other person who has impeded his rapacity. Such is the situation of this island; I assure you I wish most sincerely to be away from this place and this country, as every day produces some folly and imposition from the quarter I have been describing to you.

The Hyena and Adamant convoy are all arrived, except the Peace and Plenty victualler, who was run on shore on Long Island by a rebel privateer; some of the cargo will be saved, but a part and the vessel will be lost. We are extremely anxious about the Cork convoy. I hope in God it is safe, for should any misfortune happen to it, the army will feel its loss in a very essential manner. In my last I gave you an account of your army victuallers, and I make no doubt you will attend to them, and in future effectually put it out of Admiral Arbuthnot's power, or any other commanding officer, to act in the manner he has done. If you do not, the victuallers must return to Messrs. Muir and Atkinson, or the army will be starved. The Yarmouth will be sent home from hence, if not contradicted by Admiral Arbuthnot; however I am endeavouring to put that out of his power, as I hope to have her ready to depart with us.

With this I send you a 'New York Gazette,' and I am . . .

Sandwich: Sandy Hook. 15th November, 1780.

I have the pleasure to acquaint you that the South Carolina and New York convoys are arrived, and not above one or two missing. This has been the most fortunate supply that has made its appearance since this war took place. I must again recommend it to you to push and urge the admiralty to establish men-of-war for this service; and let them be the uncoppered ships, as the coppered ones are very unfit for convoys to deep-laden victuallers. I most sincerely wish you to attend to this service, as you are the person army and navy look up to, and not the navy board.

I am likewise to acquaint you of the immense neglects of the people at Woolwich Yard in the lading of the storeships for New York. The beds were all stowed in the hatchway, by which means a great part of them are rotten; the whole of the colours destroyed by their putting up the iron cringles for staysails in the casks with them—the iron having been wet when put up has effectually ruined them, so that out of the whole number only a few are serviceable.

The complaints respecting transports are great, and with great justice; those sent out totally unfit for service, the whole under the auspices of Mr. Wilkinson's house. Sir Hugh, I do suppose concerned with them as formerly, though you do not perceive it; I find too many proofs here for this information, as well as those which I well knew when in that department myself. While those men interfere and are concerned, the public must be robbed.

Mr. Arbuthnot's secretary follows the example of the great; he loses sight of no opportunity to rob and distress. In my last I gave you an account of such circumstance as the people chose to send me; I am now to inform you of a part of his villainy which I can personally prove, which is the purchase of fresh beef. He is supplied with it at Sandy Hook at 10*d.* York currency per pound, and charges the public 1*s.* sterling per pound; consequently he clears 5*d.* sterling, or near it, on every pound supplied. I have it from captains in Gardener's Bay, where Mr. Arbuthnot has been ever since our arrival here, that he has supplied the squadron with fresh beef, and on the same principle as at Sandy Hook. With the rapacity of this man of the navy, and others such as this fellow is, and those in the army of the same kidney, how can it be supposed that a minister and a nation can support a war? Sir, it is not possible. We must bankrupt, or other methods must be adopted.

An express arrived last night from General Leslie, who informs us that he has taken possession of Hampton, Norfolk, Portsmouth, and made an excursion up Nansemond River to the capital,[1] where he has destroyed a number of armed vessels and has reserved a ship pierced for twenty-two guns on the gun-deck, and two of twenty each. They miscarried in their attack on Richmond at the head of James River for want of pilots. This has been unlucky, as the expedition was originally intended for that purpose, the rebels having there maga-

[1] *Sc.* Suffolk.

zines of provisions and not less than 20,000 hogsheads of tobacco. We have likewise had some unpleasant accounts of a small check[1] [befallen] Colonel Ferguson and a small party detached from Lord Cornwallis. Ferguson is killed and his party taken prisoners, which has occasioned Lord Cornwallis to demand the assistance of General Leslie's army, who by this time has joined him near to Cape Fear or its environs. We shall sail to-morrow for the West Indies, leaving the whole of the American operations to Admiral Arbuthnot and Mr. Green.

The Fowey, now commanded by Captain Douglas, Sir James's son, is to sail with the convoy for England the latter end of this month, under the command of Captain Howe,[2] of the Thames; I hope you will, with his father, get him confirmed, though I have my doubts if Mr. Arbuthnot will let him continue in his command. I have got Mr. Pearson appointed purser of the Guadeloupe, who I suppose may stand in the same predicament; but probably, when he knows that he is under your protection, he may recollect himself and be civil.

We take from hence with us three transports: two laden with lumber for the use of the navy and army; a sufficient quantity for the latter to build an hospital at St. Lucia to contain the sick, and to build huts or barracks to lodge 3,000 men; and a transport for General Vaughan, who has some clothing on board.

We have had no intelligence from Mr. Hotham since we left him, but by a merchant vessel who

[1] Not by any means so small as Young supposed. It proved, on the contrary, very serious, obliging Cornwallis to fall back into South Carolina, discouraging the loyalists and 'lighting up afresh the expiring embers of the war'—Stedman, *Hist. of the American War*, ii. 215, 220–3, 232.

[2] Tyringham Howe, died 1783, a nephew of [Sir] Philip Stephens secretary of the admiralty.

arrived a week ago from St. Christopher's, who informed us of [a] heavy gale of wind taking place about the middle of October, by which means several vessels were put on shore at Basse Terre; but that there were no line-of-battle ships of the enemy in the country at that time.

Our convoy and stores being taken makes us in some manner uneasy; but we hope you will attend to us and send out supplies, running rigging, sails and slops. I wish it was in your power to order a proper room for the slops, or lay some injunctions on the captains and pursers to take proper care of them; for, in the present mode, it is astonishing to see what quantities are ruined for want of care; the bales put upon the coals, in the fish room, or in such places, where they get damp, and are rotten when taken up to be issued.

I have nothing more to say, but that I am . . .

Sandwich: Gros Islet. 12th December, 1780.

Dear Sir,—I have been favoured with all your letters, the contents of which it has been my study to persevere in; but you will see, from the sudden movements of the squadron, it has not been so much in my power to execute them. I well know your sentiments and attachment to the welfare of our country; and as far as my abilities and advice can extend, I have ever had your principles in view. If I have not been able to carry them as far as I could wish, it is not my fault; the whole tenor of my conduct I must and shall leave to the judgment of the superior officers who have been on this station, or where we have been; to them I will refer you as the most competent judges.

I thank God, that my constitution still continues good, and rest assured it shall not be spared in my country's service, though few has been more tried than mine in my present situation.

I am sorry to inform you that when we left Sandy Hook, we met with a gale of wind similar to that I represented to you when I was in the Alcide, which has disabled the Resolution, Shrewsbury, Alcide and Torbay of topmasts and a few lower yards. Rigging cut away, and sails lost of course are the common consequences, which has been done with great alertness. Had they been as alert in taking sail in in time, these disasters would not have happened; but this and many other misfortunes must attend the making young ignorant boys lieutenants, &c. We are now preparing for an expedition to the south of this isle; I hope it will be successful. I have received your letters for Mr. Ramsay and have sent them to him. This comes by the packet; I shall write you more fully in my next. Wishing you and your family health and happiness, I am, dear sir . . .

Sandwich: Gros Islet, 26th December, 1780.

Dear Sir,—I am exceedingly happy that you have at last adopted a plan for storeships. I would advise their being constructed under your own inspection, and having proper sail rooms and a room for perishable stores fixed in them; I am certain you will save a great quantity of small stores, exclusive of the first cost and the disappointment the service must have by their being damaged.

The establishing a store-house at Barbados will be of infinite use, provided a man of integrity is appointed. I cannot, from what I have heard, say much in favour of Mr. Tucker, exclusive of his political sentiments, which occasions his leaning too much to the enemy. My ideas respecting the purchase of vessels for the service agree in every sense with yours, and no one has guarded more against it; but at times he is for purchasing almost everything that offers, which I as constantly oppose, and advance such forcible arguments and reasons that I have in general gained my point, in opposition to my brother captains capturers. However, I hope by this kind of conduct I do not lose the esteem of the honourable and honest part of them, as I constantly inform them that we can neither man or equip them, as king's vessels, exclusive of the immense expense.

All our intelligence comes from St. Kitts from Dr. Ramsay and his brother-in-law, who have orders from General Vaughan to employ those they may think proper to procure it; consequently you must have it from that quarter, as I can assure [you] Sir George has no person in employ on that service, therefore there can be no charge.

I am astonished that the admiralty do not attend to the class of ships they send to this country. The Triumph and Shrewsbury are two ships totally different to the ships of the squadron; and who, if an accident happens to yards, masts, or sails, cannot be supplied with either without addition and alteration; there should be two ships at least of each class, that they might be able to lend to each other, without going into port for masts or yards. The Triumph's mainmast is unserviceable. Having no masts for her, there are at present, at St. Lucia, a foremast for a seventy-four, two lower masts and a bowsprit for a sixty-four, and not a spar of any kind, except a few small ones which was purchased lately at Barbados. Enclosed I send you the state and condition of the stores at Antigua. Our ships are now pretty near complete in masts. The Montagu has got a complete set, and will soon be fit for sea.

I must beg of you to represent to the commissioners of the victualling that the oatmeal and butter they send out in the victuallers is so much money sunk to the public; it is not wanted; and that they will not in future send any coals to this country among the salt provision casks, as the sulphurous matter insinuates itself into the provisions and destroys it, exclusive of its heating the provisions so that the pickle stinks and corrupts the flesh.

I have proposed putting the seventy-four's foremast into the Triumph, which will serve for a time at least. She will always be able to keep her station in the line of battle, but she must come home in May, therefore prepare for her. Whether the Sandwich will hold out longer than that I cannot inform you at present; the last gale of wind weakened her.

We have been on an expedition to St. Vincent, and shall refer you to Sir George's letter for an account of it. Never was there such a scene of confusion as at the embarkation of the troops; the Caribs had begun their slaughter and devastation the instant they saw the troops begin their retreat, when down came to the beach the planters, with their wives, children, and negroes. Many of them were taken on board, and the whole shore lined with those that could not be taken off. We were obliged to quit the bay in consequence of their bombarding us with two mortars, the shells of which fell very close to us; they had got our length, and would have in a little time done execution.

I suppose you have heard of Savage being captured by the Juno frigate. We sent a flag of truce for him and his people at the Grenada. In my last I acquainted you of Mr. Richards being appointed to the Suffolk; I wonder at your not mentioning him to me before. My Lord Colvill's son is now acting lieutenant in the Terrible, and as soon as an opening takes place there (which I expect will be soon) he shall be appointed. I have conveyed all your letters to Doctor Ramsay and Captain Douglas.

Admiral Parker's purchase of the frigates and storing and manning them, was not the only injury he did to the king's service; he suffered the whole of the line-of-battle ships to be neglected, and may with justice be accused of the loss of the Cornwall; he had more carpenters in his squadron than in any dockyard abroad, and never employed them in caulking and refitting those capital ships. When men do not draw with men in power, they should not be entrusted with the command of the king's ships.

P.S.—I beg your excuse for sending you a half-sheet, which I began upon and finished before I discovered it. A convoy sails from Martinique the latter end of this month.

[*Most Private.*]

Sandwich: Gros Islet, St. Lucia. 26th December, 1780.

Dear Sir,—I am sorry to be obliged to contradict my admiral's account[1] of the failure of our expedition to St. Vincent; his delineation of the expedition is very plausible, and although I detest detraction, yet I think it my duty to give you information of it, both as my friend, and a friend of our country, that we may not be imposed on by such plausible and pompous accounts.

The expedition against St. Vincent was agreed upon at Barbados immediately on our arrival there; the state of the island of St. Vincent was very authentically represented, and had we acted with propriety it must have fell, and without the loss (probably) of one subject. December the 8th we embarked, at Barbados, a company of grenadiers with two field-pieces on board of the Greyhound

[1] Printed (not verbally correct) in *Mundy*, i. 466 *seq.*

and Alcmene, and laid an embargo on the island; on the 9th we anchored at Gros Islet Bay, St. Lucia, with the Russell, Centaur, Terrible, Intrepid, Alcide, Triumph; Triton, Greyhound, Cyclops, Alcmene, and Sylph cutter; the next morning we were joined by Commodore Hotham in the Ajax, with the Alfred, Monmouth, and Vigilant. The frigates were ordered up to the Carénage to receive on board the troops for the expedition and some more cannon. The marines were taken from a squadron of six sail of the line, then intended to be commanded by Commodore Drake, to cover the expedition, to cruize off Martinique; and those marines replaced by seamen from the Ajax, Shrewsbury, and Resolution, three disabled ships who were not in a state to go to sea. Such was our arrangement first determined on; but an unsteady fit seized the admiral, and the whole was put a stop to, and orders issued accordingly.

On the 12th we were found in a different mood, and then the expedition was reassumed. Of course every effort was used to hasten it; but unfortunately, by its being put a stop to at first, the secret was discovered, and the instant it was put *en train* again, the French inhabitants of the island gave information to the Marquis de Bouillé, and the Governor of St. Vincent. The former being sensible of the state of the island, and of its being destitute of gunpowder and provisions, instantly sent a supply of both by a frigate who arrived at St. Vincent the day we left St. Lucia, which was the 14th. When we anchored in Warrawarou or Sir William Young's Bay,[1] the 16th in the morning, we found all the batteries on the shore evacuated, and the whole of their strength in the fortress and works on the

[1] Now Greathead Bay.

Morne. The troops of course landed without opposition on the 16th, and about midnight the pickets met each other, in which a few men were killed on each side, and the French drove into their works. Our troops took post close to them; but General Vaughan, with his officers and engineers, on reconnoitring the works and fortifications with the numbers in them, found they were too strong for his strength, and thought it most prudent to desist attacking it, and informed the admiral he meant to retreat and embark the troops; which was agreed to, and the ships ordered for that service who had had the troops before on board of them. So ended this expedition.

I have many other matters to relate to you of inconsistency, &c., &c., but shall suppress it on purpose to avoid giving uneasiness. I assure you I exert myself to the utmost of my power to keep our matters in order; at times they will get a little *outrée*, but in this I am obliged to you great men at home for, who have so poisoned my admiral that he really and *ipso facto* thinks and believes himself to be the very man you have represented him. God help us, how much mistaken you and he are!

Sandwich: St. Eustatius Road. 3rd February, 1781.

My dear Sir,—I have not time to give you a full account of our success against St. Eustatius. It fell, with all its appurtenances, the instant we surrounded the bay, as did all the shipping, to the number of one hundred sail, many of whom deeply laden and very rich. Five American armed ships are among the number, who are now in commission in our service; one a post ship, the other four sloops. The Mars, a frigate belonging to the States, of twenty-six eighteen-pounders, and eight nine-pounders, was captured in the Road, and is commissioned likewise. On the evening of this date, as we had got intelligence of a Dutch admiral in the Mars of sixty guns, and twenty-six sail of merchant ships under his convoy, having sailed the night before our arrival, the admiral despatched Captain Reynolds, of the Monarch, with the Panther and Sybil, in pursuit of them, who fell in with them on the 4th, and brought the Dutch admiral to action, and captured him with all his convoy. Unluckily the Dutch admiral was killed with six more, and fifteen wounded; the Monarch had only two men slightly wounded.

February the 6th.—The convoy is now in sight and several at anchor. As the Monarch is at sea and Captain Reynolds will not have it in his power to inform Mrs. Reynolds of his health, I beg you will inform her of his being well. The Alcide, Resolution, and Convert were sent to capture St. Martin and garrison it. This morning we have intelligence of that service being performed and our troops in possession; there were very few vessels there. I sincerely wish to get our fleet to windward again, as we only left Admiral Drake with six sail of the line, one of them not in a good condition; those are the Russell, Triumph, Centaur, Ajax, Vigilant, and Montagu, with the Thetis. We brought with us the Sandwich, Barfleur, Gibraltar, Alcide, Monarch, Invincible, Princessa, Prince William, Terrible, Torbay, Shrewsbury, Resolution, Belliqueux, Alfred; Convert and Sybil, frigates, two fireships, two bombs, and the bomb tenders. The latter detained us much; but as usual providence stood our friend, and although time was lost, yet no discovery was made of our hostile intentions at St. Eustatius or any of our own islands.

I have much to say to you on different cases respecting the public service, but must defer it until a more leisure moment. God preserve you!

WAL. YOUNG.

Sandwich. 8th February, 1781.

I have your favour by the Scourge, and am much obliged to you for your attention to my little family. I wrote you by the Hornet and informed you of Captain Gambier not being with us; we promise so many that it is impossible for a modest man to gain his point, and as we may probably have occasion for writers, Captain Thompson,[1] of the Hyena, succeeded. We have likewise got a Salem, *alias* Mr. Miles, who will come in play soon; at present he is agent victualler at St. Lucia. You will see what has been done respecting the Dutch business by my last, and I hope we shall be able to put some other scheme in practice as soon as our frigates join us; unfortunately they were all ordered on a particular service. The Swallow is now under sail, and I must finish with assuring you that I am . . .

Sandwich: St. Eustatius Road. 13th February, 1781.

My dear Sir,—I am still more and more embarrassed with public business. This place is filled beyond description, and how or when we shall be able to transport the whole of its traffic, the convoy and shipping, I know not. I am exceeding happy in having got Sir Samuel Hood to windward,[2] with ten sail of the line and frigates, who is to be joined by Admiral Drake with six sail of the line from St. Lucia, in order to cruize to windward of Martinique to intercept the French

[1] Edward, commonly known as 'Poet' Thompson.—*D.N.B.*

[2] So Rodney wrote on March 6th (cf. Mundy, *Life of Rodney*, ii. 42); but within three weeks he changed his mind; ordered Hood to keep a station off Fort Royal Bay, and persisted—notwithstanding Hood's remonstrances—in keeping him to leeward (*ibid.* pp. 65, 83, 85). The result, when the French fleet arrived, was little less than disastrous.

squadron of eight or ten sail of the line and a convoy; we have received intelligence of them by a small vessel which Captain Linzee[1] of the Sta. Monica has sent to us, who saw them on the 31st of December in the latitude 45° 52′ and longitude of 10° 54′, about 54 leagues distance from Cape Finisterre, steering WSW. I trust in God Sir Samuel will [be] up in time to intercept them. If he is fortunate, our campaign will not be considerable, and we shall then have it in our power to crush the trade of our enemies.

We have only one mast, a fore one, for a seventy-four in this country; I am very sure you will feel for our losses here and that at Jamaica, and how you will be able to supply us both, I know not. I wish Sir Peter would live where all commanding officers should. It most certainly would be of use, and I see nothing that he has left to do but to send the dismasted ships home under jury masts.

The Dutch ships laden here will sail in a month or less, under the Vigilant, the Dutch sixty-gun ship, and probably another of the line and a frigate. This convoy should be met at sea, on account of its immense riches. I have advised the admiral to direct the route, and inform my Lord Sandwich where our cruizers may meet them, in order to protect them.

The Marquis de Bouillé was much embarrassed about our destination. He drew from Martinique five hundred troops, and went with them in person to Grenada upon a supposition that we were going there; and from what we learn from a lieutenant of ours, who was in a cartel at that time in Martinique, that had we had a small army, that great island

[1] John Linzee, brother-in-law of Sir Samuel (afterwards Lord) Hood, a captain of 1777. According to Schomberg, he resigned his commission in 1790.

might have been captured at a very small loss. The four sail of the line who lay in Fort Royal Bay warped close under the batteries, had springs on their cables, and were apprehensive that we intended to cut them out. Such was their expectations.

I am at a loss to think what will be the consequences attending this capture. The merchants of all countries who have traded hither must be ruined. Indeed if their properties, meaning the English, should be returned to them, they must lose considerably by plunder, which it is not in our power to prevent, for want of discipline. It is almost general, both by sea and land ; I am sorry to see it ; but as every man in our service has his mode, we must eternally continue irregular; it answers no purpose for an officer to punish for practices of this kind without the whole follows the same plan.[1]

We have not found the quantity of naval stores that I expected. I suppose their stock was transported to Martinique immediately after the hurricane, for which reason I hope you will give us your attention. . . .

Sandwich: [St. Eustatius.] 3rd March, 1781.

I have been favoured with yours by the packet. In my former letter I gave an account of the surrender of this place. We might have done more; very little force would have been adequate to capturing Curaçao; that is now totally given over, and left for other people to take possession of. Since the capture of this island thirteen sail of American vessels have fallen into our hands, principally laden with tobacco and lumber. I find from my correspondents at home that you have got a

[1] On this want of discipline and want of method, cf. Kempenfelt, *post*, pp. 304–12.

pipe of madeira which was not intended for you, as I kept your pipe on board the Sandwich and had it cased as you directed; but a store I suppose will be agreeable to you, and shall keep the other for you until the ship comes home, which must take place at the end of the campaign, as she is extremely leaky.

I find I have not been sufficiently explicit respecting my good friend Sir H. Rest assured that he has been concerned with Wilkinson's house in the transports, as I am certain that, when he was at the admiralty, he constantly sent for Wilkinson, and gave him notice that transports and all other vessels for government's service were wanted; so that Mr. Wilkinson, having his intelligence a week previous to the navy board's being acquainted with the matter, he not only availed himself of this for their mutual advantage, but the people in trade were acquainted therewith—I mean such as the broker meant to serve. Another still more striking instance of their connection was that when the officers of Deptford Yard cast a vessel for her defects or being unfit for that service, private letters were sent from him, and, I believe, from a gentleman who sits on your right, to have the vessel's name changed and resurveyed. The agent house and the house of Wilkinson have large transactions in money matters; I am likewise apprehensive they are concerned. I would therefore recommend it to you never to suffer a resurvey, but to support the officers in their casting the unfit transports.

The letters for Captain Gambier, and your nephew's time shall be taken care of. I am exceedingly obliged to you and my friends at the board for their attention to my recommendation in providing for Mr. Knight and Mr. Gray.

We have lately met with an unlucky accident by the ship who came from Halifax with masts and spars. She got on shore on Goat Island, Barbuda, but luckily beat over the reef of rocks and got close into shore; the whole of her cargo will be saved, but an additional expense will attend it.

I have spoke to Sir George about Lord Colville's son, who I shall get appointed to the Terrible, where I have had him acting lieutenant for some time.

We have found an immense quantity of cordage, canvas, and naval stores at this place, and are sending it up to English Harbour as fast as possible, which will be of use to you at home, and give time to replenish your magazines.

I congratulate you on the marriage of your daughter,[1] and I am, . . .

Memorandum: in Middleton's Writing.

[*Endorsed*: Account sent me of the English and French fleets off Tobago.]

The fleet has experienced a loss in Captain Young's death,[2] for I believe there is not another man breathing so calculated to control and guide to fame a character that Nature never intended should be either a hero or man of business. By the papers which have come to our hands from England, I am sure there is not a man in the fleet but what is at a loss whether to give way to concern or ridicule at the infatuation of his country. We are so convinced that so little has been done when so much might have been done, and what has been done so badly done, that all praise is too bad to be laughed at. Instead of that profound secrecy and rapid

[1] Diana, Middleton's only child, married, 20th Dec. 1780, to Gerard Noel Edwards, afterwards Sir Gerard Noel Noel. *Cf.* Peerage, *s.n.* Gainsborough.

[2] Died 2nd May, 1781.

attack of the important St. Eustatius, if we had not been the most lucky people in the world we should not have taken it. It was known to every sailor in the fleet previous to our departure from St. Lucia, that St. Eustatius was the object. Three days were lost in preparing scaling ladders, towing useless bombs and fireships, to attack a place that might have been taken by two frigates; in which time a large convoy sailed. You may judge of the puffing incorrectness in the 'Gazette' when I tell you that instead of 3,000,000*l.* sterling, the whole amount will not exceed 500,000*l.* Curaçao, that ought to have been taken the same day, and for which service Sir S. H. offered himself, remains still to be taken, though they were not informed of the war for six weeks after the capture of St. Eustatius. We are now just returned from an unsuccessful attempt to relieve Tobago, which has surrendered at discretion. Tidings arrived that the island was threatened by three or four ships of the line and some frigates. Tuesday, Admiral Drake sailed with six sail of the line for its relief, fell in with the whole French fleet, and returned the Saturday following, 2nd June. Sunday, the 3rd, Sir G[eorge] weighed with twenty sail of the line and five frigates, and stood with a press of sail for Tobago.

Monday evening, being within five or six leagues of the island, a small schooner was sent on shore, and returned next morning with an account of the island's being taken; the same morning the Barfleur made the signal for seeing the French fleet to leeward. Soon after the British fleet tacked and edged down towards the enemy, who I think was not more than twenty-two sail of the line and one fifty, with four frigates. The signal was made to prepare for battle, still standing on with the starboard tack with all sail set, the enemy keeping their wind on the same tack in a scattered line. Evening closed in; the enemy about three leagues upon our lee quarter, fine light night, topgallant fresh breeze. At eight, the enemy made signals with rockets and guns, and soon after we lost sight of them.

Saturday, 9th, anchored in Carlisle Bay, Barbados; thank God all alive. The loss of Tobago—our returning without a fight—makes some little rumpus in this part of the world. There be some who say the whole fleet should have sailed the moment the first intelligence was received, by which we might have taken their detachment and saved the island; others that we never shall have such another opportunity (being to windward) of attacking them.

I send you facts and dates. Those who have any knowledge of sea matters may judge.

CAPTAIN FREDERICK MAITLAND[1] *TO MIDDLETON*

Elizabeth: Gros Islet Bay, St. Lucia. 5th July, 1780.

Dear Middleton,—I have been favoured with your three letters within these few days, in the last of which you take notice of the reports spread to my prejudice.[2] From what you have said, I have taken every method I can to find out the author of that anonymous letter, hitherto without effect. I have consulted several of my friends here (Admiral Rowley, George Balfour, &c.), and they are of opinion I can do nothing more than I have already done. I then went to Sir George Rodney, shewed him the letter, and informed him that I was much hurt by having my conduct represented in such a light. He declared he never had seen it before, and disapproved very much of that part of it that I took notice of concerned me; said he did not blame any person, or rather captain; but that he only declared he thought he had not been properly supported by people of higher rank in the service, by extending the line and not obeying signals. The captains (he said) were obliged to obey their admirals' signals, and he had said nothing against any individual but

[1] A younger son of Charles, 6th Earl of Lauderdale, a captain of 1759. In the action of 17th April, 1780, he had the misfortune to be, in the Elizabeth, one of the seconds to Rear-Admiral Hyde Parker, with whose conduct Rodney was greatly dissatisfied.

[2] *Cf. ante*, p. 71.

the one he had confined,[1] and seemed to be sorry that the letter gave me so much uneasiness. The captain of the packet coming in with letters, and some other gentlemen at the same time, I took my leave and said I would wait upon him again; he replied that he would be very happy to see me at any time. I told George Balfour what I had done, and he said there could be nothing more done. Old Parker is gone home with the convoy; I expect no favourable report from him.

I was so bad of a nervous fever at Barbados, the ship left me behind three weeks ago, and I only returned two days since, upon hearing that the French and Spaniards intended an attack upon this island, although I am yet very weak. We have ships looking into Martinique every day; they have from thirty to thirty-three sail of the line; we, now twenty-three; hope soon to have more, when I suppose we shall pay them a visit, if they do not come to us.

I should certainly have insisted upon a court-martial if Parker had not gone home, as you seem to think that the best method. My station was a cable's length ahead of Parker; instead of which, by Carkett's going on, I was a mile ahead, and Uvedale[2] as far ahead of me. Carkett and he had the three headmost ships, and I the next two, the headmost one of which was the French vice or rear admiral[3]—he had a blue flag with a white cross at

[1] Captain Bateman of the Yarmouth; but the statement is incorrect; for Rodney severely reprimanded Captain Carkett of the Stirling Castle and tried the officer in command of the Montagu—Lieut. Appleby, the captain being wounded—by court-martial.—See Appendix A.

[2] Captain of the Ajax. According to Troude and Chevalier the three headmost ships of the French line were Hercule, Artésien, Sphinx, all of 74 guns.

[3] Robuste 74, Comte de Grasse, Chef d'Escadre. After the battle of Ushant (27 July, 1778) D'Orvilliers reported that in

the main topmast head,—and his second [1] astern, a 64 or 74; Admiral Parker had but one ship opposed to the Princess Royal, Albion and Terrible, (I do not mean to insinuate, that it was their fault, but they were so situated). There was a mile distance, between the French admiral and his second ahead, which was the third ship in their line. When they began to fire, I was near abreast of the ship astern of the French admiral, and I kept on till I got upon that ship's bow and a little abaft the French admiral's beam. I was then engaged with both, as our admiral [2] was so far astern; and [there being] such a distance between the French admiral and the ship ahead of them, I thought it my duty to endeavour to keep as near between these two ships as possible, until more of our ships came up. I accordingly shortened and made sail, as near as I could with the French admiral, by shortening or making sail as he did.

When the ship [3] abreast of the three [4] ships astern of me bore up, the ships abreast [5] of me made a little more sail, by filling their mizen top sails, &c. I did the same as soon as possible. At this time our admiral, who had shot up within half a mile, had got his main topsail lowered, made my signal to make more sail; which I immediately did, by loosing the main sail and setting it; our jib and fore topmast stays were cut, and main top gallant stay; all the other sails were set, and we should soon have

action, when the ensign was obscured in the smoke, the blue flags of command of the rear squadron were liable to be, and actually had been, mistaken for the corresponding blue English flags. They were consequently ordered to be charged with a white cross; 'et cela s'observa durant toute la guerre d'Amérique.'—Rey, *Histoire du Drapeau*, ii. 579.

[1] Magnifique 74. [2] Parker. [3] Triton.

[4] Princess Royal (flag), Albion, Terrible.

[5] Robuste (flag), Magnifique.

passed the two French ships, but in ten minutes the sternmost of the two bore up, right before the wind, and his admiral soon followed him. Upon the last ship bearing up, when a little upon my bow, we luffed up to rake him, and then bore up to endeavour to cut off the three headmost ships, who likewise bore away right before the wind. Admiral Parker at first bore after me, but soon hauled his wind again, and either repeated the signal for the line a cable's length asunder, by firing a gun, or made it afresh if the signal was hauled down before; upon which I was obliged to haul up and get into my station ahead of him. Uvedale's signal was made that he was out of his station, because he did not immediately haul up. The ship astern of the French admiral seemed to be much disabled when she bore away, and no other ship fired a gun at either of the two. I forgot to tell you, the two ships were under their topsails and fore sail; sometimes their mizen top sail aback, and sometimes the French admiral's main top sail aback. Soon after hauling up, Admiral Parker made the signal to tack, and we joined the centre which was at some distance astern.

This is as near the state of the case as possible, as I can very well remember every motion, and can prove every part of it. Sir George blames Admiral Parker for going too far ahead, and I mentioned to several of my officers I thought that was the case, before we began to engage. Every officer in the fleet disapproves much of Sir George Rodney's letter and they think he has injured every one of them. Since writing the above, I have been informed by some here that the anonymous letter was wrote by one Ramsay,[1] who was on board of the Sandwich in the action, and is now at St. Kitts; if

[1] The chaplain, friend of Middleton's; though presumably Maitland did not know this. Cf. *ante*, p. 46.

so, he deserves to have his gown tore off his back; but this is not certain.

I have taken the liberty to enclose a letter to Mrs. Maitland, as she thought her last one had been opened; and after you have done with this, you will be so kind as [to] send her the account of my situation, as I have described it to you, as I have not been any way particular in her letter. I think I wrote you when at Barbados, by the Cerberus, of our two last skirmishes. We had very little action there, both times, as it was the van that suffered most, and our division was in the rear.

Since writing the above, I have considered that anonymous letter more particularly, in which he says, the Ajax, Terrible, Princess Royal, Albion, Grafton, &c., put the enemy's van in disorder. As for the Ajax, she was certainly ahead with the Stirling Castle; the Princess Royal and Albion had but one ship and the Terrible no one at all opposed to her in the line, which may be seen by her having no men either killed or wounded. At the same time I do not mean that the captain was to blame; it was owing to his situation in the fleet; but it shows what a scoundrel the fellow is. I cannot recollect any reason why he should say I hauled out of the line, as I always had Uvedale and Carkett open upon my weather bow; only, when the French admiral bore away before the wind—he was a little upon my lee bow at that time—I then luffed up to bring my whole broadside to bear upon his stern, and then bore up immediately again, to cut off the three ships ahead. He likewise takes notice that the Princess Royal bore down to assist the Sandwich, &c., which was never the case till we all tacked and joined the centre, as I informed you in the former part of this letter.

Everybody seems to be writing to their friends

upon this occasion, and some may to the admiralty, but I write to none but you, as I never had the honour to correspond with any at that board except Lord Sandwich, and that only upon business of the service. If you find any part of my letter proper to be communicated to his lordship, or any other way, I give you full authority, as I am certain you are a proper judge and will do nothing that may do hurt. We have now got accounts of the French and Spanish fleet having sailed from Martinique with the Spanish transports, but have not yet learned where; about 33 sail of the line, &c.

9th July; 10 at night.

I am one of five sail going to-morrow under the command of Commodore Drake. We expect Walsingham every day, when we shall certainly follow the French, though we shall still be inferior, if in conjunction with the Spaniards.

I beg you will make my most respectful compliments to Mrs. Middleton, Miss Dy,[1] and Mrs. Bouverie, and believe me to be, dear Middleton,

Yours most sincerely,

F. M.

Elizabeth: Jamaica. 11th August, 1780.

Dear Middleton,—Since my last letter to you by the packet which we left with Sir George Rodney, I have nothing new, only the Spaniards have left the French at the Cape,[2] 27 sail of the line strong, but I suppose they will not continue long there. I have the pleasure to inform you, the Elizabeth is one of the ships that is to come home with the convoy.

[1] Diana Middleton.

[2] Cape Français, now Cape Haytien; the capital and seat of government of the French part of Hayti.

In my former letter, I endeavoured to explain my situation to you in our first action; it is therefore unnecessary to repeat it again; I shall only say in this they do me great injustice that suppose I hauled out the line, or kept back more than I thought it my duty as a good officer. When the signal was made to bear down and close the enemy, both the French vice-admiral[1] and his second astern was rather before my beam, for which reason I could not go in a direct line down, as they were going on, or I should have fallen in with and engaged the only ship that the three ships astern of me had to engage (viz. the Princess Royal, Albion and Terrible), and the two ships[2] ahead must have had five;[3] instead of which, I engaged the French vice-admiral[4] and his second[5] astern, and was upon the admiral's quarter and [the] other ship's[5] bow and beam all the time, till that French ship[5] bore up; but I have already informed you in my former letter, as near as I could. At the time I began to edge down, the enemy began to fire and we soon returned it; and from that time till the French ship[6] bore away from the three ships astern, I do not remember taking any notice of them, as my attention was mostly taken up with the ships I engaged and those ahead.

By my first edging away it brought the Princess Royal upon my lee quarter; and from the smoke, &c., I saw no more of her till she had shot up nearer us. At this time, Admiral Parker made my signal to make more sail; upon which I loosed my main

[1] De Grasse was third in command, as was denoted by his flag—blue with a white cross; but the French line was reversed, and he thus commanded the van.

[2] Stirling Castle and Ajax.

[3] Hercule, Artésien, Sphinx, Robuste, Magnifique.

[4] Robuste. [5] Magnifique. [6] Triton.

sail and set it (which was before bunted) and should soon have passed the French admiral, as I outsailed him before ; but his second [1] soon after bore up, and he afterwards followed. I informed you in my former letter, the French admiral, by filling his mizen topsail quickly, had got a little upon my bow, and when he bore away, I luffed up, to bring our whole broadside to bear on him, and immediately bore up to cut off their three headmost ships, as I informed you before. As for Carkett and Uvedale, they were ahead, and I am told by Carkett, Uvedale was upon his weather quarter ; a good part of the time he could not fight great part of his foremost guns. Carkett hailed him several times to shorten sail. I do not mean any ill to Uvedale, but it shews he did not do his duty better than other people, and yet a partiality shown.[2]

I hope to hear from you upon my arrival at Portsmouth. I beg my best respects to your good family ; may God bless you ;

And believe me to be sincerely yours,

F. M.

[1] Magnifique.

[2] To Mr. Stephens, Rodney wrote that Captain Uvedale's state of health did not permit him to remain on the station, and he was therefore sending him home with the despatches, in company with Captain Bazely of the Pegasus; but there can be little difficulty in using his name and that of the Ajax to fill in the blanks left by General Mundy in Rodney's letter to his wife (*Life of Lord Rodney*, i. 289; ii. 378). Uvedale, who was a captain of 1760, had no further service, and was superannuated in 1787.

SIR SAMUEL HOOD TO MIDDLETON

Barfleur: forty leagues S. from St. Eustatius.
4th May, 1781.

My dear Sir,—I have had a distant action with a French squadron, under the command of the Count de Grasse, consisting of twenty-three sail of the line to my eighteen. My utmost endeavours were ineffectual for getting nearer; I therefore invited the enemy to come to me by putting the squadron under their topsails; and though I am conscious of no one omission, and of having done everything that was in my power for the support of the honour of the British flag, which I flatter myself will be readily acknowledged by Rear-Admiral Drake and every captain and officer under my command, yet my mind is not quite at ease, fearing an attack may be made upon St. Lucia before I can get there. I never once lost sight of getting to windward, and tried every method, but it was totally impossible; and though the French admiral had so great a superiority and his choice of distance, he has not, I thank God, no one advantage to boast. The Count de Grasse was in the Bretagne,[1] and brought with him three of eighty guns and the rest seventy-fours, except one. I trouble you with an exact similar detail I gave to Sir George Rodney, and I own to you I am not a little proud of my

[1] De Grasse had his flag in the Ville de Paris. The Bretagne was not in the West Indies during the whole war.

conduct while in sight of the enemy's fleet, whatever may be thought of it in England. I congratulate you on your daughter's marriage; beg my best compliments to Mrs. Middleton, and that you will believe me, with great regard and esteem, my dear sir, your very faithful and obedient humble servant,

SAM. HOOD.

Enclosure

Hood to Sir George Rodney [1]

Barfleur: at sea, 40 leagues South from Eustatius.
[*Copy. Signed.*] 4th May, 1781.

Sir,—At 7 A.M. on Saturday, the 28th of last month, his Majesty's ship Amazon, being to windward of Point Salines, discovered a very large fleet; and at 9 her signal of it was repeated to me by the Russell, which ship I had just ordered to St. Lucia, having one hundred and thirty sick on board, and she came back again to me. I immediately made the signal for a general chase to the SE, in order to bring all the ships up to the windward, and at 10 I formed the line ahead at 2 cables' lengths asunder. On opening Rock Diamond, saw nothing of the fleet but from the masthead, which were then upon a wind to the southward. Captain Finch [2] very properly, so soon as he saw his signal repeated, stood back to reconnoitre the fleet. At 12 he returned near enough for me to see his signal for an enemy of superior force; and upon my desiring to know how many ships of the line

[1] The bulk of this letter was published in the *Gazette*, and a paraphrase of it is given by Beatson (v. 179 *seq.*); but most readers will prefer Hood's nervous, though often inaccurate, language to the platitudes of a pamphleteer.

[2] The Hon. Seymour Finch, captain of 13th February, 1781; died 1794.

there were, he answered, nineteen. A little before two Captain Finch came on board and informed me that he saw 19 sail of the line very distinctly, and two others of two decks, that he thought were armed *en flûte*; the number of frigates he could not ascertain, as three only were drawn out from the convoy; that the convoy was very numerous, and the whole standing to the northward; which was the situation we saw part of them in at sunset from the masthead, most of them being to the northward of Point Salines. I sent Captain Finch immediately to tell Rear-Admiral Drake I desired to see him. Upon his coming on board, I told him I should continue the line ahead, and get to windward as much as I could, by carrying all my plain sail, and be close in with Fort Royal at daylight, as it was uncertain which way the enemy would come; which he was pleased to say was the best I could do.

I ordered Captain Finch to windward again, to endeavour to get sight of the enemy, and upon distinctly seeing them, to make certain signals I gave him, that I might know whether they were upon the starboard or larboard tack, or coming before the wind. Just after sunset I tacked the squadron all together, stood to the northward, and kept close in with Fort Royal all night.

I saw nothing of the enemy or Amazon at daylight. A little before 9 the Amazon joined me; the enemy, then in sight, coming down between Point Salines and the Diamond Rock. Made the signal for a close line, and to prepare for action. At 9 the enemy appeared forming the line of battle; 20 minutes past 9 the Prince William joined me from Gros Islet Bay; and as I sent for her but the night before, Captain Douglas's[1] exertion must have been

[1] Stair Douglas, a captain of 1762. Died, 1789.

great, and does him much credit, to be with me so soon, having the greatest part of his crew to collect in the night. 27 minutes past 9 hoisted our colours, as did the French admiral and his fleet. At 15 minutes past 10 made the Shrewsbury's signal to alter her course to windward, she being the leading ship; but soon perceived the wind had shifted, and that she was as close to the wind as she could lay. At 35 minutes past 10 tacked the squadron all together, the van of the enemy being almost abreast of our centre, and at 11 began to fire, which I took no notice of. At this time the ships in Fort Royal Bay slipped their cables and got under sail. At 20 minutes past 11 tacked the squadron all together, and repeated the signal for a close order of battle; at 25 minutes past 11, finding the enemy's shot go over us, hoisted the signal for engaging, and in passing, our van and the enemy's rear exchanged some broadsides; at 40 minutes past 11 the enemy tacked; at 45 minutes past 11 made the signal for the rear to close the centre; at 55 minutes past 11, finding it impossible to get up to the enemy's fleet, I invited it to come to me by bringing the squadron to under their topsails.

At half-past 12 the French admiral, in the Bretagne,[1] began to fire at the Barfleur, which was immediately returned, and the action became general, but at too great a distance; and I believe never was more powder and shot thrown away in one day before, but it was with Monsieur de Grasse the option of distance lay, and he preferred that of long shot. It was not possible for me to go nearer. At 1 I made the signal for the van to fill, the French admiral having filled and drawing ahead; at 17 minutes past one made the Shrewsbury's signal (the

[1] In error for the Ville de Paris.

leading ship) to make more sail, and set the top-gallant sails; at 34 minutes past one repeated the signal for a close line of battle; and finding not one in ten of the enemy's shot reached us, I ceased firing. The enemy did the same soon after; but their van and ours, being somewhat nearer, continued to engage; and though the French admiral had ten sail astern of him and three others to windward, he was backward in making a nearer approach. The merchant ships at this time were hauling in close under the land, attended by two ships of two decks, supposed to be armed *en flûte*, and two frigates. At 18 minutes past 3 the firing ceased between our van and that of the enemy. Made the Shrewsbury's signal to make more sail, in order to get to windward of the enemy; at 45 minutes past 4 sent Captain Finch to the Shrewsbury, to order Captain Robinson to keep as near the wind and carry all the sail he could, so as to preserve the line of battle; and to return back along the line, to acquaint every captain of the same. At 57 minutes past 5 the packet going to Antigua, which had kept company with the squadron, came within hail to acquaint me, by order of Rear-Admiral Drake, that the Russell was in great distress, having received several shot between wind and water; that the water was over the platform of the magazine, and gaining upon the pumps, and that three of their guns were dismounted. At 18 minutes past 6 made the Russell's signal to come within hail, which was answered. The enemy's fleet, consisting of 24 sail of the line, at this time about 4 miles to windward.

At half-past seven Captain Sutherland[1] of the Russell came on board, whom I ordered, if he could

[1] Andrew Sutherland, Captain of the Diadem in 1793; he went out to the Mediterranean with Hood, and was appointed Commissioner at Gibraltar in November 1794.

possibly by exertion keep the ship above water, to proceed to St. Eustatius or any other port he could make, and acquaint Sir George Rodney of all that had passed. At 45 minutes past 9 the Lizard came within hail to inform me, by the desire of Captain Sutherland, that he had bore away.

On Monday, April 30th, at daylight, found the van and centre of the squadron separated at some distance from the Barfleur and rear, owing to flattering winds and calms in the night, which would not allow us to keep the Barfleur's head the right way, and she went round and round two or three times, while the other ships had light airs; and finding the enemy's advanced ships steering for our van, made all possible sail towards them and threw out the signal for a close line of battle. The enemy's line a good deal extended and scattered. At 7 the squadron under my command being pretty well formed, the enemy's advanced ships hauled off. At 56 minutes past 7 made the signal for the rear to close the centre, as the enemy seemed to show a disposition to attack it. At 35 minutes past 8, having very light airs of wind, the squadron was thrown nearly into a line abreast; made the signal for continuing in that form, lest by endeavouring to regain the line ahead it might become extended. At 11 made the signal for a line ahead, at two cables' lengths asunder; the wind, backing to the eastward, favoured my forming in that order, the better to receive the enemy, then about 3 miles to windward. At 14 minutes past 11 made the signal for the rear to close the centre. At 12, falling little wind again, and all the ships being thrown into a line abreast, made the signal for a line abreast, to keep the squadron as close together as possible; at 25 minutes past 12, the wind blowing steady at SE, made the signal for a general chase to windward, with a design of weathering the enemy, which I should certainly have succeeded in had the breeze continued; but the wind dying away at 4 I found it impracticable to weather the enemy, and therefore made the signal for a line ahead; and having been informed that the Intrepid made so much water they could scarce keep her free, and that the Centaur was in the same state, owing to the number of shot between wind and water, and that her lower masts were very badly wounded; which, added to the loss of the Russell from the line, and from the knowledge I had of the state of the ships in general, having upwards of 1,500 men sick and short of complement,[1] I judged it improper to dare the enemy to battle any longer, not having the least prospect of beating a fleet of twenty-four sail of the line of capital ships; and knowing the consequence of my being beaten would probably be the loss of all his Majesty's possessions in this country, I thought it my indispensable duty to bear up, and made the signal for it at 8 o'clock. At 10 brought to for the squadron to close; at 40 minutes past 10 made sail.

At 5 A.M., the 1st instant, saw the enemy s fleet astern about 8 or 9 miles distant. At 26 minutes past 5 brought to for the Torbay and Pocahontas to come up, which were within reach of the enemy's guns; and the former received a good deal of damage in her masts and rigging; at 45 minutes past 7 the enemy ceased firing upon the Torbay. Sent the Amazon to tow the Pocahontas up; at 8 made the signal for a close line bearing north and south of each other. At 29 minutes past 12 made the signal and brought to upon the larboard tack, and made the signal for the state and condition of

[1] This important detail was (very properly) not made public at the time, and has not been published since.

the squadron ; the enemy bearing east, standing to the northward. 33 minutes past 3 made the signal for a close line north and south ; at 4 the enemy tacked to the southward, and were standing that way at sunset.

In the evening, though it was almost calm, the main topmast of the Intrepid fell to pieces over the side. At 7 made sail to the northward, it being the opinion of the officers of the squadron acquainted with this country that it was the only way of getting to windward, as the currents run very strong to leeward to the southward of St. Vincent's.

I am very much concerned to acquaint you that Captain Nott of his Majesty's ship Centaur, and her first lieutenant[1] were killed in the action. I put Captain Smith[2] of the Pocahontas to command the Centaur, Lieutenant John Davall Burr to command the Pocahontas, and Mr. George Bowen[3] to be lieutenant of the Centaur. My present intentions are to send the disabled ships to St. Eustatius and to proceed with those in good condition to St. Lucia, if the French should not have made an attack upon it and succeeded; if they have I shall then go to Carlisle Bay, Barbados.

I send the Hon. Captain Finch with this letter, with orders, if he should not find you at St. Eustatius, to proceed to windward of the islands to Barbados, and to put the captains of such of his Majesty's frigates as are cruising which may fall in his way upon their guard. And if you should see fit to stop me from proceeding to windward, Captain Finch will be able to form a pretty clear judgment

[1] James C. Plowden. [2] Edward Tyrell Smith.

[3] Brother of James Bowen, master of the Queen Charlotte on 1st June, 1794, and of Richard Bowen, captain of the Terpsichore, killed at Teneriffe on 24th July, 1797. George died, a captain, in 1817.

where I may be met with from the winds he may have.

I think it very much my duty to say that the zeal and exertion of Rear-Admiral Drake, and the captains, officers, and men I had the honour to command, were such that if Monsieur de Grasse had thought fit to have brought his Majesty's squadron to close action, and it should have pleased God to have given him the victory, I trust he would not have found it an easy one, sickly and short of complement by death as the ships in general are, and great as the superiority of the enemy was against us.

Herewith I transmit an account of the state and condition of the squadron under my command, a list of the killed and wounded, and the defects of the ships materially damaged. Marin and Vaudreuil served under De Grasse, all with their flags at the main topmast-head, and by seeing 24 sail of the line on the evening of the 29th and only 23 at noon, the ships supposed to be armed *en flûte* are probably of the line.

Hood to Middleton

Barfleur : Carlisle Bay, Barbados. 24th June, 1781.

I had the honour of writing you a few lines on the 4th of last month, which you will in all probability receive with this, as Sir George Rodney was so unkind, not to say illiberal, as to forbid anyone's sending a line by the Snake sloop which he sent away express. If no accident befalls the Snake in her passage to England, you will probably ere this know that I had a skirmish on the 29th of April in sight of Fort Royal, with a squadron of twenty-three sail of the line (to my eighteen) under the command of the Count de Grasse, in the Ville de Paris, and not the Bretagne, and the admirals with him were Bougainville and Chabert,[1] and not Marin and Vaudreuil.

In the evening of the day on which I courted the enemy to battle, the Russell was obliged to quit the line in great distress, and to seek her safety as she could; but I remained with seventeen, within three miles to leeward of the enemy, offering to renew the fight till the next night; when finding the Intrepid and Centaur could no longer keep their stations from their leaks, owing to the number of shot holes under water, and that the Shrewsbury, Montagu and Torbay had their lower masts very badly wounded, I judged it right to bear away, and made the signal for it at eight o'clock, and stood to the northward the next night. When I got near to St. Eustatius, I ordered the Intrepid, Torbay and Centaur into that road to repair their damages, and proceeded to windward myself with fourteen sail, as fast as I could, in hopes of being able to reach St. Lucia before the enemy, apprehending they would make an attack upon that island.

Between St. Kitts and Antigua I joined Sir George Rodney on the 11th, and the next day we anchored off the latter island for men and stores, from whence we sailed the 14th at night, and the next day and the following the disabled ships joined, except the Torbay. On the 23rd we arrived here, found St. Lucia had been attacked and the enemy obliged to abandon it, and the Torbay came to us a few days after. On the 26th, at half-past eleven

[1] Bougainville, first a mathematician and lawyer, then a soldier and aide-de-camp to Montcalm at Quebec in 1759, then a captain in the navy, and at this time chef d'escadre; Chabert, captain of the 80-gun ship Saint Esprit, was not a flag officer, though he may have acted as such in the battle.

at night, intelligence was received from Tobago that the island was attacked by nine sail, three of which were supposed to be of the line. On the 28th, in the evening, Rear-Admiral Drake sailed with six ships of the line, three frigates and three smaller vessels; and on the 30th, in the morning, he fell in with twenty-one sail of the line under De Grasse, who made the land at the same hour our ships did. Mr. Drake very wisely retreated as fast as he could, and returned off this bay the 2nd instant at night; and next morning early Sir George Rodney sailed with his whole force (twenty of the line, five frigates and five smaller vessels) determined, as he told everybody, to give the enemy battle wherever he should meet them. Indeed he sent me a very formal message by his captain to that effect just before he sailed.

We made Tobago the next afternoon. At 11 A.M. on the 5th, the signal was made in the Barfleur for fourteen sail in the south-west, and soon after several more were seen, to the number thirty, standing out from Great Courland Bay.[1] At noon the commander-in-chief was informed, by one of the small vessels he sent to reconnoitre and get intelligence, that the island surrendered so soon as Rear-Admiral Drake had retreated from the French fleet. At four in the afternoon we were so near the enemy as plainly to distinguish twenty-four sail of two-decked ships, three frigates and three cutters, standing upon a wind to the northward, the same as we were. At six the enemy were about nine or ten miles directly to leeward of us, in a very irregular and extended line ahead; at eight they made signals by rockets and guns; at eleven we lost sight of them from the Barfleur, and at daylight not one was to be

[1] In Tobago.

seen from the mast head. On the 8th, in the evening, we made Barbados, when Sir George Rodney made the signal for Rear-Admiral Drake and his division to go into port, with three of his own division, and next morning Sir George and the rest of his fleet came to anchor here.

The French fleet got into Fort Royal the 18th, and were there seen on the 22nd—thirty ships of war, twenty-five of which of the line; and the Hector is at Grenada without a head, foremast or mainyard, which were carried away by the César's falling on board of her off Tobago. The Thetis, Santa Monica, Sybil and Scourge sloop very fortunately called off St. Lucia in quest of me, having heard of my action, by which the island was most undoubtedly saved; for four thousand troops were landed and the island invested by twenty-four sail of the line. The Thetis was lost in going into the Carénage, by the over-eagerness and zeal of the pilot to get her in as soon as possible, and to a flaw of wind off the highland.

This will be taken to England by her late commander,[1] but how long it will be first I cannot say; Sir George Rodney very politely made me an offer of the choice of two seventy-fours for him, but the situation of his private affairs and Mrs. Linzee's bad state of health make his going home absolutely necessary. I beg my compliments to Mrs. Middleton, and am, with real truth and regard, my dear Sir . . .

[1] Robert Linzee, Hood's brother-in-law. In 1793 he was in the Mediterranean, as commodore, with Hood.

Rear-Admiral Graves to Sir George Rodney[1]

[*Copy.*] London: off Sandy Hook. 2nd July, 1781.

Vice-Admiral Arbuthnot having obtained leave to return to England, leaving me in the command of the naval force in this country, I have the honour to forward by Lieutenant Delanoe, in the Active brig, his Excellency General Clinton's messenger; also my despatches containing the latest intelligence obtained here, as well as that from Europe. The importance of that obtained here, which was taken from an intercepted post, will show you the apprehensions of a considerable force expected from the French commander-in-chief in the West Indies, in concert with whom Monsieur de Barras seems to act; and will demonstrate how much the fate of the country must depend upon the early intelligence and detachment which may be sent by you hither, upon the first movement of the enemy. I shall most certainly keep the squadron under my command as collected as possible, and so placed as to secure a retreat to New York, where our stand must be made, and will keep cruizers to the southward; we are strong at Charleston and in the Chesapeake, Virginia. The French have the addition of a ship of fifty-four guns. We are for the present weaker by the absence of the Royal Oak, now heaving down at Halifax, in lieu of which the Warwick has arrived, sickly and not yet fit for service. The vice-admiral goes home in the Roebuck. . . .

[1] This, and other copies of letters to or from Hood on the station, must have been enclosed in his letters to Middleton; but it seems better to preserve the natural sequence of the story, and place them here in chronological order.

A. *Hood to Rear-Admiral Graves*

Barfleur: off Cape Henry. 25th August, 1781.

[Printed in *Hood's Letters* (*N.R.S.* iii. 27).]

B. *Rear-Admiral Graves to Sir S. Hood*

[*Copy.*] London: Sandy Hook. 28th August, 1781.

I have this moment received your letter by the Nymphe, acquainting me of your intention in coming here with the fleet under your command. It was not until yesterday that I had any information of your having sailed, which came privately from Lieutenant Delanoe, now prisoner at Philadelphia, taken on his passage to this place.

I very sincerely congratulate you upon your safe arrival. We have as yet no certain intelligence of De Grasse; the accounts say that he was gone to the Havana to join the Spaniards, and expected together upon this coast; a little time will show us. I have sent up for pilots to bring your squadron over the bar, which should be buoyed to render it safe. To anchor without would neither be safe at this season of the year, nor prudent, on account of its being quite exposed to an enemy as well as to the violence of the sea.

De Barras's squadron was still at Rhode Island by our last accounts, ready for sea; they had embargoed everything and disembarked the prisoners from a cartel ready to come to us. All the American accounts are big with expectation, and the army has lately crossed to the southward of the Hudson, and appear in motion in the Jerseys as if to threaten Staten Island. For my own part, I believe the mountain in labour; only, now that you are come—

My squadron is slender and not yet ready to

move, or I should not hesitate upon your coming over the bar: as we are circumstanced it is a clear point. I meet the general to-day at Denis's, Long Island, upon a consultation.

The Princessa I understand draws twenty-six feet water; it is too much to come over the bar, therefore I have sent up two transports to come down for her guns. Perhaps to put them in the frigates may save time.

Joseph Hunt[1] *to Middleton*

[*Private.*]

Barfleur: Sandy Hook. 29th August, 1781.

Sir,—I have the honour to acquaint you of the arrival of Rear-Admiral Sir Samuel Hood on the coast of America with his Majesty's ships and vessels named in the margin—[Barfleur, Princessa, Alfred, Shrewsbury, Invincible, Monarch, Alcide, Terrible, Centaur, Resolution, Montagu, Ajax, Belliqueux, Intrepid; La Nymphe, Santa Monica, La Fortunée, Sybil; Salamander, Jane.]

The squadron sailed from St. John's Road, Antigua, on the 10th instant, and made the Capes of Virginia on the morning of the 25th without meeting with the least circumstance of moment during the voyage; but on the evening of the 26th one of the advanced ships spoke with a brig from Jamaica, which informed us that on the 28th of July the Count de Grasse, with his whole fleet, consisting of thirty sail of the line, was at the Cape, and that the Jamaica convoy only waited his departure to pursue their voyage to England. From this circumstance we know that, at the above period,

[1] Hood's Secretary, but the letters appear to be quite independent.

no detachment could have been possibly made to this country, which we are taught to expect as a certain event; and therefore, our previous arrival on the coast will operate greatly in our favour, as it will not only effectually enable the commanders-in-chief to counteract the motions of the enemy, but will also allow of their adopting such measures as will be most efficacious towards preventing a junction of their squadrons, which cannot fail to lessen the French interest in the Colonies, and will, in its consequences, prove a decisive blow to the American cause, which, from all accounts, is in a tottering state and verging towards its decline.

The squadron under M. de Barras continues at Rhode Island and consists of the ships named in the margin,

> I have been disappointed in my endeavours to obtain this list, therefore refer you to that sent home by Admiral Arbuthnot after the action, with the addition of a ship of fifty-four guns.

all of which composed Ternay's squadron, and those marked x single bottoms, which cannot fail being in a bad state and must require great repairs. I am therefore apt to conjecture the intention of the enemy was to relieve those ships after having, in conjunction with them, made some great effort in favour of their allies. Our arrival will, I trust, avert the blow; and as, from the state of the French fleet in the West Indies, I imagine they will not venture to detach more than twelve sail (about the number they had coppered), it is very probable we may find ourselves in superior force; and for your better information I have annexed the list of line-of-battle ships in this country.—[London, Robust, Royal Oak, Bedford, America, Europe, Prudent; Adamant, Warwick, Chatham.]

I flatter myself you will find the above state of things tolerably exact, and that it will enable you to form an opinion of our affairs. You may be persuaded, Sir, I shall never neglect an opportunity of conveying you every information I may be possessed of, consistent with the delicacy of my situation. With every sentiment of respect, I have the honour to be, Sir,

Your much obliged

and most obedient, humble servant,

JOS: HUNT.

Barfleur: off the Delaware. 2nd September, 1781.

In addition to the letter I had the honour to write you on the 29th ult., I beg leave to acquaint you that Admiral Graves crossed the bar the 31st, with the ships named in the margin—[London, Royal Oak, Bedford, America, Europe; Adamant]—and formed a junction with our squadron. The same evening the whole fleet put to sea, in hopes of interrupting the expected detachment of the enemy to this coast. I have the honour . . .

JOS: HUNT.

Hood to Rear-Admiral Graves

Barfleur. 13th September, 1781.

[*Copy.* Printed in *N.R.S.* iii. 34, 35.]

Hood to Middleton

Staten Island. 30th September, 1781.

[The same, with a few verbal differences, as the letter to Jackson dated 'Off the Delaware, 16th September,' (*N.R.S.* iii. 28–31). The account of the fatal battle of 5th

September is so interesting that these differences have a more than usual importance. P. 29, line 1, after 'the signal for battle was hoisted' read, 'The van of the enemy was to windward of their centre, and their centre to windward of their rear, pretty considerably.' Line 5: read, 'The London had the signal for close action flying, as well as the signal for the line at half a cable, and lay with her main topsail to the mast, notwithstanding the French ships were pushing on to their van.' Line 15: read, 'On the 6th it was calm, or very light airs the whole day, and in the evening Mr. Drake and I were sent for on board the London.' Line 11 from bottom: 'if possible' is omitted. Two lines lower: 'I fear to be cut off—the enemy's ships there,' omitted. P. 30, line 10: read, 'from the mastheads of the Barfleur.' Line 12: read, 'to write to Mr. Graves or not.' Line 22: read, 'no frigates had been particularly ordered, though we had many with us.' Line 7 from bottom: 'and his brave troops' omitted. Two lines lower: read 'passed by unattended to, and that De Grasse would now bar the entrance against us.' P. 31, line 5, 'alternative was.' The remainder is omitted, and instead we have—]

When the Terrible was in this country last year with Sir George Rodney (and I am persuaded had that admiral led his Majesty's squadron from the West Indies to this coast, the 5th of September would I think have been a most glorious day for Great Britain) she was twice ashore and has been leaky ever since. Those leaks were increased last March by the Alcide running on board of her at sea; and the firing of her guns in action had so affected her, that it was difficult to keep her from sinking in smooth water; and had she met with the least bad weather, or one of her chain pumps had failed, she must inevitably have gone down; and as a gale of wind was daily to be apprehended, all her officers and men with such stores as could be saved were ordered to be taken out and the ship set fire to.

With all good wishes to you and yours, I am, with most perfect regard and esteem . . .

Hood to Rear-Admiral Digby

[*Secret. Autograph Copy.*]

Barfleur: at sea. 31st October, 1781.

My dear Admiral Digby,—As a vast deal may probably depend on my going from this coast as strong as possible, and if I can but get away before De Grasse leaves the Chesapeake, I shall have a good prospect of intercepting whatever part of his fleet [he] may take or detach to Martinique, by cruizing a short time to the eastward and in the latitude of Deseada.

And to prove I have no view of reaping any kind of emolument from the ships of your squadron or depriving you of any, and that my only motive for wishing all your line-of-battle ships to accompany me to the West Indies during the winter months is the good of our royal master's service, I am ready to sign articles equally to share in prize money with you from the day I leave the coast of New York until the 1st of next,[1] or until the ships of your squadron return and make some part of the coast of North America in the spring, as you may most approve. I think it right in me to make this proposition, and it rests with you to accept or reject it; and if what I suggest meets your approbation, will it not be right to give out that your squadron is going to cruize off Rhode Island?

I am ever, with great regard and esteem,
My dear Admiral Digby's
Most sincere and faithful, humble servant,
SAM. HOOD.

[1] So in MS. Name of the month omitted.

Memo. by Rear-Admiral Graves

[*Copy.*] London: at sea. 6th November, 1781.

When the signal for the line of battle ahead is out at the same time with the signal for battle, it is not to be understood that the latter signal shall be rendered ineffectual by a too strict adherence to the former. The signal for the line of battle ahead is to be considered as the line of extension for the fleet, and the respective admirals and captains of the fleet are desired to be attentive not to advance or fall back, so as to intercept the fire of their seconds ahead and astern, but to keep as near the enemy as possible whilst the signal for close action continues out; and to take notice that the line must be preserved parallel to that of the enemy during battle, without regard to a particular point or bearing.

THOS. GRAVES.

[On the dorse of this copy of the Memo., is written in the same hand.]

It is the first time I ever heard it suggested that too strict an adherence could be paid to the line of battle; and if I understand the meaning of the British fleet being to be formed parallel to that of the enemy, it is, that if the enemy's fleet is disorderly and irregularly formed, the British fleet is, in compliment to it, to form irregularly and disorderly also. Now, the direct contrary is my opinion; and I think, in case of disorder and irregularity in the enemy's line, that the British fleet should be as compact as possible, in order to take the critical moment of an advantage opening and offering itself, to make a powerful impression on the most vulnerable part of the enemy. According to Mr. Graves's Memo., any captain may break the line with impunity when he pleases.

Hood to Rear-Admiral Digby

Barfleur: off Sandy Hook. 10th November, 1781.

[*Copy. N.R.S.* iii. 53, 54.]

Hood to Middleton

Barfleur: in Carlisle Bay, Barbados.
11th December, 1781.

On my arrival in this bay I received several letters from Captain Thompson,[1] but nothing he has written to me can induce me to approve his going to England without orders, as he knew I might be hourly expected, the Ranger brig being arrived with letters from me to the governor-general Christie and the senior captain—the latter of which he received—signifying my intentions of hastening with his Majesty's squadron under my command to this island.

I say without orders, as he has none from me to that effect, and I cannot perceive that he had any from Sir George Rodney, even to come from the captured settlements of Demerara, Essequibo, and Berbice committed to his care.

I cannot look upon the petition of the merchants to be any justification to him, and I find only three sail of ships belonging to this island went with him; but even admitting that there was danger to the trading ships remaining in this bay when the king's service required his going away [with] the frigates, the Carénage at St. Lucia was a place of safety for

[1] Edward (commonly distinguished as 'Poet') Thompson. In his absence from his post, the Guiana colonies were recaptured by the French. He was tried by court-martial on the charge of having left his station without orders, but was honourably acquitted.—*D.N.B.*

them; and though when Captain Thompson got to St. Kitts, and found it reported that St. Eustatius was retaken, he quits the idea of going to the relief of Tortola, and being determined, before he went from thence, to go to England, moves off immediately and leaves the trade of Antigua behind him.

It is my duty to state facts as they are represented to me, and it remains with their lordships to determine upon the propriety or impropriety of a captain's going such lengths without orders.

Barfleur: Carlisle Bay. 13th December, 1781.

Ten thousand thanks, my dear Sir Charles, for the very obliging and truly friendly letters you had the goodness to write me in July and August, and cannot express how much I feel myself flattered by your approbation of my conduct on the 29th and 30th of April. I most sincerely congratulate you on the mark of royal favour you have lately received,[1] which I am persuaded is the more acceptable to you on account of Mrs. Edwards—at least, I judge of you by myself.

What a sad event has happened in America! A strange fatality seems to hang over us; for had Mr. Graves have kept all his ships collected and ready, as he promised, he might have been stronger off the Chesapeake by five sail, including the Warwick, Chatham and Assurance; and if Captain Gidoin had not gone into Port Royal with the Torbay and Prince William,[2] contrary to his orders—as he was only to see the Jamaica trade off the island, and then make the best of his way to North America—he might have been at New York as soon as I was. When I got off the Chesapeake

[1] Middleton was created a baronet on 23rd October, 1781.

[2] Having gone in, the two ships were detained by Sir Peter Parker.

on the 25th of August, I despatched a frigate with the letter, marked A,[1] and on my getting off the Neversunk on the 28th at daylight, I received that marked B,[1] which made me very uneasy; and though I was at a great distance I immediately took to my boat and got to Denis's in the afternoon, where I found the general and admiral talking upon a plan of destroying the French squadron in the Chesapeake. They expressed great surprise at seeing me. I told Mr. Graves the motive of my taking so long a row arose from the letter I had received from him that morning, as I could not bring myself to think it right that the squadron under my command should go within the Hook; 'for whether you attend the army to Rhode Island, or seek the enemy at sea, you have no time to lose; every moment is precious.' My arguments prevailed, and he promised to be over the bar next day. That same evening an account was received that De Barras had put to sea with all his ships, as well as transports. On the 31st, in the evening, Mr. Graves came out with the London, Bedford, Royal Oak, Europe, America, and Adamant, having left the Robust and Prudent in the East river; and he had detached the Warwick, Chatham, and Assurance, a little before I appeared, and long after he wrote me the letter marked C.[2]

I arrived here on the 5th, and Captain Inglis having sent away the packet to England the day before with an account of De Grasse's arrival at Martinique—though he knew I might be probably expected every hour, which must greatly alarm at home—I thought it right to make known my arrival as soon as I could, and therefore determined to despatch the first small vessel I could put my finger on; and by a paper you will herewith receive, you

[1] *Ante*, p. 121.

[2] This has not been preserved.

will know everything respecting my situation and the situation of things here.

I will do all I can for the honour and advantage of my king and country; no one can do more. The want of bread is a most serious misfortune, and I fear is not to be remedied till the convoy arrives from England. The conduct of Captain Thompson is most unaccountable in going to England without orders, and taking with him the Amazon, and after receiving the letters I herewith send you, when one of them gave him reason to expect I should be here in a few days. I have stated the circumstances to the admiralty; for whenever an officer under my command departs from the great line of service on the score of private considerations, I shall think it my duty to take notice of him. He is very much belied if he has not been playing strange tricks at Demerara, and has not large concerns in the convoy he brought from thence and was so determined to carry to England, without regard to the king's service. Upon my arrival here I found he had given leave to Captain Curgenven and his lieutenant to go to England to save their lives. I have appointed Lieutenant Dixon to be captain of the Drake, and to Mr. Twysden to be her lieutenant, having first given an order for his passing. The young man cannot be better placed at present, Captain Dixon being a most amiable man and very excellent, in whom Mr. Twysden will see nothing in any part of his conduct that is not worthy of his imitation; but if either you or him has a wish for his being in a frigate by-and-by, I will with pleasure so place him, if the power of doing it should remain with me. By the next packet I will send you his commission and certificate of his passing.

By Captain Taylor, who arrived on the 11th, express from England in the Proserpine, and went on immediately to Jamaica, I find Sir George Rodney is about to return, though by what their lordships' order to me contains, I have no reason to think so; though they do not address me as commander-in-chief.

I perfectly agree with you that most improper purchases have been made upon this station, and shall take care no imputation shall lie against me on that score. We have several vessels here that are not of much use; for if their bottoms are not kept clean they will be liable to be taken; and whenever they go to Antigua their crews desert, and before they can be remanned become foul again. I therefore submit it to your consideration whether it would not be right to send out thin copper for their bottoms; they will then be of very great use; for without small fast-sailing vessels to run from island to island, the service here cannot be carried on in the present situation of things. I shall trouble the board with three lines upon this subject. I write now in great haste, but you shall hear from me again by the packet. . . .

P.S.—Mr. Patterson, whom you recommended to me, has been but eighteen months in the king's service; it is therefore impossible he can be made. If he chooses to be a master, I will make him one; he is a very good man, and I should be glad he was qualified to be a lieutenant.

Enclosure.

Barfleur: in Carlisle Bay, Barbados.
10th December, 1781.

[A full abstract of the letter to Stephens of the same date (*N.R.S.* iii. 48–51).]

Middleton to Hood

[*Very rough draft.*[1] *Endorsed.*]

[14 January, 1782.]

Your favour of the 14th December from Barbados, accompanied by a duplicate of the 30th September off Staten Island, were received the 10th and gave us the pleasure of knowing Barbados continued still in our possession. Your letter and papers relative to the unfortunate skirmish off the Chesapeake did not reach me, and but for those just received I should have been ignorant of many of the circumstances of that day's transaction. Lord Sandwich had communicated to me your opinion on it, but not so fully as to make me understand where the particular error lay. He shewed me at the same time Admiral Graves' private account, and which, not knowing the blunder that had been committed, appeared modest, with very little implication of censure. The not taking possession of the Chesapeake in preference to an action with a superior fleet seemed strange conduct when the object of the expedition was to succour Lord Cornwallis; but, till I received your account and observations, on the tenth, I had not the least idea of your situation and the opportunity missed in consequence of it. This circumstance has been talked of by officers returning from America, but very little known to the public in general. The not doing more was imputed to the inferiority of the English squadron, and, instead of censure, negative praise has accompanied the conduct of that day.

The admiralty will, I am persuaded, continue

[1] Full of erasures, interlineations, and contractions, making it very difficult to read. Such of the erasures as have any meaning, and seem to tell of a thought which it was judged better not to put too plainly, are given in square brackets.

passive on the subject, unless parliament [or the consideration of Lord Cornwallis's capture brings it out,] or Mr. Graves himself brings it forward, and which I do not think probable. I have the pleasure, however, to assure you that your conduct—party excepted—is much commended. The scene you are now in becomes important, but I am afraid will offer no laurels. I told you in my last how little probability there was, at the end of last summer, of Sir George Rodney returning to the West Indies, though I could not give my reasons. We are, however, under the influence of strange politics, and what appears most improbable at one hour is determined on the following one. The force fitting out here is great [but not so much so as I could wish, and I have endeavoured by every means in my power to make it greater], but as usual, will be too late to prevent an attack and too weak to hinder its effect. This [circumstance] error I have endeavoured to expose by every means in my power, and succeeded in part; but there is such a fatality attending on our measures that nothing can effectively prevail. The keeping up an insufficient Western Squadron impoverishes every other service and keeps us inferior everywhere; whereas confining it to two-decked ships and sending all the three-decks to your part of the world [in order to attack the enemy], the enemy, in the execution of this scheme, may be attacked to advantage. But ignorance always produces obstinacy, and the islands must be the sacrifice.

The detention of Sir George Rodney will, unless you can intercept Vaudreuil, will give a [fair] decided opportunity against some of the Leeward Islands, if De Grasse is at liberty to make use of it [in preference to Jamaica]. If he is not, they may continue safe for one year longer; but unless our plan of operations, as prepared here, is much amended, I see no prospect of maintaining them longer.

I must now thank you, which I do very sincerely, for your attention to Mr. Twysden and making him commission. I think he cannot be better than where he is. I observe what you say of Mr. Patterson, and how impossible it is to serve him under such circumstances. His friends have been misinformed, and I shall inform them of it by the first opportunity.

The ships to leeward have orders to join you to windward. While the fleet is entire there is a chance left. That broken, we are undone everywhere.

My best wishes attend you, and I am, with perfect esteem and regard, most faithfully yours.

Hood to Sir George Rodney

[*Copy, signed.*]

Barfleur: Carlisle Bay, Barbados. 14th January, 1782.

The naval force of the French in these seas is, and has been for some weeks past, thirty sail of the line, two fifties and seven frigates, the greatest part of which has been twice off St. Lucia, several days each time, but made no attack; and by a despatch vessel which arrived this morning from St. Kitts I received a letter, dated the 10th, from Governor Shirley, in which he informs me the enemy's fleet, amounting in the whole to upwards of forty sail, were then in sight from the hills, standing in for that island.

His Majesty's force, now here under my command, is twenty of the line, with which I am about to get under sail to seek the enemy, and to do the best I am able for the relief of St. Kitts. My rendezvous is St. John's Road, Antigua, and I am in hopes to be joined by the Prudent in going to that island; she parted with Commodore Affleck, who arrived here from New York on the 12th; had been off English Harbour the day before the commodore called there, and there is reason to fear she returned with a sprung mainmast. The Royal Oak is also in English Harbour, but without a lower mast, so that I have no prospect of any service from her. The Russell sailed from that port a second time with the Whitby armed ship on the 3rd, and I am sorry to find, by the master of the Despatch schooner from St. Kitts, that both sailed from thence on the 9th in the evening, and were standing into Basse-terre Road the next morning, having seen the French fleet, so that there is great reason to fear they will be taken, unless they should immediately bear away to leeward.

Hood to Middleton

[*Holograph.*]

Barfleur: between Deseada and Antigua.
20th January, 1782.

Knowing my situation, my dear Sir Charles, I am sure you will pity me. On the 25th of November . . .

[What follows is, with few exceptions, the same as the letter to Stephens of the same date (*N.R.S.* iii. 59–62); but the following differences may be noted: On p. 60, 'The contractor's agent for victualling his Majesty's navy was without bread, pease, or flour—not a pound of bread was to be got, of which the squadron has been at half allowance for several weeks, has now but fourteen days', and only flour in that proportion;' and goes on, 'If the contractor or his agent—if the fault does not lie with the former—is not made a public example of, government deserves to suffer. I do not know anything of Mr. Blackburn, the contractor, but I have a very bad opinion of his agent at Barbados, Mr. Shirley, who, I fear, is not so good as he should be.' P. 60, line 11 from bottom, after 'attempt to land' add 'but striving to get to windward.' Two lines lower down read, 'Captain Harvey, a very diligent and good officer, who commanded at St. Lucia.' Line 4 from bottom read, 'the Lizard joined me with information that the whole French fleet was gone to leeward, except one ship.' P. 61, line 8, for 'on the 10th' read 'on the 12th.' Bottom line, 'carried to St. Kitts,' add, 'How very unlucky all this!' P. 62, line 18, 'President' should be 'Prudent.' After 'as they may' the present letter continues—]

I am now got round Deseada, as are all the ships, and hope to get good sight of the island and be seen before dark. Herewith you have duplicates of papers I troubled you with by the Ranger brig. I will not close my letter till I have heard from Antigua.

Never was such weather remembered in this country as we have had for several weeks past; every frigate I have sent to sea has returned a mere wreck. Pray send out copper for all the small craft here; they will be otherwise of no sort of service, but, on the contrary, a nuisance. I wrote you fully upon this subject by the Ranger; I have not now time to do it. When the French fleet was at sea I had not a single frigate; all were shifting their masts and rigging. I was obliged to purchase two or three schooners for despatch vessels, to be commanded by a lieutenant with 25 men; and for that purpose they are infinitely better than larger vessels. I have been under the necessity of hiring others; Captain Harvey has been forced to do the same.

The Invincible is in a miserable state and must be sent home soon, or she will be a coffin for all that are in her; but, to do Captain Saxton justice, he says but little about her. Indeed, my dear Sir Charles, all our ships go to ruin for want of caulking, and some method should be hit upon to furnish a hundred caulkers for the use of the fleet; and I am told they are to be got, and those that are good, if government will pay their value (which appears to me no more than reasonable) in case they are killed in action, or from accident in working. Indeed any expense would be amply answered by the great preservation it would be of to the ships. I wish you to consider this matter seriously; the subject requires it.

[The letter ends thus abruptly. It looks as if there ought to be another sheet; but, if so, it is missing.]

Sir Samuel Hood to Major-General Prescott[1]

[*Copy, signed.*]

Barfleur: Basseterre Road, St. Christopher's.
27th January, 1782.

It appears to me of great importance to the king's service to possess a post on shore, and I beg to submit it to your serious consideration. I can land two battalions of marines of 700 each, rank and file; the 69th Regiment of 500 rank and file, which, with the troops in the frigates, including officers, would make a body of 2,400; and you might have as many guns, 12- and 9-pounders, as you please. It would certainly, I should imagine,

[1] Prescott, in the Fortunée frigate, had just arrived from Antigua with the 28th regiment and some companies. It was an addition to England's misfortunes that, at a time so critical, it should have fallen to this man to command the land forces in co-operation with the naval contingent. His incompetence on this occasion was only a prelude to his insolence at Guadeloupe in 1794.—See Tucker's *Memoirs of Earl of Vincent*, i. 124.

make a diversion in favour of Brimstone Hill, and very much distress, puzzle, and embarrass the enemy. The ground where the flag-staff is seems to be a proper spot. I beg your thoughts upon the business, and whether such a post is not to be maintained with the above number of men; but, even admitting it is not, I can see no harm in landing it for a short time, because your retreat can always be secure, which I should take care of, and very much attend to.

If this proposal has not the good fortune to receive your approbation, I shall be inclined to land a party of marines to rout the French from Basseterre, hoist the English flag, and summons the chief magistrates to come to me; they may probably only wait to be called upon to depart from their capitulation with the Count de Grasse and the Marquis de Bouillé.

I have the honour to be, with every sentiment of regard and esteem. . . .

Major-General Prescott to Sir S. Hood

[*Copy, signed.*] Fortunée. 30th January, 1782.

Sir,—Captain Christian has done me the honour to deliver your message. I now think that as the enemy have so completely invested Brimstone Hill that no reinforcement can be thrown in, that the troops that composed the garrison at Antigua are of consequence there. I likewise take the liberty to inform you that there is no post at Nevis that can be possessed, for want of water, artillery, and some cover. If you think proper to keep the flank companies of the 13th regiment until this particular service is over, I hope you will be so good afterwards to land them at Antigua. The weakness of the garrison there, from the very great mortality that prevailed for some months past, makes me request this more earnestly as essential to the king's service.

I beg leave to wish you every success and honour, and to assure you that I am, with very great respect,

Sir, your most obedient and
Most humble servant,
ROBERT PRESCOTT.

Sir Samuel Hood to Major-General Prescott

[*Copy, signed.*]

Barfleur: Basseterre Road, St. Kitts. 30th January, 1782.

Sir,—In all matters respecting the shore, I can only humbly suggest, and readily submit to your better judgment and determination, and as you are of opinion that the taking possession of Nevis can answer no salutary purpose, and your presence with the fleet can be no longer of essential use, from the impossibility there is of throwing in succours to Brimstone Hill; and the king's service making your return to Antigua highly necessary for the protection and defence of that island, I will direct the Captain of the Drake to receive and carry you either to St. John's or English Harbour, as winds and weather will make most convenient, as soon as I can take from her the ordnance stores she has brought from Antigua; and I shall embrace the first favourable opportunity of sending to you the troops you embarked—at least the 28th regiment, if not the two companies of the 13th also.

I have the honour to be, with every sentiment of regard and esteem . . .

Hood to Middleton

Barfleur: Basseterre Road, St. Kitts.
7th February, 1782.

The enclosed copy of a letter I have written home will inform you of my present situation after three brushes with Count de Grasse within these ten days. I am in no fear of the enemy's present force, though it consists of thirty of the line, two fiftys, and seven frigates; but what will become of me, if it is reinforced before Sir George Rodney appears, God knows! What a glorious turn would have been given to the king's affairs here, had Kempenfelt been directed, in case of falling in with the French armament and finding its destination, to have pushed on to Barbados! But it avails not to look back; I will do the best I can, and am confident of being well supported by every captain under my command; but I was a good deal dissatisfied with one or two ships on the 25th, in coming in here, for not paying strict attention to my signals (which were repeated and enforced by Commodore Affleck) for making more sail and closing the centre. Had they done it, not a tenth part of the shot could have been fired to any effect upon the rear by the enemy they did, but we suffered very little.

I daily expect yams from Antigua as a succedaneum for bread. The Antigua troops are got safe back in the Convert and Fortunée. By our seeing thirty two-decked ships one day, and but twenty-nine on another, I suppose two or three are constantly watering at Old Road. Is it not wonderful—though it is no less true—that though I have been here above ten days, I have not received a message or a bit of paper from any person upon the island except Mr. Shirley on Brimstone Hill? We are striving to save people against their inclinations.

The French fleet have fagging business; not a day passes without splitting sails.

Hood to Mr. Philip Stephens [1]

Barfleur: Basseterre Road, St. Christopher's.
7th February, 1782.

[*Copy.*]

My last letter, which I put on shore at Antigua on the 22nd of last month, and will probably accompany this, will fully explain my situation and that of the enemy to that date. The design of the Count de Grasse was most undoubtedly against Barbados, could he have got to windward; but failing of that, owing to strong easterly winds and a lee current, he bent his course to this island.

The moment his views were made known to me, I quitted Carlisle Bay and got off English Harbour with all the haste in my power, where I could only hear of a formidable attack being made upon St. Christopher's, without any certain information either of the enemy's sea or land force. The squadron having then but fourteen days' bread, I anchored in St. John's Road to get what flour I could as a succedaneum for bread; and the Prudent having joined me, I sailed on the 23rd in the evening with twenty-two sail of the line, and was close off the south end of Nevis at daylight next morning, when I directed the squadron to be formed in order of battle with a design of attacking the enemy at anchor, if I saw it practicable to any advantage. But the signal for the line ahead was no sooner thrown out than Rear-Admiral Drake made that for

[1] The matter of this letter is reproduced in Beatson, v. 450 *seq.*

speaking with me and brought to. I did the same, and soon learnt he only repeated the signal of the Alfred in the rear, and that that ship had run on board the Nymphe and almost cut her asunder. It was represented to me, each had received so much damage as to be unable to keep the sea. I immediately ordered a survey on both, and was happy to find the Alfred could be put in a state for present service in the course of the day and following night, but that the Nymphe could not. I therefore shifted the troops she had on board to another frigate, and ordered her to English Harbour, where she arrived safe. This misfortune to the Alfred obliged me to remove her from being the leading ship into the centre of my line, and to place the St. Albans in her room.

That morning the look-out frigate ahead fell in with and took a very large king's cutter of sixteen six-pounders, but seven months old, and commanded by a knight of Malta. She is named L'Espion; she came from Martinique about thirty hours before, and was full of shells and other ordnance stores. In the afternoon the Count de Grasse quitted this road, and kept a few miles to leeward of me the whole night. At daylight we plainly discerned thirty-three sail of the enemy's ships, twenty-nine of which, of two decks, formed in a line ahead. I made every appearance of an attack, which drew the Count de Grasse a little from the shore; and, as I thought I had a fair prospect of gaining the anchorage he left, and well knowing it was the only chance I had of saving the island, if it was to be saved, I pushed for it, and succeeded by having my rear and part of the centre engaged.

The enemy gave a preference to Commodore Affleck; but he kept up so noble a fire, and was so supported by his seconds, Captain Cornwallis and

Lord Robert Manners, that the loss and damages sustained in those ships were very trifling, and they very much preserved the other ships in the rear. The Prudent had the misfortune to have her wheel shot to pieces the first broadside, which occasioned her loss to exceed that of any other ship. Would the event of a battle have determined the fate of the island, I would without hesitation have attacked the enemy, from my knowledge how much was to be expected from an English squadron commanded by men amongst whom is no other contention than who should be most forward in rendering services to his king and country. Herein I placed the utmost confidence, and should not, I fully trust, have been disappointed.

I anchored his Majesty's squadron in a close line ahead; but Commodore Affleck having acquainted me that the Bedford had driven off the bank, I ordered her into the van. Next morning, about eight o'clock, I was attacked from van to rear with the whole force of the enemy (twenty-nine sail) for nearly two hours, without having the least visible impression made upon my line. The French ships then wore and stood off again, and in the afternoon began a second attack upon my centre and rear, with no better success than before; since which the Count de Grasse has kept at a safe distance. Many of the French ships must have suffered very considerably, and the Ville de Paris was upon the heel all the next day, covering her shot-holes. By information from the shore, the French ships have sent to St. Eustatius upwards of 1,000 wounded men.

I think my situation perfectly secure here against the enemy's present force, superior as it is, and am happy to find by a letter I have received from Governor Shirley, that Brimstone Hill, to which his excellency retired, is in the most perfect security. I have not a thought of moving, and think the Count de Grasse will not venture to attack me again, unless he should attempt something by fire vessels, which I am prepared against as much as possible. If therefore Brimstone Hill can hold out, which I have not a doubt of, the Marquis de Bouillé, who landed with 8,000 men upon the island, as well as the Count de Grasse, will, I think, be glad to retire.

When I sent an officer to Brimstone Hill he was accompanied by one from General Prescott (who embarked with the 28th regiment and two companies of the 13th from Antigua, at my request, knowing well Brimstone Hill and every part of the island), who brought the following message from that brave old soldier General Fraser: 'That as he had taken the trouble to come with troops to his assistance, he should doubtless be glad of the honour of seeing him, but that he was in no want of him or his troops.'

Upon my being acquainted with this spirited message from General Fraser, I proposed to General Prescott his taking a post on shore in the vicinity of Basse Terre, and offered to land two battalions of marines of 700 each rank and file, with the 69th regiment, which, with the 28th regiment and the two companies of the 13th, would make a body of 2,400 men. His answer was he did not think it practicable to maintain a post, but was sanguine in his wishes to be put on shore with his Antigua troops and the 69th regiment. They were accordingly landed on the 28th; immediately got into action, and drove the enemy with considerable loss. He remained on shore all night, and next morning the Marquis de Bouillé appeared at the head of upward of 4,000 men; but not caring to attack General Prescott on a hill he possessed just to the eastward of Frigate Bay, where he landed, led his troops back to his encampment under Brimstone Hill; and as it then appeared to me that no solid purpose could be answered by the continuance of our troops on shore, I submitted it to the general's consideration whether it would not be advisable to re-embark; and he readily concurring, all were taken off that evening without the loss of a man. The general had about forty killed and wounded in his skirmish with the Irish Brigade. General Skene landed with the 69th regiment and had his full share in putting the enemy to the rout.

All communication being now cut off with Brimstone Hill, and it being General Prescott's opinion no post could be taken and held on Nevis (which I submitted to the general's consideration), I thought it expedient, as did the general also, to send him and the Antigua troops back, as that island was entirely stripped and defenceless; and they sailed in the Convert and Fortunée on the 1st instant. On that day the Tisiphone joined me, and I immediately dispatched a sloop to Jamaica with the duplicates Captain Saumarez[1] brought from Rear-Admiral Kempenfelt, as I propose the Tisiphone shall return to England with an account of the situation of things here, which I think of importance their lordships should know.

It is impossible for me to think of moving hence at present, with an idea of going to windward of the islands, with De Grasse's fleet (now consisting of thirty two-deck ships) constantly in sight. Not that there would be any difficulty in doing it, but Antigua would in that case become an easy prey. I am sorry to say the king's squadron has but a very few days' bread; and though we make a tolerable shift

[1] The future Lord de Saumarez.

with flour at anchor we should not be able to do so well at sea. I am endeavouring to procure a quantity of yams from Antigua and Anguilla, and have a prospect of succeeding. Surely Sir George Rodney will soon be here. I have impatiently and daily expected him since the middle of last month.

Herewith I send the copy of a letter I left at Barbados for him, also copies of letters between General Prescott and me, my line of battle, and an account of the killed and wounded. I have much pleasure in telling you his Majesty's ships under my command are very immaterially injured in their masts and yards; perfectly healthy, and the people in the highest spirits.

Hood to Middleton

Barfleur: at sea. 23rd February, 1782.

My dear Sir Charles,—

[Virtually the same as the letter to Stephens of 22nd February, printed in *N.R.S.* iii. 89-98, to —— 'Sailed on the 22nd to seek Sir George Rodney at Barbados, get water and a supply of bread from the convoy, which I hope will be arrived.' It then continues—]

The Fortunée and Pegasus, which I left to watch the French fleet, have joined and report that thirty-six sail of the line, six frigates, and upwards of fifty sail of brigs, sloops, and schooners sailed from Basse Terre Road on the 20th in the evening,[1] and 21st in the morning, and steered for Martinique. Captain Christian saw the rear of the enemy's fleet at the same time he saw me, and returned with the Pegasus immediately to watch the enemy's further motions. Never, my dear sir, was a man in

[1] Slight differences in these details.

command in more trying situations than I have been, but, I trust, I have not disgraced the British flag in either, and it is in points of difficulty only an officer can show what he is made of and is equal to. I have had many flattering compliments paid me from all quarters, which has helped me under the great fatigue of body as well as of mind I have laboured. What a melancholy circumstance it is to be labouring to protect men who wish not to be protected, and who for the greater part (I mean the residents of the island only, and not the proprietors of estates living in England) seem to prefer French to English government. It is by the actions of men alone we can judge them.

I am, my dear Sir Charles, with best compliments to Lady Middleton . . .

Mr. Hunt to Middleton

Barfleur: off Point Salines, Martinique.
17th March, 1782.

Sir,—As Captain Cornish will not be enabled to avail himself of this conveyance, I cannot therefore deny myself the pleasure of acquainting you that he is in perfect health, and at present under Sir Samuel Hood's orders on a cruize to windward off Martinique. We sailed from Gros Islet Bay early yesterday morning with his Majesty's ships named in the margin [line of battle: Royal Oak (starboard), Montagu, Prince William, Shrewsbury, Valiant, Barfleur, Monarch, Belliqueux, Warrior, Yarmouth, Arrogant (larboard); Champion, Zebra], all of which are complete to four months of every species of provisions, and equally well off in point of stores, the safe arrival of the Whitby at St. Lucia having furnished the several demands of the squadron.

We left Sir George Rodney with the remainder of the ships in Gros Islet Bay, but as their most material wants had been supplied, and those which stood in need of new masts [Centaur, fore mast; Monarch, bowsprit; Alfred, bowsprit], or other repairs out of the respective artificers' hands, I make no doubt but the whole squadron will be completed and able to put to sea in a state for offensive operation in a week at farthest, which, from the accounts we have received from Martinique, will precede the enemy several days, a circumstance from which the greatest advantages may, and I trust will, accrue.

The state of the French islands in regard to provisions is truly deplorable, and their distress so great that they were under the necessity of sending the cartels with General Fraser, and the garrison of Brimstone Hill to St. Dominica to procure provisions for their voyage to Europe. St. Eustatius, although returned to their hands,[1] no longer proves the *mère nourricière* it once was; the supplies from the Danish islands very precarious and by no means equal to their wants, and from our present superiority of force liable to be entirely cut off; [whilst] such as they used to receive from our own islands, through the treachery of a few individuals, have been in a great measure prevented by the extraordinary vigilance of General Cunningham at Barbados and of the naval department at St. Lucia.

The enemy labouring under this immediate distress, the intercepting of their convoy cannot but be considered as an object of magnitude; and, should we be so fortunate as to succeed, would absolutely reduce many of their islands to famine, independent of the great turn it would give to affairs in this part of the world.

[1] Captured by Bouillé, 26 Nov. 1781. Chevalier, i. 262–3.

The Marquis de Vaudreuil, who brought the Triomphant out to this country, and who, it is said, possesses the most distinguished abilities, will (we are taught to believe) supersede the Count de Grasse in the command of the French fleet. In a little time I shall, however, be able to speak with more precision, and will not fail to communicate to you that, as well as every general information that may come within my knowledge. Captain Curgenven has been returned some days. Sir George Rodney has detained him from going home, with a view, I hope, of giving him rank in this country.[1] General Matthew is embarked on board the Formidable, and people pretend to anticipate——

Sir Samuel Hood has sent his return of appointments to the admiralty, and Mr. Twysden's passing certificate in order to his being confirmed. The first commission he received was dated the 5th December, 1781; but that being prior to the date of his passing order, which was the 8th, it has been altered to that date in the return, as was also the commission transmitted you by Sir Samuel in January last. I very particularly mentioned this to Mr. Twysden himself, and begged of him to inform you of it; but lest he should have forgotten, I have taken the liberty to trouble you on the subject.

Annexed is Sir George Rodney's line of battle. He has already bought two sloops of war into the service, and appointed captains, &c., to them—Sir Charles Douglas's son[2] one of the former.

The line of battle annexed is omitted, being the same as that given by Beatson (vi. 324) and Schomberg (iv. 399), excepting that the Shrewsbury and Intrepid are named in

[1] He was posted to the Prothée on 13th April.

[2] William Henry Douglas, posted on 15th April. On his father's death in 1789, he succeeded to the baronetcy; and died, a vice-admiral, in 1809.

place of Magnificent and Agamemnon. These two had recently come out with Rodney, and were in the line on the 12th April.

Captain Savage, from a slight indisposition, has been prevented making a trial of his scheme for watering the ships, by conveying fresh water into their boats in five-fathom water. If he should succeed, much time and labour will be saved; and it will also prevent the seamen from poisoning themselves with the strong liquors they contrive to get on shore in spite of every precaution.

You will have been informed of the Invincible's being sent to Jamaica to refit. The Intrepid is equally bad, but no determination has yet, I believe, taken place with regard to her. The Convert is ordered to English Harbour. She is indeed in a very bad state, and it will be dangerous to do more than to make her tight and put her in a condition to go home with the summer convoy.

I beg leave, sir, through your medium, to present my respectful compliments to Admiral and Mrs. Gambier, and I have the honour to be

Your most obedient, humble servant,

J. Hunt.

Hood to Middleton

[*Private.*] Barfleur: Gros Islet Bay, St. Lucia.
31st March, 1782.[1]

My dear Sir Charles,—As I feared, foretold, and laboured to prevent, the French armament got safe to Fort Royal by making Deseada and running down

[1] With the exception of the last paragraph this is virtually the same as the letter to Jackson of the same date (*N.R.S.* iii. 95–99). The verbal differences are, however, sometimes suggestive.

between Dominica and Martinique.[1] If I had been asking the greatest boon for myself I could not have been more earnest in my entreaties to Sir George Rodney, upon my return from the Cul de Sac, to divide his force, station one-half off Deseada and the other off Point Salines; but he would not listen to it, said the French always made Point Salines; to the contrary of which I took the liberty of giving him some late instances, and added that admitting there was the greatest probability that the enemy's expected convoy would make Point Salines, and but a bare possibility of its making Deseada, I humbly submitted whether it would not be prudent to guard against that possibility; for allow the armament to come into these seas escorted by fourteen sail of the line, you can have two squadrons of eighteen sail of the line, which will admit of four sail to play upon the transports and storeships and still have ship for ship with the enemy; but I do not think it likely they will come so strong, and the destruction of their transports seems to me an object of the greatest importance. To this Sir George was perfectly silent. On the 8th the February packet arrived, which took a brig from Bordeaux bound to Martinique the day after she was out, and was informed by the prisoners that the armament from Brest was then about to sail; and, as a Dane had arrived here in twenty-nine days from Spithead, I could not help suggesting to Sir George whether the French convoy might not be daily expected. His answer was, oh, no; he was sure it would not sail before March. I gave in to the probability of it, but thought it very possible to happen otherwise; and as the greatest part of his fleet was as ready for sea as they could be till our storeships and

[1] *Cf.* Chevalier, i. p. 288.

victuallers arrived, I expressed my wishes in the strongest manner to be allowed to cruise off Deseada and between that island and Dominica. After receiving three different orders, each making the ships to go with me more or less than the other, I went to sea on the 16th with eleven sail, but I was limited from five to ten leagues to windward of Point Salines. On the next day I spoke with Captain Ford of La Nymphe frigate from Antigua, where a ship was arrived which sailed from Spithead under convoy of the Princess Caroline on the 11th of last month, and parted company the same night in a snowstorm, and on the 14th she was spoken with by the Arethusa, and received written information that he had fallen in with twelve or fourteen sail of the line and six frigates, having under convoy 100 sail of transports and storeships. I despatched the Nymphe to Sir George Rodney without detaining her a moment. On the 20th in the afternoon I saw Sir George to leeward, and at midnight received from him the arrangement No. 1 [1] for the fleet's cruising, and at the same time a private note from Sir George, to which I replied that I rejoiced most exceedingly he had been pleased to extend his ships so far to the northward, for that the commander of the French squadron must be a madman to think of coming in sight of St. Lucia, knowing, as he must, the force of the British fleet, which would naturally be upon the look out; but at 8 A.M. on the 22nd, not more than thirty hours after I got his cruising arrangement, he sent me the letter No. 2,[2] which I trouble you with, to show the unsteadiness of the man; and, as a further proof of it, he did not send Commodore Affleck and the two sixty-fours to the northward

[1] *N.R.S.* iii. p. 99. *Cf. post*, p. 265. [2] *Ibid.* p. 100.

until the 26th, nor do I believe that a single frigate was stationed off Deseada; for the first intelligence Sir George received of the arrival of the French armament in Fort Royal Bay on the 20th was by an English officer, who came from Martinique in a cartel, and got to the Formidable on the 28th. We may from luck (of which we have not hitherto been blessed with a common share) yet do something to retrieve our country's misfortunes, but am afraid we cannot expect it from judgment or by acting upon any rational well digested plan, which the present situation of the king's affairs in this country makes absolutely necessary. Every scheme in my humble opinion should have been had recourse to, and every risk have been encountered for intercepting the Brest armament; having fortunately effected that, the greatest difficulty would have been surmounted; but turn one's eye now which way one will, difficulties, and those in the extreme, stare us full in the face. How Sir George Rodney could bring himself to keep his whole force to guard one path, when half of it was fully equal to the service, and to leave another (which appeared to me the most probable the enemy would take) without any guard at all, is matter of the utmost astonishment to me. I have really fretted myself ill; for nothing short of a miracle can now retrieve the nation's affairs in these seas. On the 28th in the evening I received orders to proceed to this place, and anchored with my division at sunrise next morning. Sir George and his division came in yesterday, but Admiral Drake still remains out, which I am sorry for, and wish he was in also, that the whole might be ready to act together on the spur of a moment; for I cannot see the least service his division can do at sea, beyond that of watching the enemy at Fort Royal, which two or three frigates would do as well; and I think in the present hour no unnecessary risk should be run for crippling a ship of the line, as every one will most assuredly be wanted, and their not being kept all together, with as few wants as possible, may be of the utmost bad consequence. The force of the enemy lately arrived at Martinique is three ships of the line and three frigates with 6,000 troops (every one of which ought now to have been at this port). Four sail of the line parted company with the above, and are gone to the Cape; and five of the line, with 3,000 troops, to the East Indies. All sailed from Brest together the 10th or 11th of last month. Thirteen sail of Spanish ships of the line, with 9,000 troops, are said to rendezvous at Guarico, and are there to be joined by the four French ships lately gone to the Cape, as well as by De Grasse (who has now thirty-three sail of the line in Fort Royal Bay, ready for sea), and the Marquis de Bouillé with the troops from Martinique; all this makes it highly necessary, in my humble opinion, for Sir George to keep his whole force together (after giving a substantial convoy to the regiment, storeships, victuallers, and trade destined to Jamaica, and I think the sooner they are gone the better) in perfect readiness for sea, in order to follow De Grasse the moment he starts. Though I am writing, I know not when an opportunity may offer of sending my letter, but I like to be prepared upon all occasions when I can; though I should not be surprised to find a vessel despatched to England without my knowing anything of it—well acquainted as I am with the commander-in-chief.

In further support of my argument for the fleet's being divided I observed there could be no objection from the Count de Grasse; for should he venture to come out, in whatever force he may, and go to the northward of Martinique, the squadron off Deseada could find no difficulty in making a junction with the southern one; and if he should go out to the southward of Martinique, the squadron off Point Salines could as easily join the northern one; so that nothing dangerous could be apprehended from the enemy at Fort Royal from a division of the British fleet. With every affectionate wish to you and yours . . . .

[*Private.*] Barfleur: Gros Islet Bay, St. Lucia.
3rd April, 1782.

My dear Sir Charles,—Three of Admiral Drake's division having crippled their masts in the night of the 31st past, the whole are now called in, which I very much rejoice at, and hope we shall all be in excellent order for service before the enemy quits Fort Royal.

What Sir George Rodney proposes I cannot say, but from what I hear from those who have the goodness to come to me (for I have been confined to my cabin for some days) he seems to have no plan. He told Admiral Drake yesterday he would go to windward, that De Grasse might not know where he was; and to others, almost in the same breath, that he would push to Jamaica directly. 'Well, but, Sir George,' says a pretty shrewd captain of my division, then present, 'suppose De Grasse should think the force already in the neighbourhood of Jamaica, equal to the conquest of the island, aided by a body of troops he very possibly has sent, or may send, and remains in force at Fort Royal; what will become of all these islands?' His answer was, in his accustomed off-hand strain: 'Oh damn these islands; Jamaica is of ten times more consequence than all of them put together.' His manner of talking is, to be sure, very extravagant and extraordinary, but without much meaning.

What occurs to my mind as most advisable to be done in the present situation of things, is to send away the 14th regiment, storeships, &c., to Jamaica (and would to God they had not been detained here an hour), with five or six sail of the line in addition to the Princess Caroline; go with the rest off Fort Royal; offer Count de Grasse battle, and block him up, if he should not feel bold enough to come out. Sir George calls the force there thirty-six sail of the line, but I reckon upon no more than thirty-three serviceable ships; but admitting it to be thirty-six, I should be very happy to meet the noble Count with a line of battle of thirty-three, had I the honour of commanding his Majesty's fleet. I have had daily apologies from Sir George for his not being able to come to see me; says he will pay his respects the first leisure half-hour he has. When he comes I will openly and candidly express my sentiments to him, if he will give me an opportunity.

Since writing the above, Sir George has been with me above two hours. I never found him more rational, and he gave me very great pleasure by his manner of receiving what I said respecting the future operations of the fleet; and if he does not depart from what he seems now to be perfectly satisfied to be right and proper in our present situation, he will soon be off Fort Royal, with thirty-three or thirty-four of the line, and despatch the rest at the same time to Jamaica as convoy to the 14th regiment, storeships, victuallers and trade destined to that island. But there is, I am sorry to say it, no great reliance to be placed in a man who is so much governed by whim and caprice, even in matters of the highest importance to the welfare of the State.

6th April.—A ship of my division returned last night from off Fort Royal and picked up a canoe with six negro deserters, which were taken on board a frigate in the Chesapeake. One is a sensible, intelligent fellow, who says, that upwards of nine thousand troops are embarked—and that De Grasse is certainly to sail with his whole fleet on the 8th to join the Spaniards for an attack upon Jamaica. If the 14th regiment and five sail of the line were there—which we can very well spare—I should feel very comfortable; for by a vigilant look out (and in Sir George's place I should like to see with my own eyes) I trust we shall bring the enemy to battle. What I most fear is, De Grasse will have a great start of us.

Ever and affectionately yours,

SAMUEL HOOD.

Sir George Rodney to Hood

[*Private.*] Tuesday Evening: 9th April, 1782.

[*Copy.* *N.R.S.* iii. 109.]

Hood to Sir George Rodney

Barfleur: off Dominica.

[*Private.*] 6 A.M., 10th April, 1782.

[*Copy.* *N.R.S.* iii. 110.]

Sir George Rodney to Hood

Formidable. Wed. Eveng. 10th April, 1782.

[*Copy.* *N.R.S.* iii. 111.]

Hood to Rodney

Barfleur. 11th April, 1782.

[*Copy.* *N.R.S.* iii. 112.]

Rodney to Hood

Formidable. 12th April, 7 P.M.

[*Copy.* *N.R.S.* iii. 112.]

Hood to Middleton

[*Private and confidential.*] Barfleur: off Guadeloupe. 13th April,[1] 1782.

Rejoice, my dear Sir Charles, Rejoice, and give God thanks. His Majesty's fleet has given such a beating to that of France, as no great fleet ever had before. On the 9th, my division had two actions, at a short space of time distant one from the other, with the whole of the enemy's van and centre, between the islands of Guadeloupe and Dominica, while the greatest part of our centre and the whole of the van[2] were becalmed under the latter; and had De Grasse known his duty he might have cut us up, by pouring a succession of fresh ships upon us as long as he pleased; but being very roughly handled and to windward, he hauled off, and our fleet joined in the evening. Here Sir George did not show[3] much judgment in separating his fleet. The next morning the French ships were very far to windward. Sir George carried a stiff sail all day, neared them very much by sunset, and intended to have carried a plain sail all night; but by a blunder in Charles Douglas,

[1] A good deal of this letter is repeated in that to Jackson of 16th April (*N.R.S.* iii. 101–108); the differences are interesting, especially in the story of this great day.

[2] So in MS. The letter to Jackson has 'the rear.' It was Drake's division, and Drake was junior to Hood; so that in ordinary course his division was the rear; but on the 12th, which, as he wrote, was very fresh in Hood's mind, it was the van.

[3] In the letter to Jackson the 'not' is omitted—surely by a slip of the pen.

in making the signal for the leading ship to shorten sail, which was under her topsails only with the mizen topsail aback, the fleet lay to the whole night; at least the centre and rear did so; Captain Byron can best tell what the van [1] did, as he was employed the whole night in carrying messages between the chief and third in command. At daylight, only a few of the leewardmost part of the French fleet could be seen from the masthead. We again worked to windward; and next morning, by a most fortunate shift of wind, we could look up to three or four of the enemy's ships, which brought the whole down to succour them, and they formed on the contrary tack to our fleet. Every ship on both sides was engaged. Sir George Rodney cut through the rear of the French line. So [2] soon as my division (which was then the rear one) had passed the sternmost of the enemy's ships—which it was a considerable time in doing, it being almost calm—I perceived the signal for the line was hauled down; upon which I got my boats out, and towed the ship round towards the enemy; made all the sail I could (for we had, immediately after, a little breeze), and threw out the signal for every ship of my division to do the same; and we took the César, Ardent and Ville de Paris. Observing the Ville de Paris to edge towards the Barfleur, I concluded De Grasse had a mind to be my prisoner, as an old acquaintance, and therefore met his wishes by yawing [3] towards him. As soon as I got within random shot he began to fire upon me, which I totally disregarded till I was satisfied by firing a single gun from the

[1] Here the letter to Jackson has also 'van'; but the reference is clearly to Drake's division.

[2] This is Hood's punctuation; and though that is often very wild, in this instance it seems correct.

[3] On the 16th he wrote 'looking.'

quarterdeck that I was fairly[1] within point blank, when I opened such a tremendous fire as he could not stand for more than ten minutes, when he struck.

This was at sunset, and my boat had scarcely got on board, when Sir George made the signal and brought-to, and continued to lay to the whole night.

After the glorious business of yesterday, I was most exceedingly disappointed in and mortified at the commander-in-chief. In the first instance, for not making the signal for a general chase the moment he hauled that down for the line of battle, which was about one o'clock; had he so done, I am confident we should have had twenty sail of the line before dark; instead of that, he pursued only under his topsails, the greatest part of the afternoon, though the flying enemy had all the sail set their very shattered state would allow. In the next, that he did not continue to pursue under that easy sail, so as never to have lost sight of the enemy in the night, which would clearly and most undoubtedly have enabled him to have taken almost every ship this day. But why he should bring to because the Ville de Paris was taken is not to be comprehended.

At sunrise this morning I went on board the Formidable to pay my compliments, and to try, if possible, to remedy the mistake that had been made; and I so far prevailed upon Sir George to leave the ships of his own fleet, which were most disabled, to take care of the prizes and carry them to Jamaica, and to push on in search of the enemy with the rest.

Had I, my dear Sir Charles, have had the honour of commanding his Majesty's noble fleet yesterday, I may, without the imputation of vanity, say, the flag of England should at this hour have

[1] 'Well' on the 16th.

graced the sterns of upwards of twenty sail of the enemy's ships of the line.

I herewith send you a short correspondence between Sir George and me; and had he been my father, brother or the dearest and best friend I had, I could not have proved myself a better second, or have been more open, candid, and sincere in all I have suggested to him, from my zeal and ardour for our royal and most gracious master's service, and my extreme veneration and love for his sacred person, in competition with which, no consideration in the world can ever stand.

I lamented to Sir George this morning that the signal for a general chase was not made when that for the line was hauled down, and that he did not continue to pursue, so as to keep sight of the enemy all night; to which he only answered 'We have done very handsomely.' I could therefore say no more upon the subject. I said the same afterwards to Sir Charles Douglas, upon his paying me compliments upon the conducting my division. His answer was, 'Sir George chose to pursue in a body.' 'Why, Sir Charles,' I replied, 'the signal for a general chase was the best mode of doing it, with proper attention, if it was Sir George Rodney's wish; because, if a ship is too wide upon the starboard wing, you have a signal to make her steer more to port; if a ship is too wide upon the larboard wing, you have a signal to make her keep more to starboard; if a ship is too far ahead, you can, by signal, make her shorten sail; if a ship is astern, and has not all her sail set, you have a signal for her to make more sail; and if Sir George was unwilling to have his ships engage in the night, for fear of their firing into one another, the white flag at the fore topgallant masthead, before dark, calls every ship in, and that signal, followed by the one for the form of sailing, the fleet might have gone on, in sight of the enemy, in the most compact and safe order, for completing the business most gloriously.' Upon which he said not another word and walked off.

So far is pretty much a duplicate of what I wrote you by the Andromache.

April 16th.—My patience, my dear Sir Charles, is now fairly exhausted; for notwithstanding Sir George Rodney seemed most perfectly satisfied, from what I took the liberty of suggesting to him on the morning of the 13th, of the very great propriety of pursuing with all possible eagerness, and gave orders accordingly in my hearing, adding he would wait for nothing, and upon my leaving him made sail, in less than four hours he changed his mind, and brought the fleet to; and here we now are in the same spot, off Guadeloupe. It has indeed been calm some part of the time, but we might now have been above twenty leagues further to the westward.

It is very much to be lamented that Sir Charles Douglas is so very weak, and irresolute; he is no more fit for the station he fills than I am to be an archbishop. In a great fleet, the duty of a first captain to a commander-in-chief is that of being an honest and candid counsellor and adviser to him; and there ought to be a perfect good understanding with and confidence in each other, which I am sorry to say is by no means the case on board the Formidable; and sure I am that if Sir George Rodney, from whim and caprice, should give orders in his cabin for any signal to be made that would inevitably throw the fleet into the greatest confusion or even into danger, Sir Charles has not fortitude and resolution sufficient to open his lips in remonstrance, but would implicitly obey it.

I have been witness to his receiving orders that

have appeared to me to be big with absurdity, and he has gone upon deck to direct their being executed; upon which I have more than once said, 'I believe, Sir George, you are unacquainted with some circumstances respecting the orders you have just given to Sir Charles Douglas'; which I have related, and he has immediately acknowledged it, sent for Sir Charles, and asked him, why he had not mentioned what he had just heard from me, which makes the directions he has given highly improper, and they have been put a stop to. Now what I did was most certainly the bounden duty of the first captain. But all is confusion on board the Formidable, and not the least degree of attention paid to order and regularity. Things that are of much importance to be done out of hand are neglected, and others of a very trifling nature, and of no sort of consequence whether they are done to-day or to-morrow, there is often the greatest hurry about; and orders are so frequently given and contradicted, that we don't get as forward in storing and refitting in three days as we might in one, with steadiness and a little method. In short, I not only am witness to these unpleasant circumstances, but am teazed about them, as often as a captain comes near me; which I cannot remedy to any great purpose; for as often as I attempt to bring things a little to rights and succeed, it is for the moment only, as they constantly revert to their former irregularity and confusion. Sir George Rodney requires a monitor perpetually at his elbow, as much as a froward child.

My health has suffered very much from seeing things go as they do, and I shall in no long time be tossed overboard, if I continue in my present situation; for I am of that frame and texture that it is totally impossible for me to be indifferent, where the service of my king and country is so materially affected.

Sir George Rodney seems to be satisfied with having done enough as probably to save Jamaica and keep his popularity alive; but, good God! not to avail himself of the manifest advantage his most complete victory gave him is not to be thought of with any degree of temper. We might as easily have taken the whole of the French fleet as we did the five sail (probably a ship or two might have got off, but I am confident not more than three could have escaped had they been properly pursued), which would most effectually and substantially have retrieved the misfortunes of poor old England, have set her on tip toe, and have humbled France in the extreme. It is truly mortifying to think what a glorious turn might have been given to our royal master's affairs, with common exertion and management, not only in this country, but at home, and how shamefully was the opportunity neglected.

I find all this wasting of time here is to take the Ville de Paris to Jamaica with him. Such is the vanity of the man, he can talk of nothing else, and says he will hoist his flag on board her. Would to God she had sunk the instant she had yielded to the arms of his Majesty! We should then have had ten better ships in lieu of her.

What think you of Sir George and his first captain to suffer so great a fleet to put to sea without a rendezvous? and in pursuit of an enemy's fleet, when either a victory or a defeat must unavoidably have occasioned a separation? Strange as it may appear, it is no less true. Not a rendezvous was given out till the 13th, when the Royal Oak, Alcide and Centaur, with the prizes Glorieux and Hector, had parted company. Very luckily the Alert brig fell in with them; whose captain, having heard Sir George Rodney say he should proceed to Jamaica with his whole fleet, told Captain Burnett of the

Royal Oak of it, and I suppose they are gone for that island.

What can we expect under such conduct, without the all powerful hand of Providence aids us? She was beneficent and assisting in the extreme from the 8th to the 12th, which if I live to see you, you will I am sure acknowledge. Curgenven has got post, but I know not for what ship; I believe he at present commands the Ville de Paris. Adieu. Respectful compliments to Lady Middleton and Mr. and Mrs. Edwards; and believe me always . . .

Sir George Rodney to Hood

Formidable. 17th April, 1782.

[*Copy: in Hood's writing. N.R.S.* iii. 132.]

Hood to Middleton

[*Private and confidential.*]

Barfleur: off Alta Vela, St. Domingo.
22nd April, 1782.

My dear Sir Charles,—

[What follows agrees closely (*mutatis mutandis*) with the letter of the same date to Jackson (*N.R.S.* iii. 131, 132). Even the concluding sentence is in effect the same:—'I am, my dear Sir Charles, with all good wishes to Lady Middleton, *and with every real regard*, Your most faithful, obedient *but much mortified humble servant*, Sam Hood.' It will be seen that the words in *italics* are here added. The letter of 24th April (p. 132) is here given as a postscript, as far as 'keep one's temper with him.' It then continues:—]

I am now standing in for Port Louis[1] to re-

[1] Indifferently called St. Louis, Baie de St. Louis, or Puerto San Luiz.

connoitre it. I had very handsome thanks on the 22nd from Sir George for making him acquainted with the merits of Curgenven; he is become a mighty favourite, and I think takes post for the Ville de Paris. I believe Captain Domett[1] will be the bearer of this letter (at least Sir George told me he should), who is as good an officer as any in his Majesty's navy, and has seen more real service than perhaps any officer of his standing; he is truly brave, cool, and determined, with an excellent understanding. He has been my signal officer some months, and is well qualified to answer any questions you may incline to ask him; I have desired him to take as early an opportunity as he can of waiting on you. He is appointed captain of the Ceres.

[With this is enclosed Hood to Rodney, 22nd April (*N.R.S.* iii. 133), *verbatim copy.*]

Captured Letter

Letter[2] addressed to Monsieur P. F. Ancel Gauvel and Son, merchants at Havre de Grace.

[*Translation.*] 22nd April, 1782.

My dear Uncle,—I do my duty in sending you an account of the action we have had with the English the 9th April. We were assured that they

[1] William Domett, an old follower of Hood and his brother, was posted in the following Sept., and served his whole time as captain, either as flag-captain or captain of the fleet. He died an admiral and G.C.B. in 1828. See *D.N.B.*

[2] This letter and the papers annexed are presumably those referred to (*post*, p. 178), as captured in the Ceres. It is a pity that we have not the originals, for the translation of the story of the battle, however literal, is frequently obscure.

consisted of forty-five ships and we were but twenty-nine; we were however thirty-four when we sailed, two of which went with the convoy to Guadeloupe. We had thirty in the first action against forty-five. The Auguste and another of ours were two leagues to windward of us during the action, said to be becalmed. We should not certainly have sought a second action after knowing how much superior they were to us had it not been for the Zélé and the Jason, who were disabled; and by endeavouring to preserve them we were obliged to bear up before the wind, which led us to an action, which for this very long time has been unparallelled, and our poor Glorieux has paid the tribute, though we flatter ourselves our enemies have likewise felt the effects of the battle.

On the 14th and 15th, the English fleet were distinctly seen from Guadeloupe to be but thirty-nine in number, though they were once fifty, including frigates; which makes us believe they have likewise lost some. Their manœuvres make us hope that they have been roughly handled, since they did not pursue us; we have therefore reason to hope that our expedition will not yet fail. We have sixteen Spanish ships at St. Domingo with 8,000 men, and we think it is intended for Jamaica. I am well and have only time to assure you that I am, during life, with all possible respect,

Your very humble and obedient
servant and nephew,
M. P. F.

Captured Narrative

An account of the action of the French fleet commanded by the Comte de Grasse with the British fleet off Guadeloupe and Dominica on the 9th and 12th April 1782.

[*Translation.*]

Monsieur de Grasse's intention was to have sent the convoy from Fort Royal by night, escorted by two ships of the line and two frigates, that they might be advanced before us, as we were retarded by the St. Esprit, which was not ready for sea. The convoy went out on the night of the 6th and 7th of April, in the hope that they would pass unnoticed by the enemy; which however did not happen as was imagined; they having got sight of the English, were obliged to put back again the same day. This determined the admiral to sail without the St. Esprit, having learnt on the 8th inst. that the English fleet had sailed from St. Lucia; at the same time observing four ships and a frigate of theirs watching our motions. The whole fleet got under way in the evening from Fort Royal, consisting of thirty-four ships with our convoy. At 9 we got sight of the enemy; at 10, all our convoy being out, we steered for Guadeloupe, where we were to take another convoy. During the night we steered N and NbE, with a fresh breeze at east; at 5 in the morning, we perceived the English fleet to leeward of us in line of battle; at twenty-five minutes past 6 the admiral made the signal for the convoy to anchor under Guadeloupe. Between 7 and 9 o'clock the French fleet made several movements to form the line of battle, and also to favour the convoy in getting to anchor at Guadeloupe before the action. At seven past 9 the admiral gave orders to the whole fleet to form with the admiral in the same point of bearing as best corresponded with the intended position. At 9^h 50^m the signal was made for action tc the ships the most advanced, and to make the attack on the enemy's van. At 10, the signal was made to tack together; at twenty-five past 10 the signal was made for the commanders of the 2nd and 3rd divisions to charge themselves with manœuvring and conducting their own squadrons; at 37^m past 10, the above signal was annulled; at 53^m past, the signal to the Destin that she was not in her station and ordered him into it. At 58^m past 10 the firing ceased throughout; at 3^m past 11 the signal to haul to the wind and reserve the fire; at 24^m past 11 the signal to close the line; at 41^m past 11 the firing recommenced in the rear; at 4^m past 12 the signal for the van to keep close to the wind; at 15^m past 12 the van began to fire, as did all the line, and at 47^m past noon the action became general; do. the signal for a close line; at $\frac{3}{4}$ past noon the van and centre, very close to the enemy, most vigorously engaged; at 12^m past 1, the Pluton shot away the main topmast of the enemy's van ship, and her main yard came down upon deck; at 17^m past 1 the Triomphant made the signal for the 2nd squadron to haul the wind together; at which time the English ship that had lost her topmast bore up before the wind. At 4^m past 2 the firing ceased, when part of the English ships bore up, which made us think they had suffered much maltraitée. We then saw they had thirty-nine or forty ships at least, five of which of three decks, and we were [in] all but thirty; the St. Esprit at Martinique; two ships with the convoy, the Auguste, with another whose name is not known, were not in action; those that were distinguished themselves most gallantly. The

Triomphant and the Pluton signalised themselves the best. The Pluton engaged during two hours with a ship of eighty guns, whom he made bear up. The Marquis de Vaudreuil[1] performed the most gallant manœuvres that could possibly be done, having bore up three times in the fire; but finding himself so galled by his opponent and three others that attacked him that he would have been cut up, had he not tacked; in doing which he was twice raked, but he afterwards repaid them well for it. While the fleets were in action, the general sent a tender to order the convoy to get under way from Guadeloupe; who immediately shaped their course for St. Domingo, and at six in the evening the sternmost of them were not in sight. We remained cruizing off Guadeloupe from the 9th to the 12th, the better to facilitate the convoy getting on before us, well knowing that the English watched with attention our motions; in which they did not fail. We still continued plying to windward, the better to favour the convoy's escape; and considering our advantageous situation from having the wind, and knowing the superiority of the enemy, I believe it was not the general's design to risk a second action, knowing that if we were not successful we must fail in our expedition.

The 11th, at 4 in the morning, we spoke the Triomphant, who[1] directed us to inform the general that he had given orders to his division to force sail; and to ask the general if it was his intention to weather the Saints; also to enquire if the convoy was gone. The general's answer to us was, that whatever signals Monsieur de Vaudreuil should make were well; that he intended to pass to windward of the Saints, and that the convoy went away the day

[1] Le Marquis de Vaudreuil, chef d'escadre; nephew of the Vaudreuil, Governor of Canada in 1759.

of action, and that, at five in the morning after, not one of them were to be seen. This is what made me conjecture that he had no intention to seek another battle, but rather to pursue the object of the expedition; but the misfortune was that one of his ships had lost her fore mast, which rendered her unable to keep company, and was on the point of being carried off by the enemy. This obliged the general to bear up with his fleet, to follow and protect the disabled ship, who was under the necessity to bear away before the wind, and engaged us in a second action, which proved the hottest and most vigorous that has happened for a century past.

Having bore up the whole night, we found ourselves brought down to fight with the English, who at five in the morning (of the 12th) were ready to receive us. At 6 the general made the signal to prepare for action. At 7^{m} past 7 he gave orders for the fleet to pay attention; at the same hour he made the signal *de ralliement*, to form the order of battle reversed on the larboard tack; at 40^{m} past 7 the signal for the whole to bear up together on the bearing specified—SSW.; at 8, a quick cannonade commenced; at 6^{m} past 8, the signal to close the line; at 8^{m} past 8, to haul the wind together, which was not well executed, by reason of the advantage of situation given up to the enemy. They then fought on contrary tacks. The general had reason to hope for much success, the fire being as brilliant from one as from the other. We were cutting up the rear of the English, while their van had passed and had not wore to give them aid. The action continued violent, and at the instant that we reckoned ourselves master of the field of battle, we perceived the Glorieux had lost her main and mizen masts. At $\frac{1}{4}$ past 9 the Ville de Paris and all our van were close to the rear of the enemy, keeping up a quick-fire. La Ville de Paris had her main topsail cut in two, when she immediately began to bend another and went to the assistance of the Glorieux, who kept up an incessant fire. Two ships of three decks at 9^h 37^m carried away his fore mast and bowsprit; at 10, we saw an English ship that had lost her fore mast, another her topmast. At 10^h 15^m the van of the enemy wore; at the same time the general gave directions to make an attack upon the rear of the enemy. At 10^h 45^m an English ship lost her main topmast and two others their jib-booms. At noon, the Richmond [frigate][1] bore up in the fire, to take the Glorieux in tow, but was forced to quit her; several of our ships attempted to succour her, but they were obliged to bear up likewise, by the number of the enemy that fell upon them, they being three against twenty-three, which was the cause of abandoning the Glorieux who was protected, and throughout shewed every mark of distinguished bravery to the very last moment. From this time the two fleets kept a quick fire, without ceasing, till half-past 6 in the evening. At 9 we saw a large fire bearing SbE; at 9^h 45^m, we saw the explosion of a ship,[2] but did not know whether she was English or French. We have apprehension for the Sovereign; we are however told that the French fleet had made towards St. Domingo, and the English were seen trying to fetch St. Lucia or Antigua to repair their damages, who have been very roughly handled.

Herewith annexed is an account of their state as seen from the island of Guadeloupe.

> Here follows a list of 19 British ships that had suffered in the action the loss of masts and yards.

[1] Captured from the English off the Chesapeake, on 9th September, 1781.

[2] *Sc.* the César.

Forty-two sail were then counted, though they were once forty-nine in number. It is not known what is become of the others. Of our own, no positive accounts have been heard.

I thought to have given you pleasure by this account, for which reason I am in a hurry to send it, as to-morrow we set sail for St. Domingo.

Inclosed is the number of our ships that did not come into action.

The first cripple ship described has no yard rigged, but the spritsail topsail yard; her maintopmast unrigged, her topgallant mast down and no sails bent.

Hood to Middleton

Barfleur: off the Isle Navassa. 30th April, 1782.

[*Private and confidential.*]

My dear Sir Charles,—

[Essentially the same as the letter to Jackson of the same date (N.R.S. iii. 135–7). The differences are merely verbal and unimportant, down to 'from a goat's tail.' It concludes—]

I now hourly expect a ship from Sir George and will keep my letter open till she comes. In the meantime, adieu!—

Barfleur: at sea. 9th May, 1782.

With most eager expectation have I looked out, to no purpose, for a ship from Sir George Rodney, from the 1st instant to this hour, and am exceedingly at a loss to account for my disappointment. The Prince William which I detached to cruize between Cape Tiburon and the Isle of Vache,[1] returned to me

[1] Isle la Vache, or by the buccaneers, indifferently Isle of Ash, or Cow Island; near the south-west end of San Domingo.

on the 7th at night, with certain intelligence that four of the French ships of the line, which were put to flight on the 12th of last month, arrived in a most shattered condition on the 21st at Curaçao, but not finding the means of refitting there, were getting under sail on Thursday last (the 2nd), supposed for Cape François; and that two Dutch ships of war, one of sixty-four and the other of fifty guns, with upwards of sixty sail under convoy, were reported to sail with them (and which had been ready some time) for Port au Prince, there to wait till the French convoy was ready to sail from Cape François. This immediately determined me to divide his Majesty's ships under my command into three little squadrons, for the greater chance of intercepting the enemy. Rear-Admiral Drake is gone off the Isle of Vache with six sail of the line; Commodore Affleck, with the same force, through the Mogane[1] passage and to return off the east end of St. Domingo, in case the Dutch should be able to fetch the Mona Channel, and then push to the northward for Europe, without stopping at St. Domingo; and I shall take my stand with the remaining seven sail off Cape Nicola, so that I am in hopes one or other of the squadrons will be lucky enough to fall in with the crippled ships of the enemy and so valuable a convoy.

Sir George Rodney having left a great number of prisoners in every ship of the squadron he was pleased to put under my orders when he parted for Jamaica, I have detached the Yarmouth and Montagu to Port Royal with the greatest part of them, in order that our water may hold out about three weeks longer; and by those ships I sent Sir George a copy of my order to Mr. Drake and the commodore, that he might make any alteration in,

[1] Mariguana.

or addition to, the arrangement I have made for annoying the enemy, to the best of my judgment, having never served in these seas before.

Since Sir George Rodney left me I have been obliged to send the Canada, Alfred and Prothée to Port Royal, being much disastered in their masts and yards, and short of water; and from the same motives, exclusive of the necessity of getting rid of the prisoners, the Montagu and Yarmouth were sent away yesterday morning. The Warrior has not joined since the 19th of last month, and the Belliqueux is supporting the frigates on the service of reconnoitring the harbour of Cape Français.

May 9th, 6 P.M.—The Alarm has this moment joined me with Sir George's despatches. I shall therefore send her away immediately, and can only add that I am most truly. . .

Barfleur: at sea. 12th May, 1782.

[*Private and confidential.*]

My dear Sir,—The captain of the Alarm (who joined me on the 9th in the evening with the commander-in-chief's despatches to go by the Ceres, which proceeded for England immediately), having told me that a packet, with Captain Burnett on board charged with Sir George's duplicates, was to leeward, and directed to speak with me if he can conveniently, I prepare a few lines to go by her, and will by that conveyance trouble you with copies of two letters I have written to you since Sir George Rodney left me; and if she does not join me, I shall probably fall in with Sir Peter Parker in his way to the Windward passage, as I hear he is to sail with the trade on the 15th, having his flag on board the Sandwich.

I am grieved to relate to you my friend Inglefield's misfortune; after boarding the César of seventy-four guns in the most heroic manner, under my eye, a rascal of a marine corporal [1] went below in the course of the evening in search of rum, and in drawing off a can, with a lighted candle in his hand, it caught fire, and the noble prize was instantly in a blaze not to be extinguished, and blew up about nine o'clock; by which melancholy accident the Centaur lost two lieutenants, her boatswain, a midshipman, and twenty-four of her best seamen, and a lieutenant and seven marines. Her loss in battle was eight killed and fourteen wounded. There never was more spirited conduct than that shown by Inglefield; it has covered him with honour. Sir George Rodney spoke of it to me in the highest terms of approbation, and I make no doubt will do ample justice to his very gallant behaviour in the representation he makes of it.

Oh, my dear Sir Charles, had Sir George done what he might and ought, we should all most probably have been peaceably at home by our firesides in the course of another year! How he can stand the reproaches of his own mind, if he is not perfectly callous, for doing so little, when a vast deal of honour and glory might so easily have been gathered for his poor country, almost a bankrupt in both, I cannot reconcile. The French could never have rose again this war; America would have shaken off her unnatural connection with them; Spain, in all human probability, would have seen her error, and have been glad of the first opening to have withdrawn

[1] Hood presumably knew what he was writing about, and his evidence may be considered decisive, in corroboration of that of Sir Gilbert Blane to the same effect (Mundy, ii. p. 244); but the story put abroad was that the delinquent was a French sailor (Beatson, v. p. 475), which—as it certainly was after the ship was in our possession—has always seemed highly improbable. Just forty years before (1742), the 60-gun ship Tilbury was burnt in almost exactly the same way, on the same station.

herself; and England would have been the admiration and envy of every court in Europe. Now, the whole business will be to come over again; for farther than the glory of his Majesty's arms having appeared with lustre, and the danger probably removed for the present from Jamaica, I can see no great benefit can arise from so perfectly complete and unrivalled a victory. The very important and favourable opportunity that has been lost for raising Great Britain's glory is melancholy in the extreme to think of, and there is no dwelling upon the subject with any degree of temper.

I send you a literal translation of an intelligent French seaman's letter,[1] taken in the Ceres, which gives a more just account of the actions than I apprehend De Grasse will do, who honoured me with his particular attention on both days, as the French seaman expresses; for my division was the van on the 9th and the rear on the 12th. The reason the Frenchman assigns why he supposes his Majesty's fleet was roughly handled is not a bad one,[2] but very natural, though by no means just; for we had five or six and twenty sail of the line at least as fit to pursue in the evening as they were to commence to fight in the morning, when compared to the very shattered state of the enemy; and I do not believe there were three French ships that would have resisted farther than the discharge of their guns, which were loaded, either in the water or air, as they might chance to be pointed; indeed they had not the means of resistance left. The Ville de Paris's powder was very near exhausted, which her captain told me when he came on board, and further

[1] See *ante*, p. 169.

[2] It is generally adopted by French writers; *e.g.* Chevalier, i. p. 324: Les Anglais trop maltraités . . . pour nous poursuivre, passèrent la nuit en panne sur le lieu de combat.

said he was sure it was the case of every French ship. I most pointedly told this to Sir George next morning, but he was not to be stimulated to a pursuit, which is matter of astonishment not only to me, but, I believe, to nine-tenths of the captains and officers of his fleet. I have received the most undoubted intelligence that the four ships which put into Curaçao had scarce a round of powder left.

I find my conduct is done ample justice to in a Jamaica newspaper, which I flatter myself you will be pleased to know; what follows is an extract from an account some officer sent to the printer. 'The sea never produced a scene more navally beautiful, or the service an exertion more heroically animated, than that of Sir Samuel Hood pressing to action. So impetuous, incessant, and irresistible was his fire, that just as the sun set, the guns of the Ville de Paris were silenced by that gallant rear-admiral, and Monsieur de Grasse struck the flag of France, which he had nobly defended, to the victorious Barfleur.'

How, in God's name, could the commander-in-chief pick up such a first captain? I will venture to say the list of the royal navy does not produce one more unequal altogether to the duties of the station.[1] He is totally unqualified; has no method whatever; puzzles at everything, and orders and counter-orders

[1] Douglas was an excellent French scholar, and as such had been specially attached to Saunders's staff in 1759. If there is any truth in the story that he had been formerly in the Dutch service, his linguistic accomplishments would be a high recommendation. But he had been made a baronet for his distinguished service at Quebec in the spring and summer of 1776; and Rodney could not have been ignorant of the many improvements he had introduced into naval gunnery, which—it can at least be argued—had much to do with the victory of 12th April. It may, perhaps, be thought that the harshness of Hood's opinion was suggested by a disordered liver. Cf. *post*, p. 207.

perpetually, so that the service of the fleet is interrupted and delayed in a most unheard-of manner. He has a memory that does not last him from the commander-in-chief's cabin to the quarter-deck, and three or four memorandums are given out one after the other for one and the same purpose in the course of twenty-four hours. All this I have in complaint most grievously in every letter I receive from Jamaica, but I can speak to it from experience. I believe him a very good-natured, worthy and brave man, but he is certainly in a character he is totally unfit for. The business that seems to claim his first and greatest attention is to take advantage of favourable moments to push up his followers, whether qualified and deserving or not. I will give you one instance out of many that have come to my knowledge—he got his clerk, who has not been a year in his Majesty's service, to be appointed purser of the Ville de Paris, a first-rate—the *ne plus ultra* of reward to a worthy man, who has been a purser twenty or thirty years. This is not paying attention to the commander-in-chief's character, which must suffer by such appointments.

May 20th.—Yesterday noon the Licorne joined me, accompanied by a French frigate from Cape Français, with two hundred English seamen, Admiral Vaudreuil, the commander-in-chief, having accepted my proposal for an exchange of prisoners, man for man. Captain Cadogan was at the Cape four days, and received and treated with the utmost politeness and attention. I herewith send you a very exact account of the combined forces of France and Spain on St. Domingo. All the French disabled ships are now arrived except the Zélé, which is at Guadeloupe in a wretched state. The four that went to Curaçao got into Cape Français the

12th. The account Captain Cadogan and his officers give of the very battered condition of the enemy's ships is not to be described; and they say not one half of them can be put to sea on any service whatever for some weeks.

Captain Cadogan fell in with Commodore Affleck (whom I detached with six sail on the 8th) about six or seven leagues to the windward of Cape Nicolas, yesterday morning, not having been able to get farther owing to calms and light airs northerly; and as he was told by Captain Cadogan that the Dutch convoy had been left in the Mona Channel on the 10th, standing to the northward for Europe, he concluded he had no chance of overtaking it before his water was all expended, and thought it best to rejoin me, which he did last night; and as the water of the ships in general is very short indeed—some having not more than six days supposing all the remaining casks to be full, and it often proves otherwise—I am now taking the whole to the commander-in-chief at Port Royal, Jamaica, and hope to join him to-morrow.

If the commissioners of the victualling will not send out their bread in water-butts and puncheons—which I urged them to do in the strongest manner last year from America—his Majesty's ships in general cannot keep the sea for more than a month at a time for want of casks, of which the wear and tear is immense in this country; and as we are not obliged to go from the Windward Islands to Jamaica and North America, I foresee fatal consequences will arise to the king's service if a supply of water casks are not sent; and though the board has been silent to my letter, I know it got safe as the ships in which I sent it, as well as those that conveyed a duplicate and triplicate of it, arrived in England.

Since writing the above, I have caused all the

prisoners brought from Cape Français to be examined, and found two which came from Curaçao in the Hercules, and both flatly contradict what the captain of the Pluton reported to Admiral Vaudreuil, of his leaving the Dutch convoy in the Mona Channel, and are positive that the only vessel, which sailed with the four French ships, was a Dutch snow, which the Pluton took in tow the greatest part of the way, and that they left the Dutch men-of-war and the convoy at Curaçao, where most of the latter had been waiting fifteen or sixteen months; that no ship had arrived from Europe since the rupture with Holland, and that provisions and all European commodities were exceeding scarce and bore very advanced prices.

The French ships could not fetch the Mona Channel by eight leagues, and were obliged to work up. The Spanish ships at Cape Français have their sails bent and are in all respects ready for sea; but Monsieur de l'Eguille [1] says it will not be an easy matter to get them to sail without the French. I understand there is not even the appearance of any cordiality or scarce any intercourse between the French and Spanish officers or seamen.

The report the released prisoners make (who were all in the French fleet during the actions, and compelled to pump the ships) of the number of killed and wounded is incredible; scarce a ship lost less than one hundred men, many between two and three hundred.[2] The letters I have intercepted

[1] Probably the Chevalier Froger de l'Eguille, lieutenant de vaisseau. He came out to the station in 1779, and may have been in charge of the naval establishment at the Cape. *Cf.* Lacour-Gayet, ii. pp. 624, 636.

[2] According to Lacour-Gayet (ii. p. 433), on board the Ville de Paris alone, there were 400 dead and 600 wounded. De Grasse was left on the poop with only two officers, but still he refused to strike his flag, and the English sailors were obliged to

from Curaçao respecting the carnage on board the four French ships which put in there exactly correspond with what the English seamen say. The captain[1] of the Hercules and seventy-eight men were killed, upon which the second captain quitted the fight early in the day.[2]

7 P.M., 20th May.—The Unicorn has joined me with despatches from Sir George, and I find a packet is about to sail to precede Sir Peter Parker and the convoy. If she is not gone I shall give this to Captain John Linzee, who goes in her; poor fellow, he has lost his ship off Tortola, but I hope no blame is to be imputed to him, and that the misfortune was not to be avoided. If he is gone, Sir Peter will have charge of it. I pushed hard to get in to-night, but could not effect it. I send you an extract from a private letter from Sir George Rodney, received by the Unicorn.

Adieu! Ever and most affectionately yours,

SAM. HOOD.

do it. As most of the known details mentioned by this writer are certainly erroneous, we are not called on to accept this exaggerated estimate of the numbers; and the evidence that the Ville de Paris struck her flag to the Barfleur is quite conclusive (*Cf. ante*, p. 161); but it may be, and probably was different with regard to the French admiral's flag of command. Chevalier (i. 306) quotes de Grasse as writing: 'J'étais réduit à un tel état que les ennemis, le 13 au matin, pour amener le pavillon de commandement, furent obligés de couper les mâts, de crainte, en y montant, d'être entraînés dans la mer ou écrasés par leur chute.'

[1] Chadeau de la Clocheterie; the same who, as a lieutenant, four years before, commanded the Belle-Poule in her celebrated action with the Arethusa. His father, commandant en second of the Sérieux, was killed in the action off Cape Finisterre on 3rd May, 1747 (Lacour-Gayet, i. 171).

[2] Chevalier de Coatlès, lieutenant de vaisseau. He was admonished by a 'conseil de guerre' 'pour n'avoir pas fait tout ce qu'il était possible de faire' (Chevalier, i. 314).

Barfleur : Port Royal, Jamaica. 22nd May, 1782.

My dear Sir Charles,—The Ajax having increased her leaks from two feet to four feet an hour while she was for England, it was thought expedient to send the Russell in her room, and occasioned Sir Peter Parker to stop at Bluefields till she was ready. This gave me an opportunity of sending my letter to you to Sir Peter, and to add a few lines by that excellent young man, Captain Saumarez. I arrived here with the squadron under my command yesterday, and Sir George finding himself, as he was pleased to say, so ill as to be unable to attend to the refitting the squadron (though he is undoubtedly as well as I am), and obliged to go into the country, he has put the whole under my command—an arduous business upon my shoulders ; but it is my duty to obey, and I will do my best. The confusion things are in from one cause and another is beyond conception, and though the fleet has ample employment for five hundred artificers for some weeks, this yard is short of forty—a melancholy circumstance ; but I have given the most pointed directions that no lower mast shall be taken on shore that can possibly be made serviceable as it stands.

I am, my dear Sir Charles,
Your very sincere and faithful
SAM. HOOD.

Intelligence concerning the Dutch Convoy.

Licorne. 18th May, 1782.

On Sunday, May 12th, 1782, the following French men-of-war came into Cape Français.

Le Pluton	74 guns
L'Hercule	74 ,,
Le Marseillais . . .	74 ,,
L'Eveillé	64 ,,

They came from Curaçao ten days before in company with a Dutch convoy of about sixty-four sail of merchant ships, escorted by four Dutch ships of war, bound to Europe, two of which were frigates.

I was on board the Triomphant at dinner with Monsieur Vaudreuil, when the Captain [1] of the Pluton came on board and informed the French admiral that he had parted with the Dutch convoy two days before in the Mona passage, and that they were steering to the northward with a fair wind.

THOMAS CADOGAN.

Depositions of English Prisoners

Mr. John Hay, late gunner of his Majesty's sloop Antigua, says—

He was taken prisoner on the 11th May, 1781, when the French laid siege to St. Lucia; was carried to Martinique, and confined along with the ship's company in jail at St. Pierre; from thence he was embarked with 180 English prisoners on board the Pluton, part of which number were sick soldiers taken out of the hospital at St. Lucia. From the Pluton he was sent, with twelve others, on board the Diadem, of seventy-four guns, Captain Montclair; [2] and upon refusing to do the duty of the ship, were fed upon bread and water. An English prisoner, John Watson, mate of the Bee brig, belonging to Bristol, at that time in a bad state of health, was

[1] Comte d'Albert de Rions, everywhere spoken of as an able officer. He became chef d'escadre in 1784; and in 1789, when the Revolution broke out, was commandant at Toulon, where, and afterwards at Brest, his experiences were exceedingly unpleasant (Chevalier, ii. 6–16). M. de Rions resigned his command, and did not serve again. He was made a contre-amiral in 1792, and died in 1802 (Lacour-Gayet, ii. 635).

[2] Comte de Monteclerc.

seized upon the capstan and beat in the most cruel manner, with sticks, on the body and soles of the feet, till he was quite insensible; after which he was, along with the master's mate of the Santa Monica, put into irons, without any reason but that of refusing to work. All which was done by order of the second captain; but since the action of the 12th April, they received better treatment.

About noon of the 12th the Diadem ceased firing; but being closely confined below in both actions, does not know for certain what place in the line she was; but supposes her to have been the twelfth ship. They had 17 men killed on the 9th and 120 on the 12th. He further says, that he was informed by the captain's secretary, who spoke tolerable good English, and from other reports believe it to be true, that the captain, between five and six o'clock in the evening of the 12th, ordered all hands to be turned up, and told them that the admiral had made the signal for ships to come to his assistance, and asked them if they were willing to go to his support; which they (as well as a number of the officers) peremptorily refused to do. The latter part of the action in the forenoon the men did not stand to their quarters, but run down into the hold. On the 12th there were, including soldiers, 800 men on board; and on their arrival at Cape Français, there did not appear to be above 500—300 being said to be killed and wounded. On the Diadem's ceasing firing she had not more than six rounds of powder left; and was informed that throughout the whole fleet, no ship had more; some indeed had none at all.

William Harvey, late belonging to his Majesty's ship Iris, says:—He was eight months a prisoner on board the Sovereign. She sailed from Martinique in company with the French fleet on the 8th April, but got aground in Fort Royal Bay, where she remained till the morning of the 9th, and sailed immediately to leeward. On the 11th, she joined their fleet, and on the 12th was the third ship in the van. She was not much engaged; had 30 men killed and 50 wounded. He says, he was in the action off St. Kitts, when she had 30 men killed. At leaving Martinique they left the St. Esprit in the carenage, without a single gun on board. The Sovereign is coppered half-way up.

John Dowling, late belonging to his Majesty's sloop Surprize, says:—That he was 11 months prisoner on board the Bourgogne, of 74 guns, Captain Sherry;[1] that she had 15 men killed on the 9th; 70 killed and 90 wounded on the 12th. He heard the captain of her wanted to strike the colours, but some of the officers persuaded him not; that the Burgogne had part of her bowsprit shot away; and at ceasing firing, had only three rounds of shot left.

Hugh Mitchell, late belonging to his Majesty's sloop Surprize, says:—He was prisoner on board the Hercules, which sailed from Curaçao in company with the Pluton, Eveillé, Marseillais and a Dutch snow called the Curaçao, in the beginning of this month; and left the Dutch fleet there, consisting of a 60-gun ship, a 50, a frigate, a 20-gun ship, and about 200 sail of merchantmen, 60 or 70 of which were Dutch, all loaded and ready for sea. The French ships were four or five days on their passage to the Mona, and made one tack to the eastward on the coast of Hispaniola, to enable them

[1] Comte de Charitte.

to fetch through. At their leaving Curaçao, the island was in great want of provisions; and in their passage from thence to Cape Français, the Dutch snow sailed so badly that the Pluton was obliged to take her in tow. The reason of the Dutch fleet not sailing from Curaçao, he heard, was that they expected a visit from Admiral Rodney. The men-of-war and merchantmen had their sails bent and appeared to him to be in readiness for sea. The Hercules was in action an hour and three-quarters on the 12th; had her captain and 70 men killed. At ceasing firing, the men collected their bags, broke open the steward's room, and got intoxicated with liquor, and were determined to strike their colours to the first ship that fired upon them.

Joseph Baker and James Osborne, both prisoners on board the Hercules, agree in every circumstance with the account given by Hugh Mitchell and Robert Brown, and add:—That there was but a small quantity of powder and only two rounds of shot for the upper deck remaining on board after the engagement of the 12th; that they were supplied with more shot on their arrival at Curaçao from the Dutch ships. The Dutchmen there, who could speak English, informed them that they had been ready to sail for Europe these 16 months past; that they had requested the commodore of the four French ships to convoy them home, which he refused. They further say the four ships arrived at Cape Français on Saturday, the 11th May.

Robert Brown, also a prisoner on board the Hercules, corroborates every circumstance mentioned in Hugh Mitchell's deposition.

Hood to Middleton

Barfleur: Port Royal, Jamaica. 10th June, 1782.

I snatch a moment to give you my sincere thanks for your affectionate letters by the April packet, which were brought here the 2nd instant. The general approbation my conduct has met with affords me pleasure not to be expressed, and I can with truth assure you there is nothing I so much pant after and am ambitious of as the flattering and distinguished honour of being thought well of by my king and fellow-subjects.

Sir George (in which he has some subterfuge; for the present and late captain of the Formidable, who were with him yesterday, say he is as well as when he went on shore, and much better than when he left England) has declined all business, finding himself, as he says, unequal to the fatigue of refitting the fleet, &c. The whole weight, therefore (the Rear-Admirals Rowley and Graves being at sea), is thrown upon me, which is heavy and arduous in the extreme; for there was scarce a ship but had her lower masts, yards, and bowsprit so wounded as to be obliged to be sent on shore or fished as they stood. However, I have the satisfaction to say, all are now in their proper places, and I hope and trust every ship will be ready for sea in most perfect good order in ten days. The artificers of the yard, as well as those of the fleet, have exerted themselves in a most wonderful pleasant and cheerful manner. I am regularly in the yard every morning so soon as a man can see to use a tool, where I tarry some hours, and return again after dinner till the day is fairly closed; and I can venture to say that more work was never done in the time by the same number of men in any yard in England. The artificers are called over by candlelight, and diligently work fourteen hours every day; I have therefore ordered them to be paid two for one, which I trust will be approved, and when I have more time, I will write to the board upon the subject.

A French fleet of merchant ships, under convoy of eight of the line, left Cape Français for Europe on the 3rd instant. The intelligence was brought yesterday by the Actæon, which I thought right to give notice of to the admiralty and to any squadron or cruisers we may have at sea near home. The Unicorn sails with it; God grant she may arrive in time for the enemy to be intercepted. I have only time to write more than just to tell you that I have received a very polite letter from Lord Keppel, dated the 6th of April, in which his lordship begs me to believe he is sincere and in earnest in telling me that no endeavour on his part shall be wanting to make my situation honourable and pleasant to myself. I am in great haste, but most affectionately. . . .

P.S.—This was intended to go by the Unicorn, but a breeze springing up my boat could not catch her. This comes by the Lion schooner, with a duplicate of my letter to the admiralty.

Captain Barbor[1] was taken ill on Sunday night last, and was dead at ten this morning; his fever was violent in the extreme. I am sorry to say the fleet begins to be sickly, but I hope and trust we shall recover when we get to sea. This is a vile place; we can get no refreshments for our people, but in so scanty a manner as is not to be conceived by those who have been[2] at Jamaica.—June 12th, 8 P.M.

[1] Robert Barbor, captain of the Fame. The so-called memoir in Charnock (vi. 348) misspells the name, gives a wrong date of the death, and shows a curious ignorance of the details of the life.

[2] So written; but surely the meaning is 'who have not been'?

Report by Captain Merrick,[1] *on the French and Spanish Fleet at Cape Français*

16th June, 1782.

French Ships, 14 in number: 5 of 80 guns, 8 of 74, 1 of 64.

1. Triomphant: Le Marquis de Vaudreuil, commander-in-chief; 80 guns, coppered; fore mast and bowsprit fished, yards and topmasts down, and sails unbent.

2. L'Auguste: Le Comte de Vaudreuil,[2] second in command; 80 guns, coppered; main mast and bowsprit fished, yards and topmasts down, and sails unbent.

3. Le Duc de Bourgogne: Le Chevalier de L'Espinouse, third in command; 80 guns, coppered; main and mizen masts fished, yards and topmasts down, and sails unbent.

4. Couronne: 80 guns, coppered; main mast fished, fit for sea.

5. Languedoc: 80 guns, not coppered; fore and mizen masts fished, fit for sea.

6. Northumberland: 74 guns, coppered; mizen mast fished, fit for sea.

7. Magnanime: 74 guns, not coppered; main and mizen masts and bowsprit fished, fit for sea.

8. Citoyen: 74 guns, not coppered; fore mast fished, fit for sea.

9. Pluton: 74 guns, not coppered; fore and mizen masts fished, yards and topmasts down and sails unbent.

10. Bourgogne: 74 guns, not coppered; all the lower masts and bowsprits fished; the hull in bad

[1] William Augustus Merrick; commander, 13th Sept. 1779; captain, 19th April, 1782; died at Naples, 18th Dec. 1785.

[2] Brother of the Marquis.

condition, yards and topmasts down, and partly unrigged.

11. Le Palmier: 74 guns, not coppered; fore and mizen masts fished; in very bad condition, heaving down at a careening hulk.

12. Diadème: 74 guns, not coppered; all her lower masts fished; on the point of sailing.

13. Marseillais: 74 guns, not coppered; all her lower masts fished; on the point of sailing.

14. L'Eveillé: 64 guns, coppered; bowsprit fished, fit for sea.

Spanish Ships, 11 in number: one of 96 guns,
10 of 70 guns.

Eleven sail of Spanish ships of the line, under the command of Don Solano,[1] in excellent order and fit for immediate service. The San Luis, flag ship, originally of 80 guns, converted into a three-decker[2] by mounting a tier of brass 8-pounders on her gangways; the rest of the ships are of 70 guns.

Sailed with a convoy for France, on the 31st May, 4 sail of the line, 3 of them very leaky; the 4th under jury masts. Sailed from the Cape on the 8th June, 5 French ships of the line; joined 2 Spanish do. off Cape Nicolas Mole, and were all seen on the 10th standing towards Port au Prince.

At Cape Français,	French ships of the line .	14	25
	Spanish do. .	11	
At Port au Prince,	French ships of the line .	5	7
	Spanish ditto .	2	
	Total number . .		32

[1] Don José Solano, Marqués del Socorro, jefe de escuadra; the Spanish commander-in-chief.

[2] In a similar way the Santísima Trinidad of twenty years later has often been spoken of as a *four*-decker.

At Cape Français the Néréïde and Amazon, frigates, 104 sail of merchant vessels, 27 of which have their sails bent, and are preparing for the next convoy.

The French ships have been very sickly since their arrival at the Cape. The hospital return on the 15th June amounted to 2,317 men of the wounded in the late action. A proportion of 7 in 10 have perished from locked jaws; and the daily number of deaths upon an average of the last fortnight has amounted to 23.

The Spanish army, under the command of Don Gálvez,[1] originally consisting of 13,000 men, are quartered upon the inhabitants of the plain, to an extent of near 20 miles from the Cape. They have suffered much from sickness, particularly in those regiments lately arrived from Europe; on one plantation, where 170 men are quartered, 83 only were fit for duty.

The French army of 6,000 men are partly embarked in the ships of war, and partly quartered in the town. The regiments embarked are healthy, compared to those doing duty on shore; that of Touraine alone having 327 men in the hospital.

The Marquis de Bouillé sailed for France in a frigate on the 3rd of June, and the artillery, military stores, &c., intended for the expedition against Jamaica are landed from the ships of war, and deposited in the arsenal at the Cape.

Hood to Middleton

Barfleur: Port Royal, Jamaica. 21st June, 1782.

I wrote you two short letters very lately; one by the Unicorn, the other by the Lion schooner. The

[1] D. Bernardo de Gálvez, mariscal de campo.

latter carried a duplicate of my letter to the admiralty by the former, to make known the sailing of a fleet of merchant ships from Cape Français on the 3rd, under convoy of eight ships of the line.

Sir George Rodney still continues on shore and leaves the refitting his Majesty's fleet to me, together with the other duties of the port, which has been a most heavy and arduous task indeed ; but I thank God I have pretty well got through it, and hope every ship (the Ajax excepted) that was in action will be ready for sea in three days from this date. An accident in careening the Invincible, by her mainmast giving way, has been a great clog to us, as we were obliged to make her almost an entire new one, which is now in, and she will heave the first side out to-morrow. So soon as she can be got from the wharf, the Ajax will take her place, and the Shrewsbury must follow her. Both must be careened to have their leaks stopped, to enable them to proceed to England in safety.

Sir George having expressed his wish to me for a dozen sail of the line to join Admiral Rowley off Cape Nicola Mole, I ordered Mr. Drake to put to sea with that number on the 16th.

I had the honour of a very polite letter from Lord Keppel by the April packet, dated the 6th, after he had taken his place at the head of the admiralty. Herewith you have a copy of it.[1]

Sir George Rodney seems determined to go home, and probably he may soon be relieved by an old vice-admiral, if not by an admiral of the blue ; I reckon upon Sir Robert Harland[2] or Admiral Pigot,[2] but am perfectly indifferent who it is, with respect to myself, and shall not repine if I am relieved also ; however, be that as it may, I shall

[1] Not found. [2] See *D.N.B.*

do my best for the honour of my king and country in whatever situation is allotted me; and notwithstanding conclusions may be drawn favourable to me from Lord Keppel's letter, I do not flatter myself with being in the command. Nor is it to be coveted, as things have been lately managed and marred; for instead of their being smooth and pleasant, as they might have been, they will still be laborious and rather hazardous to an officer's character, unless his Majesty's fleet is always superior to that of the enemy; and for this obvious reason; our islands are totally in a defenceless state, and those of the French strong and regularly fortified and full of troops; the chief command is not therefore a situation to be envied.

My mind as well as body has been hardly worked; and having no responsibility upon me, the task of obeying will be no ways difficult, though I can never feel indifferent where the glory and credit of our royal master's name and that of my country is not properly attended to.

As word is just brought me that a packet and a convoy from England are coming in, I shall drop my pen for the present, though I expect no letters by the former, as any coming to me will be in [the] Barbados packet, the contents of which I hope we shall get in a few days.

June 22nd.—Though I had no letter by the packet, I had several very pleasant ones by the Preston, and amongst which was one from you, particularly joyful and flattering to me; and I hold myself much obliged to our friend Laforey for his very favourable opinion of my abilities, and the very distinguished mark of his friendship in mentioning me so very handsomely in his letter to you. I long for the contents of the May packet to Barbados, as I trust I shall find in them another of your kind and

O 2

cheering letters written in that month, and I begin now to expect a frigate daily, in consequence of what happened on the 12th of April. I congratulate you on the success of Admiral Barrington; the intercepting that convoy was a lucky event,[1] and must tell advantageously for us.

I believe I have mentioned to you my desire of having a compliment paid to Vaudreuil, by returning his nephew who fell into my hands on the 19th of April in the Mona passage; he was captain of the Ceres. I made a pointed request to Sir George Rodney by letter upon the subject so soon as the circumstance came to my knowledge, and trusted it would have had weight; but on my arrival here I found the young man embarked and sailed for England, and as the Marquis de Vaudreuil had been pressing with me, by letter, to have his nephew with him, I obtained permission to send the Germain sloop to Bluefields where the convoy was anchored, in hopes of recovering him, and succeeded; and having sent the Germain with him to the Cape, I received the letter from the marquis of which you have now a copy.[2] I flatter myself, my dear Sir, you will not think I acted improper; when we can show civility and attention it is my opinion we ought to do so, even to our enemies. But another very strong reason weighed with me, which was a favourable opportunity of sending an acute and able officer to Cape François, that we might have the best account possible of the state and condition of the enemy's fleet there, &c.; and I trust the clearness of the report brought me by Captain Merrick, whom I pitched upon for this service, will show I did not make a wrong choice. Captain Merrick's account

[1] Off Ushant, 19–20 April.

[2] This has, unfortunately, not been preserved.

(which you will herewith receive)[1] proves the one we had before received respecting the strength of the convoy which sailed from the Cape for Europe on the 3rd, to have been very erroneous.

I am just told that Admiral Pigot may be hourly expected in the Jupiter.

The very great and cheerful exertion of the artificers of the yard demanded some strong mark of approbation from me; I have therefore directed the naval storekeeper to pay them two for one, which I flatter myself the board will approve.

I am sorry to relate to you of a very melancholy accident that happened here this morning. Between one and two o'clock the Mersey storeship was seen to be on fire abaft; the signal for all boats was immediately made, but I dreaded the most fatal consequences to the king's fleet; but by very great exertion of the boats, and the ships nearing[2] to her being brisk in slipping their cables, she was towed clear (though she was to windward of the whole fleet) without injuring a single ship; which was really most wonderful and providential, for she was soon in one blaze from her decks to her masthead. The most material part of her stores were out, but several sails, cordage and spars of the smaller kind were burnt. How the sad accident happened I have not yet been able to learn.

Sir George is now come to Port Royal, to all appearance perfectly well, but still declines interfering in the fleet's equipment; he will, however, transmit a state of it to their lordships, and I suppose announce when he means to put to sea. The sailing of the convoy is deferred till the 10th of next month.

I am in pain for the ships I sent out with Admiral Drake, as it has blown exceedingly strong

[1] *Ante*, p. 191. [2] It is so written.

for several days, and though they have been beating ever since they sailed, they have not got five leagues to windward. I wish they were all back again that we might go out in force, as I fear some of them will come in crippled and be wanting masts, which we have not to give them, at the time Sir George is about to move. Besides, not a ship has now more than five weeks' bread, and some not as many days' peas—surely, therefore, they had better be in?

I beg my respectful compliments to Lady Middleton, and am, . . .

June 23rd.—Poor Innes has done his best, but he is unequal to the business we have had to do, having no method, or a memory that will serve him from day to day. As I feared and foretold, five of Mr. Drake's squadron—three of the line and two frigates—are come in with crippled masts; this is distressing in the extreme.

Barfleur: Jamaica. 8th July, 1782.

My dear Sir Charles,—I have had the pleasure of writing you several letters lately; the last by a packet which has been sailed a fortnight, but was not out of sight three days ago, owing to the strong easterly winds and lee current which have prevailed for a long while. The king's fleet has been perfectly refitted some days, except the London and Conqueror, and I have been taught to expect I should ere this have been at sea with a part of it; but I am still safe moored, and perhaps shall so remain some time longer, as our commander-in-chief seems to be at a loss what to do, and is whiling away the time in hopes of a despatch from England. The convoy was fixed for sailing the 24th of last month, but put off to the 10th of this, and we have worked night and day to get the French ships ready to become a part of it; it is now said the convoy will not depart from the island before the end of the month, though I speak from common report only and not from any authority.

Sir George Rodney called upon me on the 2nd in the evening (for owing to a sad broken shin which I got in the yard, I have been under the necessity of keeping my leg up, and must continue to do so some days longer, though it is in a fair way to be well, if I am not imprudent in putting it too soon to use), previous to his going ashore to be ready to dine with the merchants at Kingston, who have raised by subscription from Jew, Turk, &c., upwards of 1,500*l.* for a grand entertainment for the commander-in-chief. I feel some consolation from my misfortune, as it unavoidably prevents my going without giving the shadow of offence, having but one foot I can put to the ground; though I do not think I could have mustered resolution to have made one of the party if I had not been lame, for I have no notion of heating myself into a fever at a dinner with 300 people in a burning dusty town—as I am told Kingston is; but I made a point of sending my captain, secretary, and two lieutenants to stop the tongue of envy.

I find my name was particularly distinguished by the whole company, notwithstanding I told Sir George as well as one or two of the principal gentlemen, upon the first idea of an entertainment, that it would be much more for the credit of both parties to have the subscription money laid out in necessaries for the poor seamen who stood much in need of such assistance and attention; but the vanity of the one, and the very inordinate passion for feasting of the other were strong bars against my advice taking effect.

There is to be another entertainment on the 10th,

at Spanish Town, and a ball the next night at the King's House. The dinner, I hear, is to be very superb, and in a different style to that given at Kingston. Spanish Town, I find, is the metropolis of the island, where the Assembly meets and the courts are held, and it seems the people hold those of Kingston very cheap. I have not had my foot on shore but in the naval yard, except for a few hours that I went to return the governor's visit at his country house, nor shall I attempt it in my present situation; though I am inclined to go to Spanish Town for a day to call upon a few gentlemen who have politely marked me with their attention.

I am much vexed we have not yet got our letters from Barbados by the May packet; for though they could bear no later date than the first or second of that month, yet I think they must contain interesting information beyond that brought by the Preston, as no letter I received from Captain Leslie was written after the middle of April.

Sir George Rodney is just returned to the Formidable, and as I have sent Captain Knight with a string of memorandums for Sir George's information, and to say I am ready for sea whenever he pleases, I shall drop my pen till he comes back.

Captain Knight is returned, and Sir George has honoured me with a visit. He still talks of ordering me to sea in a day or two; but I perceive his mind is embarrassed, and that he will not leave this island till he hears from home. The Ramillies, I find, goes to Bluefields to-morrow or next day, and I think it is meant he shall there wait till the end of the month; but really this [is] mere guess of mine.

With every good wish to you and yours. . . .

The Conqueror will have her fore mast in to-morrow, and the London on Saturday. I have daily expected to see Admiral Pigot[1] in the Jupiter for a fortnight past, as I understand she sailed early in May.

Lord Hood to Middleton

Barfleur: off the Havana. 5th August, 1782.

We got off this port a few hours since, and while laying to for the Jupiter and Enterprise to reconnoitre the harbour, I availed myself of the opportunity of making my first visit to the commander-in-chief, and of returning those of Sir Samuel Drake and Sir Edmund Affleck; and on my getting back to the Barfleur, I received a note from Admiral Pigot to inform me that the Captains Pasley and Payne saw seventeen sail of men-of-war in all appearance ready for sea, eleven or twelve of which they were very certain to be of the line; so that Solano must have retreated hither from the Cape, instead of going to America, as was given out, and probably had a design upon the Jamaica convoy. We shall therefore wait here till it comes (which will probably be to-morrow) and protect it through the Gulf. I therefore, while I have leisure, take up my pen to scribble a few lines more to you, trusting we shall see the convoy, as I wish you to know everything respecting things here, and you may rely upon it, that in all I say, truth will be distinctly adhered to on every occasion.

Upon my receiving Admiral Pigot's rendezvous on the 18th of last month (which was first, Cape Antonio on the Island Cuba; then the Capes of Virginia, and thirdly New York), I took the liberty of sending him a few lines, not being able to move

[1] Admiral Hugh Pigot relieved Rodney on 13th July.

out of my cabin, to the following effect: 'If you find the enemy in force at the Havana, I suppose you will judge it right to cruize off that port, till you have secured safety to the Jamaica convoy through the Gulf passage; and, if I understood you clearly, when you last honoured me with a visit, you proposed to reconnoitre the coast of Florida, and to satisfy yourself the enemy's fleet had not stopped at Augustine. Should not therefore your rendezvous, after passing Cape Antonio, be off the Havana; then Augustine, previous to your being looked for off the Chesapeake?' He thanked me for the hint, and fixed his rendezvous accordingly. Two sail, a ship and a brig, are standing towards the Havana from the western quarter. The Jupiter and Enterprise are gone after them, I shall therefore throw aside my pen for the present.

August 6th.—No convoy yet appears. I find by Admiral Pigot, Mr. Graves left Bluefields without his sailing orders, upon the representation of the masters of ships then there,—for his orders were carried thither by a small schooner from Lord Rodney, and are now on board the Formidable—by which he left the Jason and Glorieux behind him. The Jupiter lost sight of the ship she went in chase of in the night, and fell in with two polaccas from Marseilles, bound to the Bay of Campeachy. The Enterprise took the brig, an American privateer cruizing for the Jamaica convoy; the ship was her consort, called Le Comte de Grasse, which was again seen this morning early and chased on shore not far from the entrance of Havana harbour by the Tartar; and upon the Jupiter's coming up, her own people set fire to her; soon burnt to the water's edge and blew up.

I wish very much to get hold of a small coaster

or two, that we might know for certain whether Don Gálvez with his troops came from the Cape with Solano's squadron; for from that knowledge something material may be gathered respecting the enemy's designs after the hurricane months are over. I gave a hint of this to Admiral Pigot last night, finding a coasting schooner within our reach in the morning was neglected to be got hold of. Adieu, my dear Sir Charles, . . .

August 8th.—No appearance as yet of the convoy, which leads me to imagine Admiral Graves has recollected himself, and waited off Cape Antonio for the captured French ships and the remainder of the trade, as I understood the convoy was not to have departed from Bluefields till the last day of the month. It is I think beyond a doubt that Don Solano and his squadron are at the Havana; and I wish much to be certain whether General Don Gálvez and any number of the Spanish troops remained at the Cape, or returned with Solano, before we pass the Gulf. Now the question is, what can be Vaudreuil's plan with his ten sail of prime ships? He put to sea in company with Solano from the Cape; if he is gone to America, he will have done his business before we can get there, and be secure against any attack unless he can be met with in deep water. Should he be gone to Europe, Admiral Pigot can, I fear, do but little good upon the American coast; but he must go to New York to complete his water and the provisions of his fleet, as far as the king's magazines will allow. But is it unlikely that Vaudreuil, as well as Solano, may have had an eye upon the Jamaica convoy and the captured French line of battle ships? for by the instructions to the captains of the American privateers (the Schuylkill taken and Le Comte de Grasse destroyed) from a James Seagrove at the Havana, the people there well knew the convoy was to sail from Jamaica between the middle and end of the last month, and the privateers were to look out for, and endeavour to fall into the rear of it, to pick up stragglers or such as may be following to overtake the convoy.

Now, having turned all circumstances very seriously in my mind, I will candidly confess my ideas. The king's squadron now consists of twenty-four ships of the line, the Jupiter and four frigates. I would direct a flag officer, with ten or eleven ships, the Jupiter, and two frigates, to push on towards Bermuda and cruize forty or fifty leagues to the south-east of that island for sixteen or eighteen days, then repair to New York; and[1] proceed with the rest, (after the convoy was through the Gulf) to that port, reconnoitring the Chesapeake as I went along. This squadron would probably therefore have filled water, &c., before the other arrived, which would be saving time, and preventing much confusion; for the powers of New York are by no means equal to the completing so large a fleet at one and the same time.

Well then; supposing there is no object for the fleet upon the American coast, I should in that case hasten to sea again and make the best of my way off Cape Français; then divide the fleet (the Invincible is expected to join every day, and I suppose the Monarch and Anson will come to us at New York), station one half off that port, keeping the 50-gun ship and a frigate between it and the Mona channel, and the other [half] between the Caycos bank and Inagua. This would give a very fair chance for preventing a junction between Solano

[1] *Sc.* [I would].

and Vaudreuil, should an attack upon Jamaica be still intended ; and upon receiving intelligence to be relied upon, that the design was given up, I would then push away to windward, taking care to despatch a frigate immediately to Barbados, and order her commander to join me at New York as expeditiously as possible ; and I would direct another frigate from that quarter to cruize for me between the Cape and the Caycos bank, that I might not be ignorant of the exact state of the enemy and the islands to windward.

But should I find Vaudreuil harboured upon the coast of America, I would leave a force sufficient to watch him and proceed with the remainder off Cape Français, to guard that port against Solano's entrance, or Vaudreuil's—should he escape the squadron cruizing against him. This I shall communicate to Admiral Pigot, if he will condescend to do me the honour to ask my thoughts.

August 9th.—I begin to suspect the convoy passed us in the night by keeping upon the Florida shore, to avoid coming in sight of the Havana; and it was on that account I much wished Admiral Pigot to have stationed a couple of ships between Bahia Honda and the dry Tortugas, so that Mr. Graves should not go by unseen ; but the admiral is so very intent upon keeping his fleet together that he will not suffer a single ship to be out of his sight, or push to get hold of a small coaster or two for fear of a frigate's getting on shore; but if he will risk nothing, and suffer himself to remain in ignorance of what is very material for him to know, he will do nothing but from the chapter of accidents. But don't you think it highly expedient that a small two-deck ship and a frigate or two should have been ordered to have preceded the fleet off the Havana, by way of getting intelligence?

The Germain sloop joined this morning; left Bluefields the 29th of last month, when the Monarch was under sail for Port Royal attended by the Fox frigate. The Captain of the Germain spoke with Admiral Graves on Monday the 5th, ten leagues to the westward of Cape Antonio; the Glorieux and Jason had not joined the admiral, but were not above a dozen leagues astern, which the Germain saw the day before; and as the Hydra, with several ships left behind, were following to overtake the convoy, I suppose Admiral Graves would lay-to, or make moderate sail, till the two captured ships and the trade were come up.

Surely no other man in the world but Lord Rodney would have deprived the convoy of such strength as the Resolution and Montagu, and have taken the Nonsuch, Anson, Flora and Alert sloop from Admiral Pigot, to protect his own person through the Windward passage, and, I am told, means to take the two latter with him to England as well as the Resolution. His flag is in the Montagu, which I shall not be surprised if he shifts to the Resolution or Flora before he passes the latitude of Bermuda. I believe the world never produced such another man; one should have thought any rational person in his lordship's situation would rather have taken his passage in the Jupiter. If any accident befalls the convoy which the above two seventy-four ships would have prevented, he will have much to answer for.

Lord Rodney has not lived in France for nothing, for I defy any Frenchman living to have written a more gasconade account than his lordship has done in that of the action of the 12th of April;[1]

[1] Rodney's despatch, dated 14th April, is printed by Mundy, ii. 255–8, and does not by any means seem to call for this severe criticism.

for except what he says respecting the behaviour of the officers and men of his Majesty's fleet, there is scarce one whole line of truth; which I gave him a pretty broad hint of, when he did me the honour to show me his letters the next day; to which he answered, 'You must consider my letters are for the public at large.' 'I do so,' says I, 'and it is upon that very score, I think your account should be perfectly genuine, and not such as will allow any officer of your fleet to say things did not happen as you represent; for I should apprehend if the public became sensible that some particular parts of your letters are not right, will it not make the whole liable to be suspected? His answer was: No matter for that; did I wish any alteration? 'Not a syllable,' I said, 'respecting myself,[1] if you mean that.' He said he did.

The daily declarations of Vaudreuil and all the officers at Cape Français to Captain Merrick and Captain Ball[2] were—'We cannot deny you gained a most complete victory on the 12th of April; but you, on your part, must acknowledge you knew not how to make use of it.' Nothing was ever more true, which will be an everlasting disgrace to the commander-in-chief.

August 12th.—Since my confinement by the accident to my leg, I have been very much indisposed with a complaint I have long laboured under in my stomach and bowels;[3] but keep this to yourself, for if my wife knows it, she will be miserable.

This morning I had a note from Admiral Pigot,

[1] 'The noble behaviour of my second in command, Sir Samuel Hood, who in both actions most conspicuously exerted himself, demands my earnest encomiums.'

[2] Alexander John Ball. See *D.N.B.*

[3] His correspondence speaks of this as early as 1750. See *D.N.B.* 264b.

who had been alarmed by a letter he had received from the Lieutenant-Governor of Jamaica, informing him of the arrival of two transports with near 400 troops on board (part of those which came from Charleston), which had sailed from Antigua for St. Lucia, under convoy of the Prudent, Rotterdam and Magicienne; and that Major Maxwell and the masters of the transports said that, after having parted company, they saw under Dominica a fleet of thirty-six sail, amongst which were several men-of-war; that presently after, they saw six sail more, seemingly in chase of the first; to one of the latter they made the private signal, which, being answered, they stood towards her, but as she presently began to engage, they bore away for Jamaica. I presently satisfied the admiral about this fleet; and made it clear, next to a certainty almost, that it must be two frigates from Marseilles, with that part of the trade they had not left at Tobago, St. Vincent, and Grenada; for this convoy was seen but a few days before off Grenada. By having recourse to certain facts and dates and many little circumstances, things which appear alarming at first, are easily reconciled to be unworthy of attention. I took this opportunity of observing to [the] admiral as follows: 'May not Vaudreuil be cruising to intercept the Jamaica convoy and the captured men-of-war? and may not Solano have retreated to the Havana on the same errand? for if he had not some immediate object in view, he would not be laying at this season with all his ships in that perfect readiness for sea. That I had been thinking a good deal of the enemy's probable designs, and what was most likely to check them; and that if he had a wish to know my thoughts they were very much at his service, and that I should be extremely happy if he could make them useful.' Admiral Pigot immediately sent me word, he would call upon me, and on his coming on board, I put into his hand, the substance of what I have suggested to you, with my name to it; he expressed himself much obliged, but what the effect will be, time alone can show.

August 13th.—Yesterday the frigates, assisted by the boats of the fleet, chased a ship and two brigs into a small creek a few leagues to the eastward of the Havana, where they found two other vessels; the three former and one of the latter were brought off; the fifth, an empty vessel, was burnt. The latter is a Spaniard, laden with mahogany; the others are Americans from Baltimore, with flour; all armed. They sailed with eleven others, under convoy of a ship of twenty-two guns, which they parted with fourteen days ago, and are now astern. A signal is just made for a fleet in the north-west. I shall therefore conclude, and am, with great truth and affection, my dear Sir Charles, most faithfully yours,

HOOD.[1]

[*Secret and confidential.*]

Not yet through the Gulf of Florida.
21st August–7th September, 1782.

[Virtually the same as the letter to Jackson of the same dates (*N.R.S.* iii. 138–51). The concluding lines on 21st August (p. 141), about his wife and family, are not here; on 24th August, p. 142, 5 lines from bottom, 'German' ought to read 'Germain'; p. 144, line 13, 'annleer' ought to read 'an ulcer'; on 30th August, p. 148, line 3 from bottom, for 'command for want of practice' read 'duty, having never had the command of a squadron before, or scarce seen salt water since the year '63?'; p. 149, line 3, for 'chance of rendering a good account both of the' read 'chance of destroying both the'; and line 11, for 'not disastered' read 'in a perfect state.' On 5th September, p. 150, the names filled in are given at

[1] The first letter so signed.

length; line 19, after 'combined fleet' read 'till he was reinforced. As a battle must, I think, take place, God grant the victory may be decisive, and brilliant to his lordship.' Other differences are trivial, but the letter to Middleton ends on 7th September with the sense of the first paragraph on p. 151, as a postscript.]

Hood to Middleton

New York. 5th October, 1782.

I troubled you with a long narrative of different dates by the Southampton, which left this port the 15th of last month, and I hope and trust is now within a few days' sail of England. We have been upon the tenter-hook of expectation of news from your side the water for some time past, and still continue to be so; the latest letters from London bear no fresher date than the 6th of July. I most devoutly pray God grant we may soon hear that an administration is fixed which has the confidence of our most gracious master and the whole nation. Such a ministry would, I hope, set us firm upon our legs and enable us to subdue our host of enemies.

The Warwick, with Prince William on board, returned here the 27th of last month, with a very large French frigate named L'Aigle,[1] which was forced on shore in the Delaware. Her masts were cut away and attempts made to destroy her, without effect. She carries twenty-eight 24-pounders (English guns) on her main-deck, and sixteen 9-pounders on her quarter-deck and forecastle; she came from Rochefort, and had on board several French generals and other officers and 90,000*l.* in money; the former got ashore, and took with them all the cash except about 4,000*l.* La Gloire of thirty-two guns was with her, but, drawing less

[1] See Appendix B.

water, beat over the shoal and escaped to Philadelphia.

I have not words to express to you how very much his royal highness is improved in every respect. His appearance delighted me most exceedingly, and I really believe has grown a full head since I left this coast last year; the very kind, polite, attentive and manly manner in which his royal highness was pleased to receive me was flattering in the extreme. On the 30th my friend and old acquaintance Colonel Musgrave arrived here in the Diomede from Charleston, and has brought the blue ribbon for Prince William.

I have the pleasing satisfaction to tell you that the exercise I take mornings and evenings gives me hopes to believe I shall again become so stout as to enable me to acquit myself in the discharge of my duty to my wishes, to the end of this year at least.

The situation of things in this country is truly distressing, and altogether beyond my comprehension; I will not therefore say one word about them, except that the poor loyalists are distracted at the near approach of the miserable lot doomed for them. The packet is said to sail to-morrow, but I will keep my letter open in case it should not. . . .

The Lion and Vestal were in company with the Warwick.

October 8th.—The packet is still here and does not sail till the morning. By the last account received of the state of Vaudreuil's squadron,[1] it will not be in a condition for sea before the middle of next month, so that I suppose it will be my lot to remain here some time longer; but I speak from guess only, having not heard a syllable of any move-

[1] Arrived at Boston on 4th August, and remained there till 24th December.

ment of his Majesty's fleet, and I am afraid our intelligence is not much to be depended upon. This account was received yesterday, though dated Boston, the 17th of last month. Is it not strange we should remain in ignorance, when by a little attention and looking forward we might easily know all that would be useful to us?

Vaudreuil sent the Iris[1] to this port about a fortnight ago, and her commander was not suffered to come out of his ship—why, I cannot conceive. It was very much my wish he should have seen our fleet, which was then in the most perfect, well-looking order. Besides, it is very much our interest to encourage an intercourse with the French fleet by our most judicious and discerning officers. We can lose nothing by it, and may gain considerably, for the commanding officer does not send a ship to sea or the army make a move but it is known to the enemy immediately, as we are surrounded by their friends, without having a single friend amongst them that can venture to bring or send any information, however well they may be inclined. Captain Traversay, of the Iris, a very well-bred young man, was charged with many complimentary messages from Vaudreuil to me; and as I found he was not to be permitted to come up above Sandy Hook (which is behaviour quite different to that given to officers I have sent to the French commander-in-

[1] The story of this ship is rather exceptional. She was a 32-gun frigate, built by the American colonists as the Hancock; was captured in her first cruise, July 1777, by Sir George Collier in the 44-gun ship Rainbow, was bought into our service and renamed Iris (Beatson, iv. 280; *D.N.B. s.n.* Collier, George). In Sept. 1781 she was captured by De Grasse off the Chesapeake, and as Iris remained in the French service. In 1793 she was a powder hulk at Toulon, and was carelessly or ignorantly burnt by the Spaniards, with several thousand barrels of powder on board (James, i. 86, 91).

chief at Cape Français), I thought it right to send my captain to wait upon him, which he took very kindly, and seemed much mortified to be confined to his ship. Had he been treated with a little civility and given a dinner or two on board our ships, any captain who might have been sent from hence would, I am certain from experience, have been received and treated in the same manner in Vaudreuil's squadron.

No August packet yet arrived, which is distressing to us all in the extreme. . . .

Hood to Middleton

New York. 14th October, 1782.

The very extraordinary behaviour of Monsieur de la Touche[1] has occasioned a delay to the packet of some days, and allows me the pleasure of giving you a few lines more.

The Fortunée and Champion arrived yesterday with an account that they saw in the evening of the 9th a fleet of twenty-five sail, nine or ten of which were judged to be of the line, in the latitude of the Delaware, fifty-seven leagues from the shore, and steering SSE, or thereabouts. This brought me the honour of a note from Admiral Pigot desiring my opinion. I immediately waited on him on board the Formidable. Upon receiving the admiral's note it struck me that this fleet could be no other than a convoy of transports from Halifax to South

[1] M. de la Touche, made prisoner in the Aigle, had been allowed, on his parole, to reside in Long Island. He had made himself comfortable there, and when the cartel for France was ready to sail, he very insolently refused to go on board. The ship sailed without him, and he was afterwards, with but scanty consideration, sent to England in the Carysfort. It is a curious story. (See Appendix B.)

Carolina, which sailed on the 1st instant; and upon conversation with Captain Christian I was pretty confident of it, and Admiral P. became equally so; I was not at all displeased at the report, as it will operate as a spur; for I have not liked the idea of six and twenty sail of the line lying inactive here so long, while the French had a squadron in the neighbourhood and sent ships to sea to drive our cruizers from a sight of Boston Harbour.

I was glad of it on another account, as it enabled me with much propriety to suggest my thoughts very fully. Admiral Pigot proposes to sail in a few days to the West Indies with half his force, leaving the other half with me to watch Vaudreuil, and I hope he will order me into Boston Bay. If I am told to do as I like I will certainly go there, and finding the enemy in no condition for sea will stretch to Halifax by way of keeping up our water for three or four days, and from thence I can not only follow Vaudreuil better than from this port, but more advantageously watch his motions.

The Spanish general with the greater part of his troops are undoubtedly at Cape Français, where preparations are making for some enterprise. I shall therefore, if I am not ordered to the contrary (which I have mentioned to the chief), when I quit the American coast, steer directly in the track to the island of Hispaniola; and if I am so fortunate as to get hold of Vaudreuil, I shall be satisfied of having lived to a good purpose.

We are all miserable at not hearing from England since the first week in July.

Ever and affectionately yours,

Hood.

Hood to Admiral Pigot

[*Autograph copy.*] New York. 17th October, 1782.

Dear Sir,—I take the liberty of sending you the result of the enquiries I have been able to make since I came to the West Indies, of the track ships in general take in going to Cape Français from the coast of North America, and as you have done me the honour to ask my opinion in your present situation, I will very candidly say what I should do was the king's fleet under my command. I would as expeditiously as possible proceed to Carlisle Bay, Barbados, with half the line-of-battle ships now here, and so soon as they had completed their water, go to St. Lucia for twenty-four hours, and from thence to St. John's Road, Antigua; and not finding any reason to suspect a design from the enemy against his Majesty's islands to windward, I should stretch away to the northward, and cruize from twenty to thirty leagues to the northward of the Caycos island, until I received intelligence of the situation of things at Cape Français and the Havana, which intelligence would guide my further proceedings; and as I went to the southward I should detach the Jupiter with the Germain or Lively off the Havana, the former to return and cruize at the above-mentioned bearings and distance from the Caycos island so long as her water would last, and the latter to make all the despatch possible to Barbados, calling off English Harbour in her way, and leaving with Commissioner Laforey whatever intelligence her commander may have to communicate. The other half of the line-of-battle ships, left upon the coast to watch the motions of Vaudreuil's squadron, should put to sea at the same time with you, and proceed into Boston Bay to take a view of the enemy; and not finding the French ships in a condition for sea, to go to Halifax for a few days in order to keep their water up; then return again into Boston Bay for another look at the enemy, and from thence proceed off New York; and upon sending a frigate in, and receiving no intelligence to make a longer stay of his Majesty's squadron necessary, and the season being then such as to render any attempt from the enemy by sea impracticable at this port, the squadron should make the best of its way off the Caycos island, and not finding any frigate there to communicate intelligence, it must be sought for by sending a ship or two off Cape Français; and from the information the commanding officer receives, his conduct must be guided.

I always wish and mean to be perfectly explicit and unreserved in any opinion I might be asked for, and never to shrink from it, and am therefore willing upon every occasion to give it from under my hand; and as I cannot see any possible advantage to the king's service to arise from my remaining in this harbour, and a great deal may by my going to sea —as it will give a chance not only for intercepting the French ships from Portsmouth, but such as may be coming from Europe to Boston—I cannot help repeating my wish to follow you from hence as soon as possible. But if you think otherwise, I beg to submit to your consideration whether it would not be advisable for the ships you intend to leave with me, to remain at Staten Island till within two or three days of the time you propose I shall sail, in order to keep their water complete with the greater ease and convenience, which is a material circumstance.

Admiral Pigot to Lord Hood

[*Copy in Hood's hand.*] Formidable. 17th October, 1782.

My dear Lord,—I am much obliged to you for your very friendly letter and opinion, and although I may differ in one point, be assured it only proceeds from my idea of the situation of things at this place. I mean that of your following to sea a day or two after me; therefore wish you to stay until the next spring tide, and agree with you that it will be quite as well your keeping the ships at Staten Island until within two or three days before the next new moon. Another reason for my wishing your not going immediately with me is that of my orders, which are almost positive, to keep a fleet equal, if not superior, to the enemy as long as they continue upon the coast. The words of the part of the order, as far as relates to staying here, are as follows:—

'You are to remain in North America until the first full moon in October, or so long as the enemy's fleet continues in those seas; and when you return to the Leeward Islands, you are to leave a superiority to the naval force of the enemy remaining in North America.'

Upon considering this it goes almost to a positive order not to quit this coast while the enemy is upon it; and nothing but the want of proper places to shelter ourselves can justify us in it. I know you have the order; but as you possibly might not recollect every particular is my reason for sending you this; not from my disagreeing with you in opinion—for my own idea is that ships of our magnitude should not be trusted to the last moment and thereby be brought into difficulties.

I entirely agree with you in every other part of your letter as to cruizing and sending out ships for intelligence, unless something should arise to make a change necessary.

Note.—I admit we should not quit the coast, leaving the French ships behind, while the season will allow them to act; but I think it would be more creditable to go and look at the enemy than to remain useless at New York. Another strong reason is, we can get no intelligence to be relied upon; and before we may know that the French ships are gone from Boston, they may be half way to the West Indies. The intercepting them in their passage is what I think we should look to.

HOOD.

Hood to Middleton

Barfleur: Staten Island. 31st October, 1782.

I give my many thanks for your few friendly lines by the September packet. Lord Keppel has full credit with me for so readily complying with Lord Howe's wish in behalf of my brother,[1] who I hope and trust will never give his lordship any cause to be dissatisfied with his conduct.

In my last I told you of Admiral Pigot's having been alarmed at an account brought here, that an enemy's squadron had been, early in the month, seen upon this coast; but that he was soon made easy in his mind about it. As the time of the admiral's departure from hence drew near, and being, I believe, thoroughly convinced I had no wish but for the good of the king's service, and of course for his honour and character, he asked my opinion of what was best to be done in his then situation; upon which I wrote him the letter you will herewith

[1] Alexander, afterwards Viscount Bridport; at this time a rear-admiral in the Grand Fleet, under the command of Howe.

receive, and I also send you his answer.[1] The orders he gave me corresponded with his letter; they are dated the 18th; and on the 23rd, a few days after the August packet arrived, that part respecting my proceeding to Halifax was annulled, and I was directed to wait here, so long as it was proper for his Majesty's squadron to remain upon the coast of North America.

This correspondence between the commander-in-chief and me will, I flatter myself, prove that my conduct is consonant to your wishes and to our royal master's service. Admiral Pigot and I have lived upon the best terms possible; my sentiments have ever been expressed most clearly and without reserve, having no private view to gratify; and I believe the admiral to be very perfectly satisfied with me; for however I may have differed in opinion with him in some material points, I never lost sight of keeping up a most cordial unanimity in the fleet, and I may venture to say greater harmony never existed in any fleet than in the one under Admiral Pigot's command. As my putting to sea must very probably, for a few months to come, depend upon the motions of the French squadron at Boston, it is impossible for me to say when I shall sail.

Duplicates of the despatches the Carysfort brings will, I understand, be forwarded some days hence in a packet, when I will give you a few lines more. I will now only add my best wishes to you and yours, and that I am with real regard and esteem . . .

The force under my command consists of twelve of the line and three frigates, and I may possibly be joined by the Magnificent from Halifax before I quit the coast.

[1] 17th Oct. *ante*, pp. 215, 217.

Hood to Rear-Admiral Digby

[*Copy.*]

Barfleur: Staten Island. 10th November, 1782.

Having this moment received the intelligence I herewith send you, it appears highly necessary I should put to sea with his Majesty's squadron under my command as soon as possible, and I beg to submit to your consideration whether you should send the Lion with me, and whether something should not be detached immediately to Charleston, with orders for the troops there to proceed to Jamaica. I shall be glad you will direct the master attendant to place the buoys for the ships going to the Hook without one moment's loss of time.

If I hear anything between this and the morning I will then have the honour of waiting upon you and Sir Guy Carleton.

Rear-Admiral Rowley to Admiral Pigot (or the Commanding Officer at New York)

[*Copy.*] Ajax: Port Royal, Jamaica. 8th October, 1782.

The enclosed papers, No. 1 and 2, are copies of intelligence I have procured from a prize schooner, captured by his Majesty's ship Ulysses, and bound from the Havana to Cape François with letters and 60,000 dollars; also some intelligence from the Cape. You will therefore see the necessity of a force being immediately sent for the protection of this valuable island; and doubt not but you will give every assistance in your power, by sending such ships as you may judge necessary for its defence. No exertions on my part shall be wanting.

The Spaniards, from every report, certainly intend to rendezvous at Cape François with their fleet, the latter end of this month or early in November. Governor Campbell writes by this express to Sir Guy Carleton for what assistance is in his power to send. The force we have now here are sickly; but should assistance arrive before the enemy are able to proceed, I doubt not but their intention will be baffled. Since your sailing I have sent a small squadron down to the Musquito Shore, and have the pleasure to inform you that the squadron and troops which accompanied them have retaken Fort Dalling and the settlement of Black River. Fort Dalling was stormed, and sixty-five Spaniards out of sixty-seven were killed by the Indians; the remainder of the Spanish troops at Black River, amounting to 700, capitulated; the squadron captured only one polacca ship, with provisions and a few soldiers.

This letter will be delivered you by Captain Hulke, of his Majesty's sloop Duguay-Trouin, and I am to request you will despatch him back for this place as soon as possible, as I shall be very anxious for his arrival. I had the pleasure to receive your letter dated 23rd of August last, but his Majesty's ship Sybil has not yet arrived.

Enclosure, No. 1.

Captain Spry to Rear-Admiral Rowley

[*Copy.*]

Ulysses: off Turk's Island. 27th September, 1782.

Dear Sir,—Having this moment received some letters from Captain Douglas, which were found on one of the prisoners (taken in the schooner about a week ago), which, containing some information relative to the intentions of the Spaniards to return to the Cape the latter end of October to join the

French in an attack on Jamaica, I have judged it my duty (though she would have been of great use to me on my cruize) to send the prize to acquaint you with it. I also send you many other letters in which you probably may find other corroborating intelligence. When the prize sailed, there was at the Havana seventeen sail of the line and two frigates ready for sea; and one of the Spaniards informs me that a few days before he sailed, a packet arrived with intelligence that Mr. Bonet (the late admiral at the Havana) had arrived about six weeks ago at Martinique with twelve sail of the line and ten thousand troops. If this part of the intelligence is true,[1] I suppose you will hear of it from St. Lucia or the Windward Islands. I should suspect that the Spaniards have not abandoned their design on Jamaica, by Don Gálvez and his troops being certainly at the Cape. I shall proceed off the Old Cape, and if I should obtain any intelligence of consequence, shall despatch the Licorne to acquaint you with it.

I am, with great respect, Sir,

Your most obedient, humble servant,

THOMAS SPRY.

[1] It wasn't. El Teniente General D. Juan Bautista Bonet, who was Governor of the Havana in 1779, when war was declared, had very little naval force under his command, and seems to have gone home in the latter part of 1780. He commanded a division of the Spanish fleet in the rencounter off Cape Spartel on 20th October, 1782. Solano, who brought out 12 very sickly ships of the line in June 1780, touched at Martinique, and, in company with the French fleet, went on from there, in July, to Cap Français and the Havana. It does not appear that he or his squadron was near Martinique afterwards. Fernandez Duro, *Armada Española*, vii. 283–292, 344; Chevalier, i. 192, 193, 327; Lacour-Gayet, ii. 344, 435.

Enclosure, No. 2.

Extract from Secret Intelligence, dated Port au Prince, 31st August, 1782. Received [by Rowley], 3rd October, 1782.

During my stay both at the Cape and here, I examined the troops with some degree of attention. The men, Frenchmen and Spaniards, are fine looking fellows; but the Spaniards are as superior to the French in discipline, as the latter are to the former in cleanliness. Never have I seen troops fire and manœuvre better than the Spaniards; they are ever on the parade and employed.

You may depend on a blow being immediately to be struck by the Spaniards and Americans against Bermudas; the latter complain much of the interruption of their trade this summer; they say their trade has suffered more this year from English cruizers, than during the whole course of the war. God increase their confusion! They are particularly exasperated against the Bermudians.

Rear-Admiral Digby to Hood

Information received at New York. 12th November, 1782.

Portsmouth. 12 October.

Was on board a French 74 and passed close by the other two French 74-gun ships, namely L'Auguste and Le Bourgogne, the last of which is equipped, the other two repairing as fast as possible; a new main mast making for one and almost ready; it was expected that the Pluton would soon sail for Boston.

Boston. 19th October.

The French admiral's ship lays off the long wharf; has her damages repaired, by putting a piece, sixteen feet long, in her keel, making a new rudder, &c. &c. Two ships, of 74 guns each, in the harbour; their hulls nearly repaired, no topmasts up, nor yards across as yet. Three more ships of the line between Nantasket and the town; their damages mostly in their hulls, together with the loss of small spars. Three ships of the line repaired and occasionally cruising with two frigates; the whole fleet furnished with duck in Boston; and by late arrivals from Holland, they are all supplied with cordage; their bread is baking and provisions preparing; but as yet they have not taken in their water. From all circumstances, it is beyond a doubt they are bound to the Windward Islands in the West Indies. From the best accounts, they will not be ready to sail till the beginning of December next; but it is impossible to get an exact knowledge of their time of sailing.

The fleet will be well equipped and have several merchantmen under their convoy; the new 74-gun ship[1] given by Congress to the French king was to be launched at Portsmouth the 16th of October, and to remain there till next spring.

Connecticut. 7th November.

The French army are marching towards Boston, and, as it is imagined, to embark from thence; the first division was fifteen miles NE from Norwich this day.

Connecticut. 8th November.

The last division of the French troops marched through Coventry this morning on their way to Boston.

[1] L'América. Chevalier, i. 326.

Sir Guy Carleton to Lord Hood

[*Copy.*] New York. 12th November, 1782.

My Lord,—I enclose for your lordship's information an extract of a letter I have written to Lieutenant General Leslie, and that of another to Governor Campbell, and I most gladly take this occasion to express my very high esteem of your lordship, and to wish you, upon a personal as well as public account, all the success and honour which your public character warrants us to expect. It is with great regret that my attentions here will not permit me to pay my duty to his royal highness personally, and to wish your lordship, which I very sincerely do, a prosperous voyage.

I have the honour to be . . . .

GUY CARLETON.

Sir Guy Carleton to Lieutenant-General Leslie, commanding at Charleston

[*Extract.*] New York. 12th November, 1782.

In consequence of information received yesterday from Governor Campbell, that the island of Jamaica is in imminent danger of a speedy attack, I have judged it expedient to send a body of troops there without delay. You will therefore make the necessary arrangements for sending to that island, immediately after the evacuation of Charleston is completed, the 3rd, 63rd, 64th and 71st regiments and the companies of the 82nd and 84th now under your command. The senior officer of those corps, who is to take the command of the whole, will proceed, under convoy of such ships of war as the admiral shall appoint, to Jamaica, and put himself under the orders of the officer commanding the king's troops on that island. You will make such arrangements relative to the staff to go with this corps as you may judge expedient. You will give orders for the remainder of the troops from Charleston, including the 60th regiment, to proceed to this place, observing the directions I have already given.

Sir Guy Carleton to General Campbell, Governor of Jamaica

[*Extract.*] New York. 12th November, 1782.

I yesterday received your Excellency's letter of the 7th October by his Majesty's sloop Duguay-Trouin, in consequence of which I despatch immediate orders to Lieutenant General Leslie commanding in South Carolina, to send to Jamaica, the moment the evacuation of Charleston is completed, the 3rd, 63rd, 64th, and 71st regiments, six companies of the 82nd, and two of the 84th, amounting to 42 commissioned and 10 staff officers, 133 sergeants, 70 drummers and 1,315 rank and file; which I expect will be ready to sail on the arrival of the despatch. These are all the British there, except some detachments of very considerable[1] numbers, whose regiments are in this district or prisoners.

The relief sent you on this occasion, and so early in the season, exposes the king's service in other parts to difficulties and danger, which the importance of Jamaica, together with a full confidence that your alarm is not premature, only renders excusable. I trust your Excellency's judgment and zeal for the public welfare will induce you to look first to the safety of your own island, and delay sending detach-

[1] So in MS. In error, apparently, for 'inconsiderable.'

ments to the Spanish main, which may weaken your defence, occasion your calling for larger reinforcements of regular troops, and can produce no solid advantages to the state, until it is more able to extend its possessions, and secure such conquests.

I must request that as soon as the king's service will permit, your Excellency will send to the northward, not only the companies of the 82nd and 84th, but all the weak and sickly regiments under your command, which may be replaced by others, complete, in good health, and in other respects more fit for service. I should think the beginning of the hurricane season, when the king's fleets come to North America, the most proper for this measure. They might likewise on their return take under their protection the troops destined to replace them.

Hood to Middleton

Barfleur : New York. 13th November, 1782.

My dear Sir Charles,—By a vessel which arrived here from Jamaica on the 10th we had an account that the Duguay-Trouin sailed two days before with despatches from the commanders-in-chief by sea and land to those in that character here. I immediately wrote to Rear-Admiral Digby the letter you will herewith receive.[1] On the 10th the Duguay-Trouin came in, and so soon as I had opened and read the despatch addressed to Admiral Pigot,[2] a copy of which I now send, I waited on Sir Guy Carleton and Admiral Digby, and signified my intention of putting to sea the moment there was water to pass the bar, unless Admiral Digby gave me orders to the contrary; which he does not care to do, though he will not speak out upon the

[1] *Ante*, p. 220. [2] From Rowley, *ante*, p. 220.

propriety of my sailing, and suggests danger to this port from Vaudreuil's squadron after I am gone, though it cannot be in a condition to put to sea before the middle of next month, if before the beginning of January, according to very recent intelligence the admiral sent me, which he said might be depended on. Sir Guy Carleton said not a word against my going, and very candidly observed that, even admitting danger to be evident here, he could not think it should stand in competition with that which threatened so valuable an island as Jamaica; but he cannot part with a soldier from hence. Whether the Carolina troops that can serve in the West Indies (for some cannot, according to the agreement made at the hire of them) will be ordered, as I suggested in my letter to Admiral Digby above mentioned, I cannot say; but if the whole could be sent to Jamaica, I should apprehend the near approach of winter, and the danger the transports will run, in coming upon this coast next month (for they cannot be here before the middle of it), of being dispersed and driven to various islands, would be very sufficient reason for their going all together immediately, as any part could be sent back in the spring.

I go to the Hook to-morrow, and hope and trust to be over the bar the 16th, as I think I shall then find water enough to cross it without risk. I never knew good to come from procrastination. Had half the king's ships (agreeably to what I took the liberty to suggest to Admiral Pigot, which I sent you[1]) gone and taken a stand in the fair way from the Havana to Cape Français, the Spanish squadron would most likely have been intercepted. As it is, Don Solano will most probably have the start of

[1] *Ante*, p. 215.

me, a fortnight at least; but I hope otherwise, and shall push to the southward as fast as possible. I know I am inferior, but shall not mind a ship or two.

I can hear nothing of the Magnificent from Halifax, and I know I shall not have the Lion, though she will be useless in remaining here. His royal highness is vastly well, in fine spirits, and appears perfectly happy.

The whole of the French troops in this country are by this at Boston, to embark for the West Indies. I mentioned my readiness to receive Mr. Legge to Admiral Digby. He said he would consider it; but I find he means to keep him at New York the winter.

P.S.—I am well aware I shall probably be overmatched, not only in line-of-battle ships but in frigates also, which I have represented to Admiral Digby, and sent him the exact state of the squadron, which is more than seven hundred [short] in eleven ships; for the Prince George being then in the North River with the rear-admiral's flag on board, I had no return from her. But in case of misfortune, which may possibly happen, I herewith trouble you with letters written upon the state of the squadron, in consequence of the information that has been received, without producing the addition of a man or ship; and upon my desiring the Albemarle, which came yesterday from Quebec and not belonging to this station, Admiral Digby, in return, desired me to send one of my frigates to Charleston, to strengthen the convoy with troops from thence to Jamaica, which I have done. I have, I trust, acquitted myself with propriety in humbly representing what appeared to me to be right for the king's service, so that no blame can justly fall upon me if disaster, arising from want of sufficient force, should happen.

Hood to Admiral Pigot

Barfleur: at sea, off Sandy Hook. 22nd November, 1782.

[*Copy*. *N.R.S.* iii. 153.]

Hood to Rear-Admiral Rowley

[*Copy*.] Barfleur: at sea. 26th November, 1782.

As I think the chance is far better for intercepting Vaudreuil's squadron from Boston off the Old Cape,[1] a little to the westward of Cape Samana, on the east end of Hispaniola, than off the Caycos Island, where I told you, by the Duguay-Trouin, I should cruize; as I shall, off the Old Cape, be in a fair way to intercept any reinforcements from Europe, and of joining Admiral Pigot—as he will probably think it right to come to leeward—to whom I have despatched a frigate since I left New York on the 22nd instant; I embrace this opportunity of the Santa Margarita, whose commander I have given the Young William mast ship in charge, to convoy her to Port Royal.[2] And as the Santa Margarita is belonging to the squadron under the command of Rear-Admiral Digby, I trust you will not detain her, but

[1] Cape Viejo Français. After consulting officers who knew the West Indies, Hood was, in this, coming back to the practice of the Seven Years' War, when off Old Cape was the regular station for intercepting enemy's ships outward bound to Cape Français.

[2] So in MS. It looks as if the transcriber had omitted a line, or a few words, such as 'of letting you know the intended change of my rendezvous.'

allow Captain Salter to return to North America, agreeably to the orders he has received from me, solely for the purpose of protecting the mast ship to Jamaica.

27th November, 1782.

I believe I omitted to tell you in the letter I had the honour of writing you last evening, that I had ordered a frigate to cruize and look out for any ships from Admiral Pigot or you with intelligence, off the Caycos Island, as I there intended to take my stand when I wrote you by the Duguay-Trouin from New York; but upon conversing since with officers who have served much upon the Jamaica station, I find that though the French ships of war with their trade from Cape François go out into the sea through the Caycos passage, yet [they] seldom or ever return that way back, but go to the eastward of the Silver Keys and make the west end of Porto Rico or Cape Samana. I confess myself ignorant of the track the French ships generally take among the Keys, and therefore am ready to listen to those whom experience has better informed.

I hope I shall soon have the pleasure of receiving intelligence from some of your cruizers, whose orders I shall not interfere with to my own emolument in any respect. I have but one frigate with me except my repeater, having sent the Endymion to strengthen the convoy with troops from Charleston to Jamaica. My force in line-of-battle ships is twelve, the same number Vaudreuil has; but should I fall in [1] with a reinforcement coming from Europe or Martinique, I shall become very inferior to him, as he has not a ship under a seventy-four, and I have four of sixty-four. Therefore I beg leave humbly to submit to your judgment whether it would not

[1] So in MS.; but clearly the meaning is 'should *he* fall in with, or be joined by.'

be right to send all the serviceable ships of the line to me from Port Royal. Vaudreuil could not, I think, leave Boston before the end of this month, if so soon by a few days; all the French troops in America are at Boston, to embark in the French squadron.

Hood to Admiral Pigot

[*Copy.*] Barfleur: Cape Samana WSW, 20 Lgs. 4th December, 1782.

Sir,—I have the honour to acquaint you that I have by accident just fallen in with the Licorne, whose commander is charged with despatches [1] to you, with which I send him on without loss of time. They denote Jamaica to be in greater danger than ever. Captain Douglas was first to go to New York, and not finding you there to proceed to Barbados, and from thence to St. Lucia in search of you; but as I think he will probably get notice where you are, and may be soonest met, from Commissioner Laforey, I have directed Captain Douglas to send his boat ashore at English Harbour, and desired the commissioner not to detain him a moment.

By the accounts you will herewith receive, I stand a chance to be abominably thrashed. How unlucky the Magnificent is not with me, and that Rear-Admiral Digby was deaf to my application for the Lion! But I will do my best, and rely upon that providence which has hitherto so kindly assisted me.

I shall endeavour to learn as soon as I can, whether the Spanish squadron is got to the Cape or not. If they are not, I will cruize in sight of the Cape to windward, and take my chance for meeting that squadron, or the one from Boston, separately.

[1] They follow this letter.

But I must be more wary if it is, and not suffer myself to be entangled with an enemy's squadron of equal force, in sight of a port where a superior one rides, and can come out upon me.

Rear-Admiral Rowley to Admiral Pigot

[*Copy.*] London: Port Royal Harbour, Jamaica.
11th November, 1782.

Sir,—As I think it of the utmost consequence for the preservation of this island, that the enclosed intelligence No. 1 should be immediately forwarded to you, I doubt not but you will give every assistance in your power to frustrate any attempts which the enemy may make; and from every account I can learn, they certainly mean to attack this island in a very short time, should not the arrival of a reinforcement put a stop to their present exertions for that purpose.

His Majesty's ship London arrived here the 28th ulto., she having had an action with a French ship of the line, and enclosed I send you a copy of Captain Kempthorne's letter [1] to me respecting the action; but for further particulars I cannot say, until the arrival of the Torbay, which I expect every hour; but it is, I believe, certain that the ship run on shore, and will not be recovered to the enemy.

I shall not send home the Ajax as intended with the convoy, which is to sail the 25th instant, but keep her and the Torbay ready to join you, should you wish me to send them.

As this place is bare of every material for refitting the London, there being neither spars nor cordage in store, nor can they be procured, I am

[1] The substance of this letter is given in Beatson's *Naval and Military Memoirs*, v. 527 *seq.*

afraid it will be a long time before she is refitted, but you may depend I shall use every exertion in my power to get her as forward as possible. The fireship is in want of such timbers to repair her that it will be impossible to accomplish it, as they cannot be procured here.

I despatched to you last month the Jamaica and Post Boy to the Windward Islands, and the Duguay-Trouin to New York, by the return of which vessels I shall be in hourly expectation to receive some letters from you. . .

You will receive this from Captain Douglas, of his Majesty's ship Licorne, and am to request you will despatch him back to me, as soon as the service admits, as I want every cruizer to watch the enemy's motions.

I have the honour to be, with great regard,
Sir, your most obedient, humble servant,
Jos. Rowley.

P.S.—I am happy to congratulate you on the loss the Spaniards have sustained at Gibraltar.

Secret Intelligence, No. 1.

On the 30th October an express arrived at Cape Français which left Brest the 20th September, and has brought orders from the Court of France to prepare for the reception of 10,000 men under the command of the Marquis de Bouillé, who are immediately to sail with a convoy of fifteen sail of the line for the Cape; it may be depended upon that the object of this armament is to unite with the Spanish at Cape Français, and to proceed immediately for the attack of Jamaica. In consequence of this express, the commissaries are collecting bread and beef for the fleet and army, and great preparations are making at Port au Prince and Cape

Français for the reception of the expected troops. Orders were also despatched about the 1st of November to Port au Prince and the other parts of St. Domingo, to put a stop to the loading of any merchant vessels for Europe, and it is said that a general embargo will take place for the purpose of securing a quantity of shipping for the intended expedition.

By several ships arrived from Cadiz, the combined forces have sustained a considerable loss in their late attempt against Gibraltar; generally supposed to amount to 6,000 or 7,000 men. The Spanish fleet under Don Solano was daily expected from the Havana at the Cape.

To Captain Smith,[1] *of the Fury*

[*Copy.*] Barfleur: at sea. 5th December, 1782.

By the Right Honble. Samuel Lord Hood, Rear-Admiral of the Blue, &c., &c., &c.

Whereas three considerable squadrons of the enemy's line-of-battle ships are daily expected at Cape Français—one from Europe, another from the Havana, and a third from Boston—according to the intelligence I have received from Rear-Admiral Rowley, Governor Campbell, &c.; and it being of the greatest importance to the king's service that ships should be stationed at different places to look out for, and give me notice of, the approach of either of the said squadrons:

You are hereby required and directed to proceed with his Majesty's sloop under your command, through the Turk's Island passage, go round the Caycos Island at about ten leagues distance, and

[1] William Sidney Smith, afterwards famous as the defender of Acre.

return to me through the Caycos passage; and if in performing this service (which you are on no account to be diverted from by chasing) you should fall in with any of his Majesty's cruizers, you will not only show to, but leave with, their commanders a copy of the letter you will herewith receive; you will look out for me off the Old Cape, or between that and Isabella Point, about eight or ten leagues from the land.

Lord Hood to the respective Captains whom Captain Smith, of the Fury, may fall in with, or such others as this Letter may be shown to

Barfleur: at sea off the Old Cape. 5th December, 1782.

[*Copy.*]

[The first paragraph down to 'squadrons' verbatim, as in the order to Captain Smith.]

I am very earnestly to desire that such of his Majesty's captains as may be cruizing amongst the Keys will be vigilant in looking out for the Spanish squadron or the one from America, and not lose one moment's time in coming to me, in case of falling in with either. I shall be exact in keeping off the Old Cape, or between that and Isabella Point, about eight or ten leagues from the land. Exact and particular attention to this service is of that vast importance that I trust every other consideration will give way to it, and the respective captains will so place themselves as to give me early notice of the approach of an enemy's fleet through the Keys; and whatever captain this letter is shown to is requested to communicate and give a copy of it to such others as he may meet with.

To Captain Parry, of the Actæon

Barfleur: at sea. 9th December, 1782.

By the Right Hon. Samuel Lord Hood, Rear-Admiral of the Blue, &c., &c., &c.

[*Copy.*]

[The first paragraph down to 'squadrons' verbatim, as in the order to Captain Smith.]

You are hereby required and directed to proceed with his Majesty's ship under your command, as expeditiously as you can, to the northward of the island of Mariguana, and between that and the Caycos Island, keeping a most vigilant look out for the Havana and Boston squadrons, and upon discovering of either, you will make all possible haste to join me between Isabella Point and Monte Christi; you may expect to see L'Aimable to the northward of the Caycos Island, and in case you do, you will please to direct her commander to confine his look out to the Turk's Island passage, and you will attend to that of the Caycos. You will continue upon this station as long as your water will last, and then return to me; and as this duty is of the greatest importance to the king's service, I trust you will not be diverted from a strict attention to it by chasing to any distance.

Hood to Rear-Admiral Rowley

[*Copy.*] Barfleur: off Monte Christi. 12th December, 1782.

Sir,—I hope ere this you will know, either by the Endymion, which is part of the convoy to the troops Sir Guy Carleton has ordered from Charleston to Jamaica, or by the Santa Margarita which I detached with a mast ship on the 27th of last month, that I am in this neighbourhood, with a squadron of the king's ships under my command, consisting of a dozen of the line ; but lest you should not, I detach the Fury, being short of water and provisions, with this letter.

I passed the bar of New York the 22nd of last month, the first moment I was able after the Duguay-Trouin arrived, and was off Cape Samana the twelfth day. The next morning I met the Sybil and Fury ; the first I detached to reconnoitre Cape Français, and the other through Turk's Island passage to return through the Caycos passage, in order to inform any of your cruizers where to find me, in case of their falling in with an enemy's squadron. The Sybil came back yesterday and is now stationed off the Old Cape. Not a single ship of war is at Cape Français, except one frigate careening. I have also fallen in with the Actæon, Alarm, Diamond and Bloodhound, and herewith I send for your information a copy of the order I have given to each commander ; I am in daily expectation of being joined by the London, Monarch, Torbay and Ajax, and must beg you will be pleased to send me the Endymion and Santa Margarita, with such other cruizers as may come with the troops, as I have but one frigate to chase ; for I cannot suffer a line-of-battle ship to go from me on any account, expecting (as you must be sensible I must) to have a superior force to contend against.

By the superior sailing of La Fortunée I got hold of the Licorne on the 4th, for Captain Douglas, taking the squadron under my command to be the Spanish one, pushed before the wind as fast as he could, not being furnished with the private signals of the Leeward Island fleet ; and so soon as I had read the despatches he was charged with, sent him on to Admiral Pigot, whom I expect to see or hear from hourly.

Hood to Philip Stephens

[*Copy.*]

Barfleur: off Monte Christi. 15th December, 1782.

I passed the bar of New York, with the king's squadron under my command, on the 22nd of last month, and immediately despatched the Germain sloop to Admiral Pigot with a letter, of which the enclosed is a copy.[1] The Young William mast ship sailed with me, and having on the 27th fallen in with his Majesty's ship Santa Margarita on her return from a cruize, with her bowsprit and mizen mast sprung, and going to New York, I ordered her commander to take the Young William under his convoy, and proceed with her to Jamaica, as she was a great clog to the squadron, and must have been towed the whole way.

On the 4th instant, being about fifteen leagues to the eastward of the Silver Keys, by the superior sailing of one of my frigates I spoke with the Licorne, whose commander, not having Admiral Pigot's or Rear-Admiral Digby's private signals, and taking us for the Spanish squadron, made away to leeward as fast as possible. He was first to go to New York, and not finding Admiral Pigot there, was to follow him to Barbados. I herewith send you a copy of the despatches he was charged with, and without keeping him three hours, sent him on with the originals to my commander-in-chief at the Leeward Islands.

At daylight next morning I was within five leagues off Cape Samana, and having that day spoken with the Sybil frigate and Fury sloop (which had come through the Mona passage the evening before), the former I sent immediately to

[1] *N.R.S.* iii. 153.

reconnoitre the harbour of Cape Français, and the latter through the Turk's Island passage; and herewith I transmit a copy of my order and letter to the commander of the Fury.

On the 9th the Sybil returned and reported a single frigate only at the Cape, and that upon the careen. At the same time I was joined by the Actæon, Alarm, and Diamond frigates, and the Bloodhound sloop; the latter I detached to reconnoitre the Havana, as I could hear nothing of the Spanish squadron; the Actæon I sent to the northward of the island Mariguana, and between that and the Caycos; the Alarm to cruize north from the island Desecheo,[1] in the Mona passage, from five to fifteen leagues distance; the Diamond to reconnoitre the harbour of St. John's, in the island Porto Rico, where I had been informed two frigates with a great number of merchant vessels under convoy (which sailed from France on the 6th of September, and parted with the remainder of the convoy off Martinique, and were bound to Cape Français) had arrived; and the Sybil I stationed off the Old Cape, having shifted my rendezvous from thence a little to windward of Monte Christi, which gave me a better chance for intercepting the enemy's ships should they come through either of the island passages.

I send you also for their lordships' information a copy of my order to Captain Parry of the Actæon; and I gave a similar one to the other commanders, so that I trust no squadron of the enemy's can escape my seeing it.

[1] Zachio in MS.

Hood to Middleton

Barfleur: off Monte Christi. 23rd December, 1782.

My dear Sir Charles,—As I am about to send the Alarm frigate to Jamaica, I write you a few lines by her in order to take the conveyance of the first packet from that island, and the papers I herewith trouble you will inform you of the measures I judged right to take for intercepting one of the enemy's squadrons. God grant they may be productive of success to the arms of his Majesty.

I am happy in telling you that Prince William enjoys most perfect health, and keeps a keen look out for Don Solano from the Havana, as well as for Vaudreuil from Boston.

The Spanish force at the Havana on the 29th of last month, was thirteen of the line and four frigates, all ready for sea; and four of the line and one frigate were on a short cruise, but expected back hourly. It seems they go out in small squadrons for a few days to air and exercise; but I every moment look out for a later account, as I sent the Bloodhound sloop, which sails well, on the 9th instant to reconnoitre the harbour.

No tidings of the Magnificent, nor have I heard a syllable from Admiral Pigot. I have frequently announced to Rear-Admiral Rowley of my being here, and flatter myself with being reinforced by all the ships of the line at Jamaica that are ready for service, fully confiding my brother rear-admiral will not hesitate to send them.

We are informed by the master of a Spanish cartel from Cowes to the Havana, which carried the Providence garrison to England, that the king's fleet, under the command of Lord Viscount Howe, has defeated the combined one and taken and destroyed a dozen capital ships. Joy, much joy, to you on this great event; it is the higher joy to me, as I hope and trust my brother came in for his full share of the glory. We give the more credit to this account, having the evening before spoke with a neutral ship from Marseilles, which had been boarded by the combined fleet on the 15th of October off Malaga, and by the English one, without the Straits' mouth, on the 18th, whose master and crew declared they saw the battle commence between five and six in the evening of the 20th, and heard a most terrible cannonade till midnight. Our cartel informant said the Santísima Trinidad, with Don Cordova on board, was lost, and every soul perished in attempting her safety by flight. May all the king's enemies be so panic-struck by the terror of his Majesty's arms![1]

With every good wish to you and yours,

I am, my dear Sir Charles,

Your very affectionate and faithful, humble servant,

HOOD.

P.S.—The Spanish 80-gun ship, which sailed from Cape Français the beginning of last month, is at St. John's, Porto Rico, with that part of the convoy bound to Cape Français, &c., &c., which left France the 6th of September, waiting a re-inforcement to protect them to the places of their destination. The Jupiter, which Admiral Pigot detached in his way to Barbados to reconnoitre the Havana and then join me, has, I am told by a neutral, taken seven prizes, some valuable, particularly a ship from Guiana laden with indigo and other rich articles. Pasley has been very lucky indeed; he is deserving of it.

[1] It is scarcely necessary to remind our readers that this account of the 'rencounter' of 20th October, 1782, is absurdly inaccurate. Cf. *N.R.S.*, xx. 219; xxxi. 30–32.

Barfleur: off Cape Français. 19th January, 1783.[1]

I thank you for your two affectionate letters of the 7th and 28th of August which were brought me from Barbados by the Alcide about a fortnight ago, with above one hundred others, which were very reviving cordials, as I had received but one letter from any part of my family of later date than the end of April; but by this conveyance I heard of their being all well on the 5th of November. I wished much for a few lines from you written in that month, and flatter myself I shall not be long without being indulged with other letters from you.

I am grieved to the heart to find that there is still as much distraction in England as ever, which must infallibly, sooner or later, work our ruin. We have accounts of peace from various quarters. It is an event I shall have cause to rejoice at, on many accounts, with respect to myself; but whether I shall have solid reason to do so for my poor country, I very much doubt; being clearly of opinion, considering all things, formidable as the combination is against us, we shall, I fear, never again be in so good a condition for retrieving the national honour as at present. Nothing, I am confident, is wanting but unanimity at home, and having a regard to whom you trust your fleets and armies; and without that, all is over with us as a great and powerful kingdom, and it matters not whether we have peace or a continuance of war. It comes to one and the same thing, with this difference only—that by peace, the evil will be somewhat at a greater distance, but according to my conception, sure and certain; for if it should please God to prolong my days to another

[1] Some of the sentences in this letter are repeated in nearly the same words in the letter to Jackson of 29th January (*Hood's Letters*, *N.R.S.* iii. 155–161). The two letters are, however, essentially different.

war some years hence, I shall look to the event of it with fear and trembling, unless by the all-powerful interference of the divine providence we become an united and rational people. After a ten years' peace, we shall scarce have a lieutenant that will know his duty. Our situation at present is bad enough in that respect; it will then be abundantly worse, as we have so many ignorant boys in that station, which, from being any time ashore, will become more ignorant and probably not so well disposed towards improvement, and the few qualified officers we now have will then be past active service.

At midnight on the 11th of this month, I was joined by the Actæon, one of Rear-Admiral Rowley's ships, which I had taken the liberty to station to the northward of the Caycos island, to look out for the enemy; whose commander informed me he had on the 8th, in the afternoon, seen a large fleet steering for the Caycos passage, which was either French or Spanish; and that he counted fifteen large ships, and afterwards saw a frigate, with French or Spanish colours hoisted, bear down to two neutral vessels which he had spoken with that morning.

I immediately examined how the winds had been between the 8th and 11th; and finding the fleet could not fetch Cape Français, I concluded it would steer for Cape Nicola Mole or the Bight of Leogane, and bore away; though I was pretty confident in my own mind (and told Captain Parry so) the fleet seen was the transports from Charleston going to Jamaica; but he was so positive of its being either French or Spanish, and that fifteen were of the line, I was under the necessity of attending to his information; but neither seeing or hearing anything of an enemy's ship, and after ordering two frigates to reconnoitre Cumberland Harbour,[1] the only place the squadron could take shelter in, I hastened back to my station to windward of the Cape, and very fortunately nothing had arrived while I was away but an American frigate from Europe.

28th January: off Cape Tiburon.

On the 19th instant at night I received certain intelligence that the Marquis de Vaudreuil was off the harbour of St. John's, Porto Rico, on the 16th, with ten sail of the line. I immediately did my utmost to get to windward, but the wind and current being strong against me, I could gain but little ground. On the 23rd I was informed the enemy was still off St. John's on the 21st. On the 24th, at three in the morning, when I should have gone near to fetch the east end of Hispaniola, a large French ship, with masts and 250 soldiers on board, came under the stern of my repeater, taking us for the French squadron.

She sailed from Portsmouth in New Hampshire on the 29th of last month, with the Auguste and Pluton, and Amazon frigate, and parted company, in a south-east gale, with the two line of battle ships three days after they came out. On the 22nd they got off St. John's, and were informed by a pilot, that Vaudreuil had bore away to leeward the night before, on being joined by the Auguste and Pluton; and upon the return of the Amazon's boat from the shore, she bore away also, after ordering the transport into St. John's; but on her working up to the harbour's mouth, a sudden squall carried away her main topmast, which caused her to bear up for Cape Français.

Upon receiving this intelligence I made all

[1] Guantanamo. The English name was given to it by Vernon in 1741.

possible sail to the westward, taking it for granted that Vaudreuil had gone through the Mona Channel, with a design either of harbouring at Port Louis on the south side, or coming round the west end of the island to Nicola Mole, unless he should go to the Havana to join Don Solano, and come in great force together to the Cape, which I think not at all unlikely; and though I was well satisfied the French squadron could not have passed me unseen, the Cape and the Mole were examined as I came down. I have now but a small chance indeed, for a meeting with Vaudreuil; but in order to enable the king's squadron under my command to keep the sea ten or twelve days longer, I availed myself of a few hours' calm to distribute a little water and bread to those ships which were most in want. Some had only bread for two days, and but a few tons of water. We have had no supply of the latter since the 14th of November, and when we reach Jamaica, not a ship will have more than three days of bread, pease, rum or water; but I thank God we are tolerably healthy, though the scurvy has taken root in two or three ships. Twelve weeks will be a long time to be at sea in this country, and more particularly as the squadron is so very short of water casks.

February 1st.

I left the America and two frigates to guard Cape Français, and have sent the Prince William to look into Port Louis. When she returns, I must make the best of my way to Port Royal, leaving the Alcide and Prince William (which joined me from to windward on the 11th of last month) to cruize off the Cape for a fortnight, having left them water and provisions sufficient, as the America will be obliged, from her wants, to be in port by the 10th instant, which will be probably about the time I shall get there. If, when Sir Richard Hughes got to Barbados, the commander-in-chief had not found it necessary to keep the squadron there, and had come with, or detached it hither, St. John's in Porto Rico might have been guarded as well as Cape Français, which must have secured Vaudreuil's squadron to us; but I am confident the admiral thought it improper to do it. The force to windward is 23 of the line, and the Leander; the admiral therefore might have come with or sent ten sail, and have left a superiority to Vaudreuil; but it was next to a certainty that his destination was for the Cape. However, Admiral Pigot might see good and substantial reason for expecting a formidable squadron of the enemy's from Europe; though I cannot help thinking that, let the force which will come from that quarter be more or less, it will not touch at Martinique but come directly to the Cape; but when an officer does that which human prudence as well as sound judgment suggests, he ought to submit with becoming fortitude. There is no guarding against misfortune. I communicate to you fully and freely, and with an unbounded confidence; you will not, I therefore trust, commit me to any one.

On the 10th of last month, at daylight, the Torbay made the signal of distress from leaks; and upon my going to her, am sorry to acquaint you that I found she had struck upon a shoal the preceding night, knocked her rudder off, and received other very considerable damage. I knew of this shoal, and, from a journal I have of De Grasse's, that the Ville de Paris struck upon it last year; it lays six miles nearly NW from Monte Christi. I have had boats upon it to sound, and find it runs NW and SE about three-quarters of a mile, and about half a mile broad; but none of the pilots ever heard of it. There is a good channel within it.

I was always cautious how I approached the Mount on that bearing, and tacked the squadron at sunset at the distance of four leagues; but the Torbay, very unfortunately, stood on near four hours after, and struck upon it at half past nine. I find she had split her maintopsail in the afternoon, which occasioned her to drop astern, and I suppose lost sight of my lights. I took out her water and provisions and ordered her to Port Royal, attended by the Actæon, as she made a great deal of water, and probably will never be able to leave that port; for when she joined me, she made from three to four feet water an hour in the finest weather.

I am very sorry also to acquaint you, that the Invincible, though so lately hove down as in July, is so extremely leaky and weak, she can cruize no longer, and is by no means in a condition to be carried into action; and I am clearly of opinion that was I to meet an enemy's squadron superior in numbers and force to the one under my command, it would be far better she was out of the line of battle than in it. Her hand pumps have never rested an hour since we came from New York, which cannot keep her free in the smoothest water; and under reefed topsails, which we often are (and obliged to strive hard to keep our stations, so as to command the port of Cape Français—the current sets so strong to the westward), she gains upon the hand pumps from four to five and six feet water every four hours, which has jaded her people exceedingly. I therefore propose to dispatch her to English Harbour, when I bear up for Jamaica or receive any certain account of the enemy's squadron, that she may be patched up for a passage home in the summer, at such time as Admiral Pigot shall direct; for was I to leave her at Jamaica, she would in all probability remain unnoticed for months, as

I understand the Shrewsbury has not been yet hove down, though nine months in the harbour.

On the return of the two frigates which I sent to Cumberland Harbour in Cuba, where they saw nothing, I got a certain account that my conjecture to Captain Parry was right; for the fleet he saw and made report of to me, was the transports from Charleston under convoy of three frigates, neither of which ever saw the Actæon. This will show you what sad consequences may arise from a loose report of a fleet that is not looked at near enough to ascertain with certainty whether it consists of men-of-war, or merchant ships. I am the more concerned at it, as Captain Parry is looked upon to be a very solid and judicious officer, notwithstanding the mistake he has now made.

I have never made a request for leave to return home, but I had a letter wrote to the admiralty to that effect previous to my sailing from New York; but upon the king's laying his commands upon me to receive Prince William under my care and direction, in so very flattering a manner, I had not room to hesitate, and threw my letter into the fire. Peace must now accomplish my wishes; but should it fail to take place, I cannot possibly remain in this country much longer.

* What a lucky escape have I had in the affair of Westminster! and how wisely has my son acted in withdrawing my name as a candidate. Many people like sport to answer particular passions, but few regard what becomes of the man who makes it; and though I am not insensible to the unmerited hostile behaviour of Mr. Fox, I feel myself obliged to him as the occasion of my being saved from ruin.

* From here to 'enough to adhere to them' (bottom of next page) is virtually the same as in the letter to Jackson of 29th January, 1783. *N.R.S.* iii. 155–66.

I do assure you, my dear Sir Charles, poor as I undoubtedly am, I would sooner have given 500 pounds than have stood a contest, even had I been sure of succeeding, for a twentieth part of the money. A seat in the House of Commons, I have no ambition after, and will never offer myself for it anywhere. If there should be public spirit enough left in any corporation in England to make choice of me as its representative, from perfect free will of the electors, well![1] If not, I shall be full as well satisfied. I shall ever most carefully and studiously steer clear, as far as I am able, of all suspicion of being a party man; for if once I show myself of that frame of mind—whether for or against a minister—unbecoming a military servant of our royal master's, I must from that moment expect to lose every degree of consideration in the line of my profession, which ever has been, and ever will be, the first and greatest object of my wishes. I revere my king; I have much affection for my country; and the pride and glory of my remaining days will be to assist both with my feeble services to the utmost extent of my abilities; and I am vain enough to think that I am in some small degree qualified, but abundantly more so from inclination, to fight the battles of my country upon my own element, but acknowledge myself totally unfit to fight the battles of a minister in a house of parliament; and even if I had abilities equal to the task, I think it an employment derogatory to the true character of a sea officer, whose highest ambition is to stand well in the good opinion of his sovereign and fellow subjects. These are my sentiments, and I hope and trust I shall have fortitude enough to adhere to them; * for had the free and unbiassed voice of the people carried

[1] He was returned for Westminster, at the head of the poll, in the general election of 1784.

my election against all opposition and without a shilling expense to me, it would have distressed me beyond measure, with such a colleague;[1] besides the business of so large and populous a place as Westminster would have been more intricate and burdensome than I could have undertaken, and must have loaded me with insupportable vexation and trouble.

As I shall not have a moment's leisure from refitting the squadron at Jamaica, I am preparing my letters before I go in.

Port Royal. 5th February.

I anchored the squadron here this forenoon and had the pleasure to receive three of your kind letters of the following dates: 6th and 22nd November, and 3rd of December. They were very lately sent from to windward, and brought from home by the Anson, Nymphe and November packet. A packet sails hence so soon as my letters are ready; she shall not wait an hour for me; and I have told the admiral and governor my letters are ready, so that if she was detained on my account, she must depart soon.

We seem pretty much to jump in opinions; and what one says to the other bear corresponding ideas as much as any two men's can do, at so great distance from one another. Our next accounts must be decisive of peace or war.

I have the pleasure to assure you Prince William is in fine health and seems perfectly happy; and I should be unjust as well as ungrateful, not to say all that is handsome of his royal highness for his great attention to me, as well as for the desire he manifests of doing what I recommend.

[1] Fox; who was, however, his colleague in 1784.

With every affectionate wish to your whole family,

I most truly am, my dear Sir Charles, . . .

Barfleur: Port Royal. 28th February, 1783.

I wrote you on my arrival here early in the month, and have now the satisfaction to tell you, notwithstanding the difficulties I have met with from a want of stores, the king's squadron under my command is within twenty-four hours ready for sea, except the Bedford and Alcide. The former's main mast is still on shore making almost new, but I am told by the commissioner, who attends very closely to the duties of his office, that it will be ready to launch to-morrow night; and the latter's fore mast is totally unserviceable, but by taking the fore mast from the Torbay, she will be ready as soon as the Bedford. I have been obliged to strip the Torbay and Shrewsbury of every serviceable store they had, and I am afraid I shall be under the necessity of doing the same by the Ajax, and in part by the Monarch, though I am cautious of meddling with the latter till the last moment and it cannot be avoided, as it may become absolutely necessary to take her to sea with me, bad as she really is. The three others are all to pieces, and I think it would be a great saving to government totally to dismantle and put them out of commission, as they will not be worth the amount of the men's wages when they get home. The Shrewsbury is at this hour in the state she was ten months ago, with difficulty kept above water, owing to a preference being given, from time to time, by the artificers of the yard, to every ship upon the station that had occasion to go to the wharf or had any work to do.

Upon my coming here, my principal aim was to live in harmony and to avoid every kind of dispute with Admiral Rowley; to which end I came to an explanation, clear and explicit, and I must do him the justice to say that nothing has been wanting on his part to forward the refitting of his Majesty's squadron, which he left wholly to me; and at my desire (for without it I could not succeed) directed the commissioner to attend to any requisition I should make for refitting the squadron under my command in preference to all other ships.

Every spar in the ship I sent from New York that would make a topmast or topsail yard for a line-of-battle ship had been every one expended before I arrived; and although I took a transport with a number of masts in, which came from Portsmouth for the use of the French squadron, the least of them is large enough for the lower mast of a frigate; and the stores here have neither sails or cordage such as we want; but by stripping the Torbay, Shrewsbury, and Ajax, we shall go to sea in good order, and I hope to get out the end of next week, if I hear nothing from England or Admiral Pigot to hinder me.

I propose going off Cape Français, from thence off St. John's, Porto Rico, and then through the Mona Channel off Curaçao, but my motions must be guided by what I hear of those of Solano and Vaudreuil; for although I have reason to believe, if reports are to be credited, that the latter has taken shelter at Curaçao, it is by no means certain, nor can I find that the former has left the Havana. A frigate and small vessel are gone to reconnoitre each port, which I hope and trust will be back before I put to sea; if not, I shall keep a look-out for them as I work to windward.

I dread what may happen to many of the king's

ships, if we have not peace to occasion their being called home to have their bottoms inspected; for on being obliged to unhang the Barfleur's rudder, her stern post and plank, for five feet under water was eat by the worm in a manner not to be conceived, owing to there being no copper under the braces, as I imagine. That is a circumstance which requires to be attended to, and if it should not be thought convenient to copper under the braces, great care should be taken in coppering over them. The Alcide is as bad as the Barfleur, and more than half her rudder is so eaten that an iron rod could be pushed through it with ease. The accident last year to the Alfred, by running on board the Nymphe,[1] has given such scope for the worm, that her bows are quite destroyed; several plank had not half an inch left sound; however, by getting her bow as much out of water as was possible, I trust she is effectually cured to run this year out.

I beg my very respectful compliments to Lady Middleton, &c., &c., and that you will be assured of my being, with great truth and regard,

My dear Sir Charles,

Your most faithful, humble servant,

HOOD.

Prince William enjoys perfect health.

Hood to Middleton

Barfleur: at sea. 9th April, 1783.

My dear Sir Charles,—On the 21st of last month I was joined by the Tobago sloop to the eastward of Cape Maysi,[2] despatched with a letter

[1] See, *ante*, p. 143.

[2] The eastern point of Cuba. Hood writes, quite distinctly, Maize; but the Barfleur's log gives the position at noon on the 20th, Cape Tiburon SSE¾E., lat. 18° 48′; and on the 21st,

from Captain Cotton of the Alarm, to inform me that they had fallen in with the Spanish squadron from the Havana on the 8th at night, working through the Gulf, supposed to be bound to Cape Français, where they had been expected some time. This put us in high spirits, in hopes fortune would enable us to make a glorious finish to the war; but cruizing to windward of the Cape until the 4th instant, when hostilities had ceased in these seas, without seeing an enemy, and having accidentally heard that an express-boat from General Bellecombe had been at sea some days looking for me, with a despatch, without joining, I thought it right to show that attention to the Governor of Hispaniola of sending my boat on shore to receive his commands, and availed myself of that opportunity of letting Prince William see the first city in the West Indies.

His royal highness was received and treated with every possible mark of honour and attention. Nothing could exceed the politeness of General Bellecombe or that of Don Gálvez, the general of the Spanish troops, which Prince William has made known to the king; and I herewith send you the copy of a letter Don Gálvez wrote to the prince, which he gave to Captain Merrick (to whom I entrusted his royal highness) to be delivered after they were embarked.

Prince William landed about noon, and having dined with the governor at one o'clock, all the officers both French and Spanish were presented. After dinner, his royal highness visited every place deserving notice, attended by General Bellecombe, Don Gálvez, the officers and principal inhabitants; and on entering the park of artillery, his

Cape Donna Maria SW$\frac{1}{4}$W., Great Cammate (Cayemites) SE by E$\frac{1}{2}$E.

royal highness was saluted with twenty-one guns. In the evening they went to the opera, and from thence to the governor's house to supper, where Madame Bellecombe had assembled Madame Gálvez and a great number of other ladies. After supper there was an elegant ball, at which his royal highness danced till one o'clock, then went to bed till six, and returned to the Barfleur to breakfast, charmed with what he had seen, and the politeness and attention with which he had been received and treated. Six thousand men under arms, which made a most excellent appearance, lined the streets on both sides from the governor's house to the water's side, the officers saluting as his royal highness passed; and as soon as the boat put off, twenty-one guns were again fired from the shore, and the same number from the Andromaque frigate (which had arrived the evening before from Brest, with an account of the ratification of the preliminary articles of peace on the 3rd of February) as his royal highness rowed by her, and immediately after, every French and American ship in the harbour that had guns saluted.

I am now steering for Jamaica, that no time may be lost in my proceeding to England, after I have orders so to do. I propose going through the Gulf, to show his royal highness the Havana, and hope to have the much wished-for happiness of being home in the month of June, the thoughts of which have done me a monstrous deal of good, for, in fact, I can scarce keep upon my legs.

I am exceeding anxious about his royal highness. He employs all my thoughts respecting his future disposal until he is of age. The West Indies is the very worst place he can serve in, in time of peace. I think full half the year might be very advantageously employed in making a voyage round England, Ireland and Scotland. This would give his royal highness a knowledge of our own coasts and principal harbours; and if it is thought right to send a squadron annually to sea, by way of exercising and disciplining the men, his royal highness should be with it. Next he might make a trip to Newfoundland, and touch at Cadiz and Lisbon in his way home. This would also employ more than half the year; and the third year he might make a voyage to the Mediterranean, visiting the different ports by sea, from Gibraltar through the Faro of Messina to Malta, and even as high as the Greek islands.

The ship I am now standing towards, I take to be a Jamaica packet going to England. I therefore write in a great hurry to catch the conveyance of her, and shall therefore only add my best and warmest wishes to you and yours; and in full hopes of the pleasure of seeing you soon,

I am, my dear Sir Charles,

Your very affectionate, &c.,

HOOD.

Enclosure No. 1

Don Bernardo de Gálvez to Prince William Henry

Translation.[1]] Cape. 6th April, 1783.

Sir,—The Spanish troops, being dispersed in quarters in the country, have been deprived of the happiness enjoyed by the French of saluting your royal highness under arms, neither have they been able to testify those marks of respect and consideration due to you, a disappointment which will be ever regretted by them.

[1] Another translation, with at least one cruel blunder, is printed in Schomberg's *Naval Chronology*, ii. 138.

I have in prison at Louisiana, the chief of the Natchez revolt, with some of his accomplices; they were guilty of a violation of their parole, as well as their oath of fidelity. For these crimes a council of war, founded upon the laws of equity, have condemned them to death, which sentence only waits my confirmation, as governor of the colony, to be put in execution. They are all Englishmen. Will you then, Sir, since it is not in our power to show your royal highness any other attention, accept their pardon and their lives, in the name of the Spanish army and of my king? This is, I believe, a present of the greatest worth one prince can offer another.[1] Mine is of a truly generous disposition, and will approve my conduct. In case your royal highness deigns to interest yourself about these unfortunate people, I do myself the honour of enclosing an order for them to be given up immediately on your sending any vessel you may think proper to Louisiana to signify your commands. It will be very flattering to us if this should prove agreeable to you.

I have the honour to be most respectfully, Sir,
Your Royal Highness's most humble
and obedient servant,
B. DE GÁLVEZ.

Enclosure No. 2

General Bellecombe to Lord Hood

[*Translation.*] Cape. 6th April, 1783.

Sir,—I am impressed with a just sense of your excellency's politeness in sending Captain Merrick

[1] Schomberg's version is, 'It is, I trust, the least present that can be offered to one prince in the name of another.' Unfortunately, we have not the original.

to know the object of the vessel's mission which you had been informed I had sent to look for you.

The despatches she had on board were only duplicates of those Monsieur le Marquis de Rouvray was charged with, who had the honour of paying his respects to your excellency; and I am informed that the vessel in question fell in yesterday with the fleet under your command.

I am very sensible of the compliments of congratulation your excellency so obligingly makes me on the return of peace, and I participate very sincerely of the satisfaction which so liberal a mind as your excellency's must feel at seeing an end to the public calamities. The king's frigate, the Andromache, which arrived this day, has brought out the formal ratification of the preliminaries of peace, which confirm the account of hostilities ceasing in these seas on the 3rd instant.

His Royal Highness Prince William Henry will perpetuate this happy event by the distinguished honour he has conferred upon me, a happiness I did not expect; and I regret extremely that his royal highness, surprising me so agreeably, did not allow me time to receive him with that magnificence with which I could have wished to celebrate an event so flattering to the colony and so honourable to myself.

I have the honour to be, with every sentiment of respect and esteem, your excellency's most humble and obedient servant,

BELLECOMBE.

Hood to Middleton

Barfleur: Port Royal, Jamaica. 17th April, 1783.

My dear Sir Charles,—On the 14th instant, two days after my arrival here, I had the pleasure to receive your affectionate letters of the 30th of December and 25th of January, for which I give you many thanks. Whenever I have the power, I shall not want the inclination to be serviceable to any friend of yours, and the young man you mention in the Endymion shall be attended to. I wrote you so lately as the 9th, that I shall not take up much of your time now, but I cannot let a ship sail without sending you a few lines.

The Cormorant, which brought your letters and had her last orders signed the 26th of February, brings certain accounts that Lord Shelburne, &c., &c., &c., were out, and that the Parliament was adjourned to allow time for forming a new administration. When will the misfortunes of our poor country have an end?

Lord Howe wrote to Admiral Pigot the 26th of February (private) to say he would have orders for the disposal of the king's ships under his command soon, and that it would be expected he should visit all the islands ceded by the peace before his return to England.

I have infinite pleasure in telling you that Prince William is perfectly well and a most delightful youth; conforms to my wishes most cheerfully. His royal highness has the goodness to give me his confidence without reserve, and listens with attention to what I say to him, as I never fail to point out whatever little thing I cannot quite approve. He is rather of a volatile turn of mind, and apt now and then (very natural to the age of 18) to be run away with by his vast flow of spirits; yet he is easily restrained, and gives me the most heartfelt satisfaction. He has not a wish to go from the Barfleur without me, or to be out of my company when we are on shore, which is very seldom. His royal highness has visited Cape Français, where he was received and treated with every mark of respect, politeness, and attention. I mean he shall see the Havana also, whether we proceed immediately home or are called to windward by Admiral Pigot.

On my arrival here to wait the admiral's orders, I directed the respective captains of the squadron to complete their provisions to three months, get their water on board as soon as possible, and hold themselves in readiness to proceed to sea at the shortest notice, which I made known to Rear-Admiral Rowley the moment the squadron anchored, and at the same time gave him an account of the state and condition of it; when he was pleased to desire I would direct the senior captain of the king's ships I ordered to Rochfort, as they had neither long-boats or launches, to have an officer constantly on shore to see that no damage is done to the watering-place, to preserve order, and prevent disputes with the soldiers; which I complied with; but next evening I received from Rear-Admiral Rowley an order to put myself under his command, and he issued a similar one to every captain, with directions that they immediately made a return to him of all officers acting who had not served their full time. What a misfortune it is, my dear Sir Charles, to have anything to do with men who are guided by whim and caprice, instead of common sense! How strange and unaccountable the conduct, when an admiral and commander-in-chief of a great fleet detaches a squadron upon a particular service, under the direction and management of a junior flag, who is to repair after a certain day to this port to wait further orders, for the rear-admiral commanding here to take the said squadron under his command, when he cannot possibly receive any direction about it! But so it is, and it is my duty to represent it to my commander-in-chief as well as to the admiralty. I shall not say a word to the rear-admiral upon the subject, but strictly obey his orders. This proves how very necessary it was for me to come to an explanation with Rear-Admiral Rowley in the manner I did (having some little idea of the man's mind) when I came here to refit early in February, for I immediately told him [he must take] the responsibility of refitting the squadron, or leave the business entirely to me, directing the commissioner to attend to my requisitions in preference to other works; and I have given him the same credit for it at home as if it was a voluntary act.

Vaudreuil has been most exceedingly frightened, and such is the situation of his ships that scarce two are fit for offensive action,[1] and I am very clear the Havana squadron would not have found it an easy matter to have effected a junction with the one of France; but it is unnecessary and of no avail now to reason upon this business. I will therefore only[2] trouble you more than to express my most sincere wishes for a speedy, cordial, and perfect unanimity at home, as the only means left for the salvation of our poor distracted and seemingly devoted country; to offer my affectionate wishes to you and yours, and to assure you that I am, with very true regard, my dear Sir Charles,

Most faithfully yours,

Hood.

[1] This must refer to the intelligence brought by the Albemarle (see Appendix C), for he can hardly have had any other report on Vaudreuil's squadron.

[2] So in MS.

SIR G. B. RODNEY[1] TO MIDDLETON

[*Holograph.*] Formidable: St. Lucia. 5th April, 1782.

My dear Sir,—It is impossible for me not to snatch a few minutes to tell you how we go on in this part of the world. All our diligence availed not; the enemy fought very shy; and when I concluded they intended to come in full force, and was prepared to receive them, as you will perceive by the disposition I made of the fleet, behold they made Antigua, and crept close along Guadeloupe, and Dominica.[2] What provokes me is that the whole fleet was at sea, Sir S. Hood and his division off the north end, mine and Drake's division to windward of Point Salines, and several frigates between Martinique and Antigua, at the very time the enemy made the islands—and yet not one saw them. 'Tis provoking, but never mind it; their fate is only delayed a short time, for have it they must and shall.

Thank God, by the arrival of the convoy from England, the fleet are now complete in their stores

[1] In 1833, as a contribution to the strange controversy on 'breaking the line' then started by Sir Howard Douglas, Sir J. Deas Thomson sent copies of this letter, of Sir Charles Douglas's *Narrative*, 28th April, 1782 (p. 274) and of his letter, 4th May (p. 283), to the United Service Journal, in which they were printed (part i. pp. 510 *seq.*). Buried in an old and obscure magazine, they have been but little known; and a careful collation with the originals shows several instances of careless copying or attempted correction of the language.

[2] As to which, cf. Hood, 31st March; *ante*, p. 151.

and provisions, and in the highest spirits; and by my intelligence this day the enemy have embarked their troops and near ready to sail. You may be sure I shall watch them attentively, and notwithstanding the very great repairs that many of the fleet I found here were in want of, such has been the diligence of each officer in his different department that all will be ready and complete this very night, though many bowsprits and several lower masts were wanting when we arrived from our cruize.

The Intrepid and Shrewsbury are found unserviceable; I propose to send them with the convoy to Port Royal, to try, if possible, to put them in a sufficient repair, so as to go home with the first convoy and to assist in the defence of the island, for to keep the sea they cannot.

The great event that must restore the empire of the sea to Great Britain is near at hand; let me but live to hail my most gracious monarch but sovereign of the ocean, and then my happiness will be complete.

The whole business of the fleet is transacted here. English Harbour is of little use, and in its present situation not [to] be trusted with the naval storeships. For their better security I have directed Rear-Admiral Drake to keep them at St. Lucia. It was absolutely necessary for me to appoint a storekeeper. I wish your boards would appoint all the necessary officers; I really do not like to be answerable for any person. Adieu! and be assured that I am, with the utmost sincerity, your most faithful and obedient, humble servant,

G. B. Rodney.

General Order

[By Sir George Brydges Rodney, Bart., Admiral of the White and Commander-in-Chief, &c.]

Whereas I have received intelligence that an enemy's fleet, with a considerable number of transports with troops, are daily expected in these seas, I think it expedient for the good of his Majesty's service that the fleet under my command be stationed as follows, viz.:

Sir Samuel Hood, with his division, to cruize from fifteen to twenty leagues to windward of the north end of Martinique, stretching as far north as the latitude of Dominica.

The centre division from fifteen to twenty leagues to windward of the body of the island of Martinique, stretching as far north as the latitude of the north end thereof.

Admiral Drake, with his division from fifteen to twenty leagues to windward of Point Salines, stretching as far to the northward as the latitude of the body of the island of Martinique.

The squadrons are to keep under such moderate sail as may be just sufficient to keep their respective stations.

One line of battle ship of the centre division is to be constantly stationed midway between it and the van division; and

A line of battle ship of the rear division is to be constantly stationed between it and the centre division.

Each squadron to have a line of battle ship constantly stationed directly to windward, as far as hull down.

Commodore Affleck in the Bedford, with two 64-gun ships, is to cruize to windward of Guadeloupe, so as to be nearly in a right line with the other divisions of the fleet, stretching from the latitude of the north end of Dominica, as far as the latitude of Deseada.

The Fortunée of forty guns, the Pegasus of twenty-eight, and the Sybil of twenty-eight guns, stationed fifty leagues to windward, in the latitude of Dominica, Martinique, and Barbados, to give notice of an enemy's approach.

The Surprise, Stormont, and Barbados, stationed for the protection of Barbados and the trade thereof.

The Intrepid, Lizard, Nymph, St. Eustatius, St. Vincent, and armed schooners, at St. Lucia. The frigates to observe the motions of the enemy's fleet in Fort Royal Bay. The Alert, between the fleet and Point Salines.

The Robust, Janus, Prothée, and Triton, and four small frigates in English Harbour, off Antigua. The Prothée, after being that length, to return to the fleet.

[20th March, 1782.][1]

[1] No name or date in this copy. The disposition of the several squadrons is printed in *N.R.S.* iii. 99–100.

SIR CHARLES DOUGLAS TO MIDDLETON

Gosport, 5th May, 1779.

The censoriously acquitting sentence [1]—if it can be called by any one name in our language—having been this day passed, I take the liberty of sending, in one parcel, for your consideration, three rude partial representations of a ship's keel [2] [fitted with lee-boards on a plan I have devised. They are fixed to the keel by hinges, and heavily weighted on their lower edges, so as to hang vertically. I conceive that by these the ship will be made much stiffer, and will make less leeway].

Duke: in Torbay. July 12, 1779.

Dear Sir,—I am highly favoured in having yours of the 8th, and do thoroughly agree with you in preferring solid to hinged side-pieces to keels; as I do in being of opinion that twelve-pounders of the Carron make would answer very well on this ship's poop. But I am hopeful, for the sake of her speed and stiffness, that it [3] will be taken away altogether. Admirably, too, would 24's [4] do for her quarter-deck, three of a side, where rigging is not in the way.

[1] On Sir Hugh Palliser; not a bad summary of it.

[2] The description is very long, and is here given in short abstract.

[3] *Sc.* the poop.

[4] *Sc.* carronades.

After all the liberties I have taken, I have still more to trouble you with. By the means, then, of bolts placed in the side, right in the middle between every two guns, into which we occasionally hook their tackles, we are able to point all of them, without using a crow or handspike, where knees called standards do not interfere, full four points before or abaft the beam, which I presume is to a degree of obliquity until now unknown in the navy. This I mention to the end that such important inconvenience arising from divers of the said knees may be guarded against in future building and repairing. Moreover, could the pump-dales be made to answer going below the gun deck (the cisterns remaining where they are), a considerable accession of force, by the oblique working of two lower-deckers of a side, would be thereby acquired.

Serious indeed has been the conversation between your friend Captain Patton and me, since we came into this road. Suffice it hereby to say, we cannot help being of opinion that the state is in danger; and so much even is a great deal to be committed to paper. Nor could it have proceeded from any other motive than our humble yet ardent and impulsive zeal for the public weal.

With my most respectful compliments to Mrs. Middleton, be pleased to acquaint her that Lady Douglas has sent me the very polite letter her ladyship was honoured with from her, and that we should be very unreasonable indeed not to be more than barely satisfied with the conclusive reasons Mrs. Middleton condescends to give for not standing for our shortly expected little stranger.

May the Almighty enlighten the understandings of our rulers, who are to manage the helm of state through this thickening storm, and direct their choice in all things by sea and land; and most ardently wishing to you health and success in your generous and unremitting toils, I ever most inviolably am, with sincere respect and esteem, dear Sir, your most faithful humble servant,

CHARLES DOUGLAS.

Gosport. 5th September 1779.

Dear Sir,—In the last wherewith I took the liberty of troubling you from Torbay, I represented to you the very great inconvenience we labour under on board the Duke, from the interference of the standards with the oblique pointing of sundry of our guns on each deck, to the very considerable diminution of her force. She still continues to be of as weatherly a disposition as she was at the beginning of the late cruize; but I found myself obliged to fill more salt water than I could have wished, in order to preserve her requisite degree of stiffness; which disadvantage to her velocity cannot, in my humble opinion, be in any other way prevented but by taking a yet larger proportion of iron ballast; but as you have so little to spare, I dare not make application for any more at present.

We now dare to fire our guns without running them out, and so as to admit of the ports being shut, with certain impunity, even to the obliquity of three points before or abaft the beam. A wedge properly adapted is placed behind each truck, to make up for the reduction of space to recoil in, in firing to windward or in rolling weather. The gun first ascends the wedges by rotation, and when stopped by the cleats which cross the back parts thereof, performs the remainder of her recoil as a sledge so feebly as scarce to bring her breeching tight. In thus firing lee guns with a steady breeze and without rolling to windward, if any wedges are at all necessary two are sufficient. The bottoms thereof, to augment their friction against the deck, are pinked, tarred, and rubbed with very rough sand or with coarse coal dust. This method has, I understand, been with avidity adopted by Captain Dalrymple in the Union.

In my last, I presumed to hint to you Captain Patton's fears and my own, nor are they yet one jot abated; he'd give the world for an interview of an hour or two with you. Good, gracious heaven! Is it possible, that the sublime talents of him[1] who by his consummate skill, prudence and calm composed courage, foiled the vast superiority of D'Estaing in North America, whose conduct will, in future ages, be an object of admiration, are not to be employed in the sacred cause of our bleeding country on this stupendously important occasion?

The fleet having made good its retreat, the meditated blow of a dangerous invasion may yet be warded off. That the public danger may point out to our rulers what men and measures further to employ for that purpose, may the Almighty, of his infinite goodness and mercy grant! And to you, and good Mrs. Middleton, long health and the happiness of beholding the speedy return and long duration of Britain's glory and prosperity.

Yesterday on my arrival here, I found my dearly beloved spouse in the silent tomb; my son Frederic (this moment dead) who came into the world of healthy aspect and superior size, dwindled to a mere shadow; and my little daughter (now recovering) ill of the measles. Such scenes of sorrow are at any time terrible to a man of feeling, as a husband and a parent; but particularly so after having so recently been obliged to retire before the fleet of France and Spain. I am, dear Sir, with true respect and the

[1] *Sc.* Lord Howe.

most perfect confidence in your anxiety for the public weal, your most faithful and most affectionate servant and friend,

CHARLES DOUGLAS.

P.S.—I am just going to apply to your board to order the cutting out one port more abaft the present ones on the Duke's quarter-deck, whereby a gun, in shifting one over, may be added to the broadside; nor can it weaken her in any degree so as to shorten her duration a single hour. My carpenter is of the same opinion.

Duke: off the Dodman. 16th September, 1781.

Dear Sir,—The distances the guns of the Duke, &c., have to recoil in, being considerably shortened by the sweep-pieces fixed to the sides of the ship, and the prolongation of their carriages, it became not only expedient, but even necessary to apply some gradual, self-managing check to their recoiling, for the preservation of their breechings; and springs, to be made of well-tempered steel, were devised accordingly; with such surprising good effect that notwithstanding the shortness of the spaces which guns, fitted as this ship's are, have to run back in, their breechings are, I think I may venture to say, infallibly secured against breaking,[1] be the charges ever so great. Nor have I ever seen to break a rope thicker than 3½ inch, reeved for a breeching to a 32-pounder, a slippery deck and a weather gun, loaded with 14 pounds of gunpowder and 2 shots; and even of that size (being of about one fifth part of the strength of a respective

[1] The Namur, Mathews's flagship on 11th Feb., 1744, and the Devonshire, carrying Hawke's flag on 14th Oct., 1747, were temporarily disabled by the breaking of the breechings of the lower-deck guns.

allowed breeching) only twice, after very many repeated trials. As to the possibility of breaking a breeching of the allowed thickness, having a spring (of compression) between the parts thereof, it never enters into anybody's head on board the Duke.

One of such springs, then, dear Sir, of 9 inches diameter, being for a 24- or an 18-pounder, and having been alluded to in my last from Torbay, I shall send you by the first opportunity, and possibly it may reach you not many days after this, which conveys to you my best wishes and respects, comes to hand.

Be pleased to observe, that, for the still better checking of the gun's recoil, two of the respective shot, slung together, may be hung to the middle becket within the spring. This is observed to have a very great effect in easing the spring and lessening the shock upon the breeching, operating different ways towards those ends. One way, worthy of your notice, is by weighing down the breeching between the outer trucks and the ship's side, and thereby making the wedges, which are fixed on the sides of the carriage towards the fore parts of it, to have in some measure the joint effect of an inclining plane. These wedges were originally intended for increasing the power of the springs over the breechings; so that this effect of an inclining plane above alluded to is only a moreover lucky concomitant advantage resulting therefrom. The wedges on the carriage to be sent you from Gosport will fully show my meaning; the protuberances raised on its gun, one on each side of the touch-hole thereof, are intended to hinder the grains of powder, in the act of priming (which way soever one primes, but more especially where the horn and match are used), from falling down upon the deck—a train heretofore laid for the returning fiery sparks of one's own dry wads, when using weather guns, to set fire to.

The new form I have given to the muzzle of the model gun in question is of great consequence, by saving a motion in oblique spring, and by extending its latitude of pointing in all the four different senses of pointing guns.

The spring I have the honour of sending you is proposed to be a standard one, and I shall send two more standard ones, the one being of ten, the other of eight inches diameter, and both of good steel. I shall address them to the board of admiralty at large, and trouble their lordships with an official letter upon the occasion; nor do I despair of yet having a visit from the noble lord who presides thereat, to see guns traverse four points to the right and left without trucks, crows and handspikes; to which effect I certainly shall do myself the honour of writing to his lordship shortly after the Duke's arrival at Spithead. I send you a few more of our 4,400 now all perforated goose quills. Of such, some have been used on board the Duke so long since as early in the year 1779, answering better than those filled with common powder.

Off the Land's End. 17th September, 1781.

P.S.—To try the spring which I have the honour of sending, without firing a gun, you have but to hook a tackle to one of the small grommets through which the breeching reeves, making a rope fast to the opposite one, and to let five or six men haul and veer upon such tackle as if they were hauling a bowline. The action and reaction of the spring will thereby so strikingly appear, as not to leave the smallest doubt of its conclusive efficacy in preserving the breeching. I further observe that the expedient of hanging a weight to the small becket situated in the middle of the spring produces no sort of inconvenience in working the gun, the two shot whereof it consists keeping themselves entirely out of the way in all its traversings.

I have added to the spring two of my 2,500 flannel-bottomed cartridges; as also the small instrument wherewith, after filling with the proper composition, we perforate our never-failing priming quills; of which an ounce of powder fills about seventy; so that, including the contents of our six primers and all, twelve pounds of composition and powder together would go through an engagement of 50 broadsides of the Duke, viz. for the firing of 2,500 shot!

Farewell! When shall we get clear of our standards?

[*Abstract.*] Duke: at Spithead. November, 1781.

[He describes in tedious detail an 'apparatus' he has devised for checking the extreme recoil of weather guns, when the deck is 'slippery' and the ship—'with a great swell upon the beam'—is rolling heavily. From a weight—two half-pigs of iron ballast and two 32-lb. shot—amidships, in rear of the gun, a rope is led 'through a cleat overhead,' passes through a span connecting the muzzle-lashing-bolts, and is toggled to a sort of collar—'a grommet, with an eye formed in it by cross seizing'—which encircles the gun and goes through the breast-bolt of the carriage. When the gun recoils, it has to lift the weight against the friction, both of which can be 'augmented at pleasure.' The apparatus also helps in running the gun out—as much as two additional men on the tackles.]

Formidable: at sea. 28th April, 1782.

On Monday, the 8th instant, at 8 A.M. or a little after, being in the bay of Gros Islet in the island of St. Lucia, refitting and rewatering with unremitting assiduity, but in momentary readiness for sailing, the signal was repeated in the offing by the Alert, from the ships watching the motions of the enemy, that the French fleet, in great force and numerous in transports or trading ships, was coming out of Fort Royal.

Sir George instantly weighed, proceeded outward, and we soon got sight of twelve or fourteen sail of the sternmost ships alluded to from the masthead, standing to the northward under the lee of Martinique, which, from their fast sailing, must have been ships of war. We followed them all night, under as much canvas as we could in prudence carry, the wind blowing very fresh at NE by E. At 2 A.M. of the 9th, the St. Albans hailed, and told us that the enemy's fleet was distinctly seen from the Valiant, she being to windward of us off the north end of Dominica. We had just got sight of them ourselves, having been sufficiently aware of their proximity from the frequent nocturnal signals they had made. At 3 A.M. we brought to by signal; the weathermost of the islands called the Saints bearing N ½ W, and the north end of Dominica, N by E ½ E, five or six leagues. The French fleet bearing from N by E to North. At half-past 5 A.M. made signal to prepare for battle, and for the line ahead, two cables' lengths asunder—as also to fill and stand on; Sir Samuel Hood with the van division, having a fine breeze and a glorious prospect, making sail ahead to his station. At about forty or fifty minutes after nine the French fired upon the Alfred; she returned it, and the signal for battle was displayed.

Thus began that day's partial engagement between his Majesty's fleet commanded by Sir George Rodney, consisting of thirty-six sail of the line, and that of France of thirty-three or thirty-four (I speak from recollection and from information since gathered, for we had not time to count them), which bereaved Great Britain of that excellent citizen and officer Captain Bayne, the (late) gallant commander of the ship named.[1] I say partial engagement, most of his Majesty's ships having been quite becalmed; the whole of our rear and most of the sternmost of the van division utterly so, insomuch as never to have had it in their power to come in for any share of that fight; while the fleet of France enjoyed a commanding breeze, within the limits whereof and to windward they kept themselves as much as possible, with scrupulous attention, and at their much loved long cannonading distance.[2] Nevertheless, divers ships of Sir Samuel Hood's division were roughly handled, having had to cope with so many more of the enemy than ought to have fallen to their share.

Providence brings about mighty events by means undiscernible to men beforehand; and this day's fight, though our enemies, everything considered, had nothing to boast of, encouraged them so far as to dare to risk that general engagement[3] which they

[1] *Sc.* Alfred.

[2] Vaudreuil, who commanded this attack, wrote:—'Si nous nous fussions mis à portée de leurs caronades, nous aurions été promptement dégréés et nous aurions été battus' (Chevalier, i. 290). Douglas would then probably have added—'More fools they.' It was—and is—the rule of common sense and of tactics for the party that has the choice of the distance to take that which best suits his armament. So was it in the much-talked of action between the Phœbe and Essex; so also, according to Captain Sims, in the battle of Tsu-shima.

[3] It is never safe to give an adversary's reasons. Douglas is here certainly misinterpreting De Grasse's.

had avoided before, and which proved their ruin, on, be it ever sacred to fame, the 12th April, 1782; to give you some account of which glorious day's proceedings I am posting.

After, then, having endeavoured to keep our fleet to windward, and transposed, in the line of battle and order of sailing, the van and rear divisions, because of the damages the former had sustained, to the end that our next attack might have its full vigour if ever the enemy should give us opportunity —on the 11th, in the morning, one of Monsieur de Grasse's fleet, being of the line, was seen bearing away for Basseterre Road [1] (where we saw another) and was chased, but got in. Soon after, two ships [2] more of the enemy were discovered far to windward, having also suffered damage in the affair of the 9th, for one was employed in getting up his fore yard and the other in getting up a main topmast. To make his Majesty master of the ships alluded to, or bring Mr. de Grasse to leeward, and thereby draw him yet, if possible, into a general engagement, the signal was made for a general chase, and we all chased accordingly. In the afternoon, the Agamemnon and some others of our weathermost ships gained ground so fast, that the two mutilated ones of the enemy in question began to make signals, only three or four of the body of the French fleet being in sight from our masthead; in consequence of which signals Mr. de Grasse bore down *en corps*, our chasers still menacing their game until the count's headmost ships got very near to them, when they, as well as all the rest of the fleet, were called into close order by signal, and closed accordingly.

On the 12th, be it consigned to perpetual record

[1] Of Guadeloupe. The ship already there was the Caton; the other was the Jason.

[2] Magnanime and Zélé.

in the annals of our long injured, and I hope shortly completely avenged, country, at break of day the enemy's fleet was discovered broad on our lee bow, the wind being at ESE, our heads to the northward, and one of Mr. de Grasse's ships, towed by a frigate,[1] square under our lee, with his bowsprit and foremast prostrate athwart his forecastle. To draw him yet further to leeward, the Valiant and Monarch were sent in chase thereof, and my old acquaintance (of thirty-five years' standing),[2] the high-spirited De Grasse, edged down accordingly; Rear-Admiral Drake, now to lead on the starboard tack, pushing on with his (transposed) division to secure to us the weather-gage and thereby a general and decisive battle.

When the French admiral had got far enough down for this our purpose, the signal was made to call in the Valiant and Monarch, and they took their places in the line of battle with promptitude, the signal for the line of battle ahead and for Rear-Admiral Drake to lead with his division having been displayed some little time before. The French now also forming their line and extending themselves on the larboard tack, to regain the weather-gage, which they thought they had fully secured, because their van, from the wind having reverted to the eastward, lay up rather to windward of ours. Rear-Admiral Drake stood firmly on, in close impenetrable order, the ships composing his Majesty's line of battle being drawn up at the distance of the length of one cable from the one to the other.

[1] Zélé, towed by the Astrée.

[2] On 3rd May, 1747, De Grasse was an ensign of the Gloire, and so fell into our hands. He remained a prisoner for three months (Lacour-Gayet, i. 170). Douglas was a past-midshipman of the Centurion, but may possibly, as speaking French, have been told off to look after the prisoners.

At forty minutes after 7 A.M. the leading ships of Admiral Drake's division were fired upon by the enemy, whereupon the signal for battle and close battle was made, the Marlborough, our leading ship, having fetched the sixth or seventh ship of Mr. de Grasse's line. By the time the foremost ships of the centre division had begun to engage, the fire was heavy indeed and well supported, our ships sliding down slowly (the wind being very moderate) and closely along the enemy's line and under their lee. In stemming towards them, the commander-in-chief of his Majesty's fleet was fired upon by the eighth or ninth ship of Mr. de Grasse's line, but did not return it, the distance being too great, but began with the next; and by giving some little elevation to his guns, to good effect, still standing in a straight line with a full sail, and angling in upon the enemy in order to penetrate his line of battle, which, under favour of the vigorous impression Rear-Admiral Drake had made, the smoke and the most dreadful fire of the Duke, our immediate second ahead, the Formidable, keeping up a most insupportable, quick and well-directed fire, happily effected.

Behind the third or fourth ship astern of the Ville de Paris was the point where we cut through, the almost silenced intermediate ships having passed close to our starboard side, one [1] almost in contact therewith, about a ship's breadth from us. The immediate effect which this penetration produced was the bringing all together, almost if not quite in contact with each other, the four ships of the enemy which were nearest to the point alluded to, and coming up in succession. This unfortunate group, composing now only one large single object to fire at, was attacked by the Duke, the Namur and the Formidable wearing round upon her heel; all at

[1] The Glorieux.

once receiving several broadsides from each, not a single shot missing, and dreadful must have been the slaughter.

From this moment victory declared for the juster cause, and the Count de Grasse, who defended himself with much courage, found himself separated from all his ships, which were astern of the point of intersection in question, never to join them again. All was now a scene of disorder and confusion throughout the enemy's fleet, from end to end; whereupon the signal for the line was hauled down and the victors stuck so close [1] to their flying (late) antagonists as to leave them no time to rally or repair any part of their damages. But it would require a volume, and more time than I am master of, to recount all the handsome performances of this mighty day. Shortly after sunset the French admiral's flag [2] and ensign were struck on board the Ville de Paris, he having been abandoned by all the ships of his fleet, such excepted as were taken or otherwise destroyed, notwithstanding the signals made by the Count de Grasse, often repeated and long kept flying to the contrary.[3]

Such ships as have their guns fitted accordingly, derived unspeakable advantage from some improvements lately made in the use of naval artillery, their fire having been so very quick and so very well directed, and extending so far to the right and left,

[1] It has been seen (*ante*, p. 161) that Hood took a different view of this, and was vehement in his complaints that Rodney 'pursued only under his topsails,' and did not make 'the signal for a general chase the moment he hauled that down for the line of battle.'

[2] But see *ante*, p. 182, *note* 2.

[3] He seems to be here repeating what he had been told by De Grasse, charges which the French *conseils de guerre* denied, and for which he was banished from the court (Chevalier, i. 311–313, 322, 323).

that the French cannot comprehend how they came to lose so many men, and we so few, on the late bloody day; for they were generally so mauled by the ships alluded to as to be most part driven from their quarters before they could bring their guns to bear upon us. The fire of our centre, consisting of three three-deckers, was astonishing indeed; and the moment the Formidable penetrated the enemy's line, as many of his Majesty's ships as saw her after she got through it gave three cheers. At the same instant, the French seamen, even on board the Ville de Paris herself, fled from their quarters, crying out, 'We have lost the day! Our line of battle is cut asunder!' or words to such effect. Some little time after the Count de Grasse struck his flag, our signal for continuing the engagement was hauled down, and an end put to the celebrated general battle of the Saints, by which name certain islands situate between the north end of Dominica and Guadeloupe are called.

P.S.—The moment the Ville de Paris struck, her worthless, disorderly crew broke open the chests and trunks of all their officers, and, with lighted candles in their hands, stove in the doors of the store rooms in quest of wine and other strong liquors, to the very great danger of all on board from fire; and, moreover, killed and destroyed for their own use, the major part of the live stock belonging to the Count de Grasse, consisting of bullocks, sheep and poultry of different kinds. It is very extraordinary and no less true, notwithstanding some thousands of land forces having been on board the French fleet, only one single musket, to the best of my recollection, was fired at the Formidable—so completely were their soldiers, as well as seamen, driven from their quarters before they came abreast of us. As to the loss sustained by his Majesty's fleet, I refer you to the public account; but I think I may pronounce, from the tattered condition the flying enemies were in when they left their general, that their loss cannot be, upon the whole, less than 7,000 or 8,000 men killed and wounded. The number of prisoners borders upon 6,000, including those taken near the east end of St. Domingo, since the battle, by the (detached) van division of the fleet under the command of Sir Samuel Hood, in the Cato and Jason of sixty-four guns each, the Aimable of thirty-six and the Ceres of eighteen—deducting, however, the number slain on board all the ships taken, and the very many of those burnt in the César of seventy-four guns, she having unfortunately caught fire very shortly after she struck.

Not a single goose-quill tube[1] failed, nor did a gun require being wormed, so long as the flannel-bottomed cartridges lasted on board the Formidable or Duke; nor of the 126 locks on board the latter[2] (every lower decker having two) did a single one fail. One Kentish black flint to each served during the whole engagement, in one lock excepted. Though about eighty men short at quarters, the Duke, from the improvements alluded to, fired sometimes fully from both sides, and even with as much ease as if they had been exercising; nor did a single atom of gunpowder catch fire by accident on board of her, she having, as usual, and as now is becoming the practice, as well as the Formidable and divers other ships, used wetted wads.

[1] Tin tubes had been tried more than twenty years before, in the battle of Quiberon Bay, but had been reported as 'very pernicious things,' apt to fly out and wound the men.—Hawke to Clevland, 19 Feb., 1760.

[2] The Duke's guns had, of course, been fitted under Douglas's own eye. He had only left her about four months before the battle.

Reckoning the strength of the French fleet according to its weight of metal, it was stronger than his Majesty's by a force equal at least to that of four French 84-gun ships, to say nothing of their several thousands of supernumerary soldiers—I mean on the 9th. On the 12th, the Zélé of seventy-four, the Cato and Jason of sixty-four each, were absent, having sustained damages; so that on the 12th, according to the above standard, the fleet of France was superior to his Majesty's by the strength of two common ships of the line.[1] In frigates they far outnumbered us, and two of them—the Sagittaire and Experiment—were of fifty or fifty-four guns each.

N.B.—For some little time after we got sight of the French fleet on the 12th, in the morning the wind was, unnaturally and therefore unexpectedly, at SE; of which fortunate circumstance we availed ourselves by pushing on, in order to make sure of fetching the enemy. It then reverted to ESE, and gradually afterwards to east.

Formidable: Port Royal, Jamaica. 4th May, 1782.

Dear Sir,—In consequence of the more exact information I have had, and of my own recollection, the account I now send you differs a little, particularly as to the point in the French line of battle where we broke through, and which I had not then seen upon paper, from my last, as also in some other inconsiderable respects. Some further interesting anecdotes and remarks, too, are in this interspersed or thereunto subjoined.

The more I hear of the late battle, the more am

[1] It will be noticed that in this estimate Douglas entirely omits the English carronades, which, however, in such a close action, must have had a tremendous importance.

I satisfied, even to my own surprise, of the conclusive efficacy of the oblique fire of such ships as could give it. The Ville de Paris, for example, edging down towards our friend Cornish, thought secure in being, as was supposed by them, out of the Arrogant's line of fire, because four points on her bow, did, to their infinite surprise, in that direction receive such a broadside as had wonderful effect. Captain Gardner, of the Duke, told the admiral in my hearing that, from the improvements alluded to, he is sure that he annoyed the enemy with at least twice as many shot as he should have done according to establishment. Upon the whole, I think I may safely pronounce that, if every ship in the fleet had been so appointed, and without standards, like the Arrogant, fewer—possibly very few—of the enemy's ships would have escaped. But withal, the victory, if every ship had been taken, could not have been more clearly and decidedly ours than it was. I only allude to probable consequences, presuming that, had such oblique fire been general, few, if any, of the enemy's masts had been left standing. Lieutenant Butler (now most deservedly captain of the Alecto) says that from the middle deck of the Formidable he never fired less than two, sometimes three, broadsides at each passing Frenchman [1] before such Frenchman could bring a gun to bear on him—from such guns excepted as standards are in the way of. Our admiral informs me that he has written for the appointment of an inspector-general of naval artillery, and of Captain Cunningham as ship's captain to the Formidable. I beg leave to recommend both such appointments to your support and acceleration.

[1] The exercise, so born, continued as long as the old men-of-war and the old guns—'Ships passing on opposite tacks; three rounds of quick firing.'

Should opportunity serve, and should it be with your pleasure, I pray you read the account I now trouble you with, to Lord Mansfield and Lord Loughborough ; and be further pleased to recommend it to the perusal of General Carpenter, his lady, and Mrs. Carr, to all of whom I, for so many years, have been so much obliged ; and to whomsoever else you please. Can Lord Sandwich and Lord North have time to honour it with a reading? —as you please. Gracious heaven! what a labouring oar I have got to manage! anything whereby I may contribute my mite towards the welfare and glory of Great Britain! That you, Lady Middleton, Mr. and Mrs. Edwards, may long and in health enjoy the unspeakable happiness of seeing her wrongs avenged to the utmost farthing, most religiously prays, dear Sir, your obliged and most affectionate friend and servant,

Charles Douglas

Formidable : St. Lucia. 23rd April, 1783.

Dear Sir,—Your two very pressing letters with regard to Lord Colvill's son came in due course to hand. His time, according to his own account, expires not until the month of June; nor has he a single document whereby to make it appear that [he] ever served previous to his entry on board the Conqueror with George Balfour; consequently, were his time actually out, he, at this moment, could not, for want of such documents, be admitted to examination, none being admitted to such examination without being able to make it appear, by the usual testimony, that they have served their six years in the navy. Admiral Pigot very cheerfully took Mr. Colvill into the Formidable; and had he been susceptible of a commission, would ere now have given him one; and, in consequence of my suggestion, would, as I had done, have recommended him to Sir Richard Hughes, whom he leaves here in command; but the young gentleman does not choose to be left abroad, and therefore returns to England in the Formidable. I understand that Admiral Pigot's orders are, and have been, to make no lieutenants who have not served their full six years. Upon the whole, it never was, nor is, in my power to get Mr. Colvill made a lieutenant, nor indeed in anybody's power.[1]

That you may be informed what the late gallant Admiral Kempenfelt, who was an officer indeed, and who went to sea to serve his king and country, and not to serve a faction, thought of our oblique fire, I trouble you to read the paper herewith enclosed. Frenchmen have expressed their surprise thereat; and, ignorant as to the apparatus within, have attributed its effects to the superior width of our ports. The Leander, then commanded by the gallant captain Payne, in her late nocturnal engagement with the Pluton, of 74 guns and full of men, had, during a stage of that fight, of about 14 or 15 minutes' dura-

[1] With the vast number of instances to the contrary within his immediate knowledge—such as, among others, that of Captain Isaac Coffin, who was tried (29 July, 1782) on a charge of 'disobedience and contempt' for objecting to the appointment of three children as lieutenants of the Shrewsbury; or the still more flagrant case of Rodney's son John, lieutenant, commander, and captain within a year of his first coming to sea, while still under sixteen—it is difficult to understand how Douglas could write this, which he not only knew to be false, but which he also knew Middleton knew to be false. Still, this—if it had come off—would have been as bad a case as any on record; for young Colvill, who may have been born in 1765 (Marshall's *Royal Naval Biography*, ii. 754), but according to O'Byrne, was born in 1768, and by Foster's *Peerage*, in 1769, was an acting lieutenant in 1780 (*ante*, p. 88). It is, however, satisfactory to see that he was not confirmed till 1793.

tion, the firing at her antagonist almost with total impunity, discharging into her two shot from each gun, as fast as [it] could be loaded and fired during that space of time; and happy was it for the Pluton, that he could save himself by his heels, his antagonist having, of the two, suffered most, in masts, yards, sails and rigging; but nevertheless his Majesty's ship the Leander remained mistress of the field, and completely victorious over a French one of 74 guns.

But now that the war is over, the less said of improvements in the use of our naval artillery, of what nature soever, the better; discontinuing the same and every trace thereof; only holding it in remembrance and keeping a model or two of it is now surely best. And I beg that you may be pleased to take this my suggestion into your consideration; and if you think it of consequence to take order with Lord Howe for letting the whole improvements in allusion,[1] as fast as may be proper, dwindle into seeming disregard and oblivion.

As we have to visit Antigua and Jamaica, I despair of having, until August, the happiness of assuring you *vivâ voce*, that while I have to breathe, I inviolably am, dear Sir, your most faithful and affectionate servant,

CHARLES DOUGLAS.

[1] So in MS., meaning, apparently, 'which I have been alluding to.'

CAPTAIN KEMPENFELT TO MIDDLETON

INTRODUCTORY.

WITH one exception (p. 359) these letters from Kempenfelt are all holographs, well and legibly written, not badly spelt; but, with that, and one other exception (p. 327), they are all imperfectly dated. In only one instance did Kempenfelt give the year; and though he very commonly noted the day of the month, sometimes he gave only the day of the week, and occasionally only the hour, or not even that. In most of these latter cases nothing can be decided, though the approximate position of the letter can sometimes be guessed at. When the day of the month is given, the subject-matter of the letter, the name of the ship, the place where the ship was, the address, or sometimes the endorsement, have singly or together proved sufficient, by reference to the ships' logs or to the chronology of Kempenfelt's life; as thus:—

Joined Victory as first Captain to Sir C. Hardy	7 May, 1779
Hardy died	18 May, 1780
Admiral Geary hoisted his flag	24 May, 1780
Geary succeeded by Vice-Admiral Darby	8 Sept., 1780
Kempenfelt moved to Britannia	14 Sept., 1780
Rear-Admiral	26 Sept., 1780
Middleton made a Baronet	23 Oct., 1781
Kempenfelt hoisted flag in Victory	18 Nov., 1781
Kempenfelt hoisted flag in Royal George	7 April, 1782
Royal George foundered	29 Aug., 1782

For the rest, where the date remains absolutely indeterminate, it will be seen that the interest of the letter is quite independent of it.

[No date.]

I was in company the other day with a person who made some observations which I thought pertinent upon docks and shipping, which I have wrote down for your perusal.

More docks are required for repairing ships. In peace, many ships that want repairs, and which might be done at no very great expense if taken in hand soon, become repairless from the length of time before they can go to work upon them through the paucity of docks. This renders it impossible to keep up the navy to a proper force of serviceable ships, and greatly enhances the expense, as it requires the building of more new ships than otherwise would be wanted.

The Norfolk, a remarkable fine ship, came from the East Indies with few defects; yet being left for several years before taken in hand, was then found not worth repairing, and broke up. The same has been the fate of several other ships, lost from delay, not applying the remedy in time; for when a ship's frame begins to decay, if the defective parts are not soon removed, they infect the rest, and that with an increasing celerity.

He says that during the first eight years he was at Portsmouth, which were the first part of the last peace, not less than twenty-four sail of the line were broke up or sold.

By this slow method of repair you have scarcely ever more than half your ships properly in condition for sea.

Thinks Portsmouth and Plymouth yards should be wholly for repairs, and the yards to the eastward for building: therefore that the money laid out in making building slips would have been better employed in forming of docks at Portsmouth and Plymouth. That the canal which leads from the harbour to the boat-house might, at very little expense more than what they are at now to face it, have made three docks one ahead of the other; the depth was ready formed for it, and a short cut towards Fountain Lake—not above two-thirds of a ship's length—would have made a canal for the use of the boat-house.

Portsmouth. 28th April [1779].

Dear Sir,—The course of this court martial[1] has given me a clearer idea of the action between our fleet and that of France last summer than I had before conceived; and the different state the two fleets were in after the action confirms most strongly what I have always thought; that is, that the disabling of your enemy in his masts and rigging should have no small share of your attention and your fire. In this skirmish between the two fleets there was at least as many shot sent from us to them as they sent to us; I should think many more, as several of their ships could not open their lower ports and most of ours could.

Now let us take a view of the conditions of the two fleets after action, owing to the different directions of their fire; ours, except the red division, so totally shattered in masts, rigging, and sails that for the whole evening of that day they could not all form into a line. The French ships, on the contrary, were so little injured in these particulars that they had the perfect command of their yards and sails, and immediately after action ceased formed a

[1] On Sir Hugh Palliser. That on Keppel ended on 11 Feb. Probably, however, he means both.

regular line on the starboard tack, pointing towards our fleet, and placing those ships in their van which were the van on the other tack, as being fresh ships.

Now consider a fleet dispersed and unable to collect together, whilst the enemy, perfectly capable of manœuvring, is well formed; is not the first, in such circumstances, at the mercy of the last? Suppose you had killed and wounded them five times the number they had you, yet they having the command of motion and direction, which you had not, gave them a decisive superiority. There is no strength and force without motion and direction. Deprive a giant of one of his legs and a stripling shall master him. 'Tis plain to me that our fleet, after that action, for all the first part of the afternoon, was at the mercy of the French. Unconnected to succour and support each other, what defence could they have made against the attack of a close, well-formed line of ships? Why the French did not profit from this advantage they had, I can't conceive.

In close action such as was between most of our ships and the enemy that day, langridge[1] is certainly the most destructive shot for rigging and sails, much more so than grape. When grape goes through a sail it makes a smooth round hole, but the long and ragged pieces of langridge cut and tear a sail to rags. I think we should make use of this kind of shot. An old ship broke up furnishes ample materials for it.

I am, dear sir,
Your most obedient servant,
RICHARD KEMPENFELT.

[1] 'A villainous kind of shot . . . seldom used but by privateers.' Smyth, *Sailors' Word-Book.*

Victory: off the Lizard. 2 July,[1] [1779].

I have just time to tell you that we have received intelligence by a Genoese ship, that they saw a French fleet consisting of upwards of forty sail off Cape Finisterre the 10th of June last.[2] My situation is extremely disagreeable; I would give all the little I am worth to be out of it. Does the people at home think the nation in no danger? Where is Lord Howe at this alarming period? I can't say more; you'll divine the rest. I can foresee no prospect at present.

All seems to depend upon the abilities with which this fleet is conducted—let that be well considered.

Victory. 27 July [1779].

[*Endorsed*: 27 July, 1779.]

Much, I may say almost all, depends upon this fleet; 'tis an inferior against a superior fleet; therefore the greatest skill and address is requisite to counteract the designs of the enemy, to watch and seize the favourable opportunity for action, and to catch the advantage of making the effort at some or other feeble part of the enemy's line; or, if such opportunities don't offer, to hover near the enemy, keep him at bay, and prevent his attempting to execute anything but at risk and hazard; to command their attention, and oblige them to think of nothing but being on their guard against your attack.

1 The English fleet of thirty-five sail of the line, under Sir Charles Hardy, put to sea from Spithead on the 16th June.

2 The French fleet of twenty-eight ships of the line, under the command of D'Orvilliers, sailed from Brest on the 4th June. On the 11th they were on their rendezvous off the Cisargas Islands, where they were to be joined by the Spanish fleet. Some of the Spanish ships kept tryst, but the great body of the fleet, twenty-eight ships of the line, under Cordova, did not join till the 23rd.

Have the ministry sought for a head capable of such management and dexterity, or, do they think that ships are sufficient of themselves, without wisdom to direct and order their operations? So much indifference at so dangerous a crisis is astonishing and alarming. Adieu! The cutter is going.

Victory. 6th August, [1779].

[*Endorsed. Post-mark:* Falmouth, AV. 11.]

I have scarce time to write to you; a perpetual hurry prevails here, which, from the natural consequence of hurry, produces nothing to the purpose.

In confidence, I must inform you the confused conduct here is such that I tremble for the event. There is no forethought, therefore no events provided against; we are every day, from morning till night, plagued and puzzled in minutiæ, whilst essentials are totally neglected. An odd obstinacy and way of negativing everything proposed, makes all advice useless. There is a fund of good nature in the man, but not one grain of the commander-in-chief. I hear it often said the salvation of Britain depends upon this fleet. I never hear the expression but I turn pale and sink. My God, what have your great people done by such an appointment! I am called upon for the letter. Adieu! Not a word of this transpires from you.

P.S.—I suffer much in character, I know, for a conduct which, if people knew I had nothing to do with, they'd excuse me from censure.

Victory: Off Scilly. 9 August, [1779].

[*Post-mark:* Falmouth 18 AV.]

Dear Sir,—I have wrote you, though something soon, yet pretty freely my opinion, in a certain confidence of your discretion that it rests with you a secret. To not a soul besides have I wrote a word upon the subject. But at this alarming crisis, when our salvation seems to depend upon the good management of this fleet, the anxious concern I have for the safety of my country forces me to declare that you have placed it in hands extremely unequal to the charge. How you can now remedy the evil of this injudicious appointment I can't say.

A man who never thinks beforehand, and therefore is always under the confusion of a surprise when anything happens; always in such a hurry when he takes in hand to do anything that he never does it; puzzling himself and all about him in little detail minutiæ, whilst essentials are never thought of; not the least idea of what the officer should be, so that he destroys his own authority and those in command next under him; gives his directions to the captain of the ship [or] to the lieutenants, without their ever passing through me. It is with the greatest difficulty I can ever prevail upon him to manœuvre the fleet; he is always [so] impatient and in [such] a hurry to get to the westward, to the northward, or the southward, that he won't lose time to form a line.

An admiral who commands in chief should have the esteem, the respect, and the confidence of his officers, but our admiral fails in all these. He never associates with any of them; though good-natured, his manners are rude; his impatience is such that, when an officer comes, he almost shoves him out of the ship; he never invites any to dine with him.

I write this with a number of people talking to me; excuse its irregularity. It is to show you that in this great national charge, the command of the fleet, the person you have chose is not in any degree equal to it. Find a man if possible capable of it; and don't, in so careless a manner, destroy all our hopes. In all your consideration, let the interest and safety [of the] nation be predominant, and let any other consideration yield to that. Adieu!

Sincerely yours,
RD. KEMPENFELT.

P.S.—Not a syllable of what I have said goes from me to any person but yourself: and 'tis only the interest of Britain at this most dangerous conjuncture that has forced me to open myself in this manner. His good nature has my esteem; but for the commander of a fleet he is totally unfit.

Victory: to the westward of Scilly. 14th August, [1779].
[*Endorsed. Post-mark:* Plymouth.]

Sir,—That we have no regular system of naval tactics you know; also that tactics are as necessary for fleets as armies, to give regularity, activity and force, and that that force may be directed in the best manner. Of two fleets, if one acts by a regular system of tactics, when the other has none, I needn't say where the advantage must lay. Our enemies have theory, we were superior in practice. They are in a way to remove the difference in the last, and how will the comparison then stand between us? Our fleet, under its present deficiency of discipline for regular manœuvring and fighting, is to a fleet that acts by a well-formed system, just the same as an army composed of raw militia would be to one formed of regulars under an experienced general. The expediency of having some person at the head of the fleet capable of introducing such a discipline is become absolutely necessary, and should be immediate.

Victory: Spithead. 5th September [1779].

Dear Sir,—I have just received your last favour—I am indebted to you for many. A number of frigates are of great use in a fleet; they extend your views far round you, and in consequence your intelligence; without a strong support of this kind the enemy's frigates will cut off your fireships in time of action. Fireships, if judiciously employed, are a great additional force, if you have the wind of the enemy. In that case I think you may be sure to break their line at whatever part you please to make the attack, if you have a number of them. I really don't see the necessity of waiting till a ship is disabled before you apply the fireship. I think the best time to use them is in the very beginning of the action; the smoke covers them as well then as afterwards; and is it not best to do the greatest injury to your enemy as soon as you can, to hasten his defeat? And I think, in the line, the fireship has as much chance to succeed when the masts are standing as when they are gone, without the ship she point for bears away; and then the line is broke, and an opening made for their defeat. The very appearance of a fireship's coming to board causes a confusion which you must profit from. But fireships should sail well, or they retard a fleet much; and yet very little attention has been paid to that quality in them, most of ours sailing very bad.

We don't seem to have considered sufficiently a certain fact, that the comparative force of two fleets depends much upon their sailing. The fleet that sails fastest has much the advantage, as they can engage or not as they please, and so have it always in their power to choose the favourable opportunity to attack. I think I may safely hazard an opinion that twenty-five sail of the line, coppered, would be sufficient to hazard and tease this great, unwieldy, combined armada, so as to prevent their effecting anything ; hanging continually upon them, ready to catch at any opportunity of a separation from night, gale or fog ; to dart upon the separated, to cut off any convoys of provisions coming to them ; and if they attempted an invasion, to oblige their whole fleet to escort the transports, and even then it would be impossible to protect them entirely from so active and nimble a fleet. I think when the enemy's fleet were off Plymouth, fireships in the night, disguised in the dress of their tenders, as luggers, cutters, &c., might have been applied with success, under the management of some bold, sensible man.

Langridge shot are certainly of great use in close action, and I am glad to find they are adopted by the admiralty.

Some of our ships are very badly manned ; the Blenheim in particular. Of the frigates appointed last to the fleet, there are three or four most wretched sailers, as the Druid, the Camel, the Squirrel, &c., which the admiral, I believe, intends taking out the men, and to strengthen the worst manned ships with them, which in my opinion will be very right.

When so much depends upon this fleet, 'tis matter of great astonishment so little care was taken in the choice of the conductor. As a private man he is worthy of esteem, but as an officer, I am afraid the fleet has neither esteem for or confidence in him ; a serious thing at so critical a juncture. The fleet wants a sensible, active, and strict officer at the head of it, to brace up relaxed discipline, to give alertness and activity to it, in which consist great part of its force. There is none of that ardour remains now that upon extraordinary occasions urged everyone to try to have his ship the first ready; but there is a supine languor and indifference reigns now: it is the epidemic disorder of the nation and affects all. Adieu!

Yours sincerely,
RD. KEMPENFELT.

Victory. 19th September [1779].

Dear Sir,—As you expected, I was much surprised at what you mentioned in your letter of the 5th of August that I should have said I would offer no further advice to Sir C.,[1] an expression I never made use of, for I never thought my advice of so much consequence and am never officious to give it. As to Sir C., I have not, nor never had, any variance with him; he is good-natured, honest, has many private virtues which I esteem him for; but as an officer, you know my opinion; and when I considered that all depended upon the wise conduct of the fleet, I trembled for the event; I suffered the severest anxiety; I opened myself to you, and to you only.

If the combined fleet are in port, they'll not appear at sea in a body before the spring, I should think. Is it supposed the whole winter at Brest, or the Spaniards return home? If they all keep at Brest they'll want large supplies of provisions; much of it will go from their eastern ports; a good look out on their coast in the Channel, when the wind leads down, might have a fair chance to intercept some of them.

If a continuance of strong westerly winds should prevent our fleets going out, I suppose a strong squadron will be sent the first opportunity to the westward, on account of our home-bound West India trade.

[1] Sir Charles Hardy.

One grand object of the admiralty should be to restore a strict, orderly discipline in the fleet; for which purpose there ought to be an admiral at each port, besides the port-admiral, whose charge should be the order and conduct of the ships only. Captains should not be absent from their ships, nor lay on shore when at Spithead. The relaxation of last winter was of great prejudice to the fleet; no admiral particular to attend to their conduct, captains mostly absent,[1] and the greatest part of the lieutenants likewise; the men, left in a great measure to themselves, became riotous and licentious, and such opportunities given for desertion that the numbers lost was shameful.[2] Men must be constantly employed to keep them orderly. When ships are not fitting for sea, they should be at sea; then order and discipline gain ground, and the men keep their health better in short cruises than in port. Some better regulations should take place with respect to Haslar[3] Hospital to prevent desertion, which last winter was amazing. All our small cruisers should be kept out the winter to protect our own and annoy the enemy's trade. Last winter, when I was at the Nore, Sheerness was crowded with these sort of vessels who ought to have been at sea.

I don't think the admiralty support their authority with sufficient vigour and spirit. They should make themselves feared and respected, to make the whole under them move orderly. There is a languor and inertia hangs upon us which must be shaken off before we can act with vigour. If a proper spirit could be roused, and close attention paid to every-

[1] Attending at the Keppel and Palliser courts martial.

[2] *Cf.* Young's remarks on the want of discipline on the Leewards Islands Station in 1780 (*ante*, p. 95).

[3] Kempenfelt wrote 'Hazeler,' which is still the local pronunciation.

thing this winter that could add force to the fleet, it might next spring appear respectably formidable.

P.S.—I have mentioned that ships not a-fitting for sea should be at sea during the winter; but to save the masts and ships from injury as much as possible, when it comes to blow hard westerly, they should bear up for Torbay or some port.

A propos: A few batteries well placed at Torbay might prevent an enemy's fleet from making use of it.

[*Post-mark:* Portsmouth.] Victory. 13th October [1779].

I took the liberty last winter to mention to you that I thought it would be of great service to the navy by rendering the corps of marines much more useful, if they were trained to the management of artillery when ashore, as in action it is generally necessary to quarter the greatest part of them to the great guns.

I beg leave to say a word or two about courts martial, which, according to the present regulation, are attended with very great inconvenience in so large a fleet as the present is. For there will be almost daily demands for courts martial, by which the admirals and senior captains will be almost constantly employed on that service—an insufferable fatigue, and affording them no time to attend to other essential duties; and the admiral of the fleet's captain is taken off, for days together, on this service from his attention to the fleet, when his whole time is scarcely sufficient for it.

But if an admiral, with seven captains for instance, were allowed to be sufficient for holding a court—the captains in rotation—how would this service, now a kind of slavery, be rendered easy; and with what despatch! when by this method four courts martial, as our fleet now stands, might be held at the same time.

Victory. 17th October [1779].

Dear Sir,—Signals pointed out by numbers, and according to that method observed in those you sent me, I have been long acquainted with. They don't require many flags; however there must be three of each sort, or you can't express a number which consists of three figures of the same rank, as 222 or 333, &c., and for expedition in making the signals there should be the whole nine flags ready for each masthead. This numeral way of pointing out the signal is very convenient for those to whom they are addressed, for the ready finding out their meaning, and a very great ease to the compiler of the signals. The objections against them are that, for the most part of the signals, you have three flags to show instead of one in the common method; that ships may often be in a position not to see the flag at the mizen topmast-head; that to ships at a distance it will be more difficult to ascertain the colour of two or three flags than of one; that when signals are simple, with only one position, that, assisted by circumstances, may lead to the knowledge of the signal, though the colour of the flag may not distinctly be distinguished.

However, I think all these objections may be obviated; and in my opinion, the signals by numbers, or those by a superior flag, as used by D'Orvilliers the two last summers, are by much superior to any method we have. I could in a very few days (less than a week) arrange our signals according to both the above methods, could I have those days to myself without interruption.

You speak about keeping frigates out. Certainly none should be kept in when fit to go to sea; but that is neglected. I have frequently recommended it; and in my opinion they should cruize in pairs, or a smart sloop with them. I wanted another frigate to have been sent with the Quebec,[1] the more as she was designed to go off Ushant.

The luxury of the age, which naturally leads to pleasure and ease, has greatly infected the navy. At this season the greatest part of the captains of cruizers had rather stay in port than go to sea, an evil only to be remedied by an active and strict admiral at the head of the fleet.

It seems very extraordinary to me that we keep vessels as cruizers in the service who can't sail. 'Tis really throwing so much money away as their charge is, and losing the use of so many sailors as they employ. Of this class are the Camel, Hydra, Squirrel, Cabot, Hawke, Wolf, Helena brig, and many others whose names I don't recollect.

Neither the Alexander or Alfred[2] promise to be good ships; they neither sail nor carry sail. The faults found in the construction are that the extreme

[1] The news of the loss of the Quebec on 6th October had just come in. The Admiralty minute conferring a pension on Farmer's widow (*cf. D.N.B.*, s.n. Farmer, George) was dated 15th October. On her last cruize the Quebec had carried a reduced armament of 9 instead of 12 pounders; but it is very probable that Kempenfelt did not know that; and his suggestion was simply an answer to the new class of 18-pounder frigates which the French were fitting out. When in 1814 the admiralty answered the United States' construction of 24-pounder frigates by an order that our 18-pounder frigates should cruize in pairs, it was denounced by some writers as a shameful confession of inferiority. In reality, it was a reliance on the facts and the lessons of history, and has quite recently been recognized as such by a very capable student of strategy, tactics, and the science of naval war (*Naval Policy*, p. 282).

[2] Sister seventy-four-gun ships, launched in 1778 at Deptford and Chatham respectively. The first of them was, twenty years later, in the battle of the Nile. The other was with Rodney on the 12th April, 1782, and again with Howe on the 1st June, 1794.

breadth is too low; it goes below the load water-line. The next is that the after body is too clean[1] near the water edge, by which, when by the wind, the quarter is not supported; which also tends to make her crank and prevents the ballast being stowed near the centre, but must be placed far forward to keep those ships from sinking too much by the stern, in which case she carries a lee helm and often misses stays. I am told it is the practice of the French and of our best builders to make the after body clean under water; but at the water's edge to give a fulness to support or resist the pressure of the sail.

I am, dear Sir, much yours,
RD. KEMPENFELT.

Victory: Torbay. 16th November [1779].

Dear Sir,—I mentioned in my last my opinion of the improbability of the combined fleets coming out again this winter; for this reason, that it is morally impossible so numerous a fleet as theirs can keep the sea for any time at this season without receiving great damage. Long nights and heavy gales are formidable enemies to large fleets.

But suppose the enemy should put to sea with their fleet—a thing much to be wished for by us. Let us act wiser, and keep ours in port; leave them to the mercy of long nights and hard gales. They'll do more in favour of you than your fleet can. A large fleet never tacks or wears when it blows hard in a dark night without risking great damage. We have had occasion to do it three times since we have been out, and each time with narrow escapes.

If the wind comes to the eastward we shall proceed westward to our station, and if it should

[1] Has too fine a run.

continue a stiff and long-winded wind, we may be drove a 100 or 150 leagues to the westward, and perhaps not able to recover the Channel for six weeks or two months; a pretty situation for the fleet to be in to protect this island! and how much such a circumstance would forward the early equipment of the fleet for spring service! The fleet left Spithead with only two months' provisions. I leave it to you to judge of the prudence of risking their being drove out of the Channel so victualled.

In fine, sir, I don't suppose any person acquainted with naval affairs but sees the necessity of immediately taking in hand to prepare the fleet for the next campaign, to endeavour of having the advantage of being the first in the field.

Let us keep a stout squadron to the westward ready to attend the motions of the enemy. I don't mean to keep them at sea, disabling themselves in buffeting the winds, but at Torbay ready to act as intelligence may direct.

28th December, [1779?[1]].

Without discipline is well planned and strictly supported, a military corps or a ship's crew are no

[1] This date cannot be considered quite certain, though the agreement of the subject matter of this letter with that of the letter immediately following seems to confirm the slight indication given by the mention of the Defiance, which went out to North America in the spring of 1779, and was lost at the mouth of the Savannah River on 15th February, 1780. The incident referred to—the refusal to weigh anchor—cannot be found in any of the three logs, and it is quite possible that Kempenfelt wrote the wrong names, as he certainly did just before in the case of the Prince, an old 90-gun ship—a hulk, in fact—which was not in commission during the war. He seems to have meant the Queen, flag-ship of Vice-Admiral Harland, on board which on 9th February, 1779—not summer—there was a noisy attempt to take possession of a butt of beer, which had been placed in charge of a sentry under the half deck. The two ringleaders were tried by

better than a disorderly mob; it is a well-formed discipline that gives force, preserves order, obedience, and cleanliness, and causes alertness and despatch in the execution of business. We want in the navy such a discipline which should be general; and all commanders, &c., required to put it strictly in practice. It has been for want of this that such a spirit of insolence and licentiousness has so daringly showed itself of late upon so many occasions. That alarming mutiny the summer before last, on board of the Prince, in a large fleet, and under the immediate authority of an admiral whose flag was flying on board, was a degree of audacity never heard of before in the annals of our navy. Then the refusal of weighing anchor in the Defiance, the Valiant, the Cumberland. This undisciplined, audacious spirit showed itself upon several occasions in the Victory when we first went on board her; however, that is now pretty well suppressed. All these disorders arise from a defect in discipline.

In what order is a military corps kept on shore, when well officered! Certainly the situation of a ship's crew is more favourable to sustain order and regularity than that of a corps ashore, confined within narrow limits, without tippling houses to debauch in, and under the constant eye of their officers. But if six, seven, or eight hundred men are left in a mass together, without divisions, and the officers assigned no particular charge over any part of them, who only give orders from the quarter-deck or gangways—such a crew must remain a disorderly mob, business will be done awkwardly and tumultuously, without order or despatch, and the raw men put into no train of improvement.

court-martial on 3rd March and sentenced to receive 200 and 150 lashes respectively. This was before Kempenfelt joined the fleet, and his knowledge of it may easily have been inaccurate.

The officers, having no particular charge appointed them, the conduct and behaviour of the men are not inspected into; they know nothing of their proceedings; and the people, thus left to themselves, become sottish, slovenly and lazy, form cabals, and spirit each other up to insolence and mutiny.

The only way to keep large bodies of men in order is by dividing and subdividing of them, with officers over each, to inspect into and regulate their conduct, to discipline and form them. Let the ship's crew be divided into as many companies as there are lieutenants [1]—except the first lieutenant, whose care should extend over the whole. These companies to be subdivided, and put under the charge of mates or midshipmen; and besides this, every twenty-five men to have a foreman to assist in the care of the men, as a sergeant or corporal in the army.

Each lieutenant's company should be formed of the men who are under his command at quarters for action. These companies should be reviewed every day by their lieutenants, when the men are to appear tight and clean. He is to see that the raw men are daily exercised at arms, and the sails and rigging. The captain should review them himself at least once a week.

When it can be done, the men should always have the full time for their meals and for repose, and certain portions of time in the week allotted for washing and mending; but at all other times they should be kept constantly employed; and whatever they are exercised about, be particularly careful that they do it with attention and alertness, and perfect.[2] Labour to bring them to a habit of this, and suffer nothing to be done negligently and awkwardly.

[1] *Cf.* Middleton's orders in the Ardent, *ante*, p. 39.

[2] So in MS.

The adage that idleness is the root of evil is with no people more strongly verified than with sailors and soldiers. Motion preserves purity; everything that stagnates corrupts. When you have nothing more necessary for the men to do, let them be exercised at small-arms; it makes the men straight, gives them an easy and graceful motion of the limbs, shakes off the awkward clown, and gives that military air which shows a man to advantage.

This leads me to step a little out of the way to remark that our sea officers should be acquainted with the military art; the seaman and the soldier are two professions that should be united in the former. They should know how to form men for marching; for attacking, or defending themselves when on shore with a body of men; they should know the advantage to be made of ground, by possessing heights, hedges, houses, walls, &c.; the advantage of covering their front or flanks with rivers, ponds, morasses, or woods; how to intrench, or form a redoubt. These are things not very difficult to acquire, and are of infinite advantage to the officer who may command a party ashore in presence of an enemy.

To keep the seamen properly clothed and clean, they should be uniformed, and be obliged to possess a certain quantity of each species of clothing; which that they do, the lieutenant of the company should every Monday make a muster of their clothes. As chests cannot be allowed, haversacks should be provided as other slops, and furnished the purser. This uniformity of the seamen might contribute something to check desertion; I am sure it would keep the men in a more decent appearance. At present, their appearance in general is a disgrace to the service, very shabby and very dirty. This method which I recommend, if strictly pursued, must be attended with the most beneficial effects. The men would be kept sober, orderly, and clean, perfected in all the necessary duties; the officers, by thus daily reviewing the men, would become acquainted with the character and behaviour of each individual; he would find out the turbulent and seditious, and keep a strict hand over such.

An emulation would naturally rise amongst the lieutenants to show their companies perfect in cleanliness, discipline, and all the several manœuvres; the young landmen would very soon be made acquainted with the seamanship and fighting parts of their duty. I am certain that young landmen, with proper attention, may, in three months, if half that time at sea, be made to know every rope in the ship, to knot and splice, hand and reef, and be perfect at the management of the cannon and small-arms.

Religion is particularly necessary in the common people to preserve morals. It should, in a plan of discipline, make a part. Divine service should therefore be performed every Sunday; and I think a short form of prayer for mornings and evenings, to be used every day, would be proper. It would take up but a short time. The French and Spaniards, in their ships, have their matins and their vespers every day. Our seamen people are more licentious than those of other nations. The reason is, they have less religion. Don't let anyone imagine that this discipline will disgust the men, and give them a dislike to the service; for the very reverse will be the consequence. Sobriety, cleanliness, order, and regularity, the conveniencies resulting from these to them, will convince [them] that they tend as much to their particular benefit as to the public service.

What I have here recommended I know is not new; I have thought of it many years ago, and I know many others have done the same; but yet it is not adopted. What I want is, that it is commanded, enforced by authority, to be practised in every ship. It is easy and simple, and if strictly observed would very soon produce a most desirable change. With order and discipline you would increase your force; cleanliness and sobriety would keep your men healthy; and punishments would be seldom, as crimes would be rare.

18th January, [1780].

I believe you will, with me, think it something surprising that we, who have been so long a famous maritime power, should not yet have established any regular rules for the orderly and expeditious performance of the several evolutions necessary to be made in a fleet. The French have long since set us the example. They have formed a system of tactics, which are studied in their academies and practised in their squadrons.

Fleets, as well as armies, require rules to direct their several motions. In the movement of a fleet to perform any evolution, the way of doing it with most regularity, facility and expedition, is to be preferred; and tactics lays down rules for this purpose, by which every ship knows what they have to do when any evolution by signal is ordered, by which the whole fleet act together in concert, to the same end, by the same method; and nothing is left arbitrarily to the captains, who, without some determined rule known to all, by taking different methods for the execution, would embarrass each other.

All general movements, without they are made by established rules known to all, must be disorderly and confused, subject the ships to run foul of each other, be tedious in the performance, and imperfect in the execution. The fleet, therefore, whose motions are regulated by fixed rules, must have greatly the advantage of one whose motions have no rule to regulate them. In the one, when it becomes necessary to change the form or arrangement of it, to re-establish a line of battle disordered by a shift of wind, &c., it is done with order and expedition ; in the other, when these things are to be done, there will unavoidably be an awkward slowness in the execution, a long time of confusion before order can be restored, which, if this should happen in the presence of an enemy near, the situation of such a fleet will then be rendered extremely critical and dangerous ; for although the enemy may have the same movements to make, yet his motions will be much quicker and more orderly from the regular rules he acts by, and will therefore be in order before the other is out of confusion ; and consequently, if his situation will admit, will lose no time to profit from his advantage, but immediately attack his adversary while in disorder.

Indeed, 'tis too obvious to make any arguments necessary to show that fleets as well as armies require rules for the execution of their movements, and that the one stands in need of tactics as well as the other ; without which both are unwieldy masses, where force is lost for want of form and order. Superior address in conduct may make up for the want of numbers, but what is to be expected when skill and address are wholly on the side of numbers ?

Oh, but, 'tis said by several, our men are better seamen than the French. But the management of a private ship and a fleet are as different from each other as the exercising of a firelock and the conducting of an army. But don't let us flatter ourselves even with this advantage. The French have a vast navigation trade in which to form seamen ; and that industry and genius that leads them to the more sublime part of naval war, we may be assured won't let them neglect the lower parts necessary to the execution of the other.

Enquire of those who were in the fleet with Mr. Keppel the summer before last,[1] if the French did not manage their ships like seamen; and as to their frigates, they showed an alertness, I have been told, not equalled by any of ours. When their signals were at any time thrown out to make sail, they were in an instant under a cloud of canvas; when they returned to their admiral, or were called to him, they run close up to his stern with all sail set, when in a moment all disappeared but the topsails. If a ship was but at a small distance, if called to the admiral, she immediately spread all her sail, even to stern[2] sails if they would draw. This appears to be not only seamanship, but the brilliancy of it.

I have heard it said by some that the French out-manœuvred us, or showed more generalship in their conduct than we, the summer before last. I should suppose it to have been so, as they had tactics to direct them and we had not. There is also a vulgar notion prevails amongst us, and that even with our gentry, that our seamen are braver than the French. Ridiculous to suppose courage dependent upon climate. The men who are best disciplined, of whatever country they are, will always fight the best. The Roman troops beat those of all other nations, not because they were Romans, for their legions were composed of people from all countries; but because their discipline was superior to that of all other nations. It is a maxim

[1] *Sc.* 1778.

[2] The word is plainly written in Kempenfelt's clear writing; possibly by a slip of the pen for 'stun.'

that experience has ever confirmed, that discipline gives more force than numbers.

In fine, if you will neither give an internal discipline for your ships, nor a system of tactics for the evolutions of your fleet, I don't know from what you are to expect success, when you leave the enemy in unrivalled possession of these advantages. It certainly behoves us at this time to give our navy all the force we can; and no way more speedy, more effectual, and which will be attended with no expense, than establishing and strictly enforcing an internal and external discipline as here recommended; for all military bodies are defective in force in proportion as they are defective in discipline.

We should therefore immediately and in earnest set about a reform; endeavours should be used to find out proper persons, and encouragement offered for such to write on naval tactics, as also to translate what the French have published on that subject. They should enter into the plan of education at our marine academies.

But the most effectual way to obtain every wished for reform in your fleet is to find out a man to place at the head of it, who has genius to comprehend every requisite regulation, and has activity and spirit to enforce their execution. I am sorry to say that wealth, ease, I may add luxury—never favourable to a military character, to assiduity, fatigue, and subordination—show their effect in the fleet, and in a more particular manner call for a disciplinarian to be at the head of it.

I shall conclude with observing what an extraordinary genius prevailed amongst the French in Louis XIV's reign, to push up everything to the summit of perfection. They had no sooner created a great navy in that reign (for they never had any before), to the astonishment of all Europe, as at that time they had scarce any commerce at sea to furnish them with the materials for building, the necessary workmen or seamen to man their ships—I say they had no sooner effected this prodigy of forming a navy without the apparent requisites, than they had the quickness of discernment immediately to see (what we have never been able to see yet) the great advantage that would result in sea fights from a system of naval tactics. They had no example of it from other nations. All that had been done was the introducing of a straight line for a line of battle, instead of the curve or half moon used before. This was an improvement of the Duke of York's. They judiciously perceived that military tactics might be adapted to naval tactics in the arrangement and evolutions of fleets. They set to work about it, and completed it so well as to exhaust the subject, and so were as astonishingly rapid in perfecting the discipline and manœuvres of a fleet as they were in forming one. Père Hoste, a Jesuit, secretary to the Count of Tourville, admiral of the French fleet, was the person who undertook the task, which he executed so well that it remains still, with little alteration, the system they follow.

20 March, [1780].

The dimensions for signal flags which seems to be the most generally approved of, is that of five yards and a half in depth and nine yards in length.

In flags that are crossed, the breadth of the cross should be one-fifth part of the breadth of the flag.

Striped flags to have seven stripes; the dark colour to make the outside stripe on both sides.

Chequered flags to have three chequers breadthways, and four chequers lengthways; that end of the flag which has two light-coloured chequers with a dark chequer between them should be at the tabling[1] next the staff.

In pierced, or (more properly) bordered, flags the pierced part should be in breadth half the depth of the flag, and bordered all the way round with a quarter-part of the depth of the flag; as, for instance, suppose a red flag pierced with white, the flag four yards deep, the white part will have two yards in breadth, and be bordered round with red one yard deep.

Chequered pennants to have only two chequers breadthways and five chequers lengthways.

Coupée pennants[2] to have five divisions; the first division, or that next the staff, to be the dark colour.

Striped pennants to have five stripes; the two outside stripes to be of the dark colour.

I have enclosed the flags and pennants that we have adopted in the signals; and when two colours are used in a flag, to make the contrast stronger, we have joined the white always with the red, and the yellow always with the blue.[3] These flags which we have chose may, I imagine, be all formed out of the flags we already have.

The triangular flags are to denote the different squadrons of the fleet; and by adding different coloured pennants to them, the different division of each squadron. For instance, the white triangular flag, with a red pennant over, signifies the first division of the second squadron; a white pennant over, the second division; and a blue pennant, the third division of that squadron; and in the same manner for the other squadrons. If the commander-in-chief

[1] The hem at the hoist.

[2] Striped vertically.

[3] Driven by nature's optics to the heraldic rule which forbade metal on metal, or colour on colour.

means signals confined to one squadron only, he at the same time shows the triangular flag denoting that squadron; if he means the signals to relate to two squadrons at the same time, he shows the two flags denoting such squadrons.

[21st March, 1780.][1]

I received a letter from Portsmouth last night, after I left you, by which I find that a great part of our flags are already of the dimensions, or nearly so, of those I gave to you, and when the difference is small there will be no occasion for an alteration. I beg leave to request you will change the dimension of the depth of the flags from five yards and a half to that of five yards only; then it will stand five yards deep and nine yards long, which I find by the above letter are the dimensions of the flag I had in view as of a proper size; and I believe these dimensions will better correspond with the breadth of the bunting.

If the dimensions I gave you for crosses, stripes, chequers, &c., in flags should be found inconvenient to be complied with on account of the breadth of the bunting, I will, when I know it, adjust the one to the other. I wrote in to the admiralty board this morning about the colours. I think the breadth of bunting is twenty-one inches. If so, nine breadths is five yards nine inches, and the odd inches will be taken up in the seams; from which, nine whole breadths of bunting sewn together will make a flag just five yards deep.

[1] The dates of this and the previous letter are fixed by a letter to the admiralty of 21st March, 1780, in which he gives these corrected dimensions of the flags, and wishes that the colours of some of them should be altered to 'such as are more distinct, an account of which I have given to the comptroller of the navy.'

P.S.—May it not be proper to send to the ports where the Spanish prize ships of war[1] are, to desire that care is taken to preserve their signal lanterns, as they probably may be bought for the use of the flagships of the fleet?

26th March, [1780].

[*Endorsed*: Sent Lord Sandwich,
28 March, 1780.]

When the fleet is going to sea and the ships are cleared of chests, there is always, as you know, a great demand for old canvas to make bags for the men, an expense there is no reason should fall upon the government. It would therefore be proper, in time, to signify to the ships' crews that they are to provide themselves with such conveniences, and to direct that the pursers are furnished with them, to issue as slops; and likewise, notice to be given to those who sell slops on board of ships to provide themselves with such bags for sale. I know these are already your thoughts; I only take the liberty to remind you of them.[2]

It shows a strange neglect and indifference that so long as carronades have been proposed, and under such ascribed advantages, that sufficient trials have not been yet made on board a ship to decide

[1] Captured by Sir George Rodney off Cape St. Vincent, on 16th January, 1780.

[2] Proposal that canvas bags as an article of slops, as applied for by Captain Kempenfelt, may be allowed. 'They will be not only useful, but a considerable saving to government' (*Navy Board Letters*, 3rd April, 1780). The canvas bags for the use of the seamen have been provided and forwarded to the different ports, with directions to issue them to the pursers (*Ibid.*, 12th October, 1780). Such bags had been ordered by Middleton, in the Ardent, five years before; and very probably in other ships. The novelty of Kempenfelt's proposal was that they should be systematically issued by the pursers.

upon them, that, if approved of, we might not lose time in profiting from them. The trials would neither cost trouble, expense or time. I am inclined to think a little more weight and length, which would allow of somewhat more powder for charge, would improve the carronades, and remove in a great measure the objections against them : as, not throwing their [shot] with sufficient [force] and to a sufficient distance, endangering the sides of the ports in firing, and violence of recoil. But this by the by; but I am certain the largest carronades will be found the least exceptionable.

I shall shortly show you a scheme for artillery of different nations, for ship use, drawn up by an ingenious mathematician, who has made the science of artillery his favourite study, especially that for sea service ; a service he is well acquainted with, having been much at sea, especially in ships of war. He proposes for the tops and poops a large musketoon of three feet barrel, to carry nine musket balls, and to be mounted with a swivel on a stock. He says it will throw the nine balls as far as a musket will a single ball. Such a piece promises to be very useful for the tops, quarters, forecastle—in short, in all places and for all purposes that muskets can be used, and requires but one man to manage it. We at present have no sort of firearms proper for tops ; the swivel guns are awkward, and now condemned by everybody. The blunderbusses and musketoons won't throw their shot far enough.

Wednesday morning.

There was yesterday some conversation upon cannon, and of Robins's proposal for reducing the weight of the different natures under a 32-pounder to the proportion of that piece, according to their different weight of bullet.[1] If he is right in his principle, what he proposes would be a great advantage, especially for sea service. I'll transcribe to you what he says upon this subject.

'When the charge and the effort of the bullet are assigned, the weight of each species of cannon in a ship is, or ought to be, determined by the following circumstances :—

1. 'That they shall not be in danger of bursting ;
2. 'That they shall not heel too much in firing ;

and 3. 'That they shall not recoil too boisterously.

'All this is to be done by a proper quantity of metal properly disposed of ; and when the pieces are secured from these accidents, all addition of metal beyond is not only useless but prejudicial.'

The author takes for a standard to go by, the 32-pounders, that weigh 52 cwt. 53 lbs., which is somewhat less than $1\frac{2}{3}$ cwt. for each pound of bullet. From this he concludes that any smaller piece made upon the model of these 32-pounders, and having their weight proportioned in the same manner to the weight of the bullet, will fully answer all the purposes recited above, and will be of unexceptionable service. All ships' guns to be cast upon the model of the 32-pounders, measuring by the diameter of the respective bullets, that for each pound of ball there should be allowed one hundred and two-thirds of metal only.

The advantages of this scheme will appear by the following comparison of the weight of the

[1] *Proposals for increasing the strength of the British Navy*, one of Robins's *Tracts of Gunnery*, printed as an Appendix to his *New Principles of Gunnery* (ed. 1805), pp. 283 *seq.*

present pieces with the weight proposed by this new fabric :—

Pieces.		Weight in hundreds.		Weight in hundreds by the new fabric.
24-pounders	.	48 to 46	.	40
18 ,,	.	41 ,, 39	.	30
12 ,,	.	34 ,, 31	.	20
9 ,,	.	29 ,, 26	.	15
6 ,,	.	24 ,, 18	.	10

The changes proposed by the author are these :—

	Pounders.		Hundreds.		Pounders.		Hundreds.
For	6	of	24 and 18	new	12	of	20
,,	9	,,	29 ,, 26	,,	18	,,	28
,,	12	,,	34 ,, 31	,,	18	,,	28
,,	18	,,	41 ,, 39	,,	24	,,	40

Now all the objections that can be made against the present proposal will equally hold good against the present 32-pounders, which are known to be guns of unexceptionable service. Of the charge of powder for cannon, Robins says: 'If the powder was reduced to one-third the weight of the ball, or even less, it would be a considerable advantage, not only by the saving of ammunition, but by keeping of the gun cooler and quieter, and at the same time effectually injuring the vessels of the enemy; for with the present allowance of powder, the guns are heated and their tackle and furniture strained, and this only to render the bullet less efficacious than it would prove if impelled by a smaller charge. This quantity of powder I propose, of one-third the weight of the bullet, has for some time past been practised with the French even in battering in breach.'

The author thinks a much greater reduction in the charge than to one-third the weight of the ball might take place, and that one-fourth, or even one-fifth, of the weight of the bullet in powder, if properly disposed, is abundantly sufficient for every species of ships' guns. In a letter to Lord Anson he says: 'Small charges are much more efficacious than has been generally believed. That after a certain charge (for instance, 3½ lbs. of powder in an 18-pounder), all addition of powder will create but an inconsiderable change either in the range at an elevation, or in the force at a distance; and that the penetration of an 18-pounder with 3 lbs. of powder is more than sufficient for traversing the sides of the stoutest ships.'

Here you have, sir, with respect to the weight of cannon and their charges for sea service, the opinion of the ablest artillery officer in England at that time, and perhaps in Europe.

[Wednesday], 5th April, [1780].

[*Endorsed.*]

I don't suppose that there is an office in the whole state that is considered to be of any consequence, whose duty is so vague and undetermined as that of an admiral's first captain. If it ever had a prescribed duty, it has been lost and forgot with the disuse of the office. Some think that the origin of admiral's first captain was to have the particular charge of his squadron or division of the fleet, as the commander-in-chief's care and concern for the whole occupied too much of his time to attend to the detail of his own squadron or division.

It is certain that a person supposed to have a duty to execute, which is not laid down to him, and an authority which is not explained to him, must rest in a very awkward situation.

By what I have observed since I have been in this office, I find that there are some things absolutely necessary to render the person who holds it of any utility; and these are: First, that all orders from the admiral pass through the first captain, and who should be considered as first captain of the ship as well as to the admiral; and in consequence of that, that nothing should be done in the ship but by his direction or with his consent; otherwise there will be one authority clashing with another, contrary to that regular subordination so necessary for order in military corps. This indeed will reduce the captain of the ship's authority to little more than that of a first lieutenant in other ships; and as things now stand, what captain will consider himself in such a light?

I am much of opinion that everything would go on smoother and better, was the admiral's captain to recommend an extra first lieutenant to have the charge and pay of captain and the care of the books. Such a person would be chosen for his abilities; his preferment would depend upon his behaviour; and the due subordination that would result from this would be attended with that diligence and attention to orders as would greatly facilitate the business of the fleet.

As things stand at present, if the admiral's captain is so circumstanced as to have an admiral who will deliver his orders to the captain of the ship instead of his first captain, and the captain of the ship at the same time considers himself as independent of the admiral's captain, what a ridiculous situation is this last reduced to! He is then totally annihilated as to office, and remains a mere cypher.

In fine, sir, it is an office (that of first captain) that must be defined as to its duty, and have a clear, determined, and undubious authority, or it had better be abolished; for as it now stands no one would choose to accept of it.

Thursday, P.M. [6th April, 1780].

I shall just add a few words, which I omitted in my last letter, which are as follows: That the consequence of a person in military office is in proportion to his authority. That if a person has not authority equal to the duty with which he is charged there is an incompetency, the extent of the duty not being compatible with the limitation of the authority. But in fine, to make all co-operate well together—the admiral, his captain, and the ship's captain—the admiral should choose his first captain, and the first captain the captain of the ship.

Those movements and evolutions which I put into your hands this morning are so frequently practised in a fleet, that some rule, which is proved to be the best, should be laid down for the execution, that all captains may be acquainted with the manner, and co-operate suitably; otherwise irregularity and confusion must attend the movement. The rules laid down for the movements must be comprehended by any that know the first rudiments of geometry. There may perhaps some obscurity arise from the manner of expression. I should be glad you would mention such as you meet with. It is rough wrote; I intend to correct it.

When a fleet formed on one line wheels, or turns, as I may say, on one end—the rear ship—to form on another line of bearing, it is necessary that they occupy the same extent on this last line as they did on that they wheeled from, in order to preserve the same distance from each other; to which end the course they steer down on to the new line must cut both the lines at equal angles.

N and ESE, as in the examples given in those papers, is ten points; and NE and WNW make also an angle of ten points; so that the line of the course makes equal angles with the line changed from and the line changed to. I mention this explanation lest what was said without might appear obscure; for in all cases where a fleet is to form from one line to another to leeward of it, the half of the number of points that the two lines differ added to eight points, is the number of points you are to bear up, and gives a course that cuts both the lines at equal angles.

[*Endorsed.*] 8th April, [1780].

I waited upon Sir Charles and spoke to him about the manner of dividing the fleet, and the number of chief officers, admirals or commodores, that might be requisite upon the supposed number of ships that might be expected to compose the fleet this summer. He said that we did very well last summer in the manner the fleet was then divided, and he did not therefore see any occasion for alteration. I replied by just mentioning the conveniences of a regular division by thirds, and the inconveniences that attended any other mode; and said no more, as I knew by experience reasoning would make no impression upon him. I, with this, send you what I think the best manner of dividing a fleet according to the number it consists of.

[*Endorsed.*] 8th April, [1780].

The best manner of dividing fleets, in my opinion, according to the number of ships of the line which they consist of, is as follows:—

When a fleet consists of fifteen or more ships of the line, they should be divided into three squadrons.

From fifteen to twenty-seven sail, both numbers included, there will be no occasion for divisions in the squadrons.

From twenty-seven to forty-five sail, each squadron should have two divisions.

From forty-five sail (included) and upwards, each squadron should have three divisions. In such a fleet, where it is necessary that each of the squadrons should have three divisions, whatever rank the admirals may be of, they should, notwithstanding, bear the proper flags for a complete fleet; thus, the commander-in-chief, the red [1] or union, at the main topmast-head; the second in command, the white; and the third in command, the blue at the same place. And the admiral of each squadron to have his vice- and rear-admirals.

Instead of vice- and rear-admirals, if it should be judged expedient, may be substituted commodores having their broad pennants of the colour of the flag in the squadron in which they are, and hoisted at the respective mastheads for vice- and rear-admirals.

When a fleet consists of only fifteen sail of the line, one admiral and two commodores may be sufficient. But when there are divisions in squadrons there should be an admiral to each squadron.

[*Endorsed.*] 9th April, [1780].

You have with this a letter concerning Haslar Hospital. I am not clear whether it is in the manner you wanted.

[1] This tactical use or the three colours was the original idea, and had continued until the end of the war of the Spanish Succession; but in the long peace which followed it was practically forgotten, and the different colours ceased to have any definite meaning. Till then, the commander-in-chief, if not authorised to fly the standard, always flew the union at the main; but his vice- and rear-admirals wore the red flag at their respective mastheads, and all the ships of his squadron flew the red ensign. It was the red squadron; and this led to the commander-in-chief being sometimes—non-officially—spoken of as admiral of the red. It was no doubt an ignorant misunderstanding of this that led the admiralty in 1805 to perpetrate the horrible blunder of 'restoring' the rank of admiral of the red—which till then had never existed.

There is a book coming out on the art of shipbuilding, composed by one Marmaduke Stalkartt.[1] I have been told by a tolerable good judge, who has perused the manuscript, that it is a very ingenious piece—handles the subject full and clear. It certainly should have so much attention paid to it as to examine if it really has merit; and if it has, surely it is incumbent both with the admiralty and navy board to encourage it; and the more so as, to our disgrace, we have nothing published of our own production on that subject worth looking into.

I have long thought that premiums should be offered by government for the best productions of this kind, to excite genius and proper abilities to turn their thoughts to an object so interesting to a maritime state. That we want able designers for shipbuilding is a truth too well known. To have such, there should be an academy for educating those designed for builders in the royal navy, that they may there be furnished with a sufficient foundation of mathematical knowledge and the leading principles of the art. The want of a good foundation laid of mathematical knowledge prevents our builders from rising to eminence; for want of this light, they are often obliged to grope in the dark; they guess, because they have not mathematics to calculate certainty; when they give their bottom any particular form, they guess at the effect. More acquaintance with mathematics would give them certainty; by this, errors would be prevented, as they would know whether the means would obtain the end or not, and not, as is now often the case with them, produce a contrary effect to what they intended, and from ignorance imagined.

[1] *Naval Architecture; or, The Rudiments and Rules of Ship-Building*, fo. plates. 1781

Victory: lat. 40° 16′, 60 leagues off shore.
[18th July, 1780.]

I have nothing to write that will give pleasure. I am afraid the conduct of the fleet will not meet with approbation.

An ill-judged general chase in the evening of the 28th of June and continued the night, was the cause of springing several masts; and its consequence, of two of our ships separating, the Formidable and Bellona. Our frigates are now reduced to three. We are here cruizing between the latitudes of 40° 30′ and 39° 20′, from 20 to 70 leagues from the shore, in quest of a squadron of the enemy said to be in this station, looking out for our homeward and outward-bound trade. But this is not the track of either our East or West India ships, and I therefore conceive no station for the enemy to cruize in.

It appears to me by placing ourselves here we leave the enemy at liberty to join their different squadrons, and have put ourselves out of the way of receiving intelligence or directions from the admiralty, or of preventing any designs the enemy may have upon us at home. I therefore wish we were in your neighbourhood again. The 20th we are to make for the Channel, but it may be some weeks before we reach there. We spoke with a Portugal man-of-war of sixty-four guns yesterday, from the Brazils for Lisbon.[1] In her passage, on the 19th of June, she fell in with Admiral Graves in latitude 32° 53′ and longitude 343° from Faro, who had with him six sail of the line, one frigate, and a French East Indiaman, a prize.

P.S.—Our chief[2] is much perplexed; he wants to square his conduct to the approbation of Admiral

[1] July 18, P.M.—*Victory's Log.*
[2] Admiral Geary.

Barrington and Lord Mulgrave. But that is impossible, as those gentlemen think differently. However, he pays much attention to the advice of the former, and indeed don't take any step without it. But a man who has no opinion of his own, but acts from those of others, can never act regular and consistent.

Victory: at sea; Ushant N 31° E, 49 leagues.
8th August, 1780.

Dear Sir,—The scurvy now shows itself in most of the ships of the fleet; in some very severe; and according to the nature of that disorder, increases fast, so that there is a necessity for the fleet's going into port. Torbay, which has many advantages to recommend it, it is judged will not answer upon this occasion. How dispose of the sick? and how receive provisions and beer with any despatch there? For despatch, and the better accommodation of the sick, it would be best for part of the fleet to go to Plymouth, and the rest to Spithead; but would not a separation be dangerous? Spithead seems in the opinion of most to be the proper place; and yet, the fleet's going there will be attended with many inconveniences, which would be avoided at Torbay; so that I am somewhat disposed to think that this bay, upon the whole, would be the most eligible place.

The Inflexible, who has lately joined us, by the account I have received of her, seems replete with all the bad qualities that ignorance in construction can bestow upon a ship; plunges violent against a head sea, is very crank, leewardly, and don't fore-reach upon a wind. However, I hope means will be found to relieve her from some of these complaints, as has been done by the Alexander. My compliments to madam and miss.

[*Endorsed.*] Victory: Spithead. 19th August, [1780].

Dear Sir,—You know of our arrival.[1] The great number of sick, especially scorbutics, made it indispensable. I shall observe upon this, that, when at sea before the enemy, the fleet should every three or four weeks put into Torbay for a few days. This would keep the scurvy off, their provisions and water up; whilst you could do this, you might cruize the whole year; for, except the scurvy, the men keep freer from diseases at sea than in port, as they have neither women nor spirits, the chief causes of their diseases. By going to sea with the fleet long before the enemy can, and keeping the sea constantly, it happens that when they are in a state to take the field, you, in a disabled state, are obliged to return to port. Such a fleet as ours is, all together at Spithead, which, at best, from its situation so far from the shore and the strong tides, is not favourable for despatch in fitting, must be attended with great delay; especially as the port of Portsmouth is not provided with a sufficient quantity of necessary craft for sending water, provisions, &c., off.

If a division could have been made, a very short time would have sufficed to have put the fleet in readiness again. Four or five of the most sickly ships to have gone to Plymouth, and seven or eight of the most healthy with Admiral Digby, whose ship has few sick on board, to Torbay, and the rest then to Spithead. This would have promoted despatch, and been attended with many other conveniences. This I proposed, but the opinion of the admiral was not to separate the fleet.

I would prefer Torbay for the recovery of scorbutics to either Portsmouth or Plymouth, for a small

[1] Anchored at Spithead, 18th August, when the commander-in-chief, Admiral Geary, reported the number of sick as 2,500 sent to hospital.

squadron, where, at this season of the year, they might be lodged under tents, the communication with the shore there quick and easy, and plenty of every kind of refreshment.

Four line-of-battle ships and a frigate, which lately joined us at sea, are brought in to add to our embarrassment at Spithead. Had they been cruizing for short intervals, putting in from time to time at Plymouth or Torbay, they would have been in the way to have annoyed the enemy and protected our trade, to have kept themselves healthy and have formed their raw men by practice; and what makes the bringing these ships in the more blameable is, that we knew a convoy from St. Domingo was not far to the westward of us, having taken one that had separated from them.

I should hope the admiralty will not let those ships ready for sea remain at Spithead, but send them some short cruize, or else to Torbay; for here they only increase our embarrassment, and impede the despatch of the ships fitting.

In fine, if the admiralty will not appoint a suitable person to command the fleet, you must expect nothing but bad conduct, and, in consequence, bad success; the present person is brave, generous, and may perhaps have been a good officer; but he is wholly debilitated in his faculties, his memory and judgment lost, wavering and indetermined in everything.

I am, dear Sir, much yours,

RD. KEMPENFELT.

[Geary was seventy years old; his health was much broken, and he resigned the command on the 8th September. His old chief, Hawke, had meanwhile written to him on the 26th, from Sunbury[1] :—

[1] Charnock's *Biog. Navalis*, v. 186.

'I am greatly obliged to you for the favour of your letter of the 20th, on your arrival at Spithead; indeed, it was more than I expected, well knowing the hurry and bustle you must be in on your first coming into port. I do not wonder at the men being sickly upon so long a cruize; six weeks is long enough in all conscience; any time after that must be very hurtful to the men, and will occasion their falling down very fast. I hope in God they will soon recover, that you may be enabled to proceed to sea immediately, for by all accounts the enemy is out, so that nothing can well stir from home with safety. I wish the admiralty would see what was done in former times; it would be the means of making them act with more propriety, both for the good of officers and men. I take it for granted that the great ones will let you have no rest till they get you out to sea again.

'Although I am in a good deal of pain and much in the invalid order, yet I cannot refuse myself the pleasure of wishing you all imaginable good fortune when you go out again; and I trust in God your next cruize will prove a happy and glorious one, both for your country and yourself. My good friend, I have always wished you well, and have ever talked freely and openly to you upon every subject relative to the service. Recollect some of these passages; and for God's sake, if you should be so lucky as to get sight of the enemy, get as close to them as possible. Do not let them shuffle with you by engaging at a distance, but get within musket-shot if you can. That will be the way to gain great honour, and will be the means to make the action decisive. By doing this, you will put it out of the power of any of the brawlers to find fault. I am fully persuaded you will faithfully do your part, therefore hope you will forgive my saying so much on the subject. . . . May the hand of Providence go with you and protect you in the day of battle, and grant you victory over your perfidious enemies; and may you return with honour to your country and family again!']

[*Post-mark*: Portsmouth.] Victory. 25 August, [1780].

I have just received yours of the 22nd. The fate of the convoy under Moutray,[1] and that our fleet instead of them had not fallen in with the French and Spaniards chagrins and mortifies extremely. To reflect how near we were to the most favourable event that could possibly happen for this country—that is, falling in with the Cadiz fleet—is distracting. I begin to grow sick of everything, particularly my employ; I grow too old. I find a want of activity and quickness of recollection. I think it best to retire from business in time, and not to wait to be told that it is so.

[*Post-mark*: Portsmouth.] Victory. 27 August, [1780].

The positive order for sailing when half our people are scorbutic—probably the whole somewhat tainted—however necessary, disconcerts us greatly. The fatigue is too much for Mr. Geary; I have just left him in bed, ashore, much indisposed. This increases our embarrassment and must produce delay.

In my opinion he'll not go to sea with the fleet. It was wrong to pitch upon him, and still more so in him to accept the command of the fleet—a more arduous task now than ever since our time. What you'll do I don't know; but if the fleet is not put into able hands, you are not to expect success.

Victory. 29th August, [1780].

Dear Sir,—I find Admiral Geary does not go to sea with the fleet. I hope this will relieve me from my present employ, which is really too much fatigue for my years. The duty, managed in the best manner, is arduous; but vastly increased by

[1] 9th August, 1780.

confused and contradictory orders, and the want of looking forward to be prepared for events. Though Mr. Geary was unequal to the command, yet his declining it at this juncture will be productive of much inconvenience. It would have been with more propriety had he made known his intentions to the admiralty before the fleet came in, if he had then thought of it, which I suspect he had.

I am, dear Sir, much yours,

RICHARD KEMPENFELT.

Victory: Spithead. 6th September, [1780].

Dear Sir,—I have received your letters; the hints and thoughts in them are very just and worth attention to. I am so hurried that I have scarce time to read a letter; yours merit to be read and considered. What I have said of our chief has been mentioned by me to none but yourself; I write to no other person. I mentioned my thoughts to you from the anxiety I am under at this time which won't bear misconduct without ruin. I must acknowledge to you likewise that the place I am in is much too important for my abilities. Adieu; with more leisure you shall have more writing.

Portsmouth. 9th September, [1780].

I have just received yours with Lord Sandwich's enclosed, in which his lordship is pleased to flatter my capabilities much above their merit, and to give me a consequence I am nowise entitled to. If I have any merit it consists principally in knowing my insufficiency for the charge that is imposed upon me. My health at this time is very indifferent; but as Lord Sandwich thinks it expedient that I should go to sea with Mr. Darby,[1] I shall obey.

[1] Vice-Admiral Darby's commission as commander-in-chief was dated 8th September.

P.S.—I wish Sir William Temple's rule was better understood and practised, that a man should not be in business after a certain age, and that there is such a thing as serving down a reputation.

Britannia: Torbay. 16th September, [1780].

Dear Sir,—I have just received yours of the 15th instant. If Lord Sandwich thinks proper to honour me with a flag, I shall receive it with gratitude, and esteem it a mark of distinguished favour.

Britannia: Torbay. 17th September, [1780].

Dear Sir,—I said in my letter of yesterday, the 16th, to you that I should be glad to be honoured with a flag; but, to be candid, I do not think myself fit for active service. I find great and increasing defects both with respect to body and mind; and therefore must, as I ought to do, retire, in justice to myself and the public, and not risk the mortification of serving down the little reputation I may have acquired.

Rear-Admiral Kempenfelt to Middleton.

Britannia: Torbay. 3rd October, [1780].

Dear Sir,—I am truly sensible of the obligation I am under to you for your attention to my interest. It is a misfortune to this country that persons are not called to places of consequence, especially in our line, until their abilities are upon the decline. The evil of this struck me when I was young, and experience has more confirmed it. If you wish success in your armies or fleets, look out for persons of abilities of the middle age—I mean about forty—

to conduct them. You can't be too nice in the choice of a commander-in-chief of your fleet; order, discipline, ability, everything that gives force and consequence to the fleet depends upon him.

Lieutenant Curgenven is greatly obliged to you for your attention to him; should consider himself very happy to go out with Sir Samuel Hood.

Britannia: Torbay. 14th October, [1780].

The number of ships that suffered in their rudders by the late gale we had here at SE is somewhat extraordinary and alarming.

Though I think the composition metal is not so strong, and is more brittle than iron, yet much can't be imputed to that. Indeed, the nails of that metal don't hold so well in the wood as iron, owing to its great smoothness or polish; and the rust of iron increases its cohesion to wood. This defect of the composition nails might be remedied by roughing their surface or ragging of them. But I imagine the damage suffered was in most owing to their tillers breaking, and not being immediately ready with the chocks and spare tiller to stop the violent motion of the rudder which ensued. Ships therefore should, in such cases, be prepared and have their chocks and spare tiller in the ward-room ready.

One of the accidents that happened I conceive arose from another cause, as having tackles upon the tiller bowsed taut, as also the rudder pendants; and the chocks fixed; by which means the rudder was so closely confined that it could not yield, but felt the full force of the sea which struck it; and when it is considered that this confinement is up at the head of the rudder, it is easy to conceive that a sea striking with force on the broadside of the rudder, much below its confinement, must endanger twisting the head of it off. This was the case of the Royal George, whose rudder was confined as above; and when the wind shifted from the SE to the SW, a sea struck direct the side or flat of her rudder (as it then ranged athwart her), and broke it off short just below the head.

The method the Victory pursued seems to me the best to follow on such occasions. They had tackles on the tiller, with men on each side tending of them, and to the side towards which the sea struck the rudder, they always eased it to it by the tackles, and so diminished the force of the stroke.

P.S.—The proper dimensions of flags for repeating frigates is six whole breadths of the bunting in depth. And the proper length for all flags is one and a half of the depth—that is, when the depth is ten feet, the length should be fifteen feet.

Britannia: Torbay. 24 October, [1780].

I forgot in my letter of yesterday to mention to you Mr. Madgshon, master of the Victory, whom I take to be one of the most accomplished men of his class in the navy; a most excellent pilot for the Channel; to which is joined a clear judgment to act in all difficulties in the best and safest manner, and therefore a most proper person to be master to the commander-in-chief of the western squadron, where the safety of the fleet so often depends upon pilotage judgment.

I only give you my opinion of him; the present commander-in-chief may probably prefer his own master.

11 November, [1780].

As I find from you that there are advocates in favour of the two-decked forty-gun frigates, in preference to those of thirty-eight guns, single-decked, though of the several whose opinions I have asked upon this subject they have all been unanimous in giving the advantage to the single deck, I'll take the liberty of troubling you with my thoughts upon the subject.

Both these kind of frigates carrying the same weight of metal, we may in that point consider them of equal force whilst the two-decker can fight all her guns; one gun or two difference of a side being of little consequence. But when the two-decker is put by her lower tier, she is deprived of the greatest part of her force, whilst the single-decker retains the whole of hers. Here the equality is gone in point of force, and the two-decker becomes but of half the force with the other.

The single-decker having a deep waist, with broad gangboards, her men will be as much secured from the small shot of the enemy as the men on the lower deck of the two-decker.

The single-decker will have the advantage oi having all her men upon deck, ready to board or oppose boarding.

The two-decker will be something loftier, therefore less weatherly, than the single-decker.

A two-decker can't have so fine a bottom for sailing (which is certainly the first quality of a frigate) as a single-decker; for the two-decker must, like a line-of-battle ship, have a full body, which opposes fleetness, to enable her to carry her lower battery sufficiently above the water.

From the above considerations it seems to me that the differences between these two kind of frigates are wholly in favour of the single-decker, without any one advantage, as I can conceive, resulting from two decks, except it may be considered as one in action, her being something higher.

Britannia. 19 February, [1781].

Post-mark: Portsmouth.]

What appears the most convenient size of signal flags for large ships is five yards in breadth; and signal pennants for such ships, nine feet at the staff, three feet at the end of the fly, forty-five feet in length.

For frigates: The flags to be four yards in breadth. Their signal pennants, six feet at the staff, two feet at the end of fly, forty five feet in length.

The signal pennants to have no swallow's tail.

The length of all flags to be once and one half of the breadth.

Do you furnish the Britannia with one of Ramsden's compasses for trial?

I hope Mrs. Middleton is quite recovered.

Britannia. 22 February, [1781].

I sent you the other day the dimensions of flags and pennants for admirals' ships, and also the smaller dimensions for repeating frigates. If some sets of the smaller dimensions were made, it would save you a good deal of bunting, and us a good deal of trouble, in reducing the flags and pennants now made to the proper size for frigates.

The flags marked No. 1 on the other side [red, white, red; and blue, yellow, blue, horizontal] are for the future to be changed to the form No. 2 [same colours, vertical] as less liable to be mistaken; and the chequered red and white, and the chequered blue and yellow pennants are, for the future, to be striped red and white, and striped blue and yellow, for the same cause as above.[1]

[1] Middleton had probably acquainted him with Young's objection to the chequered flags (*ante*, pp. 69, 72), and similar objections may have reached him from other quarters.

The flags already made No. 1 may very easily be changed to the form No. 2.

[The coloured flags referred to in the following letter are twenty-eight in number, to which are added five triangular flags and ten pennants. It seems unnecessary to reproduce them in colour, but a verbal enumeration of them may be interesting. The numbers, here given for distinction, are not in the original—neither numbers nor letters are assigned to any of them.

Flags.—1, Union Jack; 2, white; 3, yellow; 4 (b), per fess, red and white; 5 (b), per fess, blue and yellow; 6 (b), Dutch flag; 7, red, white, red, vertical; 8, white, red, white, horizontal; 9, per pale, white and red; 10, seven stripes horizontal, red and white; 11, checker, 3 and 5, white and red; 12, quarterly, red and white; 13, blue, yellow cross; 14, red; 15, blue; 16, red, white cross; 17, 18, 19 (a) are 4, 5, and 6 (b), inverted; 20, blue, yellow, blue, vertical; 21, yellow, blue, yellow, horizontal; 22, per pale, yellow and blue; 23, 24, 25 as 10, 11, 12, blue and yellow; 26, yellow, blue cross; 27, red, pierced white; 28, blue, pierced yellow.

Triangles.—1, red, yellow stripe horizontal; 2, yellow, red stripe horizontal; 3, blue, white stripe horizontal; 4, white, blue stripe horizontal; 5, per pale, yellow and red.

Pennants.—1, blue, yellow, blue, lengthways; 2, white; 3, crossways, red and white, five stripes; 4, red; 5, as 1, red and white; 6, blue; 7, as 3, blue and yellow; 8, yellow; 9, hoist blue, fly yellow; 10, checker, red and white, two squares in the breadth.]

Britannia. 2nd March, [1781].

The colours you have here are those we are supplied with and use, agreeable to a list I gave in last winter.[1] The number of colours in a set are the same for all admirals and repeaters. A set consists of two flags of each sort, and four pennants of each sort. The three flags marked (a) might have been

[1] 20 March, 1780; see *ante*, p. 313.

omitted, as those marked (b) answer the purpose of them by inversion. The colours used by private ships in their signals to the admiral and in the private signals, and which all ships in the fleet now have, are the flags half red half white, and half blue half yellow, marked (b), with a red flag and a blue flag; pennants a red, a white, a blue, and a yellow, one of each sort of the flags and of the pennants, with the colours of other nations usually allowed.

The dimensions of the colours you already have had. However, I'll repeat them here.

For admirals. Flags to be five yards in breadth. Pennants to be eight or nine feet in breadth at the staff and forty-five feet in length.

For frigates. Their flags to be four yards in breadth; and their signal pennants to be six feet in breadth at the staff and forty-five feet in length.

All flags to be once and one half of the breadth [1] in length. The signal pennants are to have no swallow's tail, and to be, at the end of the fly, one third the breadth at the staff; as thus, six feet at the staff to be two feet at the end of the fly.

P.S.—As to the other part of your letter I shall take another opportunity to reply to it. If in what I have here said concerning the signals I have not fully answered your meaning you'll let me know.

Other modes of exhibiting signals might be used, which would require much fewer flags, and probably preferable to the present mode.

The dimensions of triangular flags are: breadth at the tabling, fourteen and a half feet.

Length in the middle, from the tabling to the end of the fly, twenty and a half feet.

[1] At the present time the prescribed length of English flags is twice the breadth; in the French navy it is once and one-half.

[*Endorsed.*] [9th March, 1781.]

I sent you in my last an account of the flags we use in our signals, and also their dimensions. They are such as in general we find to be very distinguishable.

Every article or order in a signal book should be numbered; and then, any ship possessed of eleven flags, different the one from the other, may express signals to any number.

It has been a common saying that it is an advantage to go by signals that we have been used to, and when a new set comes out, to say we have our trade to learn again. This style was very proper with respect to the different signals used by different admirals formerly, when the signals were jumbled together without form or order, and when a long acquaintance with them was necessary to find out the meaning of any signal that was made in the chaotic state in which they were. But when signals are formed upon a proper plan they require no study to comprehend them, and when a signal is made you can immediately turn to the article or order alluded to. If the greatest novice can't do this, the plan is faulty. When in any project for signals they appear intricate and seem difficult to comprehend, you may be sure they are faulty; what is good must be clear and simple.

Had I remained ashore this winter, which my health very much required, I think I should have been able to have rendered the signals much more perfect and useful by the helps I have received from others and my own observations. The plan I followed in the signals I made was not that I most approved of. That which I would have adopted—though most evidently the best—I could not get any of the admirals or officers of note to approve and countenance. I therefore followed in a great measure Lord Howe's mode, he being a popular character. The night and fog signals we use are almost entirely his, and both extremely defective. I would have used the French night signals, which are by much superior to anything of the kind that has yet appeared, but I was afraid of prejudice, for not an admiral I showed them to but started objections.

A scheme for fog-signals has lately fallen into my hands, which is very simple and clear, which, when I have leisure, I shall recommend for use.

I have mentioned to Admiral Darby what you desired respecting leaving stores at Gibraltar and Mahon with the naval officers.

I have seen a compass of Sir William Burnaby's, made, I think, by one Wright, an instrument maker, for standing the quick motions of a boat, much superior to Ramsden's.[1] Ramsden's will vibrate four, five, or more points in a boat with a popling swell, as I experienced some days ago with Captain Elliot; but this compass won't vibrate a point by any boat motion.

The case or box in which the needle is suspended is filled with water; the needle is japanned over to prevent rusting. There is no card upon the needle; the points of the compass are marked on the side of the box in an inverted manner—the points to the west of the N being marked to the right of it, and those to the east to the left; and if you place the compass so in ship or boat that this north point is directly forward, the point of the compass that the north pole of the needle stands at is the caping[2] of the ship. The needle in this water will turn as fast as the boat, without any fluctuating motion. This

[1] Jesse Ramsden (1735–1800), optician and mechanician. See *D.N.B.*

[2] The direction of the ship's head.

steadiness in the needle is owing to its being charged with no card, and its moving in so dense a fluid as water.[1]

Britannia. 12th March, [1781].

By your letter just received of the 10th inst. I am apprehensive you have not received a letter I some days since sent to you with all the flags and pennants we use in signals drawn out and coloured. I there informed you that all the flag-ships and repeaters in a fleet should have one complete set of signal colours. What I call a set is two flags of each sort and four pennants of each sort. That the commander-in-chief requires no more, and the others, that repeat his signals, require the same number.

In what I have said I have confined myself to signal colours only, taking no notice of the colours of foreign states allowed, or flags for marking the rank of admirals.

The dimensions of flags and pennants for signals I have repeatedly given you.

[1] Captain Ettrick W. Creak, C.B., R.N., F.R.S., has been good enough to contribute the following: 'The idea of using liquid as a damper to the oscillations of a compass due to the motion of a ship dates back to the thirteenth century, but the fault of all early attempts at a liquid compass was that the water in the "case or box" was not tightly enclosed. About 1820 Crow of Faversham invented a liquid compass with a leather elastic bottom, which allowed the bowl to be entirely filled, the expansion of the liquid being compensated for by the elasticity of the leather. Vast improvements have been made since Crow's time, and the liquid compass is now the standard compass of the navy; but Crow hit off the vital point, that there must never be an air bubble, or any freedom of the liquid to move about in the bowl. From its failure in this respect Sir W. Burnaby's compass could never succeed; and the loss of the card upon the needle would further hinder its successful action in water. The fanciful way of reading its indications would probably be a more immediate bar to its acceptance, or even to its trial as a service instrument.'

For admirals or large ships: five yards in breadth for the flags; for the pennants nine feet at the staff and forty-five feet in length.

For frigates: flags to be four yards in breadth; their pennants six feet at the staff and forty-five feet in length.

The length of all flags to be once and one half of the breadth.

The pennants to have no swallow's tail and to be at the end of the fly one third of the breadth at the staff.

The triangular flags for distinguishing the squadrons are fourteen and a half broad at the tabling, and twenty and a half feet in length at the middle part.

[No date.]

You have here the numeral signals you desired as near as I can in the words of the author.

Project for signals.

Signals should be simple, clear, and easily discernible. I don't know any more perfect than those invented by M. de la Bourdonnais. He made use of broad pennants as more readily fixed to any part than flags. He fixes a number for each pennant; and that several pennants, each designing a particular number and, put one above another, serve as cyphers.[1] By this it is easy to know the number of each signal, because the pennants are numbered by their colours. For example:—

A pennant Red signifies 1
White 2
Blue 3
Yellow 4

[1] French, chiffres = digits.

A pennant	Red with a white fly [signifies]	5
	Red with a blue fly . .	6
	White with a blue fly . .	7
	White with a red fly . .	8
	Blue with a yellow fly . .	9
	Yellow with a red fly . .	0

With this arrangement an infinite number of signals may be made. There should be three or four pennants of each sort, in order to express the same number three or four times at once; as, for example, the signal of 33 or 444 or 8888. These signals are made indifferently from any part of the masts or rigging, preferring that part from whence they will be best seen. The uppermost pennant signifies the first number,[1] the second pennant the second number, the third the third number, and the fourth the fourth number. For example, No. 170 is fixed upon to order boats to be manned and armed. This signal is made by throwing out three pennants one above another in the same place; the first [uppermost] red, the second white with a blue fly, and the third [lowest] yellow with a red fly. The signal will be seen in this manner:—

Red pennant . . .	1	170	Boats manned and armed.
White do. with a blue fly .	7		
Yellow do. with a red fly .	0		

If you would make several signals at the same time from the same place, you separate each signal with a small red flag, which serves as a comma between the signals.

Care should be taken that the colours of the pennants are bright and striking, as a deep blue, a scarlet red, an orpiment yellow, and a clear white.

[1] The left-hand number; the lowest flag is the place of units, and so, gradually upwards, tens, hundreds, thousands,

You form a table of all the signals, placing in the first column the numbers as they stand in their natural order, and in the second column you write in alphabetic order what each signal means. For example:—

575 . . abordons l'ennemi.
576 . . abandonnez le vaisseau que vous battez.

You will observe to reserve for the fighting signals the first numbers, as they will then be made with one or two pennants only. As there is frequent occasion at sea to make demands, the ship to whom we make the demand should answer immediately to the question by a signal affirmative or negative, Yes or No, without further preamble.

Signals by day when the ships are at a distance the one from the other.

For this purpose we use pennants and flags, and employ the four colours, white, red, blue, and yellow, as the most distinguishable; and we show them from the ensign staff, mizen peak, mizen topmast flagstaff, main topgallant flagstaff, and fore topgallant flagstaff; observing, that for the first number, which answers to hundreds—for we don't go farther in these signals—we make use of two pennants, the one white and the other blue; the second number, which is the tens, is known by the pennants red and yellow, and the third, or units place, is marked by the flags one yellow and one red; and to show the cypher or figure for each of these places you make use of the pennants or flags assigned for them in this manner. For example, for the place of hundreds, a white pennant at the ensign staff denotes 1; ditto at the mizen peak, 2; at the mizen top flagstaff, 3; at the main topgallant flagstaff, 4 ; at the fore topgallant flagstaff, 5 ; then the blue pennant at the ensign staff, 6 ; at the mizen peak, 7 ; at the mizen top flagstaff, 8 ; main topgallant flagstaff, 9 ; fore topgallant flagstaff, 0 ; and so the same with the colours appointed for the places of the tens and units.

Our author is concise, but not very clear, in this description. I will therefore describe it, after a manner of my own, which I believe will render it more comprehensible.

Suppose, for example, the signal 123 is required. You look for the colour in the first column, or place of hundreds, answering to No. 1, and you'll find it to be a white pennant at the ensign staff ; next look for the colour in the second column, or place of tens, answering to No. 2, and you will find it to be a red pennant at the mizen peak ; lastly, look in the third column, or place of units, for the colour answering to No. 3, and you will find it to be a yellow flag at the mizen topmast flagstaff ; and so in the same manner for any other numbers.

Some examples :—

The signal answering 333 you'll find to be a white pennant, a red pennant, and a yellow flag, all three at the mizen topmast flagstaff, to be placed one above the other, that for the hundreds uppermost, next the tens, and that for units' place undermost ; so for 333, the white pennant is uppermost, next the red, and the yellow flag below.

Signal numbered 105 is a white pennant at the ensign staff, a yellow one at the fore topgallant-mast flagstaff, and a yellow flag below the pennant at the fore topgallant flagstaff.

Again, signal No. 297 is a white pennant at the mizen peak, a yellow pennant at the main topgallant flagstaff, and a red flag at the mizen peak.

For the place of hundreds, a white and a blue pennant	For the place of tens, a red and a yellow pennant	For the place of units, a yellow and a red flag	Place where shown from	Number signified
1st No.	2nd No.	3rd No.		
White pennant	Red pennant	Yellow flag	Ensign staff	1
Do.	Do.	Do.	Mizen peak	2
Do.	Do.	Do.	Mizen topmast flagstaff	3
Do.	Do.	Do.	Main topgallant flagstaff	4
Do.	Do.	Do.	Fore topgallant flagstaff	5
Blue pennant	Yellow pennant	Red flag	Ensign staff	6
Do.	Do.	Do.	Mizen peak	7
Do.	Do.	Do.	Mizen topmast flagstaff	8
Do.	Do.	Do.	Main topgallant flagstaff	9
Do.	Do.	Do.	Fore topgallant flagstaff	0

Signals by night.

Signals by night should be made by lights and cannon, to which we assign some convenient number. For example, suppose each light to signify one and each cannon fired seven, then to make the signal for No. 17 you fire two guns and show three lights, from any part where they will be best seen: six lights and four guns expresses thirty-four.

When we don't choose to be heard at a distance, we make use of false fires instead of cannon.

We make use of sky-rockets sometimes to let our companions know where we are, but they should never be used as signals because they are liable to fail, and then we are under the necessity of sending off others, which may perplex and embarrass the signal: and they are very apt to fail when it blows hard.

This manner of making signals by night is more simple and clear than any others, for you have only to count the number of lights shown to know what the signal of the gun or guns mean, whereas, if the lights are confined to particular places to express their meaning, we can't always distinguish the places they are shown from, especially if we view them obliquely, from abaft or before; and sometimes the place is such from whence the lights are shown, that they are only visible to the ships to windward, being hid from those to leeward.

Wednesday [? 14th March, 1781].

I send you a numerary table for night signals as now used in the French navy. You'll perceive they are upon the same principle as their day signals, made with two flags, a superior and inferior. The small table, at the upper part of the page to the left, shows the guns and lights used to express the numbers of the flags in the large table; thus, one gun and one light signifies No. 1; one gun and two lights, No. 2; one gun and three lights, No. 3; three guns and one light, No. 4, &c.; six guns and one light, No. 7, &c. The flags in the large table are placed to help the conception by showing the affinity of these with the day signals, the only difference being that lights and guns are substituted to represent flags.

These signals consist of two parts That first made expresses the number of the superior flag, or that at the head of the table; that last made, the number of the inferior flag, or that on the left side of the table. The French, in the same table, use one gun for the first column, three for the second, and six for the third. This, when the number used in both parts of the signal is seven or more, requires twelve guns; an inconvenient number, the reason for which, I suppose, is, that after the first three numbers, the guns and lights added together make the number they are intended to signalise; but this is a small advantage to compensate for such a number of guns.

If, instead of one, three, and six guns, we use one, two, and three guns, then the numbers seven, eight, and nine would be expressed with three guns instead of six. As the manner of signifying the number of the flag is so very simple, there is no person but who could retain it in his memory without having recourse to the table to find it. This method of exhibiting night signals is certainly very simple, easy to make, easy to be understood, and much less liable to be mistaken than any that have been yet in use amongst us.

Night signals composed of two parts, separated by a certain number of rockets or false fires.

The table annexed may be epitomized—so :

Number of Lights	Number of Guns		
	1	2	3
1	1	4	7
2	2	5	8
3	3	6	9

Portsmouth. 23rd November, [1781].

It will be difficult to fix any kind of rendezvous free from objections. If it's confined to one spot, the enemy, either by their cruizers or neutral vessels, will soon be informed of it, and then you must not expect to meet with any outward bound but what are of superior force. And if you from time to time change your cruizing station, which promises the better chance for falling in with the enemy's outward bound, your cruizers detached from the fleet, separated ships, &c., will not know where to find you. And if you give two rendezvous—say a northern and southern—both in the track we may suppose ships from Brest would take for the West Indies—they will partake of both the above objections in some degree. Upon the whole, that of changing from time [to time] the cruizing stations promises best to answer the purposes of the cruizers; and make those changes regular with respect to time, except the change arises from intelligence received.

24th November, [1781].

Dear Sir,—I this morning by express received my orders to sail as soon as ready, with the object for which I am sent out, as you informed me before. It says: 'to sail with ships[1] as soon as they are

[1] So in MS.

ready, or with such part of them as I may think necessary for the service.' To be sure I shall think the whole necessary, when they tell me the enemy's escort is eighteen sail of the line, four of which armed *en flûte*. The Plymouth ships are not arrived. I have heard only from the Namur there, and that gives me no prospect of her being ready soon. Does the admiralty mean I should go to sea with fewer ships than they first appointed? There are but two frigates here of those appointed. I needn't notice to you the necessity of a number of such upon the service I am going on. We shall not be ready with all the ships these two or three days; the high winds have interrupted so much.

Frigates at Portsmouth—

Success . . } Daphne . . }	Ready, and on home service.
Minerva . .	The same.
Alarm . . .	I don't know her destination.
Scourge (sloop)	Ready; on no service; would be useful.

Plymouth—

The Medea ready at Plymouth.

Endorsed by Middleton.

27 Nov., 1781.

Answered. Wrote Lord S[andwich] that no seaman would undertake this service with so inferior a force on their own opinion, but would readily sail if ordered to do so.

Advised giving such orders, or sending Bellona and Fortitude to join Ad. K[empenfelt], as the Downs Squadron would certainly gain strength as they came down Channel in case the Dutch sailed.

Portsmouth. 25th November, [1781]

I wrote to you in haste yesterday to save post. I am much obliged to you for speaking in favour of young Nicholson; he is acting in the Nonsuch; you expressed yourself as if he was in the Inflexible.

By letter last night from Lord Sandwich I am not to expect the Namur or Hercules, and perhaps not the Ocean. I have heard nothing from her. This will be a great reduction of the force the squadron was named at, and not adequate to insure the success of what they so ardently wish for. If we should fall in with them, we should have a force sufficient to cope with their ships of war, while others at the same time fall upon the convoy. Frigates may not be sufficient for that purpose without they are numerous, as the enemy will probably have several of that class with them.

There is a prospect that we shall go out very scanty of frigates. Of the six that are ordered under my command there are only two here—La Prudente and Monsieur. Two are out at sea, cruizing; and two are at Plymouth, which I have heard nothing from. The repeating frigate—or frigates, for there should be two—ought never to be sent out from the fleet; line-of-battle ships you can't venture from you to look out, especially at this season, without risk of separation, and that risk must not be run when you expect to meet an enemy of force. There are no sailing cutters here of the fleet, except one just come from Plymouth and is now repairing; the rest, as I mentioned before, are to the eastward refitting. I inquired of Sir Thomas Pye about them, and at my request he sent an order away immediately for them to repair here; but if they don't arrive, we should have something in the stead of them, as armed cutters, &c. Sir Thomas has two tender cutters that wait on him—the Peggy and the

George, or Young Hazard; if the others don't come, we should have them. I request you'd urge that they let us have what frigates they can. As to any vessels joining us on the rendezvous, it is too precarious to be the least depended upon.

As the enemy's squadron is of such force as fourteen of the line complete in guns and four armed *en flûte*, does the admiralty mean I should go to sea deficient of the number they appointed? If they would have me go to sea with what ships of my squadron are here, I wish they had ordered it; then I should clearly have known what to do. But the words of the order are these: 'You are, therefore, so soon as the ships under your command, or such a number of them as you shall judge necessary, shall be ready, hereby directed to proceed to cruize,' &c. I wrote to Lord Sandwich yesterday to let him know, from the force of the enemy, I judged the whole squadron that was appointed would be necessary. Perhaps I ought to have wrote to this purpose a public letter to the board. Now, as the orders stand, if I proceed to sea without the whole of the ships put under my command, and the design proves abortive through want of an adequate force, the blame will be fixed upon me. In the letter I received from Lord Sandwich last night, he is pressing for my sailing, and says: 'I fear there is no chance of your having the Namur, and I am fearful of the Hercules; but if you stay for them, the object you have in view will [be] at an end.' Now, if the admiralty (or Lord Sandwich) think it expedient I should go to sea with what ships of the squadron are here, why is not an order sent to me for that purpose? It would give me satisfaction to have their order for the lowest number of ships they think I ought to sail with.

The Medway's pay-books are not down. She was in course of payment the last time she sailed; and if not paid now, I apprehend the men will be rusty about it. When I first came down, I gave out a memorandum to know what ships came in course of payment, in order to make them attentive to get the same done in time.

Minuted in Middleton's hand: Ad. Kempenfelt on scarcity of ships and frigates, and desiring explicit orders. Answered: That I had applied to Lord Sandwich on receiving his letters of 23rd and 24th.

Tuesday morning: [4th December, 1781].

[*Endorsed*: 5th Dec^{r}. [Wednesday].
Addressed: Sir Charles Middleton, Bart.]

I was looking yesterday into a treatise upon cordage or rope-making, wrote by the celebrated Du Hamel. It is a large volume in 4to., in which he seems, with the assistance of several ingenious sea officers and experienced artists in that business, to have considered the subject very fully and accurately, to have made a vast number of experiments in order to approach near perfection in that manufactory. This shows how attentive the French are to improve everything that relates to their marine, and affects one with concern at our negligence in these things.

The present wretched state of our cordage calls loud for an inspection, and reform in the mode of fabricating it. I believe with us no man of science or genius ever considered it worth his while to trouble his head about rope-making; it has wholly been left to low mechanics. On the contrary with the French, they have justly considered it as a most essential part in the equipment of a fleet, and therefore their minister of marine recommended the consideration of it, and how it might be improved, to some of their most ingenious sea officers at each royal port.

Monsieur du Hamel begins with direction to distinguish the best hemp, the best manner of cleaning and preparing of it, and that the yarns are not spun too thick and be of equal thickness throughout; that the strands are but moderately turned or twisted, which gives strength as well as suppleness to the rope. He gives you a number of experiments made in different ships between his new improved cordage and the old cordage. That his new cordage, by its suppleness, works with one-third less men than the old cordage; that it never kinks or gets into knots; that it runs much freer in the blocks; that it is one-fourth part less in weight; the masts and yards are therefore eased of so much top-weight; that it is one-eighth part smaller, consequently presents a less surface to the wind. By several trials, which he particularly mentions, this new cordage was found to sustain one-third more weight before it broke than the old cordage; at the same time this new cordage was one-fourth less in weight than the old; and, therefore, if it had been of equal weight, would have been just double the strength of it.[1]

I think this treatise of Du Hamel well worth consulting by any person who may have the inspection and direction of rope works, as they will there find a number of useful observations and experiments upon that subject; and that there is great reason to suppose that a much stronger and [more] manageable cordage may be made by a proper mode

[1] The arithmetic is difficult to follow; but it seems to amount to this: that a new rope $\frac{7}{8}$ of the size of the old will be $\frac{4}{3}$ of the strength, and only $\frac{3}{4}$ of the weight.

of fabrication, without any additional expense or labour; I may say at less expense than what we now make.

Victory: at sea; Ushant, N 59° E, 62 leagues.
14th December, [1781].

Dear Sir,—The 12th instant, Ushant bearing N 61° E, distant fifty-three leagues, the look out frigate to windward made signal soon after day for a fleet in the SE, the wind then in that quarter. Made signal for the two-decked ships and frigates to chase. At nine we perceived they were going large to the westward; at half-past ten, observed several of the line ahead and to leeward forming in order of battle; upon which made the signal for the line; but having a prospect of passing between the enemy's ships of war and part of their convoy, I continued a press sail with the view of cutting them off, and succeeded in part. Several struck to us; the exact number I can't tell, but I suppose upwards of twenty; believe some of which were not taken possession of, night drawing on, it blowing fresh and the weather thick.

By crowding sail to cut the convoy off from the line-of-battle ships, some of our ships became very far astern, so that to form a line proper for action before dark would have been impossible. After collecting the ships together, I made sail on the same tack with the enemy, and at daylight in the morning saw them to leeward of us, in much the same position as in the evening before, but able to discern them more distinct. They were in line; we formed ours, but their superiority to us was such that I could not think of hazarding an attack. Besides we must have engaged to windward, and the weather was such we could not have opened our lower deck ports to leeward; they might have done theirs to windward.

De Guichen was within an ace of suffering a most ridiculous disgrace—that of having all his convoy taken from him before his face. He, with the ships of war, was to leeward of the convoy; the weather was rather hazy, the convoy took us for part of their fleet, and I believe their ships of war for part of the convoy. We stood into the convoy upon the larboard tack. De Guichen was not above two points upon our lee bow; had he stood towards us on the starboard tack he would have fetched us, and by that manœuvre obliged us to quit the pursuit of the convoy, to have tacked to close the rear ships we had separated from, to have got in proper form to have received him.

Had I waited for the slow-sailing ships it would have been dark before we could have got near the enemy, and the convoy would all have escaped. Had we been sufficiently furnished with frigates and armed cutters, De Guichen might have returned to Brest, for then almost the whole of his convoy must have been taken. Had I that day known the superior strength of their squadron, and that it was such that I could not in prudence risk an action with, I should have made a general chase of it, and in that case very few of their transports would have escaped; for had any number of our ships been half an hour's sail ahead of us—and many would have been more than that, had the signal for the two-decked ships continued out—they would have got in time between the convoy and the ships of war to have intercepted them. You must excuse haste.

Victory's Log.

[Official No. 2589.]

1781. *12th December.* A.M.—At 8 Tisiphone made the signal for a sail in the SE, and soon after for a fleet of fifteen sail. Made the signal to tack. Cleared ship. Found the fleet to be a large convoy of the enemy. In chase. The enemy's line of battle forming to leeward of their convoy, the body of them bearing WSW. Wind SEly. Lat. 47° 14′; Long. 8° 18′. Ushant N 61° E, 53 lgs.

13th December. P.M.—Fresh breeze. Made the signal to form a line ahead. At 1 the Edgar began to fire at a ship of the line running abreast her; fired a number of shot and brought-to several of the convoy. Fresh breeze and hazy. Ships employed securing several prizes. At 3 tacked per signal. At 4 joined the sternmost of our ships. Wore and stood to the southward, the tack the enemy was on, bearing W by S, 3 leagues. A.M. Strong breeze. At 8 made the signal for a line WSW. Made the frigates signal to board the prizes. Noon. The extremes of the enemy NNW to NNE, 10 or 11 miles. Wind SSE. Lat. 46° 33′; Long. 9° 30′; Ushant N 54° E, 67 lgs.

Kempenfelt to Middleton.

Victory: Spithead. 20 December, [1781].

The armament from Brest being passed; the French West India fleet arrived at that port under convoy of three crazy ships of the line the 7th instant, as all the French (prisoners) officers affirm; and the Jackal cutter informing me that he fell in with a Dutch convoy of fifty-four sail (one of which he took) NNE, twenty leagues from Ushant, who had come down the Channel escorted by two ships of war—his prisoners informed him they were bound for Brest; there remained no object, as I conceived, that made it necessary for me to continue out with the squadron. I therefore judged it would be more to their lordships' desire and the public service that I returned, that the ships might receive the repairs they stand in need of for future service. As to the destination and proceedings of the armament from Brest, the prisoners vary very much in their accounts, some asserting positively that they are all to proceed immediately to Cadiz, and from there to their further destination.

[*Signed.*] Victory: Spithead. 21st December, 1781.[1]

The report of the prisoners as to the proceedings of the armament under the command of De Guichen are very various. Some say they proceed by latitude of Madeira and there separate to their different destinations, De Guichen returning to Cadiz.[2] Others say De Guichen is to return to Brest; and one of the sea officers, a prisoner on board the Victory, with the appearance of sincerity, opened himself very freely to one of our lieutenants who speaks French, and who, from the civility and attention he showed the prisoner, has acquired his esteem and confidence. The prisoner says confidently that they all proceed to Cadiz first; that there the Spaniards are to join a certain number of ships of war and troops to those of the French designed for the West Indies, and that the object there is the attack of Jamaica. That the five first-rates, with some others, were to remain at Cadiz, and with the Spanish men-of-war that did not proceed to the West Indies form a combined fleet for home service.

[1] The only one of these letters from Kempenfelt not in his own handwriting.

[2] This was very likely the true story (Chevalier, i. 278); but falling in with bad weather, most of the ships were dismasted, and were happy to get back to Brest. Two only continued their voyage and reinforced De Grasse in the West Indies.

There seems to be more probability in this man's information than that of the other, and if Jamaica is really the object, it is to be supposed the Spaniards will make part of the force that is sent against that island; and where can their forces join so properly as at Cadiz?

Victory: Spithead. 23rd December [1781].

Dear Sir,—Some may think I did wrong in coming in with the squadron; but as the purpose for which I was sent out was over, by the armament from Brest having passed, their West India fleet arrived, and no object of consequence in view to make my continuance out necessary, I judged it would be most to the wishes of the admiralty and [to] the public service to return, as I supposed ships would be wanted for reinforcement to the West Indies and other parts; in fine, as it would be more interesting to have the squadron at home refitting for some purpose than beating the sea to no purpose.

My particular[1] interest was to remain out; some prizes might have been picked up. I returned because I thought it most for the public service. If in this I determined wrong, my judgment may be censured, but not my intention.

P.S.—The number of prisoners taken which I have had an account of are 1,342, of which 334 are seamen; the rest soldiers. Those in the Medway and some that have remained in the prizes I have had no account of yet.

[1] *Sc.* personal.

Admiral Kempenfelt's observations on the arrangement given to him by Lord S[andwich].

[*Copy in Middleton's hand.*] 6th January, 1782.

When the enemy's force by sea is superior to yours and you have many remote possessions to guard, it renders it difficult to determine the best means of disposing of your ships.

When you know the enemy's designs, in order to do something effectual you must endeavour to be superior to them in some part where they have designs to execute, and where, if they succeeded, they would most injure you. If your fleet is so divided as to be in all places inferior to the enemy, they will have a fair chance of succeeding everywhere in their attempts. If a squadron cannot be formed of sufficient force to face the enemy's at home, it would be more advantageous to let your inferiority be still greater, in order by it to gain the superiority elsewhere.

When inferior to the enemy, and you have only a squadron of observation to watch and attend upon their motions, such a squadron should be composed of two-decked ships only, as to ensure its purpose. It must have the advantage of the enemy in sailing; else, under certain circumstances, it will be liable to be forced to battle, or to give up some of their heavy sailers. It is highly necessary to have such a flying squadron to hang on the enemy's large fleet, as it will prevent their dividing into separate squadrons for intercepting your trade, or spreading their ships for a more extensive view. You will be at hand to profit from any accidental separation or dispersion of their fleet from hard gales, fogs or other causes. You may intercept supplies, intelligence, &c., to them. In fine, such a squadron will be a check and restraint upon their motions, and prevent a good deal of the mischief they might otherways do.

When the enemy are near the Channel, I should suppose the best situation for such a squadron would be to keep without them to the westward. When the enemy perceives your design of keeping the North Sea free by a stout squadron, for your trade to return home that way, it may be supposed they will detach from the grand fleet as many ships as the inferiority of your western squadron will allow, to endeavour, in conjunction with the Dutch, to turn, in that sea, the balance of power on their side.

The enemy I conceive at this time have two grand designs against us. The one, the conquest of our West India Islands; the other, at home, not confined merely to the interception of our trade, but to faovur, by their superiority, a formidable descent upon Great Britain and Ireland; and I should suppose the blow would be directed where it would be most felt by us, either against the metropolis or Portsmouth. I should rather think the latter, as less difficult from the nature of the navigation.

They will with some reason conclude that one or other of these designs will succeed; well knowing that we cannot, by our naval power, guard against both; and that if we employ a force sufficient to defeat their design in one place, we must necessarily leave the other exposed to them.

Mem. by Sir C. M.

As something must be left exposed, it appears to me that Great Britain and Ireland are more capable of defending themselves than our colonies; and that the present year will probably pass over before they discover our design in the North Sea. It behoves us, therefore, to make the best of the time allowed us.

Kempenfelt to Middleton.

Leicester Street. 11 March, [1782].

A lieutenant of the Active, who was with me this morning, says that, when attacked in Praya Bay,[1] of the guns they employed against the enemy, three were carronades, which, after some firing, broke their lower carriage or bed, and became useless. They all gave way at the inner part of the slit, where the wood is cut across the grain; this, therefore, as the weakest part of the bed, and which is liable to receive the force of the recoil, should be well strengthened, as by a plate of iron across, &c. But although the bed may be strengthened in this manner, yet attention must be paid to the spindle of the carriage, which by such recoil may break, though the bed resists.

There is no doubt but the above-mentioned accidents were from the breechings being too long; otherwise the beds could not be injured. By frequent firing the breechings will stretch; and is it not to be expected that, from the carelessness of seamen, attention will not always be paid to this in action, and that, therefore, the above accidents will often happen? Some have found that selvagee[2] breechings answer best for carronades; being formed of straight yarns they stretch less.

I conceive that the breaking of the bed or lower carriage is one of the principal evils the carronades

[1] 16 April, 1781.

[2] Untwisted hanks of rope yarn.

are liable to, and this from want of attention to the stretching of the breechings. Might not this be remedied by leaving the lower carriage or bed at liberty to recoil when, from the length of the breeching, it is struck by the spindle of the gun-carriage in firing? as, by the bed's yielding to the stroke, the force of it would be diminished. And by having the beds thus loose, what inconvenience would there be more than what attends our present gun-carriages? Besides, by having the beds thus movable you might always give them the same direction as the gun, which would prevent the lateral stroke they receive when the guns are pointed forward or aft; and the shot in my opinion would thereby go truer to the aim. You would likewise have the means of pointing your guns more directly forward or aft than when the bed is fixed at right angles to the side, as you could throw the gun close to either side of the port. When you want to secure the guns, the beds may be fastened to the side as in the present method.

Suppose, instead of mounting carronades upon a carriage and a bed, they were to be mounted upon a carriage only, to stand just in the same manner they do now when mounted on their carriage and bed; what would be the inconvenience? It would remove any apprehension of the carriages breaking. Carriages to work on a bed were used before carronades were invented. The advantage is that few men are required to manage them; but though this method of mounting may answer with the smaller carronades, I doubt whether they will do so well with the larger; and this appears to be Mr. Miller's[1] opinion, for he said he proposed his large carronades to be mounted upon a carriage only.

[1] Patrick Miller (1731–1815), said to have been the inventor of carronades, was certainly a large shareholder in the Carron Ironworks. See *D.N.B.*

I should like to have a few of the large carronades[1] on board of the Victory. To begin with, two upon each deck, forecastle and quarter-deck included. What would be best to substitute upon the poop, in the stead of small arms? Carronades upon carriages would encumber and be in the way of the main brace. Some sort of guns fixed with swivels and mounted upon stocks, that would throw musket balls to a sufficient distance, would, I should imagine, answer well, both for the tops and poop. That sort of musketoon of Mr. Miller's which takes a two-pound bullet would, I think, answer the purpose; their charge would consist of a considerable number of musket balls; such pieces are expeditiously loaded and directed.

P.S.—I have sent you observations upon the night signals in the new signal book, which shows the advantage of that method over the old one. The 130-pdr. carronade,[2] Mr. Gascoyne says, is too large for any ship's port.

[1] By *Admiralty Minute* of 3rd April, 1780, it appears that at that date 32-pdr. carronades were not on the establishment, and 24-pdr. carronades had been issued to the Victory, in lieu of the 32-pdrs. demanded. A few weeks later (5th May) it was minuted that the Carron Company had invented a carronade to carry a 68-pound ball or a shell shot of 56 pounds; and that the master-general of the ordnance was desired to make experiments with it. It was presumably guns of this type that Kempenfelt was now demanding. They do not appear to have been supplied.

[2] 'The 130-pdr.' is quite clearly written, but if such a gun was ever proposed it does not seem to have been anywhere adopted, certainly not in the navy. Bamber Gascoyne (1725–1791), a barrister and receiver-general of customs, was at this time a lord of the admiralty; but why he was considered an authority on the size of carronades or ships' ports does not appear. His daughter, heiress to his 12,000*l.* a year, married the second Marquis of Salisbury.—*D.N.B.*

ADMIRAL BARRINGTON[1] TO MIDDLETON

Portsmouth. 22nd May [1780].

[*Holograph.*]

My dear Middleton,—A man must see with my eyes, and have my feelings before he can account for my refusing the command. If our superiors had those feelings, and only their king and country's interest at heart, we might in time be ourselves again. Had I been in command, what I have seen since I have been here would have made me run mad. A total relaxation of discipline, and the rule laid down by a great man that we are all alike, must in the end be productive of bad consequences. Adieu. Yours sincerely,

SAMUEL BARRINGTON.

[1] The command of the Channel fleet was offered to Barrington, and, on his refusing it, was given to Admiral Geary. Cf. *D.N.B.*

CAPTAIN THOMAS CORNEWALL[1] *TO MIDDLETON*

Sunday [(?) 27th August, 1780].

[*Holograph.*]

My dear Friend,—Almost as soon as the ministers had acquiesced in opinion that B[arrington]n should have leave to strike his flag and retire on shore (but before it was sent to Lord S[andwic]h for his concurrence) Admiral Geary's son arrived with a private letter from his father to Mr. Stephens—saying that if government could dispense with his personal services for a week or ten days, he thought he should then be able to return to his duty and resume the command of the fleet, and that so much time would at least be necessary to restore and re-establish the strength of the recovering sick before they were fit for service. Bar[rington]n, he mentions as firmly determined to relinquish the first post, and observes that if B[arrington]n retires the utmost confusion would prevail among the officers—the discontent much increased by the promotion of Sir H[ugh] P[allise]r to Greenwich Hospital. Young Geary said Mr. Stephens seemed greatly pleased at his appearance with this letter—this was about 3 o'clock on Thursday. Mr. Stephens desired him to call again at 7, for he in-

[1] A captain of 1757; having very little service, he was passed over in the promotion of 1787, and died, still a captain, in 1796.—Charnock, vi. 222.

tended to shew it to Lord North and give him an answer; which was verbal but, in confidence, meaning exactly what you told me yesterday of government's resolution respecting B[arringto]n; but that since the admiral thought himself capable of returning to the command, all things should remain in their original state; so that B[arrington] is now acting under the chief, refitting &c. the remaining part of the fleet at Spithead.

I dined at Polesdon[1] yesterday, where I picked up this intelligence. The old chief very happy to see me and opened himself without reserve. He began with saying how much he had been obliged to B[arringto]n during the cruize; of his friendship to him, of his abilities and extent of knowledge in naval affairs. I indulged him with an unlimited scope till a pause declared he had no more to say on the subject. Just at the conclusion, the son came into the room, who was desired by his father to repeat to me the interview he had with Mr. Stephens. When that was over, the son said how very fortunate at this crisis it was that matters had taken so favourable a turn. I thought so too; and while the son remained with us I went over Bar[ringto]n in my turn. You may be sure that I was as liberal in commendation of those qualities I thought the amiable parts of his character as either of them could wish; but I could not help observing that characters, like medals, had a reversed side to examine before the description became intelligent; and that although I honoured the person who was the subject of our conversation as much as either of them, still there remained some parts of his conduct so highly reprehensible and inconsistent, they must pardon me if I differed, and differed widely indeed, in attributing

[1] A house and manor in the parish of Great Bookham, Surrey. It was then owned by Geary, but was sold by his son.

that degree of applause to his personal merit bestowed so abundantly on him. Now, says I, my good admiral, I will give one proof of it, and only one; and it shall be instanced by a comparison with yourself. I saw the old buck brighten up and the son attentive. Have you not declared a thousand times (and you have acted consistent with that declaration) that an officer, if not incapacitated by infirmities, called forth to serve his country, and with proper abilities to fulfil the summons, deserved the united reproaches of all mankind on a refusal? Yes, replied the admiral, and I shall always think so.—Well then, what do you say of your friend B[arrington]n?—He turned his wig about and was silent. My good Sir, continued I, the person of whom we are speaking has more to answer for than that; by what power I cannot say, but from the effect of that power, he has drawn over to himself a party of half at least of the officers under your command; these are trained up in discontent, and perhaps I don't go too far if I say in open contempt of every resolution sent from the admiralty. He has been caressed and flattered by his prince in the highest degree; called upon to serve his country at a time of extreme exigence; in short he has been held up in the most exalted view that ambition could desire. Upon all this he has put a cold, obstinate and inflexible negative. Is my picture at all like, Sir?—The admiral was staggered and confessed it was so.

I really believe this made a considerable impression. My view, if possible, was to detach him from, or at least not to rely entirely on, the counsels of his friend B[arrington]n, and to pave the way for better from his captain. I could go no further then, for Captain and Mrs. Williams arrived to dinner and we had no further conversation. It was particularly unfortunate for me that Captain Kempenfelt did not come to Polesdon; he was expected to dinner, but was not arrived at half past 7.—The admiral and his family will dine with us before he returns to Portsmouth, but I doubt if the visit will produce any good. I shall try however; though, to say the truth, this fever makes him appear weaker than ever. If anything profitable occurs to you on this subject let me know.

I think the admiral will hardly be sound enough for another year; he seems tottering, and training towards childhood again.[1] That may at present proceed from his illness; they are, however, attacks at his age seldom conquered without leaving debilitating proofs of their effects.

I shall be happy in hearing of the safe return of my friends at Teston. William Watt will bring on Tuesday a drawing board for Mrs. Middleton to look at; if it is not too large for her use, she will give me great pleasure by her acceptance; if she wishes to have a smaller one made, the man's name is Vercoe who fabricated mine, and lives at the Feathers, in Great Wild Street. Adieu, my dear friend.

Yours most faithfully,

THOS. CORNEWALL.

If the paper is just damped a little before it is put on the board it will become as tight as possible.

[1] He lived for sixteen years more, dying in 1796.

APPENDIX A

THE BATTLE OF 17TH APRIL, 1780.

THE MONTAGU COURT-MARTIAL.

[Public Record Office—Admiralty, Sec. In letters, 5316.]

AT a court-martial assembled on board his Majesty's ship the Russell in Basseterre Road, St. Christopher's, the 2nd August, 1780, and continued by adjournment till the 4th of the same month. Present:—

Commodore Francis Samuel Drake, President.

Geo. Balfour	Philip Affleck
Mark Robinson	John N. P. Nott
John Brisbane	James Ferguson
Robert Fanshawe	John Lewis Gidoin
Arth. J. Pye Molloy	Hugh C. Christian
William Fooks	Walter Young

The Court, pursuant to an order from Sir George Brydges Rodney, Bart., Admiral of the White and Commander in Chief of his Majesty's ships and vessels employed and to be employed at Barbados, the Leeward Islands and the seas adjacent, dated 28th July, 1780, and directed to Commodore Drake, second in command upon the said station, being first duly sworn, proceeded to try Lieutenant Robert Taylor Appleby for withdrawing, with his Majesty's ship Montagu, from the battle with the French fleet on the 17th April last, without signal or order from the Commander in Chief, or the Admiral in whose division the ship was, to the great detriment of his

Majesty's service ; to the command of which ship he succeeded upon Captain Houlton, her commander, being wounded.

The Court having considered the evidence, and maturely weighed and considered the whole, is of opinion that the charge against the prisoner for withdrawing from the action with the enemy on the 17th April last, without signal or order for so doing from the Commander in Chief or the officer commanding the division the Montagu belonged to, has been proved ; but by no means to the great detriment of his Majesty's service ; so far from it, that it has been clearly proved to the Court that the ship must unavoidably have fallen into the hands of the enemy, had she not been withdrawn from the action at the time she was.

The Court does therefore think the prisoner did his duty as a good officer upon the occasion, and we do hereby honourably acquit him, and he is hereby acquitted accordingly.

Follow, the signatures.

MINUTES OF THE PROCEEDINGS.

[The Prisoner was brought in and the audience admitted. The order for trial was read [1]] :—

First Witness: Captain Henry Bryne of his Majesty's ship Andromeda.

By the Court: You have heard the charge. Please to relate what you saw on the 17th April last relative thereto against the prisoner.—*Answer:* On the 17th April, at half-past three, I observed the Montagu to be the sternmost ship of the rear, standing to the southward, with the larboard tacks on board. A few minutes after, perceived the Montagu amidst the fire of five line of battle ships of the enemy. Whilst in that fire I observed her haul down her ensign and hoist a weft. As soon as she got out of the fire, she hauled down her weft and hoisted her ensign. Still standing to the southward, she hauled down her ensign and hoisted her weft again ; on which I wore, set fore sail and top-gallant sails and stood after her. When

[1] Passages in brackets are in abstract only.

I came alongside, I was hailed and acquainted that the ship was in a shattered condition, and had received many shot between wind and water, and desired to stay by her. I immediately asked if they wanted any men or assistance that was in my power to give them. The reply was No; but desired I would send a boat on board, which I did accordingly with my first lieutenant in her, with my compliments to Captain Houlton, that I would be happy to render him any service in my power. On the boat going alongside, Lieut. Appleby went into it and came on board the Andromeda.

I introduced Mr. Appleby and my own first lieutenant into my own cabin. Mr. Appleby acquainted me that the Montagu was in a shattered condition in her rigging, masts and sails, and several shot between wind and water; that Captain Houlton was also wounded and that the command of the ship devolved to him. I asked him what lieutenant he was on board. He told me he was 2nd, but did duty as 1st, as there was none on board; therefore he thought it his duty to come on board, to acquaint me with the state and condition of the ship, and should be glad of my advice. He also asked me how the land bore and at what distance, and whether or no it was not safe to go to leeward. I told him, By no means. If he did, he would run the risk of falling into the enemy's hands; and that, as he had asked, my advice was that he should get the ship (Montagu) ready as soon as possible; that I did imagine Sir George Rodney meant to engage the French fleet that night or early in the morning.

Q. What position was our fleet in at that time?—*A.* It is very difficult for me to tell. I could not see all the fleet.

Q. Was any signal for the line flying on board the flag ship or repeater at that time?—*A.* None that I observed.

Q. Was any signal out from the commander in chief or the commander of the division the Montagu was in, for any particular purpose, at that time?—*A.* None, that I recollect.

Q. What tack was the English fleet on at that time?—*A.* The starboard tack.

Q. As the English fleet was on the starboard tack and the Montagu on the larboard tack, can you inform the court how she came to be on the contrary tack to that of the fleet?—*A*. I do not know. I did not observe the Montagu till she was in the position already described.

Q. On what tack was the French fleet at that time?—*A*. Some on the starboard, some on the larboard; some wearing, some staying.

Q. Whether the hauling down the ensign and hoisting the weft was understood by you as a signal of distress?—*A*. I did imagine so.

Q. On a nearer inspection from you, what condition did the Montagu appear to you to be in?—*A*. She appeared to be in a very shattered condition in her rigging and sails.

Q. Can you inform the court whether the Montagu withdrew from the action of the 17th April last by design, or in consequence of order or signal from the commander in chief or the officer commanding the particular division the Montagu belonged to?—*A*. I saw no signal made for her withdrawing from the fleet.

Q. How came the Montagu engaged with those five ships you mentioned of the enemy's line?—*A*. By standing to the southward, I should imagine.

Q. Were there any of the British ships at hand to support her while in action with those five ships?—*A*. When engaging those five ships, I observed the Conqueror, Medway and Vengeance, as I took them to be; two of them tacked, one of them wore, and were standing to the south. On seeing the Montagu hoist her colours again and clear of the fire, they either tacked or wore, and stood into the fleet again.

Q. Whether the Montagu, after the advice given by you for that purpose, did use all the means in her power to rejoin the fleet again?—*A*. She did.

Q. Whether, as the English fleet and Montagu were on different tacks, you thought the Montagu at such a distance from the English fleet as to advise the towing her head round, or did the prisoner apply for that purpose?—*A*. He did not make such application, neither was it necessary, as the ship could both wear and stay, and there was wind enough.

Q. Did she appear to you to be manageable?—*A*. Yes.

Q. Did you imagine, if she had been on the same tack with the British fleet, she was in condition to have kept way with it?—*A*. I do think she could.

Q. When you first saw the Montagu on the larboard tack, did you see any other of our ships on the same tack?—*A.* None that I could observe.

Q. Had the signal for the line of battle been made that day?—*A.* It had.

Q. Can you inform the court how long it had been hauled down when you observed the Montagu to be the sternmost ship of the fleet?—*A.* I do not remember the time.

Q. You say you saw the Montagu engaged with five sail of the enemy's line of battle ships. Can you inform the court whether the enemy quitted farther action with the Montagu, or the Montagu withdrew from them?—*A.* The Montagu withdrew from them.

Q. Did it appear to you necessary that the Montagu should disengage herself from the enemy, considering the condition she appeared to you to be in, and the distance she was from the British fleet?—*A.* I did think it highly necessary she should disengage herself from those five sail of the enemy's ships she was engaged with, as she must otherwise, in ten minutes, have been taken.

Q. After the action ceased between the Montagu and the five ships of the enemy, how long did the action continue between the English and French fleets?—*A.* I do not remember.

Q. Was there any action after that?—*A.* To the best of my recollection, there was. Part of the English and French fleets were engaging.

Q. Do you think it continued long enough for the Montagu to have engaged in it, considering the situation she was in?—*A.* I think not.

Q. As Captain Houlton's being wounded occasioned the command of the Montagu to devolve on the prisoner, it is presumed there must have been an action before the period at which your evidence commences. Did you, at that time, see the Montagu withdraw from the action; or at any other time during the action of the 17th April last, excepting what you have already related to the court?—*A.* I do not remember taking any notice of the Montagu till I saw her in the rear of the fleet.

Q. In what state were the five ships of the enemy when the Montagu withdrew from them; and did they attempt to continue their attack upon her?—*A.* They appeared to be much damaged and confused, and did not attempt to continue the attack upon her.

Q. When you saw her engaged with the five ships of the enemy, what distance was she from the nearest ship of the British fleet?—*A.* I cannot ascertain the exact distance.

Q. Can you recollect what time those ships of the enemy, that were upon the larboard tack, went upon it?—*A.* I do not.

Q. In what part of the line was the partial action, which you said continued after the Montagu was engaged with those five ships of the enemy?—*A.* It appeared to be in the centre.

Q. After the signal for the line had been made that day, what other signal was made by the commander in chief, or admirals commanding the divisions?—*A.* A variety.

Q. Was the signal for close action made?—*A.* It was.

Q. Did you, at any time in that day, after the signal for the line had been made, observe a union flag at the admiral's main topgallant mast head? [1]—*A.* I do not recollect I did.

Q. How long did the Montagu continue to engage the five ships of the enemy?—*A.* I do imagine it might be ten minutes.

Q. At the time of her engaging those ships, what sail had the Montagu set?—*A.* Her fore sail, three top-sails, jib and fore top-mast stay-sail.

[1] Article XXI. of Rodney's *Instructions and Signals by Day*, commonly referred to as *Additional Fighting Instructions*, is: 'If the squadron be sailing in a line of battle ahead to windward of the enemy, and the commander-in-chief would have the course altered in order to lead down to them, he will hoist an union flag at the main topgallant mast head and fire a gun; whereupon every ship in the squadron is to steer for the ship of the enemy which, from the disposition of the two squadrons, it must be her lot to engage, notwithstanding the signal for the line ahead will be kept flying; making or shortening sail in such proportion as to preserve the distance assigned by the signal for the line, in order that the whole squadron may, as near as possible, come to action at the same time.'

Q. Did the Montagu's sails appear to be shattered *prior* to her engaging those ships, or in consequence of it?—*A.* I really do not know.

Q. Did the situation of the five sail of the enemy with which the Montagu had been engaged prevent her from tacking or wearing to join those three ships which came to support her, but tacked on her hoisting her ensign and being out of the fire of the enemy?—*A.* I already have said I thought the Montagu capable of wearing or staying; therefore, I know of no reason why she could not wear and stay then.

Q. How long was it after these three ships had tacked or wore that the Montagu stood after them to the northward?—*A.* I do not recollect the time.

Q. Are you of opinion that the Montagu could have tacked or wore sooner than she did?—*A.* I have already said she was in a condition to wear or stay. They must be the best judges why they did not wear or tack sooner.

The Prisoner had no questions to ask.

[Other witnesses from Andromeda: Benjamin Cull, 1st lieutenant; Samuel Bignal, 2nd lieutenant; Alexander McGeachen, master; George Holland, 1st lieutenant of marines; Charles Symons, captain's clerk, called but did not appear, being reported sick; John Brown, boatswain; Jacob Hager, quartermaster; John Todd, quartermaster; William Grant, boatswain's mate. Their evidence, more or less lengthy, is essentially the same as that of the captain; except that Cull deposes: that the Montagu, with her head to the southward, after being engaged with several ships of the enemy, hauled down her ensign and hoisted a weft, between half-past three and four.] 'The weft was kept flying for some time; then hauled down and the ensign hoisted again. The ensign was then hauled down and a weft hoisted a second time. She stood on to the southward while the Andromeda was running down to her assistance, and wore to the northward just before the Andromeda joined her. . . . The Montagu stood to the northward till 5 o'clock; then tacked and stood to the SE till 4 o'clock in the morning when I left the deck.' [When Appleby was on board the Andromeda, the fleets were five or six miles distant, in the NE quarter, the French about half a point to leeward of the English. Bignal agrees with this.] 'As we came near her, she wore. . . . We made sail with the Montagu northward; about 5 we both wore and stood to the southward again, and continued so all night.' [The evidence of McGeachen, Holland and Todd on this point is to the same effect—that the Montagu wore to the northward before the Andromeda spoke her. Bryne is the only witness who implies that she did not wear to the northward till later.]

[Witnesses from the Montagu: John Taber, surgeon; Scorey Barker, 2nd lieutenant; George Duff, 3rd lieutenant; the Hon. Alexander Cochrane, 4th lieutenant; Lieut. Jackson, 5th lieutenant; David Ogilvie, master; John Hudson, boatswain; and Anthony Paul, captain's clerk.]

[As the lieutenants were below, at their quarters, their evidence amounts to very little. Jackson, who was quartered at the foremost lower deck guns, says that just before the ship began to engage, 'the admiral of the division had the union jack at the mizen peak,[1] the union jack at the main topgallant mast head,[2] the red flag at the fore topgallant mast head,[3] and a half blue, half white flag under it.'[4] The one evidence which has any real bearing on the case is Ogilvie's; and this is both interesting and important. It is here given verbatim.]

Q. Do you know when and for what reason the Montagu withdrew from action with the French fleet on the 17th April?—*A.* When Mr. Appleby came upon deck and took the command, he told me that it was his orders to me to draw the ship from action as soon as possible, as the fire was so hot, and asked me what was to be done. I told him we must immediately get the fore tack on board and the fore sheet aft, and as soon as that was done, to get the main tack down and see if possible we could draw ahead of the enemy; which he immediately got done, we still keeping up a constant fire against three ships of the enemy, and they against us. We suffered greatly from their firing in passing them. The ship then drew ahead of two of them and abreast of one, when we still kept a continual fire

[1] 'Line of battle ahead.'

[2] See note, p. 376.

[3] 'Engage the enemy.'

[4] 'Engage more closely.'

at him and he at us. He seemed once to bear away and we raked him; and then we passed him and became out of gunshot, and he left off firing. The French admiral, that was our first opponent, made a signal, and they (the four ships) wore and stood to the northward, on the starboard tack, to join their fleet. We still continued on the larboard tack. We then, being to leeward of the body and centre of the whole French fleet, stood on about ten minutes and then hauled the main sail up and wore the ship with her head to the northward. The same time the Andromeda came under our stern and gave us three cheers; and run and brought-to upon our larboard bow and hoisted a boat out, which boat came aboard on our larboard side. We were then shortening sail and getting ready to repair our rigging which was damaged. Mr. Appleby then went and had some private conference with Captain Houlton; who[1] had then come upon deck and then went into the Andromeda's boat and went on board her; and in about a quarter of an hour returned, and ordered everybody to be turned about splicing and knotting the rigging, going fore and aft himself to see his orders put into execution. Captain Houlton was sitting in the ward room, and sent for the coxswain of the Andromeda's boat, and sent his compliments to the captain of her, letting him know his wounds were pretty easy.

Q. What tack was the Montagu on in the line of battle?—*A.* On the starboard.

Q. At what time did she wear to go on the larboard tack? and who ordered her?—*A.* About three o'clock, the captain, being then upon deck, ordered me to haul the mizen up, shiver the mizen topsail, and steer right down to our opponent, as he observed firing at that distance was of no use, and only expending powder and shot. The captain's orders were immediately obeyed, and we were raked twice in going down. The captain said to me, We are now as nigh as I could wish; let us bring her to on the starboard tack again and then we shall be able to give him a dose. The helm was accordingly put down and the

[1] This 'who' must mean Appleby. It is clear from Taber's evidence that Houlton was then in the stern walk, having his wound attended to.

mizen hauled out, and the sails braced up abaft, but all to no purpose; the ship came-to against her helm to port, as there was little wind. Captain Houlton then asked me what was best to be done; we must bring one broadside or other upon the enemy. We accordingly shifted the helm and brought her by the wind upon the larboard tack, where we engaged our opponent with our starboard guns. Immediately after, the French admiral of the rear division made a signal, and wore, with four others, and came upon the larboard tack; but in wearing, three of them got foul of one another, where we kept a continual fire upon them while they were in that situation. A few minutes after, Captain Houlton was wounded, being, as near as I can recollect, about twenty minutes after three. Just as Captain Houlton went off the deck, those three ships got clear of one another, and opened their whole fire upon us. I immediately sent the aide-de-camp to Lieutenant Appleby, to let him know Captain Houlton was wounded; and when he came upon deck he told me he had just parted with the captain, who was of opinion with himself that we should withdraw from the enemy and make the signal for assistance, which I believe Mr. Appleby did. I saw no British ships then in sight but the Magnificent and Andromeda. The Magnificent passed us near half a mile to windward, and discharged her larboard guns; and I believe some of her shot came on board us, as some were found with a Broad R[1] upon them; three on the lower deck and one in the quarter gallery.

Q. Was any signal for wearing made by the admiral or commander of the division the Montagu was in?—*A.* None that I saw or ever heard of.

Q. What was the condition of the Montagu when Lieutenant Appleby came upon deck to take the command of her?—*A.* She was very much damaged, both in mast, rigging, and sails; her main topsail all tore to pieces above the third reef; her main top-mast half cut through six feet above the cap; her main stay cut through all but one strand close to the mouse.

Q. Do you think her not coming round upon the starboard tack, as was required, was owing to her being

[1] The recognised way of writing a 'Broad Arrow.'

unmanageable by reason of such damage, or for want of wind?—*A*. Want of wind only, and if we had not come-to on one tack, we must have been plump on board the French admiral, he then being about musket shot from us.

Q. What space of time was there between Captain Houlton's going off the deck wounded and Lieutenant Appleby[1] coming upon deck?—About five minutes.

Q. When the Montagu withdrew from action with those ships she engaged, were any part of the English and French fleets engaged?—*A*. I neither saw nor heard so.

Q. Did it appear to you that the Montagu withdrawing from action was owing to any cowardice, negligence, or disaffection in Lieutenant Appleby, having the command of her after his captain went off the deck wounded?—*A*. By his behaviour, quite otherwise.

Q. (*By the Prisoner.*) Did you not receive an order (prior to my coming upon deck) from Captain Houlton, to get the ship out of the enemy's fire as soon as possible; which order you conceived to proceed from the situation he left the ship in when he quitted the deck?—*A*. No. A midshipman came up from Captain Houlton and told me everything must be done to fight the ship and defend her as long as possible; and rather than strike, to let her go down with her colours flying.

Q. (*By the Court.*) Did you repeat Captain Houlton's orders to Lieutenant Appleby when he came up?—*A*. I did not. Mr. Appleby was just come from the captain.

Q. Did you understand Captain Houlton's message to be that you was to defend the ship against the enemy as long as possible? or that you should continue the action under the circumstances the Montagu then was in, having it in her power to draw out of the enemy's fire?—*A*. I understood it related to the defence of the ship only till we could draw out of action.

Q. Do you think the Montagu could have continued the action to the advantage of his Majesty's service all that time?—*A*. No, not to the advantage of his Majesty's service, but quite otherwise.

Witness withdrew.

[1] He was quartered at the after main-deck guns.

[The Prisoner, in his defence, said] :—

I think it needless for me to say more than that I hope it will appear to the satisfaction of the court that I did everything in my power for the good of his Majesty's service, after the command of the Montagu devolved upon me; and as the witnesses already called have given so full an account of the matter, I will not trouble the court with the examination of any witness in my behalf.

The court was then cleared, and the sentence being drawn up and signed, the prisoner was brought in and audience admitted. The Deputy Judge-Advocate then pronounced sentence. [*As before.*]

Will. Pagett, Dep. J. Advocate.

THE YARMOUTH COURT-MARTIAL.

[Public Record Office. Admiralty, Sec. In letters, 5316.]

Minutes of the Proceedings at a Court Martial assembled on board his Majesty's ship Resolution, off New York, the 24th day of October, 1780, and from thence continued to the 3rd day of November, 1780, Sundays excepted Present :—

Commodore Sir Chaloner Ogle, President.

Captains Philip Affleck, Charles Thompson, John Robinson, Lord Robt. Manners, And. S. Douglas, J. L. Gidoin, Edwd. Thompson, Hugh Robinson, Howell Lloyd

The above members and also Mr. Howard, Deputy Judge Advocate, were sworn in, according to Act of Parliament.

Then the order for assembling the court martial and the charge against Captain Bateman, was read, as follows :—

By Sir G. B. Rodney, Bart., Admiral of the White and Commander in Chief of his Majesty's ships and vessels employed and to be employed at Barbados, the Leeward Islands, and the seas adjacent, &c., &c.

You are hereby required and directed to assemble a court martial for the trial of Captain Bateman of his Majesty's ship Yarmouth. My charge against him is that on the 17th April last, when his Majesty's fleet was engaged with that of his enemy, the said Captain Bateman, then commander of his Majesty's ship Yarmouth, withdrew from his station in the line of battle, and lay to windward of the squadron while it was in action, with his main and mizen topsails aback, and continued in that situation for a very considerable time, though his particular signal was made to make sail to get into his station, and to engage close; which signal he answered by his answering flag, but did not obey. He continued laying to windward till near the end of the action, when I was forced by his disobedience to the other signals, to make his signal to bear down into my wake.

Given under my hand on board his Majesty's ship
Sandwich, off New York, 21st October, 1780.
G. B. RODNEY.

To Commodore Sir Chaloner Ogle, &c., &c.
By command of the Admiral,
Will. Pagett.

[Mr. Edward Bright, surgeon of the Pearl, attended to give evidence that Captain Montagu was confined to his room by a bruised knee. This was admitted a sufficient excuse, and Captain Montagu's attendance dispensed with.]

Captain Walter Young, of the Sandwich, being then called in, was accordingly sworn.

By the Court. You will please to relate what you know relative to the action of the 17th April last.—*A.* I cannot ascertain the exact time relative to the signals being made on board the Sandwich, or the exact time respecting the conduct of the Yarmouth on the 17th April, as I had the fleet to attend to, and the ship I commanded in action at the same time; but to the best of my recollection, as soon as the enemy was discovered, at daylight in the morning, the signal was made for the line of battle ahead on the starboard tack, at two cables' length distance; the French fleet then with their larboard tacks on board, to leeward, between four and five leagues; the wind at

East, or E by N. At near 8 o'clock the admiral made the signal that he intended to attack the enemy's rear. Soon afterwards, the signal was made to form the line of battle and each ship to bear from the other S by E and N by W. The enemy, on discovering the position of our fleet, wore and came to the wind on the starboard tack; the ships that were now their rear became their van. On our seeing this alteration in the enemy's line, the signal was made for the line of battle ahead on the larboard tack, at two cables' length. We continued leading on that tack, the enemy on the starboard tack, until the Sandwich was nearly opposite the French admiral, who was near the centre of his fleet. We then made the signal to wear. On finding that the ships did not wear immediately on the signal's being made, the Stirling Castle's signal was thrown out to wear, who became the leading ship on that tack. Soon after, the signal for the line of battle ahead, at two cables' length, was made. Near about noon the signal was made to prepare for action; the distance from the enemy, I should suppose between 8 and 9 miles. I believe about one o'clock the signal was made for each ship to bear down on her opponent, and bring her to action, the signal at the same time out for engaging, with the signal for close action. At about half past one the Sandwich engaged the second ship astern of the French admiral, who in less than half an hour gave way and bore right before the wind, out of the line. A second ship came up and was beat out of the line likewise. Some time after that, the admiral came to me, when I was on the lee gangway, and informed me that the French admiral was on the weather bow; soon after which, I saw the Yarmouth haul out of the line, and brought-to, with her main and mizen topsails aback, to windward of our line, and continued lying-to with her main and mizen topsails aback. The Yarmouth's signal, on seeing him lie-to, was made to make more sail, which was answered by the Yarmouth's answering flag, the ship still continuing in the same situation, without making sail. The admiral then directed me to order a shot to be fired into her to make her obey that signal; in consequence of which, I ordered two guns on the upper[1] deck on the starboard side to be

[1] *I.e.*, main-deck; therefore 12-pounders.

shotted and fired into the Yarmouth. The officer and men who were at those guns told me that the guns would not bear on the Yarmouth. I then went on the forecastle and ordered a forecastle gun [1] to be fired into her. That gun the men could not bring to bear on her, as we were then bearing down on the French admiral to bring him to a closer action, being then engaged with him and his two seconds. The Yarmouth still continued laying-to, with her main and mizen topsails aback, until—as near as I can recollect—about half past three, and about half an hour before the action ceased between the French admiral, his two seconds and the Sandwich, when the Yarmouth's signal was made to bear down into the admiral's wake, which he obeyed; and in the act of wearing I saw her—the Yarmouth's—larboard main topsail yard carried away, I suppose by the enemy's shot. She came down in our wake, and kept up an incessant and good fire till the action was over.

Q. (*By Court.*) How long do you suppose the Yarmouth continued laying-to between the first and the last?—*A.* An hour or thereabouts.

Q. What distance do you apprehend the Yarmouth was to windward of the line of battle, when she obeyed the signal to bear down?—*A.* A quarter of a mile or more.

Q. Do you apprehend the reason why the admiral made Captain Bateman's signal to bear into his wake; as that does not appear to be his position in the line of battle then out?—*A.* As Captain Bateman did not obey the signal to make more sail and get into his station, the signal for close action and engaging still flying, we being then engaged with the French admiral and his two seconds and such of their guns as would bear on us, and the Suffolk, our second, being so far astern and to windward as not to take off the fire of the French admiral's second astern of him from us, the admiral thought it necessary to place the Yarmouth there for that purpose.

Q. Was it not always in Captain Bateman's power to bear away and get into his station?—*A.* As the masts, yards and rigging of the Yarmouth appeared to me not to be damaged, I saw no impediment nor know of none.

[1] A 6-pounder.

Q. Had the Yarmouth been engaged with the enemy previous to her hauling out of the line?—*A.* She had; and on seeing her engaged at too great a distance, the Yarmouth's signal was made to come to closer action; which signal for close action was never taken in from that time till the action was over.

Q. Did she obey that signal previous to her hauling out of the line?—*A.* I cannot tell whether she did or not.

Q. Did the Yarmouth appear disabled, or can you assign any apparent reason for her hauling out of the line at that time?—*A.* She did not appear disabled, nor do I know or can I assign any reason or occasion she had to haul out of the line.

Q. You have observed the Sandwich had already beat two ships out of the line. Was she afterwards attacked by the French admiral and two other ships of their line ahead?—*A.* She was.

Q. Was not the Yarmouth to windward of the French admiral at that time, and in a situation to bear down?—*A.* She was; and I saw nothing to prevent her bearing down, we, at that time, going from the wind and endeavouring to close with the Cornwall.

Q. Was not the British flag unsupported and exposed by the Yarmouth not bearing down?—*A.* The British flag most certainly might have been better supported, had the Yarmouth kept her station in the line.

Q. At the time the Yarmouth bore down and engaged the French admiral's second astern, did she appear to you to engage close, keep up a brisk fire and do her duty as a British man-of-war?—*A.* She kept up a brisk fire, but neither us nor the Yarmouth appeared to me to be sufficiently close.

Q. At the time that you say the Yarmouth hauled out of the line, what sort of line was that, or did it appear to you to be regularly formed?—*A.* The ships ahead of the line, I could see no farther than the Yarmouth. The Yarmouth, Cornwall, and Sandwich appeared to be in a good line, but the distance a little increased, from the signal being made for each ship in the line to engage her opponent in the enemy's line.

Q. What distance may you suppose the leading ship to be from the Sandwich when the Yarmouth hauled out of the line?—*A.* It was so far extended that I cannot tell.

Q. What became of the ship the Yarmouth engaged on bearing down? or was she forced out of the line?—*A.* The French admiral, at 4 o'clock, put his helm a-weather and bore away with his two seconds, the ship the Yarmouth engaged being one of them. Soon after he bore away, on my being informed the Sandwich's foretop-mast was shot through and likely to go overboard, I ordered the topsail halyards to be let go and the topsail to be lowered down on the cap. On the halyards being let go, the topmast went overboard. The mizen mast shot half through, the main mast and main yard shot through, her sails and rigging all cut to pieces, which of course did prevent our following the enemy.

Q. How long after the action was it before Captain Bateman was put under an arrest?—*A.* I believe the day after the action.

Q. When you bore down and brought the French admiral on your weather bow, how far was you from the wind?—*A.* I suppose about two or three points from the wind. The instant I saw them in that situation, I ordered the main tack to be got on board to close with the Cornwall, on purpose to repel any attempt the enemy might make upon us.

Q. Was the French admiral then close to the wind?—*A.* I believe not.

Q. The time the forecastle gun would not bear on the Yarmouth, how many points was the Sandwich from the wind?—*A.* To the best of my recollection, we were going two or three points from the wind.

Q. Do you recollect what signals were then flying?—*A.* The signal for engaging and the signal for close action.

Q. Were all those signals regularly repeated by a repeating frigate, and was that frigate in a proper situation for repeating?—*A.* To the best of my judgment they were, and she was in a proper situation for that purpose.

Q. When the Yarmouth bore down in your wake, in consequence of the admiral's signal, did she fire on the enemy as she came down, or not till she came in your wake, abreast of the enemy?—*A.* She did not fire on the enemy on bearing down, because it would not have been in her power to have brought her metal to bear on the enemy; but as soon as she came in our wake and came to the wind, she commenced firing and kept up a very good and brisk fire until the enemy bore away.

Q. In what position and distance was the Yarmouth from the Sandwich when the French admiral bore away?—*A.* In our wake, and at the distance of two or three cables' length.

Q. When the Yarmouth lay to windward of the Sandwich, you observed she had her main and mizen topsails aback. Was her mizen hauled out, or mizen stay-sail hoisted?—*A.* To the best of my recollection she had only her three topsails out.

Q. Was there any of the French ships, ahead of the French admiral, to windward of him, at the time the Sandwich brought the French admiral on his weather bow?—*A.* I saw none.

Q. (*By the Prisoner.*) Did the Sandwich bearing away two or three points to engage the enemy carry her so far to leeward as to have our van ships open with one another, to windward of the Sandwich?—*A.* I never saw any of our van ships to windward of the Sandwich, or to leeward of her; and the furthest ship that I saw was the Yarmouth.

Q. Did the Yarmouth hinder Captain Young from seeing the ships in the van?—*A.* No; the Yarmouth could not hinder me from seeing the ships in the van.

Q. Then what did prevent your seeing them?—*A.* I can assign no other reason for not seeing the ships in the van but their being extended from us, and in such a situation as I could not see them from the quarter deck, either from the weather or lee gangway.

Q. When the Yarmouth was abreast of the Sandwich, was she then at her greatest distance to windward of the line?—*A.* Yes, she was.

Q. When the Yarmouth dropped close under the Sandwich's stern, what sail had the Yarmouth set?—*A.* I cannot immediately recollect.

Q. Did you take any particular notice of the Yarmouth when she was nearest to you abreast? Did she appear then to be like a ship that was wrecked or had been in heavy service?—*A.* I recollect seeing the Yarmouth set her fore sail and bear down, with her larboard main topsail yard-arm lying over the top; but could not perceive any other damage she had sustained.

Q. When the signal was made for the Yarmouth to get into the admiral's wake, what sail had the Sandwich set?—*A.* To the best of my recollection, the main sail, fore sail, three topsails, and main top-mast stay-sail. Whether the jib or fore top-mast stay-sail was cut away by the enemy's shot at that time, I cannot recollect; but if that circumstance did not take place, they were set likewise.

Q. When the Yarmouth was close under the Sandwich's stern, do you remember if there was not a vast difference in the wind between that time and the time the action began?—*A.* To the best of my recollection, near the close of the action the wind decreased.

Q. About the time the action began, was not the enemy's van carrying a press of sail?—*A.* Just before the action began, the French admiral, then upon our beam, with his main sail hauled up, threw out a signal, which signal being repeated through their line as far as I could see it, he immediately hauled his main tack on board, and made sail, the other ships following his example.

Q. I should be glad to know what that signal was.—*A.* I do not understand the French signals, nor did I take notice of the colour of the flag, but I prepared the admiral for an alteration in the French line, and soon after saw the French admiral haul his main tack on board.

Q. What part of the ship was that signal made from?—*A.* It might be made from the main topgallant yard down and at the mizen peak at the same time. I do not immediately recollect where, not looking upon it as my duty to attend to the French signals.

Q. Was it one flag or two flags?—*A.* I cannot recollect. I paid no attention to their signals.

Q. Was not the Yarmouth in general one of the heaviest sailing ships in the fleet?—*A.* She was one of the heavy sailing ships.

Q. Did not the Grafton and Cornwall sail better than the Yarmouth?—*A.* To the best of my judgment they might at times sail better, and in general did so; but how they sailed on that day I cannot say.

Q. Did you see anything of the Grafton when you first perceived the Yarmouth's main topsail aback?—*A.* I did not.

Q. Had any signal then been given by Admiral Rodney to the ships to inform him that the signal then made was not understood?—*A*. There was no such signal established by Admiral Rodney at that time.

Q. Has there been any such signal established since?—*A*. Yes, there has.

Q. Do you know of any orders to Mr. Taylor, given at any time, to prevent any of the officers of the fleet coming to visit me on board the Yarmouth?—*A*. I do not; but on being informed that Captain Bateman had been deprived of that indulgence, I asked Mr. Taylor if he had orders from the admiral on that head. His answer to me was that the admiral thought it would be indelicate in those gentlemen to visit Captain Bateman, as in all probability they might become his judges. I afterwards went down to Sir George Rodney and asked him if he had given Mr. Taylor orders to prevent the officers visiting Captain Bateman. His answer was he had not given him such orders, and what he said to him was matter of conversation, to the same effect as Mr. Taylor had related to me. I then desired Captain Bateman might have liberty and permission to be visited by any officers of the fleet as he might think proper to receive, and Mr. Taylor had orders given him for that purpose. Mr. Iggulden, who succeeded Mr. Taylor, had orders from me to the same purpose.

Q. Was there not frequent intercourse between the Sandwich and the Yarmouth after the action, and between the action and Captain Bateman's being put under arrest?—*A*. Certainly there was.

Captain Young withdrew.

[Captain Francis Pender: sworn; was 3rd lieutenant of the Sandwich on the 17th April, doing duty as signal officer. Read the signals.

Monday, 17th April.

5.45 A.M.	General	Form line of battle ahead at two cables' length asunder; fleet on starboard tack.
6.45 "	"	Admiral's intention to attack enemy's rear.
7.0 "	"	Line of battle ahead at one cable's length asunder. Starboard tack.
8.30 "	"	Line of bearing NbyW, SbyE of each other; two cables; wind then on starboard beam.

Monday, 17th April.		
9.0 A.M.	General	Line of battle ahead at two cables; haul to the wind on larboard tack.
9.42 "	"	Repeated signal for line of battle ahead at two cables, on larboard tack.
10.10 "	"	Wear and bring to the wind on starboard tack.
10.18 "	"	Repeated do.
10.19 "	Stirling Castle	Wear; she being the sternmost ship.
10.36 "	General	Line of battle ahead at two cables, on starboard tack.
11.0 "	"	Prepare for battle.
" "	"	Alter course to port.
11.28 "	Rear division	To close the centre.
11.50 "	General	For every ship to steer for her opposite in the enemy's line, agreeable to the 21st Article of the Additional Fighting Instructions.
11·55 "	"	Engage.
Immediately after	"	Come to closer engagement.
18th April		
1.25 P.M.	"	Repeated do.
1.45 "	Yarmouth	Make more sail, she then lying to windward of the line with her main and mizen topsails aback.
2.40 "	Yarmouth and Cornwall	Come to closer action; they being both on our weather bow.
Near about that time hauled down the union jack from the mizen peak.		
3.25 "	Ships to windward	Bear down into the admiral's wake.
3.26 "	Yarmouth	Bear down into the admiral's wake.
4.0 "		Action ceased.

[Other witnesses:
Captain William Fooks, of Deal Castle, repeating frigate.
Lieutenant [George][1] Burlton, of Deal Castle.
Captain James Ferguson, of Venus, repeating frigate.
Mr. Hall,[2] master of Cornwall.
Mr. Tristram Burnett, master of Grafton.
Mr. [John Carteret][1] Lewis, master of Yarmouth.
Lieutenant [Thomas][1] Tireman, first of Yarmouth.
Daniel James, gunner of Yarmouth.

[1] The Christian names are given from the pay-books.

[2] The name Hall is quite distinct; but according to the pay-book of the Cornwall, the master was Robert Jull 1st, and Robert Jull 2nd was his servant.

Smith,[1] midshipman of Sandwich, aide-de-camp to Captain Young.

William Kent, captain's clerk of Yarmouth.

[James][2] Hankey, midshipman of Sandwich.

[James M.][2] Humphrys, master of Sandwich.

[Joseph][2] Pollard, master's mate of Yarmouth.

[John][2] Webber, midshipman of Sandwich, aide-de-camp of the admiral.

And for the defence :

[Martin][2] Benton, midshipman of Yarmouth.

William Watts, quartermaster of Yarmouth.

[William][2] Yard, boatswain of Yarmouth.

[William][2] Welsh, carpenter of Yarmouth.

Robert Rowland, quartermaster of Yarmouth.

[Matthew][2] Pinkerton, captain of the afterguard of Yarmouth.

The examination, for the most part, turns on trivial details ; the main facts, on which the sentence was passed, are neither contradicted nor explained away ; and the only evidence that seems to have any interest now is that of Lewis, the master of the Yarmouth, who was stationed on the quarterdeck, and was asked] :—

Q. Did the Yarmouth get into her station in the line, agreeable to the signal made on the 17th April ?—*A.* Yes.

Q. Did she bear down and engage her opponent, agreeable to the signal made ?—*A.* It was a considerable time before we engaged after the rest of the ships had engaged.

Q. What did that delay proceed from ?—*A.* From our not being thoroughly acquainted with the admiral's meaning.

Q. What signal was you in doubt about ?—*A.* The signal for bearing down to engage.

Q. What was your doubts ?—*A.* Whether we should bear down and engage the ship abaft the beam, or follow the commodore, who seemed to wish to engage the ships of the enemy's van.

Q. What were Captain Bateman's directions on that

[1] Cannot be identified; the pay-book shows a large number of Smiths, but not one rated midshipman.

[2] The Christian names are given from the pay-books.

occasion?—*A*. Captain Bateman seemed inclined to follow the commodore, and ordered me to count the ships in the enemy's line, beginning with the van; observing to me after I had counted them, that the ninth ship was the ship he was to engage, and which we made sail to get up with. But as the commodore left us fast, Captain Bateman then changed his determination and said he would engage the ship ahead of that with which the Cornwall was engaged. He therefore threw his main topsail aback and said he would wait till those ships came farther ahead.

Q. What distance were you from that ship you intended to engage when you laid your main topsail to the mast?—*A*. Better than a mile and a half.

Q. Was the signal then out for engaging the enemy?—*A*. It was.

Q. What was your reason for bringing-to, and not going immediately to close with the enemy?—*A*. I understood Captain Bateman's reason for not bearing down was the great distance that both our second ahead and second astern were from us.

Q. Was the Sandwich then engaged with the enemy?—*A*. Very warmly.

Q. Was the Cornwall then engaged with the enemy?—*A*. She was.

Q. Do you not think that by bringing-to, as you then did, that you neglected the support of the British flag, or to do your duty as a British man-of-war?—*A*. I think we might have done better.

Q. How near do you think you ought to have gone to the enemy before you brought-to?—*A*. We might have gone into the line and there have waited for the Cornwall.

Q. Who directed the main topsail to be laid to the mast?—*A*. The captain.

Q. Did anybody observe to the captain the impropriety of laying the main topsail to the mast? and who?—*A*. Yes. The first lieutenant and myself.

Q. Did you apprehend there would have been an impropriety in your continuing to go down, instead of bringing-to; and to have engaged your opponent in close action without loss of time?—*A*. No, provided we had taken the ship ahead of that with which the Cornwall was engaged.

Q. What reply did Captain Bateman make to you and the first lieutenant when you represented the impropriety of bringing-to so far to windward?—*A*. He said the Cornwall would soon be up.

Q. Did you apprehend that a sufficient reason for your delaying to engage the enemy and support the British flag, then in warm action?—*A*. Certainly not, as I then objected to it; and the first lieutenant mentioned he was sure we should have our signal thrown out.

. . . .

Q. At what distance did you engage?—*A*. In my opinion a very proper one until the main topsail yard was carried away.

. . . .

Q. What directions or orders did Captain Bateman give when your main topsail yard was shot away?—*A*. He ordered the men at the wheel to put the helm down, by which means we luffed out of the line and lost our station, which we never could regain during the action.

Q. How many points do you conceive the two fleets were steering from the wind, when you luffed out of your station?—*A*. Two or three.

Q. Did you then conceive the damages you had already received sufficient cause for hauling out of the line, in a general engagement, and exposing the British flag?—*A*. No.

Q. To what distance did you then haul out of the line?—*A*. Sufficient for the Cornwall to pass under our lee.

Q. Did you haul so far out of the line as not to be annoyed by the enemy's fire?—*A*. Our distance soon became increased from our line, so that no shot from the enemy could reach us.

. . . .

Q. Did you or any other officer or men express concern on that occasion, or disapprobation?—*A*. I informed Captain Bateman of our increasing our distance very fast from our line, and he asked what I would have him do: upon which I gave it as my opinion that we ought to close the line between any two ships, sooner than remain in that situation. He then wanted to close the line ahead of the admiral; but we were apprehensive of getting on board him; therefore closed the line between him and the Suffolk. . . .

Q. Do you apprehend that the Yarmouth withdrawing from the line and continuing to lie to windward for a considerable time while the rest of the squadron was in action, left the British flag unsupported and exposed?—*A.* It would have been better supported had we joined the line, and not have laid-to to windward.

Q. Did Captain Bateman during the action of the 17th April appear to you to be collected and clear, or did he show any dismay or fear?—*A.* He seemed perfectly collected, though at times rather diffident; but as for dismay or fear, I did not see the least sign of either.

[On this, and many points of detail, Lewis was cross-examined by the prisoner, but the main facts stand out clearly and uncontroverted. Tireman, first lieutenant of the Yarmouth, gave evidence to the same purport. He was stationed at the seven after guns on the main deck.]

Q. Do you remember the last signal for the line on the starboard tack, and also the signal for bearing down to engage your opponent?—*A.* I remember the first signal being made; and when the signal was made for each ship to bear down and engage her opponent, the master came and told me that the ninth of the enemy's line fell to our lot; at the same time told me the French admiral was her; and I then went forward and told all the officers and people at the guns on both decks to reserve their fire for that particular ship.

Q. When the Yarmouth obeyed the signal, how near did she approach the enemy before she brought-to?—*A.* About random shot from the nearest ship to us, when we brought-to.

Q. Did you then observe to the captain any impropriety in bringing-to at so great a distance from the enemy?—*A.* I went upon the quarter-deck and told him that the Grafton left us fast and was then at least two miles ahead of us; and the Cornwall was near as far astern, and had shortened sail and begun to engage; that we had better go down to engage the ship ahead of the one the Cornwall was engaged with. Captain Bateman said that we had better shorten sail and back the main topsail, as we should receive the fire of the French admiral and his two seconds before we got down to the ship, we meant to engage. I then said we had better edge down gradually, and not before the wind, to prevent being raked, and at the same time to go under cover of our own smoke, but by no means to shorten sail, as I was certain the admiral would throw out our signal to make more sail, if he did; or if he would shorten sail, it should be so little as to get alongside the ship we were to engage without retarding our way. He desired me to man the main clew-garnets and haul the main sail up; which I did. I then went to my quarters, and looking at the admiral out of the stern windows, I saw our signal to make more sail. I then went upon the quarter deck, and told Captain Bateman of it, and ordered our answering flag to be hoisted. Found our main topsail was aback, which I did not know of before. I heard Captain Bateman give orders to fill the main topsail; then went to my quarters again, and looking out at the admiral about four or five minutes after, I saw our pennant out again, and went and told Captain Bateman of it. He took his spyglass, went into his cabin and looked at the admiral; ordered the answering flag to be hoisted, the helm a-weather, and the after sails to be brailed up. I again returned to my quarters and remained during the action.

[The rest of the evidence is merely illustrating or confirming the facts as stated, which may be summarised by some of the answers of the master of the Sandwich, James Humphrys.]

Q. When the French admiral and his second attacked the Sandwich, was not the Yarmouth to windward at that time?—*A*. She was.

Q. Was not her signal out then to bear down and engage close?—*A*. It was.

Q. Did she do so?—*A*. She did not.

Q. Was not the British flag exposed and unsupported, by her disobedience?—*A*. It was.

[Captain Bateman's defence is very long (some 30 pages of foolscap, closely written), and comments on the evidence in detail, frequently on very trivial matters. But his account of the battle, from his point of view, is interesting.]

The Yarmouth was stationed in the line of battle between the Grafton and Cornwall; and being formed on the starboard tack, Commodore Collingwood in the Grafton, who led the centre division, was ahead. When our fleet stood to the north before the action began, the van carried so much sail as to leave the centre at a considerable distance astern, and something to leeward. The Grafton endeavoured to keep up with the van, and the Yarmouth with the Grafton. The Grafton, by suddenly making more sail and bearing away, left the Yarmouth three miles astern and to windward. The Yarmouth then carried all sail and steered such a course as would have carried her into action in her proper station to support the Grafton, had she sailed as well as that ship. The Yarmouth had been carried rather to windward of the rest of our centre ships by keeping in line with the Grafton and van, and about two miles and a half ahead of the Cornwall, by attempting to keep up with the Grafton. In this situation, rather to windward of our line of battle, distant three miles from the nearest ship ahead and two miles and a half from our nearest ship astern, the Yarmouth had the French admiral and his two seconds abreast nearly of her, and about a mile to leeward of their own line; consequently she could not engage so soon as the other ships of our fleet. Those ships of the enemy were keeping their wind with much sail to gain their line and pointing towards the Grafton. The Yarmouth continued to carry a press of sail, and was keeping away to fall in with the headmost of those three, in obedience to the admiral's general signal for close action, when her particular signal for close action was seen. Admiral Rodney had given no signal to express that the signal made was not understood.

[The rest of the statement is mainly contradicted by the evidence and the certain facts: *e.g.* that he was two miles and a half ahead of the Cornwall, when the whole body of evidence is that the Yarmouth could not close the line ahead of the Cornwall or even ahead of the Sandwich; and the great length is filled up by frequent repetitions, as *e.g.* that the Grafton suddenly left him three miles astern, and by bearing away, was something to windward of the line. The whole, both cross-examination and defence, gives the impression of an ignorant, puzzle-headed man, much surprised that his conduct is being called in question.]

[The Court having enquired] into a charge exhibited by Sir George B. Rodney, Bart., against Captain Nathaniel Bateman, commander of his Majesty's ship Yarmouth . . . and having heard the evidence and the prisoner's defence, and maturely and seriously considered the whole, are of opinion that the charge is in part proved, and they do adjudge the said Captain Bateman to be dismissed his Majesty's naval service, and he is hereby dismissed his Majesty's naval service accordingly.

But, it having appeared to the Court that Captain Bateman's misconduct did not arise from cowardice or disaffection, but from diffidence and error in judgment, the Court do therefore unanimously recommend him to his Majesty's clemency.

Follow, the signatures.

John Harrison, D.J.A.

Report on Captain Bateman's Memorial.

[**Admiralty. Minute-book, 91.**]

15th March, 1781.

[In answer to the Order in Council of 23rd February, referring a memorial from Captain Nathaniel Bateman, praying to be restored,] their lordships having carefully perused the minutes of the Court-martial, and maturely considered the same, Resolved that it be reported that this board cannot advise his Majesty to restore the memorialist.

[In 1792 Captain Bateman presented a similar memorial, which was again referred to the Admiralty, with the same ill success. He was never restored. The further course of his life and the date of his death are unknown.]

APPENDIX B

THE CASE OF M. DE LA TOUCHE.

THE story of the earlier episode in the career of M. de la Touche—to which Nelson distinctly referred when he wrote of him, 'From the time of his meeting Captain Hawkins in the Iris, I never heard of his acting otherwise than as a poltroon and a liar'—has long been before the public;[1] but though in reality quite sufficiently authenticated, there has always been some unwillingness to accept the accuracy of what seemed merely an English report. It has, too, been assumed that Nelson knew nothing more of La Touche except from that story, or after the incident so described, till he met him as an enemy and was baffled, if not defeated, by him at Boulogne. His fierce invective has consequently been denounced as betraying a petty spite or a littleness of mind derogatory to his own character. Hood's reference to 'the very extraordinary behaviour of M. de la Touche'[2] shows that there was something more, which Nelson, who was then on the station and was, in after years, admitted to Hood's intimacy, also knew; but the story of it is now here published for the first time.

When the Aigle was captured[3] (14th September, 1782), and La Touche, after doing what he could to destroy her, fell into our hands, he was almost immediately allowed to go at large on parole;[4] and whilst waiting to be sent to France, took up his residence on Long Island, accompanied, it would seem, by his mistress, whom he had brought out with him. No explanation of his conduct, as

[1] Beatson, v. 46–7.
[2] *Ante*, p. 213.
[3] *Ante*, p. 210.
[4] Beatson, vi. 347–9.

related in the following letters, is given, but the motive is suggested by a letter from Vaudreuil (21 December, 1782) to the Ministre de la Marine: 'M. de la Touche mérite que vous lui fassiez une réprimande. Il avait, dans un bâtiment à sa suite, une créature avec laquelle il vit. Les Anglais l'ayant prise, la lui ont renvoyée comme sa femme. Cela s'est su et ne peut faire qu'un mauvais effet dans un pays d'aussi bonnes mœurs que celui-ci.'[1] As it had become known that the *créature* was not La Touche's wife, no provision would be made for her passage to France in La Touche's company; and, according to his native insolence, he refused to go without her.

Rear-Admiral Robert Digby to Philip Stephens.

[**In letters, 490.**]

Abstract and Extract.

Prince George: off New York. 8th October, 1782.

[Acquaints their lordships with the capture of the Aigle, French frigate, of 44 guns—twenty-eight 24-pounders on one deck—and the Sophie, of twenty-two 9-pounders, by the Warwick, Lion, Vestal, and Bonetta; two brigs with them were run on shore, and the only one of the convoy that escaped was the Gloire, a coppered frigate of 36 guns. Unfortunately, in her escaped the Duc de Lauzun and Monsieur de Vioménil, who was to command the French army, many other French officers, and the greatest part of the money intended to pay the French army.]

The whole would have fallen into our hands, had it not been for the pilot of his Majesty's sloop Racoon, which the Aigle had captured entering the Delaware the day before, who, when they were got into difficulty, took charge of their ship, by which means the Gloire was able to escape. . . . Had it not been for Captain Elphinstone's great vigilance and knowledge of the Delaware, they would never have been able to have either taken or brought out the Aigle, commanded by Monsieur le Comte de la Touche, who had a broad pennant and was intended

[1] Lacour-Gayet, ii. 416.

to command a squadron upon this coast; and who, after he got aground, cut away his masts and scuttled his ship, but to no purpose, as she is brought off without any considerable damage to her hull; and as she is a very new ship and promises to make so fine a frigate that Captain Elphinstone has applied to have the command of her, I shall order her to be bought into the service.

Digby to Philip Stephens.

[In letters, 490.]

Prince George: off New York. 24th October, 1782.

Be pleased to acquaint their lordships that, agreeable to Admiral Pigot's direction, I have sent Monsieur de la Touche, captain of the Aigle, home by the Carysfort, which also carries the general's despatches. The motives for sending Monsieur de la Touche to England in preference to France, in the cartel, as was first intended, is that it appears from a representation of a Mr. Cramond, who is now here, that he was principally concerned in confining Captain Agnew, the Rev. Mr. Agnew, and some others belonging to Virginia, who were taken prisoners in the Romulus,[1] and who are still kept prisoners in France. He may be therefore thought a proper person to detain till they shall be released. He has also given sufficient reason, since he has been on parole upon Long Island, for taking this step; as a proof of which I send you a copy of his parole—which, you will observe, is not in the common form—and the commissary of prisoners' report; by which you will see he refused to comply with his parole, and that, I am informed, in a very insolent manner. However, he was suffered to remain on shore some days after this, by a misunderstanding between General Robertson and myself as to his confinement; and when my officer went to insist upon his embarking, and to use force if he attempted again to refuse, he came quietly with him. But this was not till after I had been obliged to send away the cartel intended to carry him to France,

[1] 19 Feb., 1781.

which had been supplied with stock and necessaries for his use.

Enclosure 1.

Parole of M. de la Touche.

I, Comte de la Touche, captain in the service of his Most Christian Majesty, lately captured on board the ship L'Aigle, and brought into this port, hereby acknowledge myself prisoner of war to the king of Great Britain; and, having permission from his Excellency Rear-Admiral Digby, commander-in-chief, &c. &c. &c., to go to the town of Jamaica on Long Island, to remain until a cartel vessel is got ready to carry me to France, do pledge my faith and most sacredly promise, upon my parole of honour, that I will not do, say, write, or cause to be done, said, or written, directly or indirectly, in any respect whatever, anything to the prejudice of his Britannic Majesty's service, until I am duly exchanged; and that when required, I will deliver myself up to the Commissary-General for Naval Prisoners, or to the person acting for or under him; and embark on board the said vessel with my whole family for France.

In testimony whereof I have hereunto set my hand and seal at New York this fourth day of October, 1782.

LE COMTE DE LA TOUCHE.

Attested by DAVID SPROUT.

Enclosure 2.

Report of the Commissary-General.

Having informed Comte de la Touche that the admiral had sent Mr. Blane, physician to the fleet, to visit him, on Mr. Blane's having reported his indisposition not so bad as to prevent his embarkation in the cartel vessel for France, Mr. Sprout told Monsieur de la Touche that it was the admiral's directions to him to desire that he would immediately prepare to embark accordingly; to which the Comte de la Touche gave for answer that he was the best judge of his own health; that he would not be the martyr of his own life, and that he positively would not go unless forced at the point of the bayonet.

DAVID SPROUT,
Commissary-General for Naval Prisoners.

Affidavit of John Cramond.

[In letters, 490.]

City of New York.—The Deponent, JOHN CRAMOND, came before me, and made oath on the Holy Evangelists of Almighty God.

On the 19th February, 1781, he was taken in the Romulus by a French 64 and two frigates, going from Charleston to the Chesapeake; as also were Captain George Blair, Captain James Parker of the engineers, Captain Stair Agnew of the queen's rangers, and the Rev. John Agnew, chaplain to the same regiment; and carried to Rhode Island, where they were all confined on board a prison ship till 2nd June, when they were sent to Boston in the frigate Hermione, Captain de la Touche, and thence in the frigate La Concorde to Cape Français, where they arrived on the 6th July. There they were kept in close confinement till the 25th October, when they were sent by different vessels to France. By the 6th of December they had all arrived at Brest, except Captain Blair, who had been embarked on board La Sensible frigate, which was found unfit for the voyage and compelled to put back. In France they were all closely confined, and refused the use of pen, ink, and paper—except Captain Parker, who was allowed to draw a bill. No one was allowed to see them, or to bring them necessaries. From Brest they were taken to St. Dinant Castle, where they remained in close confinement till the 18th December. They were then removed to Saint Malo, where Captain Parker, Captain Agnew, and the Rev. John Agnew were left on the 2nd January, 1782.[1]

[While the prisoners were on board the Hermione, they were treated by Monsieur de la Touche more like criminals

[1] Presumably Mr. Cramond was then released; but he does not say so.

than prisoners of war; and Cramond was informed by one of the officers that it was for political reasons. On the passage to Cape Français in La Concorde, he was again told by the lieutenant and by the doctor that it was in consequence of a letter sent by Monsieur de la Touche and the Congress that they were now prisoners, and would be so kept during the war.]

From this and many other instances during the deponent's captivity he verily believes Monsieur de la Touche, at the instance of the rebel Congress,[1] has been the cause of the above named gentlemen's long, cruel, and unjust confinement.

JOHN CRAMOND.

Sworn the 30th day of October, 1782,
before me,
D. MATHEWS, Mayor.

[1] It must seem more probable that La Touche had neither forgotten nor forgiven the very angry criticisms on his conduct in the action with the Iris a few months before, which had been published in the New York papers.

APPENDIX C

AN UNRECORDED SERVICE OF NELSON'S.

During Hood's last cruize[1] in February and March 1783, along the north coast of Hispaniola, the Albemarle, then commanded by Nelson, was more or less in company; and towards the end of March performed a little service which has—somewhat curiously—escaped the notice of all Nelson's biographers. It has been left to a French writer to bring it to our notice. M. Lacour-Gayet (ii. 436–7) thus describes it :—

'L'escadre de Vaudreuil à Porto-Cabello se gardait avec beaucoup de négligence. Un jour qu'une partie des officiers et des équipages étaient à terre, une frégate inconnue pénétra dans la rade. Tout à son aise, elle examina et compta les bâtiments de l'escadre. On finit par s'apercevoir de sa présence insolente. Vaudreuil donna l'ordre à la Cérès de lui donner la chasse ; il fallut deux heures à la Cérès pour mettre à la voile. C'était trop tard ; la frégate ennemie échappa à toute poursuite. Elle était commandée par un officier de vingt-quatre ans : il s'appelait Nelson.'

A reference to the Albemarle's log corroborates the French story. It would seem that on 21 March, being then in latitude 19° 28′ N, the Albemarle received orders to examine the coast of South America, presumably to ascertain the position and state of Vaudreuil's squadron. On the 22nd, at noon, her latitude was 17° 31′ ; on the 24th, 15° 34′ ; on the 25th, 14° 13′. The 26th she seems to have spent in examining Bonira (Bonaire, Buen Ayre),

[1] *Ante*, p. 253.

and on the 27th was in latitude 10° 53′. On the 28th at noon she was off Cape Blanco; and for the 29th the entry is:—

'A.M. ½-past 10, abreast of Tourine (Turiamo). 11, made the French fleet in Porto Cabello. ½-past, Porto Cabello SW by W 6 or 7 miles. Counted 11 sail of the line of battle ships, one of which wore a flag at the fore and a pennant at the main; and one do. at the mizen topgallant mast head, and several smaller vessels. Hauled our wind to the northward. Noon. Latitude 10° 38′.'

What seems a little curious, in the total absence of any letters elucidating the cruize, is that, having obtained this intelligence, the Albemarle did not make the best of her way to rejoin the fleet. On the contrary, she seems to have continued her perquisitions. On the 31st March and 1st April she was off Curaçao: on the 2nd, back off Bonaire; but on the 3rd, 10 A.M., a butt end started on the starboard bow. The carpenter was of opinion it was not safe to keep the wind. Bore away for Jamaica, where she arrived on the morning of the 7th.

Rowley was there in command and Hood came in a few days later, but there does not appear to be any written report of Nelson's intelligence. It must have been given to Rowley *vivâ voce*, and repeated to Hood; but as the order to cease hostilities had reached Jamaica on the 29th March—the very day Nelson was counting the French ships at Porto Cabello—the intelligence had no longer any practical value.

INDEX

*Names marked with * are in the Dictionary of National Biography.*

SHIPS

THE NAVY RECORDS SOCIETY, which has been established for the purpose of printing rare or unpublished works of naval interest, aims at rendering accessible the sources of our naval history, and at elucidating questions of naval archæology, construction, administration, organisation and social life.

The Society has already issued :—

In 1894 : Vols. I. and II. *State Papers relating to the Defeat of the Spanish Armada, Anno* 1588. Edited by Professor J. K. Laughton. (30*s.*)

In 1895 : Vol. III. *Letters of Lord Hood,* 1781-82. Edited by Mr. David Hannay. (*None available.*)

Vol. IV. *Index to James's Naval History,* by Mr. C. G. Toogood. Edited by the Hon. T. A. Brassey. (12*s.* 6*d.*)

Vol. V. *Life of Captain Stephen Martin,* 1666–1740. Edited by Sir Clements R. Markham. (*None available.*)

In 1896: Vol. VI. *Journal of Rear-Admiral Bartholomew James,* 1752-1828. Edited by Professor J. K. Laughton and Commander J. Y. F. Sulivan. (10*s.* 6*d.*)

Vol. VII. *Hollond's Discourses of the Navy,* 1638 and 1658. Edited by Mr. J. R. Tanner. (12*s.* 6*d.*)

Vol. VIII. *Naval Accounts and Inventories in the Reign of Henry VII.* Edited by Mr. M. Oppenheim. (10*s.* 6*d.*)

In 1897: Vol. IX. *Journal of Sir George Rooke.* Edited by Mr. Oscar Browning. (10*s.* 6*d.*)

Vol. X. *Letters and Papers relating to the War with France,* 1512–13. Edited by M. Alfred Spont. (10*s.* 6*d.*)

Vol. XI. *Papers relating to the Spanish War,* 1585–87. Edited by Mr. Julian Corbett. (10*s.* 6*d.*)

In 1898 : Vol. XII. *Journals and Letters of Admiral of the Fleet Sir Thomas Byam Martin,* 1773–1854 (Vol. II.). Edited by Admiral Sir R. Vesey Hamilton. (*See* XXIV.)

Vol. XIII. *Papers relating to the First Dutch War.* 1652–54 (Vol. I.). Edited by Mr. S. R. Gardiner. (10*s.* 6*d.*)

Vol. XIV. *Papers relating to the Blockade of Brest,* 1803–5 (Vol. I.). Edited by Mr. J. Leyland. (*See* XXI.)

In 1899: Vol. XV. *History of the Russian Fleet during the Reign of Peter the Great. By a Contemporary Englishman.* Edited by Admiral Sir Cyprian Bridge. (10*s.* 6*d.*)

Vol. XVI. *Logs of the Great Sea Fights,* 1794–1805 (Vol. I.). Edited by Vice-Admiral Sir T. Sturges Jackson. (*See* XVIII.)

Vol. XVII. *Papers relating to the First Dutch War,* 1652–54 (Vol. II.). Edited by Mr. S. R. Gardiner. (10*s.* 6*d.*)

In 1900: Vol. XVIII. *Logs of the Great Sea Fights* (Vol. II.). Edited by Sir T. S. Jackson. (*Two vols.* 25*s.*)

Vol. XIX. *Journals and Letters of Sir T. Byam Martin* (Vol. III.). Edited by Sir R. Vesey Hamilton. (*See* XXIV.)

In 1901: Vol. XX. *The Naval Miscellany* (Vol. I.). Edited by the Secretary. (15*s.*)

Vol. XXI. *Papers relating to the Blockade of Brest,* 1803–5 (Vol. II.). Edited by Mr. John Leyland. (*Two vols.* 25*s.*)

In 1902: Vols. XXII. and XXIII. *The Naval Tracts of Sir William Monson* (Vols. I. and II.). Edited by Mr. M. Oppenheim. (*Two vols.* 25*s.*)

Vol. XXIV. *Journals and Letters of Sir T. Byam Martin* (Vol. I.). Edited by Sir R. Vesey Hamilton. (*Three vols.* 31*s.* 6*d.*)

In 1903: Vol. XXV. *Nelson and the Neapolitan Jacobins.* Edited by Mr. H. C. Gutteridge. (12*s.* 6*d.*)

Vol. XXVI. *A Descriptive Catalogue of the Naval MSS. in the Pepysian Library* (Vol. I.). Edited by Mr. J. R. Tanner. (15*s.*)

In 1904: Vol. XXVII. *A Descriptive Catalogue of the Naval MSS. in the Pepysian Library* (Vol. II.). Edited by Mr. J. R. Tanner. (12*s.* 6*d.*)

Vol. XXVIII. *The Correspondence of Admiral John Markham*, 1801–7. Edited by Sir Clements R. Markham. (12*s.* 6*d.*)

In 1905: Vol. XXIX. *Fighting Instructions*, 1530–1816. Edited by Mr. Julian Corbett. (10*s.* 6*d.*)

Vol. XXX. *Papers relating to the First Dutch War*, 1652–54 (Vol. III.). Edited by the late Dr. S. R. Gardiner and Mr. C. T. Atkinson. (12*s.* 6*d.*)

In 1906: Vol. XXXI. *The Recollections of Commander James Anthony Gardner*, 1775–1814. Edited by Sir R. Vesey Hamilton and Professor J. K. Laughton. (12*s.* 6*d.*)

Vol. XXXII. *Letters and Papers of Charles, Lord Barham*, 1758–1813 (Vol. I.). Edited by Sir J. K. Laughton. (12*s.* 6*d.*)

The volumes for the current year (1907) will be *Naval Ballads and Songs*, edited by Professor C. H. Firth; and *Panoramic Views of the Battles of the Third Dutch War*, edited by Mr. J. S. Corbett.

Other works in preparation, in addition to further volumes of *Sir William Monson's Tracts*, *The First Dutch War*, *The Catalogue of the Pepys MSS.*, *The Barham Papers*, and *The Naval Miscellany*, are *The Journal of Captain* (afterwards Sir John) *Narbrough*, 1672–73, to be edited by Sir J. K. Laughton; *Official Documents illustrating the Social Life and Internal Discipline of the Navy in the XVIIIth Century*, to be edited by Sir J. K. Laughton; and *Select Correspondence of the great Earl of Chatham and his Sons*, to be edited by Sir J. K. Laughton.

Any person wishing to become a Member of the Society is requested to apply to the Secretary (Sir J. Knox Laughton, 9 Pepys Road, Wimbledon, S.W.), who will submit his name to the Council. The Annual Subscription is One Guinea, the payment of which entitles the Member to receive one copy of all works issued by the Society for that year. The publications are not offered for general sale; but Members can obtain a complete set of the volumes at the rate of one guinea for each year. On first joining the Society, a new Member may obtain a complete set at the reduced price of 12*s.* 6*d.* for each year except the last three, for which the full price of one guinea must be paid. Single volumes can be obtained by Members at the prices marked to each.

August 1907.

PRINTED BY
SPOTTISWOODE AND CO. LTD., NEW-STREET SQUARE
LONDON

4196471R00275

Printed in Great Britain
by Amazon.co.uk, Ltd.,
Marston Gate.